THE HAMLET FIRE

THE HAMLET FIRE

A TRAGIC STORY OF CHEAP FOOD, CHEAP GOVERNMENT, AND CHEAP LIVES

Bryant Simon

THE NEW PRESS

25 YEARS

NEW YORK
LONDON

Requests for permission to reproduce selections from this book should be mailed to: Permissions Department, The New Press, 120 Wall Street, 31st floor, New York, NY 10005.

Published in the United States by The New Press, New York, 2017
Distributed by Perseus Distribution

LIBRARY OF CONGRESS CATALOGING-IN-PUBLICATION DATA
Names: Simon, Bryant.
Title: The Hamlet Fire : a tragic story of cheap food, cheap government, and cheap lives / Bryant Simon.
Description: New York : The New Press, [2017] | Includes bibliographical references and index.
Identifiers: LCCN 2017014037 (print) | LCCN 2017022986 (ebook) | ISBN 9781620972397 (e-book) | ISBN 9781620972380 (hc : alk. paper)
Subjects: LCSH: Imperial Food Products. Plant (Hamlet, N.C.)—Fire, 1991. | Poultry plants—Fires and fire prevention—North Carolina—Hamlet. | Employers' liability—North Carolina—Hamlet. | Industrial safety—Government policy—United States.
Classification: LCC TH9449.H2 (ebook) | LCC TH9449.H2 S56 2017 (print) | DDC 363.11/9664930975634—dc23
LC record available at https://lccn.loc.gov/2017014037

The New Press publishes books that promote and enrich public discussion and understanding of the issues vital to our democracy and to a more equitable world. These books are made possible by the enthusiasm of our readers; the support of a committed group of donors, large and small; the collaboration of our many partners in the independent media and the not-for-profit sector; booksellers, who often hand-sell New Press books; librarians; and above all by our authors.

www.thenewpress.com

Composition by dix!
This book was set in Garamond Premier Pro

Printed in the United States of America

10 9 8 7 6 5 4 3 2 1

To my father, Robert Simon, and to his bright memory

CONTENTS

THE HAMLET FIRE

INTRODUCTION

A blessing and a curse—that's how Loretta Goodwin described her job at Imperial Food Products.

She started processing chicken tenders at the rambling, one-story, red brick factory in Hamlet, North Carolina, on September 14, 1989, not long after celebrating her fortieth birthday. She didn't mind the job as much as some of her co-workers. Maybe that's because she knew what hard work was. One of sixteen, she had left school in the tenth grade to pick cotton, tobacco, and peaches to help her family get by. In her twenties, she had served up barbecue sandwiches and cleaned other people's houses, done their laundry, and made their breakfasts and dinners.[1] She was glad to be out of the hot sun and buggy fields, and she was glad to be out of white people's kitchens and pantries. She was especially glad to leave the nursing home where she had worked for a dozen years before coming to Imperial.

Goodwin liked that she could weigh a five and half ounce chicken breast in her hand without using a scale. She liked that she could keep up with the speeding production line while others fell behind. What she didn't like about the job was the sour smell of chicken that clung to her long after her shift ended, or the ice-cold water that dripped off the meat and puddled on the floors, seeping into her shoes and then her socks. She didn't like how the ceaseless repetition of picking up and putting down frozen blocks of boneless chicken breasts made it feel like there was something inside her hands and fingers "pinching at her flesh." She didn't like how the white supervisors hollered at her and sometimes made fun of her clothes and her weight. And she didn't like that she had to ask them to use the bathroom, or that they sometimes timed her trips to the toilet with a stopwatch and threatened to fire her if she went too often or for too long.[2]

Still, Goodwin thanked God for the work. She made $5.50 an hour.

That was $1.25 above the federal minimum wage at the time. On payday, she brought home a check for $179. As a single mother with five kids, three still living with her, and no regular child support from her former husband that she could depend on, Goodwin was glad, proud even, to be eking out a living in a place where a steady job at an hourly rate above minimum wage was as hard to find as a cool breeze in the summer or a street without a church on it. "You couldn't get much else better around here," Goodwin reflected, assessing the labor market in the 1990s for black women like herself—and increasingly for white women and men across the color line as well—in her hometown and in so many other places across the country where good jobs had disappeared and unions had faded from the scene.[3]

But Goodwin's steady paycheck didn't change everything. After almost two years on the job, she remained one fall on the slippery floors, one sick child, or one missed shift because of her stiff hands away from sinking below the poverty line.

On Tuesday, September 3, 1991, the day after Labor Day, the buzzing of the alarm clock woke up Goodwin just before dawn. She didn't feel like getting out of bed that morning. Something made her feel uneasy about the day ahead. But she did what she always did. She shuffled around her rented house getting ready, avoiding the creaks in the floor so she wouldn't wake up her children. A little after 7:00 a.m., Ruby Sellers pulled up in front of the house in her puttering four-cylinder compact car. Goodwin didn't drive, so she got a ride to work from Sellers every morning. At the end of the week, she gave her gas money. They felt the thickness of late summer in the air as they rode through town under overcast skies, passing convenience stores, aging hotels in need of repairs, and the town's signature building, the Victorian-era train depot with its gables and intricate woodwork. After taking a left on Main Street, they made a right onto Bridges Street. They drove up the hill to the Imperial plant and parked a little beyond the factory in the gravel lot. As they walked inside, they didn't notice the tractor-trailer sitting at the loading dock or the driver, Rickie Godfrey, asleep at the wheel.

Once inside, Goodwin stowed her lunch in her locker and sat down in the breakroom. She started to tell her co-workers about how the local police had picked up one of her nephews on some undisclosed charge over the holiday weekend. Before all the details came out, she put on a hairnet and blue plastic smock, grabbed a pair of gloves, and took her place on the line.[4]

It was 8:00 a.m.

Usually, Goodwin worked in the packing area, loading up boxes with breaded, fried, and frozen chicken tenders and marinated boneless chicken breasts headed for Shoney's, Red Lobster, and Long John Silver's. That morning, though, the supervisor sent her to the trim room. She didn't like working there, "messin' with raw chicken," as she described the job, but she didn't say anything.

The tenders racing by Goodwin that morning were, as one of her co-workers remembered, "beautiful," "plumb and full of meat."[5] While Goodwin scraped gobs of yellow fat from the frozen chunks of chicken, the maintenance crew huddled in the processing room, studying the hydraulic system that powered the conveyor belt carrying breaded chicken tenders into the cooker at the top of the twenty-nine-foot, three-hundred-gallon Stein fryer. Over the previous couple of months one of the lines powering the belt had been misting and occasionally leaking drops of fluid onto the floor dangerously close to the burners under the fryer. During the Labor Day weekend, maintenance workers had again changed the hose that connected the machine box to the conveyor belt. But when the morning crew arrived that Tuesday and looked at the replacement hose, some of them thought that it was too long. They worried that it might drag on the floor and trip one of the women on the line or a foreman as they hurried by the area.

Part of the problem with the hydraulic system was that the maintenance men didn't have the precise factory-specified hoses and couplings to fix it. Lead mechanic John Gagnon, his co-worker William Morris remembered, had previously asked Brad Roe, the plant manager and son of the company's president and chief officer, Emmett Roe, to purchase the right parts. Morris thought Gagnon had even found a place in Charlotte, two hours away by car, that stocked those items. After checking with his father, Morris recalled, Brad Roe said no, as he historically had, because the company didn't want to pay for new and expensive parts.[6] So Gagnon kept doing what he was good at: jerry-rigging things so that the production line would keep moving and Brad Roe wouldn't badger him over the intercom, as he sometimes did, to hurry up and get things running again. Gagnon tried, as best he could, to maintain some safety standards under these cost-cutting conditions. When he had finished replacing the hose that connected the machine box to the conveyor belt on previous occasions, one worker remembered, he had tugged on it with his hands as hard as he could to make sure it held. When it did, he turned on the pressure.[7]

The equipment manual for the Stein fryer, the manual that no one at the plant could find anymore, advised repair crews to turn off its heat sources whenever someone was working around it with flammable products, like hydraulic fluids. Government health and safety officials gave the same advice. When dealing with "hazardous energy," they strongly recommended, "all power sources [are] to be shut off."[8] But the Imperial maintenance crew knew that the Roes probably wouldn't like it if they turned the burners under the fryer off because it could take as long as two hours to get it heated back up to 375 degrees, the temperature it was at that morning and the temperature it needed to be to cook chicken tenders golden brown. Turning it off might have been the safe thing to do, but it also would have meant that Goodwin and her co-workers would have been sitting around doing nothing for a while. That would cost the company money, money that it didn't have in the fall of 1991 as it struggled to pay its mounting debts and stay afloat in the brutally competitive business of making fat- and salt-filled, inexpensive, easy-to-prepare-and-eat fast food products.

Fifteen minutes or so after Goodwin started "messin'" with that chicken, she heard a loud pop and then a hissing sound, like a missile had been launched inside the plant. She looked behind her to the processing room where the noise was coming from and saw "a big streak of fire ran across the doorway." She pulled her smock over her face and started to run, but she didn't know where to go. Imperial managers had never held a fire drill before, and none of the escape routes were lit to indicate where to turn to safely get out of the building.[9]

Fire and insurance investigators would later learn that on the morning of the fire, John Gagnon and the Imperial maintenance crew decided to cut the hydraulic hose that was dragging on the ground. As they made

the changes, they shut off the hydraulic system but left the burners under the fryer on. They used a hacksaw to cut and shorten the hose before
they reconnected it to the machine box.[10] No one remembered if Gagnon
pulled on the connection this time, but the maintenance men must have
trusted that the parts would hold, just like they had in the past. Maybe
the cut end of the hose didn't fit snugly enough, or maybe it was slightly
smaller than the fitting, or maybe in a rush to keep things moving they
didn't tighten that coupling quite enough. Whatever the exact reason,
only seconds after the mechanics turned the hydraulic line back on to at
least 800 pounds per square inch (p.s.i.)—though it sometimes surged to
1,500 p.s.i.—the hose came loose and launched into a wild dance, spew-
ing flammable oil-based Chevron 32 hydraulic fluid in every direction.
The liquid hit the concrete floor with enough force that droplets formed
and bounced up and down all over the place. Some landed under the gas
plumes rising up under the fryer. The heat from the gas vaporized the
splashing oil and created the horrible hissing sound that Goodwin mis-
took for a missile.

From that point, the fire intensified, greedily feeding on the chicken
grease on the floors and the walls and the oils from the fryer and the hydraulic line.

The blaze immediately created a wall of heat and flames that split the
factory in half. Most of the women and men in the packing room and
marinating room slipped out the unlocked front door. The line workers
and members of the maintenance crew in the trim room and processing rooms ran, like Goodwin did, in the opposite direction, away from
the fire toward the side and back of the building, toward the breakroom,
equipment room, loading dock, and dumpster.[11]

No sprinklers turned on to blunt the blaze. The supposedly flame-
retardant Kemlite ceiling tiles hanging over the fryer ignited, adding another surge of heat to the conflagration. Within minutes, the fire melted
electric and telephone lines and, eventually, blew a gaping hole in the
building's roof.[12]

But for Goodwin and her co-workers it was smoke, not flames, that
threatened their lives. The thick, almost velvet-like blankets of yellow
and black smoke made it impossible to see. As the line workers, foremen, and supervisors stumbled toward the exits, tears welled up in their

eyes, and their lungs felt like there was fire burning inside of them. Without knowing it, they were sucking in lethal amounts of carbon monoxide. The poison in the air replaced the oxygen in their bloodstream, causing shortness of breath, dizziness, and weakened muscles, and clouded the judgment of Goodwin and her co-workers just when they needed to make snap decisions.[13]

Unable to see even her hand right in front of her face, Goodwin ran away from the fire, banging into equipment, vats of chicken, and bags of flour as she did. She fell down a few times and her frightened and blinded co-workers stepped on her as they fled. She got up and made it to the far end of the plant, near the loading dock, but she and the others gathered there couldn't find a way out. The truck with the sleeping driver that she had walked past an hour earlier blocked the loading dock exit. Several people banged on the trailer. One person lay down and found a tiny opening between the vehicle and the building and stayed there sucking whatever fresh air she could.

A bunch of workers went to the breakroom, but the door to the outside there was locked. A few frantically tried to push an air conditioner out through a window, but it wouldn't budge. Several stumbled back in the direction of the loading dock, "hollering and screaming," Goodwin remembered. "Somebody let us out! We're trapped in here. We're gonna burn up. We're gonna die." When they saw the truck still parked there, they moved a few feet down toward the closest doors, the ones that led outside to the dumpster and the receiving dock.

A few months earlier, the Roes, trying to stop flies from coming into the plant and workers from going out, blocked one of these exits. The other was locked from the outside with a latch and padlocks. Workers pounded and kicked at this exit, not knowing that it only opened to the inside.

Unable to escape through the doors near the loading dock or the breakroom, a pack of workers decided to hide in a nearby cooler, hoping to shield themselves from the smoke and the flames. They didn't realize that this door, the one going into the cooler, wouldn't shut all the way, and that deadly carbon monoxide gases were oozing into the chamber and into their lungs. A dozen of Goodwin's friends and co-workers would die inside there from carbon monoxide poisoning, the same thing that killed the others in the plant.

Seven more people, including several male maintenance workers, perished near the fryer and the blocked exits in the rear of the building near the equipment room and one of the blast freezers.

As Goodwin made her way in the dark toward the locked exits, Brad Roe, just back from a weekend at the coast and still wearing a white tank top with the words "Myrtle Beach" across the front, was sitting in the Imperial office when he realized what had happened. He reached for the phone, though apparently not for the keys to any of the doors. The line was dead, so he jumped into his car and raced over to the Hamlet Fire Department, just a few blocks away. He slammed on the brakes in front of the main entrance and ran inside.

It was 8:22 a.m.

"Is anyone here? Is anyone here?" he yelled.

Captain Calvin White, one of only two firefighters in the building at the time, was in the back making a cup of coffee when he heard Roe's panicked voice.

"We got a fire at Imperial Foods. Help us! Help us quick!" Roe blurted out without mentioning, White would later remember, anything about people being trapped inside.[14]

Goodwin, meanwhile, decided to stay put near the loading dock and the dumpster. Several of Goodwin's co-workers fell on top of her and some were underneath her, smothering her in a sandwich of dread and feverish prayers. Somehow, she clawed her way through the arms and legs to get near the top of the heap.[15]

Outside the plant, the people in the shotgun houses and rusted metal trailers lining the nearby streets saw the menacing streams of black and yellow smoke shooting out from the hole in the roof at Imperial. The ones closest to the plant heard the chilling screams coming from inside. They roused the driver at the loading dock and got him to move his truck. City workers rushed over with a Trojan tractor. They attached a chain to the dumpster and pried it away from the wall, creating a tight opening. When the gap appeared, someone from the inside shoved Goodwin through the hole. When she got about halfway out, someone on the outside grabbed her by her right arm and slung her to the ground where she landed, cough-ing and covered in soot.[16]

Rescuers would find three people dead near those doors, and three more in the trim room.

Goodwin squinted as she adjusted her eyes to the hazy morning light. She got up and staggered over to the parking lot where she crouched over and coughed out the soot still stuck in her lungs.[17] Trying to catch her breath, she sat down and watched what was going on around her. She saw the ground in front of the plant littered with discarded smocks and rub-ber gloves. She saw men and women stumble out of the plant, so covered in soot and smoke that she didn't recognize them at first and didn't know if they were white or black. She watched as the first two firefighters on the scene rushed from worker to worker, giving them oxygen from the airpacks they carried on their backs and in a few cases doing CPR. As more fire trucks and firefighters from Hamlet and the surrounding towns arrived, the crews put on their gear and began to enter the building.[18] Not long after the firefighters went inside, Goodwin saw them bring out the lifeless body of Mary Lillian Wall, who, minutes earlier, had been by her side near the locked door and exit leading to the trash compacter. Then they brought out Bertha Jarrell. Goodwin had grown up with her. Gail Campbell was next.[19]

As Goodwin watched the beginning of the parade of the dead, she heard the screams and wailing of family members as they found out that they had lost someone close to them. She saw police cars and ambulances racing back and forth, dodging the first TV vans on the scene, and report-ers running after the fire chief and the mayor with microphones and note pads. As she sat there a little longer and someone checked her vital signs, she might have seen a driver pulling a refrigerated tractor-trailer, used by the fire department for barbeque fund-raisers, up to the plant. For the rest of that day, it served as a temporary morgue. Before emergency medical personnel loaded her into an ambulance and took her to the hospital, she noticed a line of lumpy black body bags near the front of the building. She swore then, just as she does now, that she saw one of them start to squirm and then rise up as the person inside pulled down the zipper and climbed out alive. This may have happened, though it was more likely not to have happened exactly the way the story was told.[20]

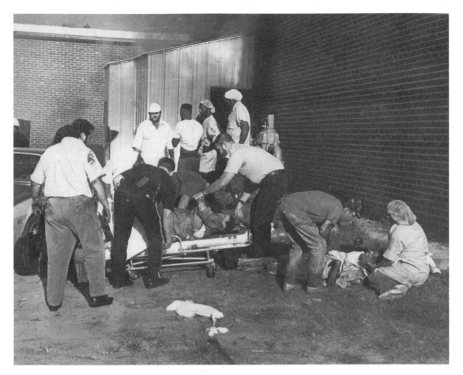

Rescuers help victims on the morning of the fire. *Photo courtesy of Tom MacCallum.*

Goodwin's retelling of what occurred with the body bags was the beginning of a rewiring of memory in Hamlet, a way of dealing, perhaps, with the trauma of senseless death. In the years after the fire, there were few facts that weren't disputed. Truth proved hard to find in the face of calculated neglect and indifference for the lives of working people, past and present, and lingering racial bitterness and distrust in the town, past and present.

Although Goodwin wrenched her knee, broke her toe, chipped a bone in her shoulder, and had a burning sensation in her lungs every time she took a breath for years to come, she was, in the end, one of the lucky ones. Luckier than those killed near the fryer or her co-workers who died from carbon monoxide poisoning in the cooler, and luckier than those who choked to death beside her by the door that was locked from the outside near the loading dock.

Luckier than the eighteen other mothers who died and left behind forty-nine orphaned children.

Luckier than recently engaged Fred Barrington Jr. Years earlier, he had left high school before graduating. On the morning of September 3, the thirty-seven-year-old man, known as a prankster, escaped from the building still wearing his hairnet, blue smock, and white apron, only to die, as the legend of the fire has it, when he rushed back into the plant to rescue his mother, a line worker at Imperial. He didn't get to her before the smoke got to the both of them.[21]

Luckier than Margaret Banks. She was found with only one of her tennis shoes still on and soot covering her nostrils and mouth and smeared over her thighs and lower legs. The single mom died of smoke inhalation and left behind in her Laurinburg home—a twenty-minute drive from Hamlet—a boy and a girl.[22]

Luckier than forty-nine-year-old Philip Dawkins, a husband and a father, and a deacon and a softball coach at Pine Grove Baptist Church in East Rockingham, who drove a delivery truck for the Lance Snack Company. He usually stopped by the Imperial plant on Mondays, but because of the Labor Day holiday, he came early that Tuesday morning to restock the vending machines in the breakroom with packs of peanut butter crackers and bags of barbeque potato chips.[23]

Philip Dawkins's son from his first marriage, Philip Jr., was a paper mill worker and a volunteer fireman for the Cordova Fire Company. He got the call that morning and put on his uniform and rushed over to the Imperial plant. Rescue workers were bringing bodies out from the cooler and the breakroom three at a time on buggies. They hauled them to the loading dock, where they lifted them down into the waiting arms of firemen and rescue personnel. That's where Philip Jr. discovered that his father was dead. Someone unknowingly handed him the body.[24]

Luckier than Jeff Webb, who left behind a four-year-old daughter, a fiancée, and a taste, his partner recalled, for "those French things, croissants."[25]

Luckier than Mildred Lassiter Moates and her husband of almost thirty years, Olin D. Moates. A mother to three boys, Mildred was working in the trim room when the fire broke out. She ran to the loading dock and kept going when she figured out the doors there were locked. Rescuers found her crumpled and trampled body in the marinating and mixing room. She was unconscious and just hanging on to life. A helicopter airlifted her and her husband to the University of North Carolina Hospital in Chapel Hill.

The stress proved too much for Olin. He suffered a heart attack right there in the hospital. He recovered, but Mildred did not, at least not fully. Suffering from nerve damage that left her feet almost permanently curled and her arms resting stiffly, nearly immobile, on her chest, she needed constant care. She could barely see and she could only take a few steps at a time, and even those were hard to do. The injuries harmed her brain enough that, according to her lawyer, she could only say "a few words at a time."[26]

Luckier than Mary Alice Quick, a mother to a boy and two girls and a member of her church choir, whose estranged husband, Martin, had also worked for a time at Imperial. By the fall of 1991, he had taken a job building a new prison thirty miles away from Hamlet. He learned about the fire on his lunch break when he stopped at a country gas station to get something to eat.

A couple of older guys, passing time hanging out in front of the store, didn't recognize him, so they asked him where he was from.

"Hamlet," he said.

"Did you hear about the fire this morning at the chicken plant?" they wondered.

Before they finished with their question, Martin was digging for change in his pocket and dashing off to the pay phone, hoping to find out that the information wasn't true. He learned that Imperial had, in fact, caught fire, but not much about Mary Alice. He went back to Hamlet right away. Once in town, he found out that an ambulance had taken his wife to Hamlet Hospital. He joined his brother in-law and kids and other Imperial families, along with a handful of pastors and preachers, in the basement of the building in a tense vigil, waiting to hear some news from a doctor or a nurse.[27]

Pastor Berry Barbour from a Methodist church just off Main Street remembered meeting the Quick family in the hospital and praying with them that day. He recalled another moment as well. Throughout the morning and early afternoon, hospital officials came down the steps and updated families on the status of their wives, sisters, mothers, husbands, brothers, and fathers. One hospital representative searched out a family and told them that their loved one had survived. Moments later, he came back with bad news. He had gotten it wrong. The Imperial worker they were waiting for was dead, he told the family.[28]

Luckier than John Gagnon, the last person taken out of the building, just after noon on September 3, 1991. On a final sweep of the factory, firefighters found the chief maintenance man by the blast freezer in the corner of the processing room, still breathing, if only faintly. They rushed him outside, where a doctor quickly put a tracheostomy tube in him, but that procedure couldn't save "Johnny on the Spot," as he was known to his co-workers. He died before he reached the hospital.[29]

Fifty-six people, line workers like Loretta Goodwin, members of the maintenance crew, and a few supervisors, escaped the fire alive, although few came away without lasting physical and psychological injuries. Twenty-five people—eighteen of whom were women, many single mothers with children, and twelve of whom were African American, like Goodwin and the majority of the laborers at the Imperial plant—died amid the explosion and profusion of smoke that day.

Around the time of the twentieth anniversary of the fire, in 2011, I first started the research for this book. Trying to find out what happened in 1991, and why, would lead me through newspaper accounts, union records, fire and insurance reports, congressional testimony, death certifications, and bankruptcy proceedings, from archives in Raleigh, Chapel Hill, and Hamlet to collections in Silver Springs, Maryland, Madison, Wisconsin, and Provo, Utah. Before all of these library visits and photocopying, however, I sat down with three retired journalists at a diner ten minutes by car from where the Imperial plant once stood. This wasn't my first time in Hamlet. Years before that lunch and before the fire, I was making my way from Raleigh, North Carolina, to Columbia, South Carolina. I intentionally got off the state highway and drove through the town of just over six thousand residents. I wanted to see what this place a shade north of the South Carolina border looked like, this small town that was remarkably, to me at least, the birthplace of both jazz legend John Coltrane and famed *New York Times* reporter and columnist—and frequent guest, when I was a kid, on Sunday morning talk shows like *Meet the Press*—Tom Wicker. Both were born in Hamlet in 1926, though on

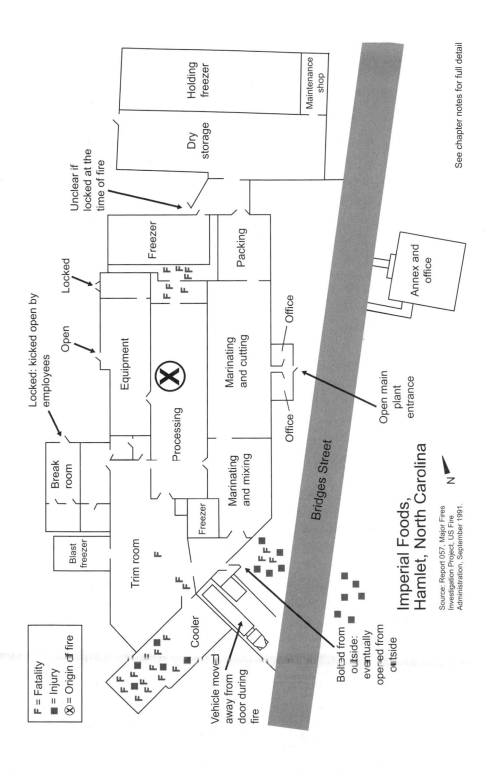

Imperial Foods, Hamlet, North Carolina

Legend:
- F = Fatality
- ■ = Injury
- ⊗ = Origin of fire

Labels within diagram:
- Holding freezer
- Maintenance shop
- Dry storage
- Unclear if locked at the time of fire
- Freezer
- Packing
- Locked
- Open
- Equipment
- Break room
- Blast freezer
- Trim room
- Cooler
- Processing
- Marinating and mixing
- Freezer
- Marinating and cutting
- Office
- Office
- Annex and office
- Open main plant entrance
- Bridges Street
- Locked: kicked open by employees
- Vehicle moved away from door during fire
- Bolted from outside: eventually opened from outside
- N
- See chapter notes for full detail

Source: Report 057, Major Fires Investigation Project, US Fire Administration, September 1991.

different sides of the tracks and of the community's then legally enforced racial divide.

On the trip back to Hamlet in 2011, I wasn't just driving around searching for Coltrane's and Wicker's spirits. I wanted to find out about the town's most traumatic moment. All three of the men having lunch with me had reported on the fire at the Imperial Food Products plant and its aftermath. They had lived most of their lives in Hamlet and the surrounding communities and were all involved in the local historical society, community politics, and economic development.

Between spoonfuls of cream of broccoli soup and sips of sweet tea, they talked about the tragedy at Imperial. They came to a quick consensus: Emmett and Brad Roe, the father-and-son business team originally from New York and Pennsylvania who owned and operated the plant, caused the fire. According to their analysis, the deaths that occurred on September 3, 1991, were the result of an unfortunate accident triggered by the greedy and careless actions of a few.

"If they hadn't locked the doors, nothing would have happened; we wouldn't be sitting here," one of them concluded as the others nodded their heads in agreement.

Underscoring the point, another of the men at the table insisted, "It didn't have anything to do with social conditions. It really was a freak accident."

Putting a period on the conversation, the last to speak on the topic added, "They were just a couple of rogue employers. There was no *social* meaning to the fire." [30]

This is one way to explain the deaths at Imperial. It emphasizes the exceptional quality of this moment and points a guilty finger directly at someone. No doubt, this makes for a good story, with clear lines between cause and effect, good and evil, right and wrong. But at the same time, it pulls the Roes, Loretta Goodwin, and Hamlet out of the stream of history and downplays, perhaps deliberately, the everyday political, economic, and, yes, social forces that shaped the decisions to the fix the hydraulic line with the wrong parts and to lock the doors. It makes the actors in the drama uniquely powerful characters in a moving morality play while obscuring what was so ordinary about this town, the Imperial plant, the people who owned it and worked inside it, and the hidden dangers that lurked there and in so many corners of America in the 1990s.

There is another, more socially informed, way to tell the story of the causes of the Hamlet fire, a way that shows, to paraphrase the poet Claudia Rankine, just how "wrongfully ordinary" this deadly moment was.[31]

This book is that other way. It argues that the Hamlet fire broke out because the nation, not just this place or these people, had essentially given up on protecting its most vulnerable and precarious citizens. It shows that in the years leading up to the blaze the United States had become a more callous and divided, less patient and generous land. Above all, America, and especially the spaces on its margins, became dominated by the idea—the system, really—of *cheap*. Cheap's central notion was that the combination of less pay, less regulation, and less attention to the economic and racial inequities of the past was the best way to solve the nation's most pressing problems. By 1991, this idea had seeped into every part of the country, every political discussion, every debate about civil rights, and every workplace and government agency until it reached the factory floor and the dinner table. Again and again, those with power valued cheap food, cheap government, and cheap lives over quality ingredients, investment in human capital, and strong oversight and regulation. But the policies of cheap came at a cost, as this story of the fire at Imperial Food Products in 1991 makes clear, a cost that hasn't been repaid in Hamlet or places like it; not yet, some twenty-five years and counting after the deaths of Loretta Goodwin's family and co-workers.

1

HAMLET

The Mello-Buttercup Ice Cream factory, with its red brick exterior and clean white tile walls inside, stood on a slightly raised plateau just up the street from Hamlet's rounded, Queen Anne–style train depot. Everything in Hamlet was close to the railroad station. Main Street. The "black" stores on Hamlet Avenue. The NAACP headquarters. The sprawling houses with tall white columns and wide front steps. The public housing project without air-conditioning. The limestone churches with steeples that reached higher into the sky than any other building in town and the cinder-block churches no bigger than a grade school classroom. Hamlet Hospital. The Piggly Wiggly. The mini-mart that doubled as a drug corner. The movie theater that once had a crow's nest where black people sat. The florist shops and hardware stores. The playgrounds and sports fields. The dance clubs and juke joints. The fire station and police department headquarters. The elementary schools and middle schools. The library and City Hall. They were all close to the station. Everything was close together in Hamlet because Hamlet wasn't that big, less than five square miles, and home to 4,700 people in 1980, when Emmett Roe first came to town. But everything was close to the station because just about every house, place of worship, and business was there because of the railroad. That included the ice cream plant.

Hamlet residents will tell you that there wouldn't have been a Hamlet without the railroad. Founded in 1873 at the junction where the Wilmington, Charlotte & Rutherford Railroad met the Raleigh and Augusta Air Line Railroad, the town didn't welcome its hundredth resident until almost twenty years later.[1] In those early days, Hamlet was known as a frontier town. Not quite the Wild West, it was still a place where card playing and whiskey drinking took place out in the open and no one said anything. By 1897, Hamlet was officially incorporated and sobered up enough that the highly capitalized and economically powerful Seaboard Air Line Railroad, known as the "South's Progressive Railway" and "The Route of Courteous Service," moved its regional headquarters to town. After that, Hamlet took off. By 1910, it had a Coca-Cola bottling company, five dry goods stores, and two five-and-dimes. Its population had jumped from 639 in 1900 to more than 4,000 in 1930. By then, the town had become the kind of place people moved *to* to get a good job and build a good life.[2]

"Well," Riley Watson, a longtime foreman on the line, remarked, "if it hadn't been for the Seaboard, Hamlet wouldn't ever have been what it is. If they hadn't built that railroad through here, and they hadn't decided to make this a big division point, Hamlet . . . might have been a crossroad, that's all."[3]

During the first two decades of the twentieth century, with Seaboard pouring money into the town, Hamlet grew into a bustling and busy transportation hub. By the end of World War I, more than thirty trains rumbled in and out of town every day. The grinding of brakes and the whistle of locomotives woke people up in the morning and put them to sleep at night. North of the depot, Seaboard built an extensive maintenance shop, then a mammoth roundhouse, and, after that, an expansive shipping yard. Following World War II, the railroad company invested $11 million in a classification yard, the first in the Southeast, where engines, freight cars, and dining cars were pulled apart and reassembled for the next leg of their journey. Eventually, seventy-two separate tracks crisscrossed Hamlet and the edges of town. Most of the trains coming through were freight trains, pulling boxcar after boxcar loaded with shirts made in Passaic, New Jersey, on their way to Atlanta's downtown department stores or coal from West Virginia headed to the port of Wilmington or timber from South Georgia destined for the furniture factories in High Point, North Carolina. But it wasn't just cargo that came through. With tourism and leisure travel on the rise in America in the years after the Civil War, Hamlet became part of a new, and by far less contentious, Mason-Dixon Line, separating New York in the cold months of winter from the sunshine of Florida. Every morning, the Orange Blossom Special pulled into the depot. Late in the afternoon it was the Silver Meteor. In between, the Boll Weevil, a local running from Hamlet to Wilmington, with stops in Laurel Hill, Old Hundred, and Laurinburg, passed through the station as well.[4]

Four thousand people—really four thousand men, mostly white men—worked for the railroad. With a virtual monopoly on moving goods across America, railroad companies and the stout robber barons who owned them piled up mountains of profits between 1877 and 1925. The conductors, engineers, and brakemen who ran the trains and maintained the tracks got a share of the wealth as well. The railroads provided their laborers with good, steady, well-paying jobs supplemented with sick pay, unemployment benefits, and pension plans. The work could be grueling and dangerous, but the companies usually abided by safety rules and put in place protections that limited risks and injuries. A job with the railroad was by far the best job a man without a college degree or a family name could get in the piney and gently rolling Sandhill sections of North Carolina that surrounded Hamlet. These jobs were even better than having a patch of land outside of town on which to grow cotton or peaches. And they were union jobs. The men who headed the Brotherhood of Railway Carmen, the Order of Railway Conductors of America, and the nation's other railroad unions did not, however, deliver fiery speeches about wage slavery and the destruction of capitalism at their annual meetings in Atlantic City and Chicago. They preached the gospel of bread-and-butter unionism, promising to lift their thick-necked and brawny members into the middle class. They fought for seniority protections, clearly spelled-out grievance procedures, and annual pay raises. Usually they won, in part because the railroads were making money in the first half of the twentieth century and the men who ran them wanted to avoid strikes and walk-outs.

Because the Seaboard and other railroads operated nationally, the railway unions fought for and won national wage scales. Unlike the steel and coal industries, there was little regional competition and no agreed upon southern wage differential. A brakeman in Hamlet got paid the same amount as a brakeman in Hannibal, Missouri, or Des Moines, Iowa. That kind of money went a long way in a small southern town. It turned these men into breadwinners and guaranteed them job stability, rising living standards, and a secure retirement. When they married, as most surely did, their wives generally stayed at home, taking care of the cooking and housekeeping, volunteering at school and church, and raising children and looking after elderly neighbors.[5]

"Hamlet became a thriving, bustling town," explained local journalist Clark Cox. And that prosperity, he maintained, was broadly shared. "Hamlet," Cox wrote, "had something that (nearby) Rockingham didn't have—a large middle class. Railroad workers were skilled, unionized, and much better paid than textile workers."[6] The money they made as conductors, engineers, foremen, and machine shop supervisors spread across the town and lifted up whole families for generations to come. Getting a job with the railroad was usually a family affair. Brother recommended brother. Fathers got apprenticeships for sons. Church members put in a good word for fellow congregants and relatives. Once a man landed a railroad job, he usually kept it for the rest of his working life.

Burnell McGirt served in the Navy during World War II. He came home and got his first and the only job he ever had with the railroad. "I hired out in May of 1946," he told an interviewer in 2009. "I worked in the signaling department until 1971, and from there I went to the roadway department. I had thirty-eight years of service with the railroad."[7]

Nat Campbell's stint with the railroad lasted forty-two years. Over that time, he always made decent money. "I was able to give my wife and children things that I probably couldn't give them if I worked anywhere else," he bragged in 2009, looking back on his years as a carman and laborer in the wheel-and-axle shop. "We always had a nice trip," he said. They had a Sears charge account, and they ran it up each year buying Christmas presents for "our young'uns." "By November of the next year," he joked, "we had it all paid up, and we had to start all over again."[8]

Once white workers—"railroad men," as they called themselves—got married and saved a little money, they bought modest brick houses and·wood bungalows to the east of the depot on Boyd Lake Road and Spring Street, and not far from the center of town, on Cherry Street and Rosedale Lane. Seaboard accountants and managers, conductors and crew leaders, the aristocrats of labor, settled even closer to Main Street, where they lived next to the high school principal and the football coach, lawyers, and store owners on shaded streets with names like Madison and

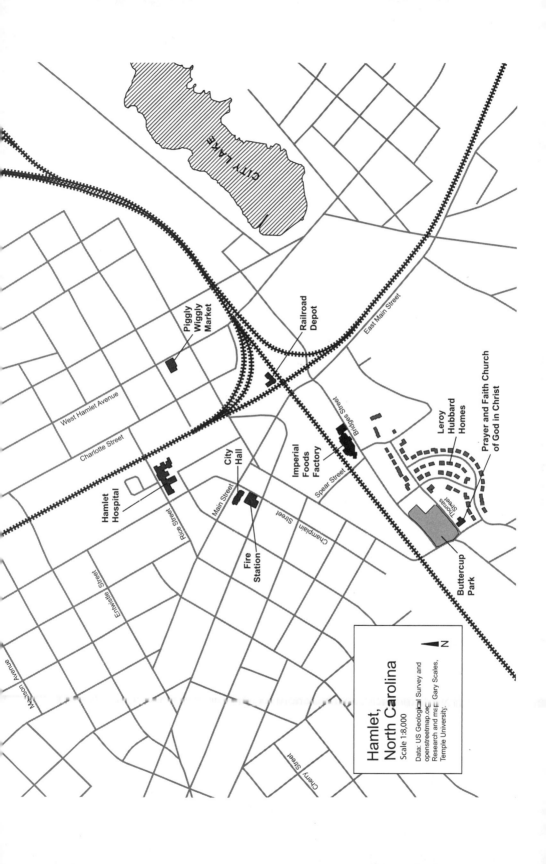

CITY LAKE

Piggly
Wiggly
Market

Railroad
Depot

West Hamlet Avenue

Charlotte Street

East Main Street

Bridges Street

Hamlet
Hospital

City
Hall

Imperial
Foods
Factory

Spear Street

Leroy
Hubbard
Homes

Prayer and Faith Church
of God in Christ

Rice Street

Main Street

Fire
Station

Champlain Street

Thomas
Street

Buttercup
Park

Entwistle Street

Madison Avenue

Cherry Street

Hamlet,
North Carolina

Scale 1:8,000

Data: US Geological Survey and
openstreetmap.org
Research and map: Gary Scales,
Temple University.

N

Hamilton, Entwistle, and Pineland, in white clapboard houses with lawns as manicured as country club greens and porches wide enough for three-person bench swings. In the spring, these thoroughfares smelled like azaleas and dogwoods, and in the fall like damp pine needles and moist oak leaves. Kids tracked along the sidewalks, trick-or-treating at Halloween and singing carols at Christmas. In the years after World War II, some railway workers moved their families farther out onto curvy streets in small subdivisions named after plantations, into what passed for Hamlet's suburbs. They parked their motorized fishing boats on trailers out front in their driveways next to their new Ford trucks, Buick sedans, and Chevy station wagons. In the backyards were brick grills and above-ground pools. In fact, one local official chuckled about Hamlet, "We had more backyard swimming pools then Beverly Hills. It was a high-income place for the South."[9]

Most of Hamlet's prosperity stayed on the white side of the town's racial divide. Thirty-nine percent of Hamlet residents in 1980 were, according to the United States Census, African American. But not many held the kinds of high-paying jobs that pulled them out to the suburbs or paid for backyard pools. On average, African Americans made almost 40 percent less than whites, and they were less likely to work on the railroads, which classified jobs along racial lines well past World War II.[10] By the time that Imperial Food Products began to relocate to Hamlet from northeast Pennsylvania, twenty-six years after the *Brown* decision, jobs were no longer explicitly segregated, the lights were off on the minstrel shows that used to play at the city ballpark, voting booths were open to everyone, and local children attended integrated schools. But when the bell rang after the last class period, the African American students still went home to largely segregated neighborhoods; they still knew that some sections of town were essentially off-limits to them and most still had little faith that the police would protect them or their property. Sunday remained the holiest and most segregated day of the week, as black families went to black churches and white families went to white churches.[11]

Yet within Hamlet's black community there was, as one local preacher noted, an "economic divide." Along Charlotte Street, a short walk from the depot, African Americans "who were doing well," doctors and teachers and families with men who worked for the railroads as porters and waiters—and later on, as employment segregation broke down somewhat, as switchmen, machinists, and mechanics—lived in tidy houses with neat stone walkways and flower-filled window boxes. By 1970, a handful of black professionals had moved away from the Main Street area into one of the neat ranch houses with aluminum carports in the tiny black suburban development known as McEachern Forest on the southern edge of town, named after a successful Hamlet African American undertaker, business-man, and politician who himself lived there.[12]

African Americans who taught in the schools, worked as janitors in the hospital, and held decent railway jobs lived in simple brick homes just north of Hamlet Avenue along Pine, Washington, and Monroe Streets. Men who worked the dirtier, but still steady, jobs loading coal, haul-ing freight, hammering rails, and washing down engines lived to south near Bridges Street, and even farther south and north, in narrow trailers, on lots cut out from forests of tall, skinny pine trees.[13] Their neighbors washed dishes at local hotels, stocked the shelves at hardware and auto parts stores, and cleaned up around the depot and the filling stations. They hauled wood and made a little extra money picking peaches and cotton during the harvest seasons. Black women—like Imperial worker Loretta Goodwin and John Coltrane's mom—no matter where they lived, including along Charlotte Street, contributed to their household in-comes by waiting tables, picking crops, and, mostly before 1980, cleaning toilets, folding clothes, and cooking dinner in the homes of white railroad workers, doctors, lawyers, and firefighters.

Many of Hamlet's African American families didn't actually live in Hamlet. They lived in the North Yard, an unincorporated section of Richmond County with a population of between eight hundred and one thousand people that sat about halfway between the Hamlet train depot and Seaboard's vast maintenance facilities north of town. Some houses in this area were neat and tidy and clustered together in family plots. Most, however, were shotgun shacks and trailers owned by politically connected white landlords, men like D.L. McDonald.

Born in 1911, Daniel Leonard McDonald graduated from high school and went right to work as a carpenter. It didn't take long before he moved up a few rungs and became a general contractor. Over the next several decades, he built hundreds of houses, from simple lakeside cabins to sprawling ranch homes across Richmond County. Between 1961 and 1978, he served on the Richmond County Board of Commissioners.[14] Throughout his years of real estate and political success, McDonald held on to a North Yard general store where he extended credit to his tenants and their neighbors. Locals called him "Jot It Down" because every time someone picked up a can of beans or a loaf of bread, he wrote it down in his book. He would add it to the rent. Then, it seems, he would factor in interest and other fees. When it came time to settle up, no one in the North Yard ever seemed to be able to get all of their debts erased from D.L. McDonald's book.

McDonald charged $50 to $100 a month for one of his three- or four-room houses in the North Yard. Most of these tin-roofed places sat a foot or two off the ground on short stacks of cement blocks. Well into the 1960s, some still had hand-dug wells and outhouses in the back. "There were so many holes in the floor," remembered Martin Quick of his North Yard rental house, "that if you dropped a penny you had to go outside to pick it up." During the winter, his family shoved crumpled pieces of newspaper into the holes in the walls to keep out the cold.

Locals knew that they could find a drink and a dice game in the North Yard just about any time of day. "If my mom got word I was there," Joseph Arnold, who lived in one of Hamlet's black neighborhoods, chuckled, "I'd be in trouble." Even if she didn't know he was there, he made sure he left by nightfall.[15]

"I wouldn't have gone over to that part of town," Josh Newton recalled. There just wasn't anything there for him, the white son of a white railroad worker who didn't drink or smoke and was getting ready to go to college. At least, that's how he looked at it at the time.[16]

When Mike Quick's family moved from the North Yard to the Leroy Hubbard Homes, the South Hamlet public housing project down the hill from the Mello-Buttercup factory on Bridges Street, he felt like a real-life version of the television Jeffersons, moving on up the social ladder. For the first time in his life, the future NFL All-Pro wide receiver lived in a place where he couldn't see the ground through the floors and his neighbors didn't walk out the back door to go to the bathroom. But he remained in a segregated neighborhood, one where most people were just getting by, though things got better for his family when he entered the fifth grade around 1971 and his mom, the family's breadwinner, landed a job as a nurse's assistant at Hamlet Hospital not far from the depot and downtown.[17]

From the time that Seaboard set up shop in town, even the people who didn't work for the railroad in Hamlet, black and white, still depended on the railroad. For years, Walter Bell shined shoes at the station. J.C. Niemeyer started in the Seaboard maintenance shops around the turn of the century. A few years later, in 1902, he left the railroad and opened the town's first laundry. J.L. Dooley, a carpenter, made his living building and repairing homes for Seaboard engineers and conductors. W.R. Bosnal and Company manufactured crossties and switches. Before refrigerated cars came into use, the Hamlet Ice Company employed fifty men, making huge blocks of ice and delivering them to the yards to keep the fruit from Florida and vegetables from New Jersey cool and fresh in transit. During World War I, runners carried platters of fried chicken, potato salad, greens, and cornbread from McEachern's Hotel, an African American–owned rooming house on Bridges Street, not far from where the Imperial plant would be, over to the depot and sold them for a quarter each to hungry black soldiers passing through town, men trusted to fight for the United States Army but not permitted to get food at the whites-only lunch counters and eateries on Hamlet's Main Street.[18]

Before the wide adoption of Pullman cars in the years after World War I, passengers didn't sleep overnight on trains. They got off at midway points between New York and Miami in places like Hamlet. Local businesses grew to meet the travel needs of these short-term visitors. Passengers in blue blazers and silk skirts stayed at Hamlet's Terminal Hotel or at the fancier Seaboard Hotel. After they checked in and freshened up, they went for a stroll along Main Street, where as one local remembers, "every store was filled and business was doing pretty well down here." They passed the banks, the Beaux Arts opera house, and the hardware store, shoe store, and jewelry shop. Next to Birmingham Drug there was a bowling alley where, as a local dentist recalled, "They had black boys in there that'd set the pins." On Saturday nights, the overnight guests mixed with local bankers and their wives, and on Sunday mornings, railroad workers and their families walked through town on the way back home from church. White men would stop by the newsstand in the depot to pick up the papers, including the *New York Times* if they wanted it, and get the latest local gossip.[19] Every once in a while, they would catch a glimpse of one of the famous figures seen on the front or back pages of papers in their hometown. When the Ringling Brothers and Barnum and Bailey Circus hit the road in the South, it would stop and exercise its lions and elephants on Hamlet's streets. During the first few decades of the twentieth century, Booker T. Washington, William Jennings Bryan, Franklin D. Roosevelt, Buffalo Bill Cody, and Jenny Lind stopped in Hamlet. And for one glorious night in 1917, Hamlet was the center of the musical world as Italian tenor Enrico Caruso performed before a packed crowd at the town's opera house.[20]

Donations from the railroads and contributions from the paychecks of railroad workers helped to create Hamlet's layered town life. The city put on a Christmas parade in December and fireworks on the Fourth of July. Downtown there were Belk's and W.R. Land's department stores and Stewart Gordon Furniture with its rocking-chair sign over the front door. There was Cromartie's and Fox's Barber Shop, three pool rooms, and two or three movie theaters showing weekly serials and Westerns to packed—and of course segregated—houses on Saturday afternoons. The money from Seaboard helped to build churches with stained glass windows and pipe organs. It paid for meeting halls and Sunday school classrooms, folding tables and stacks of collapsible chairs brought out for banquets and weddings. It funded improvements that made Hamlet schools, especially the white ones, better than most in the area. Those wages helped to lay out Little League fields with smooth infields, lush grass outfields, and electric scoreboards. It built a hospital other towns envied. Opened in 1915, Hamlet Hospital, where Mike Quick's mom worked, grew by 1940 into a four-story, one-hundred-bed facility, twice the size of the one in more populous Rockingham, the county seat of Richmond County and Hamlet's bitter rival in sports and business. According to a local historian, Hamlet Hospital was the largest medical facility in the state at the time. Patients traveled from the much larger cities of Charlotte and Greensboro, two and three hours away, to get their care there.[21]

Beginning in the 1960s, however, the economic world of Hamlet's well-dressed Main Street and landscaped residential areas began to fray.

State highways and county roads began to cut across North Carolina and the rest of the South. The post office started to use planes to move letters and postcards. Snowbirds on their way to Florida started to drive on the wide interstates paid for with Cold War dollars. Salesmen from Charlotte loaded their samples in their trunks and steered their new Oldsmobiles with electric windows and frosty air-conditioning out of their driveways to call on customers in Wilmington and Fayetteville. Truckers carried trailers full of live chickens, loaves of Wonder Bread, crates of sweet potatoes, and boxes of rolled bologna from the farms and factories to supermarkets in cities, suburbs, and small towns.

The Seaboard tried to shore up its financial health and meet the new challenges posed by jetliners, road building, and a growing trucking industry. Beginning in 1967, it began buying up smaller lines and merging with other rail companies. The early consolidations cost Hamlet some jobs as they got shifted to other hubs in the system. To stay competitive, the company cut crews, eliminated the caboose on some lines, froze wages, and introduced other labor-saving technologies. Faced with fewer riders, it reduced its passenger services, eliminating more jobs and taking visitors off the streets of Hamlet who in the past had looked round town for lunch, a souvenir, and even a taste of whiskey. Seaboard would stay in business, eventually reorganizing after another round of mergers and job transfers that moved even more positions out of Hamlet to Jacksonville, Florida, and Corbin, Kentucky. In 1986, the company would officially be renamed CSX, but by then, the best days were clearly behind the one-time "Hub City of the Carolinas." The one or two short lines that still cut through Hamlet scaled back as well during the 1970s and 1980s. In 1991, just months before the fire at Imperial, as the nation's economy sagged under the weight of a sharp downturn, there was another round of layoffs in town as dozens of longtime local workers were furloughed.[22]

As jobs, industry, and talent gravitated toward urban centers and interstate highways, Hamlet, forty-eight miles from I-95 and eighty-one miles from I 85, started to die a slow death. The signs of the area's decline could be seen from a number of different vantage points. In 1974, as double-digit inflation struck the entire country and the nation's economy began to tank, the unemployment rate for Richmond County—where Hamlet was located—rose to a staggering 24.4 percent. The local paper, the

Richmond County Daily News, reported the next year that 20 percent of area families lived below the poverty line and that the local annual wage had fallen below the state average and wasn't keeping up with incomes in urban areas.[23] By the 1980s, despite the presence of Hamlet Hospital, the county had less than half as many physicians per capita as the rest of the state averaged. Teenage pregnancies were on the rise and so was infant mortality. In 1980, the county nearly topped the state in premature deaths of children.[24]

Adding to the town's pain, over the course of the 1970s, Hamlet had fought a losing retail battle with neighboring Rockingham. A K-Mart and then a Walmart—which one Hamlet man called the "big box over yonder"—opened on the highway connecting the two towns, but both were within Rockingham's city limits and tax jurisdiction. Cars from Hamlet filled the spots in the football field–sized parking lots in front of the discount stores and at the supermarkets, buffets, and fast food outlets next to them. The wide-aisled Food Lion sold peaches and tomatoes from California and New Jersey for less than farmers could grow them a county or two away. The McDonald's churned out burgers at half the price of the grill in downtown Hamlet. Revco, the national chain with a store in Rockingham, charged less than the pharmacy on Main Street for aspirin, Q-tips, and rubbing alcohol. As paychecks shrunk and jobs disappeared, these bargains were harder and harder for many to pass up.[25]

Starting in the 1970s, as work vanished on the railroad, Hamlet and the small towns in Richmond County and across the country began to mimic the new stores popping up on the retail horizon, the Food Lions and Walmarts. Working people, like these chains, had to survive on the cheap. Prices were lower, but so were wages. With the railroad slowly laying off hundreds of men, there were fewer well-paying, benefit-rich union jobs in town and more part-time posts—or full-time positions that paid part-time wages and didn't include health insurance or retirement contributions. As pay envelopes shrunk, working people depended more and more on everyday low prices, especially with public assistance barely covering the basics and getting cut by lawmakers in Raleigh, it seemed, every year. As the jobs people held changed and their paychecks weren't what they used to be, Main Street, with its locally owned shops, became too expensive, a retail anachronism of an older time, pushing people toward the aisles of the low-price chains and away from downtown.

Another sharp blow to Main Street, to Hamlet's downtown life, came in 1975. It came like it did to so many places in the United States—with bursting flames and angry shouts. It surprised some, especially in Hamlet's white community, but not everyone.

When Glenn Sumpter moved to Richmond County in 1970 to edit the local paper, he remembered thinking that race relations there were "basically better than in Hickory," the white-majority, western North Carolina town where he had been working for years as a reporter and columnist. Locals told him that the county "had been free of racial incidents" and was slowly adjusting to the ramifications of the Supreme Court decisions of the Earl Warren era and the civil rights acts of the Lyndon Johnson years.

Any sense of racial calm would be undone around 3:30 a.m. on Thursday, June 5, 1975. That's when two Hamlet police officers drove their cruiser past the closed-up stores along Hamlet Avenue and stopped in front of the City Café, where Rhonda Scott, a twenty-year-old African American woman, was sitting on the curb with four other African Americans. They were waiting for cabs to take them home. As the police drove up, two people got into a car and drove away. That left Scott and her two friends. The white officers asked for their names. Scott didn't answer right away. She said she wouldn't give them the information until they told her why they needed it. Her cab arrived. Scott climbed in. Maybe she said something, maybe she didn't. Before the car drove off, Sergeant James Bryant grabbed the door and tried to drag Scott out of the vehicle.

According to the police report, Scott got ahold of the officer's slapjack. Trying to pry it away from her, he hit her with his flashlight and then with his .357 Magnum pistol. Somehow, the gun discharged. Bryant said he shot into the air. Scott ended up in the hospital with scrapes and bruises and a possible grazing wound on her back from a pistol shot. The police charged her with drunk and disorderly conduct.

Within hours, Scott filed a formal complaint against Bryant "for violating my civil rights, brutality, use of degrading language and gesture, and exceeding normal restraint and authority in exercising the performance of his duty." The local magistrate, however, refused to charge the police officer.

The next afternoon, a Friday, Hamlet's black community, led by the local NAACP chapter, took to the streets in a hastily organized demonstration against Bryant and the police, city leaders who refused to charge him, and the everyday indignities they endured in their hometown. Fearful of violence stoked by rumors circulating within the white community that marchers planned to show up armed with guns, the police chief issued riot gear to his men and called in twenty highway patrolmen and fifteen state troopers. The rally took place without any disturbances and the streets of Hamlet cleared without incident. But as darkness fell, the town exploded. A fire erupted at Enterprise Auto Parts. Minutes later, the Builder's Supply Company and Pinecroft Industries burst into flames. More fires broke out at the Hamlet Housing Authority and at an office owned by landlord D.L. McDonald in the county's North Yard section. The fire department received additional reports of brush fires along Bridges Street, near the eventual Imperial site. When Eugene Ross, a firefighter, pulled up to investigate, he was pelted with gunfire. It missed him but shattered his car windows and scratched his young son, who sat in the passenger seat. As Mayor Earl Covington drove through African American sections of Hamlet, rocks rained down on his car. An unnamed white woman told the police that two black men grabbed her for no reason and roughed her up.

During the next few days, an uneasy peace hung over Hamlet, largely because Richmond County Sheriff Raymond Goodman stepped in and issued a warrant charging Sergeant Bryant with "assault with a deadly weapon." [26]

The rioters in Hamlet hoped, perhaps, like rioters in Oxford, North Carolina, did in 1970, that their demonstration would "cost these white people . . . enough goddamn money they was gonna start changing some things." [27] That yearning for something different and better would not be immediately rewarded. In the political campaigns in Hamlet after the riots, a new mayor and three new city council members were elected. Not one of them was black. Money didn't rush into town to create new well-paying jobs or better housing for African Americans either.

Reverend Harold Miller arrived in Hamlet twelve years after the riots to preach at a Baptist church on the black side of town. He looked around and saw a "close-knit," "hard-working," and faithful community. It was the kind of place that wherever you went you ran into someone you knew. But it was also, Miller noted, a place that was still largely segregated and on the "decline economically." Hamlet felt to him like it was "stuck in time," in both good and bad ways.[28]

"Stuck in time." That's exactly what the producers of the gangster film *Billy Bathgate*, starring Dustin Hoffman and Nicole Kidman, were looking to find. As they sketched out the film in 1988, they searched for a location to shoot a few scenes that resembled the small town of Onondaga, New York, in the 1930s. They settled on Hamlet, in part because of the same economic decline that Miller noticed, which, as a result of the flight of business to the box stores and the riot, had emptied out the downtown area over the previous two decades. This meant that the film crews wouldn't have to relocate too many establishments or move too many cars to get the look and feel they wanted. All they had to do was pry off a few layers of aluminum siding to get down to the buildings' original stonework and facades and they were back in the past. Locals played the parts of extras strolling between shops like the men and women coming off the Orange Blossom Special might have done sixty years earlier.[29]

With its star turn at the movies, things seemed to be looking up for Hamlet. In June 1990, the National Civic League named Hamlet an All-American City. The judges praised the town for its efforts to save Hamlet Hospital, expand the local library, and stage the annual Seaboard Festival, a yearly fall gathering of craft vendors, food stands, long-distance runners, and live bands celebrating the community and its railroading past. The town heralded its new national distinction by putting up red, white, and blue flags up and down Main Street.[30]

But a movie appearance, awards, and patriotic banners couldn't stop the town's economic slide. They couldn't bring back the railroad or re-create the trickle-down effect that good-paying jobs used to have in the homes and stores of Hamlet. The movie crews had painted in one of the windows of the Terminal Hotel, "Dining Room. Best Coffee in Onondaga." For years, though, the aging inn had operated as a flophouse, renting rooms to transients by the day—and even the hour. Around the corner, For Rent signs hung in the windows of many Main Street and Hamlet Avenue stores. Some places had no signs at all, and no merchandise either, just empty and dust-filled display cases facing the street. The opera house was long gone. The movie theaters had already played their last picture shows, and the bank doors were locked tight. St. James, the Catholic church, moved to the outskirts of town near Rockingham, and its old downtown location got turned into a restaurant and caterer that by the early 1980s was on the verge of going out of business. Only a handful of other businesses were still operating along Main Street,[31] including a cluttered hardware store and an old-timey drugstore that still mixed up cherry Cokes and vanilla cream sodas to order. One of the busiest places downtown was the soup kitchen.

When the Imperial plant burned down, Hamlet's freight yards and maintenance shops employed fewer than 600 men, down from 1,500 ten years earlier and more than twice that number ten years before that. The gabled and graceful depot at the bottom of Main Street opened just twice a day, and just long enough for a speeding Amtrak train to stop for a couple of minutes in the morning and a few minutes before midnight to let off a passenger or two before hustling north to Richmond or south to Atlanta. A coin-operated metal box filled with a handful of local papers replaced the newsstand. The only people around were the stationmaster and the occasional train buff. No one was there to greet the trains with chicken dinners or opera tickets to sell anymore.[32]

It wasn't just the railroads that were in decline, nor was it simply a matter of Hamlet's commercial spaces being in the midst of decay. The economic rot was much wider. Nearby Rockingham, with its fast-flowing streams, had been a textile center since 1837, before electricity had even arrived in the county. By the end of World War II, Richmond County had ten mills that employed, by one estimate, as many as 15,000 women and men, running two and three shifts a day, churning out underwear for Hanes, T-shirts for Fruit of the Loom, and rayon bedsheets for Burlington Industries. Although textile workers never got paid like railroad workers did, the mills provided jobs, housing, and enough money to keep families afloat, especially with two or three people from each household laboring in the noisy and dusty plants. By the 1980s, however, boxer shorts from Haiti and pillowcases from Guatemala filled the racks at the K-Mart store along the highway between Rockingham and Hamlet. Jobs tending looms and spindles in North Carolina left the state and landed farther south, in Mexico, and east, in Malaysia. Several of the ones still open—Burlington Mills, L'eggs Hosiery, and Union Underwear—invested in new, automated machines, cut their workforces, and slashed their payrolls. By the 1970s, Richmond County's mills were down to 5,000 total employees. During the 1980s, the local textile industry lost another third of its jobs, and another 10 percent of the positions vanished by the time of the Imperial fire. As a percentage of total employment, textiles provided 52 percent of the county's manufacturing jobs in 1979; by 1990, this number had fallen to 38 percent, and it would keep falling as American manufacturers of yarn, T-shirts, and linens faced ceaseless competition from corporate spin-offs and upstarts in the Global South.[33]

Ada Blanchard, an African American woman employed by Imperial in 1991, worked in a Richmond County spinning mill during her high school years in the late 1970s. After that, she went up north for a decade. When she came back, she noted, "those jobs in the mills were gone."[34]

As the jobs Blanchard once knew drifted overseas and Mack trucks hauling forty-eight-foot trailers replaced railroad cars, men with jobs that could support a family and pay the mortgage on a roomy house with a porch and backyard pool were becoming a rarity in the Sandhills of North Carolina. With the good jobs gone, there wasn't as much pressure on employers to keep wage rates up. That turned Hamlet and Richmond County into a buyer's market for employers. More and more, all that was left for working people in these parts were dead-end service jobs at the places out on the highway and jobs in food-processing plants at low hourly rates and without benefits or lifetime guarantees of employment or union protections for seniority rights and safety. And increasingly the places that had jobs to offer would just as soon hire women as men and pay them less if they could get away with it.

This wasn't only a local problem. Factories were closing in well-established manufacturing centers and small towns everywhere. As the economy shifted, the nation's social contract got rewritten in fits and spurts. Under the New Deal order that held sway in the United States from the 1930s until the 1970s, policy makers shared a loose consensus about the lessons of modern American history and the obligations of government. Underconsumption, they believed, had triggered the on-slaught and dislocations of the Great Depression. Raising demand across the board, many thought, would set the stage for the nation's economic rebound and for sustained and robust growth across the country for years to come. Economic health was, above all in this view, about aggregate demand. Borrowing ideas from Henry Ford and John Maynard Keynes, New Deal government, business, and labor leaders thought a tighter labor market would produce a larger number of better paying jobs, and that the more working people made, the more they would spend, and that the more they spent, the more high-wage work there would be, for men, and prosperity for everyone else. Under Democratic presidents Franklin D. Roosevelt, Harry S. Truman, and Lyndon B. Johnson, and then under the Republican regimes of Dwight D. Eisenhower and Richard M. Nixon, the government did what it could through spending, regulations, and le-gal changes to keep the cycle of higher wages and increased purchasing power going.

With the Wagner Act, workers gained in 1935 the right to organize and collectively bargain. The Fair Labor Standards Act of 1938 set man-datory minimum wage and maximum hour standards for laborers to spread out work and boost take-home pay. During World War II, gov-ernment officials protected unions and preserved the earning capacity of production soldiers. In the postwar era, unions pressed for and won cost-of-living increases, paid family vacations, fully funded pensions, and company-provided health care. When laborers fell on hard times, the gov-ernment stepped in with worker's compensation, unemployment benefits, and retirement pay. Bolstered by the New Deal safety net, laborers and their families would, it was hoped, have some money to spend at the gro-cery store and the meat market even during hard times, keeping them-selves and the economy from hitting rock bottom. Between the 1930s and the 1970s, there was, notes the historian Bruce Shulman, "little disagreement . . . over the fundamental principles for organizing Ameri-can life," including the broad benefits of decent wages and the need for taxes to pay for the safety net that hung beneath the economy.[35]

More, then, was central to the entire New Deal social bargain. The more people made and the more they had in the bank and in their homes, the more cars and radios they bought, the better, it was believed, for everyone. At the heart of the New Deal idea of America was the working man, not so much the grizzled miner or the gaunt millhand, but the stout autoworker, the plumber, and the railroad worker. A man in work pants and steel-toed boots with a car out front, a mortgage to pay, a home entertainment system in the living room, and a swimming pool in the backyard. A wife and kids standing behind him. Christmas club and savings account books in a desk drawer. A bowling ball and fishing rod in a closet. A union pin fastened to his jacket. This man symbolized the New Deal world of *more*.

Yet, by the time the *Billy Bathgate* crew left Hamlet, the New Deal order was unraveling at breakneck speed. With global competition on the rise and the economic pie no longer growing, people everywhere in the 1970s and 1980s grumbled about taxes and social programs and who deserved government support and who didn't. Meanwhile, thirty years of steadily rising wages led some businesses to invest (again) in labor-saving technologies. Smaller, undercapitalized firms, which were proliferating, looked (again) for cheaper workers. As they did, many of the jobs that had sustained white men as breadwinners—like those on the railroad—disappeared, replaced by positions flipping burgers, taking orders at fast food restaurants, processing chickens and pigs, and changing beds in hotels and hospitals. In this new economy, employers, especially ones operating in competitive industries that didn't require huge capital investments in equipment and physical plants, searched for larger pools of cheaper labor. They didn't care who swam in them. The more people looking for a job the less they would have to pay and the less say workers would have about their working conditions. The first thing employers looked for as a sign that they were in the right place for less expensive and less boisterous laborers was the lack of a union.

Southern boosters, businessmen, and commentators created a myth about the region. They told people that southerners didn't like unions, that they wouldn't bend their stiff red necks to the yoke of organization. They used numbers to back up their portraits.[36] In the 1970s, only 14 percent of nonfarm workers in North Carolina belonged to a union, as compared to 30 to 40 percent in Pennsylvania, Ohio, and Michigan. Like all myths and like all statistics, these numbers hide as much as they reveal. Throughout the 1930s and 1940s, southern workers pressed their employers for pay hikes and improved conditions. They walked off the job and staged massive region-wide strikes. As late as the 1980s, Houston construction workers were plastering their pickup trucks with union stickers, Birmingham steelworkers were wearing union pins on their overalls, and CSX workers in Hamlet were proudly declaring their allegiance to their unions.

"I believe in unionized labor," Hamlet's Burnell McGirt told an interviewer for a local oral history project in 2009. "I belonged to the Brotherhood of Signalmen," he proudly added. Another Hamlet resident (and southerner), Walter Bell, declared, "You can't beat the union. Because if you didn't, the company will take advantage of you." His neighbor, Jimmy Stricklin, thought that everyone, not just union members, benefited from organized labor. Unions, he said, made sure there were no children in the mills and people had money to spend downtown. When Josh Newton's dad's railroad union went out on strike one time in Hamlet, his cousin crossed the picket. That relative never got another invitation to the Newton house again.[37]

The issue with the South, then, was not that southern workers didn't like unions. It was that the region was late to industrialize, lacked investment, and didn't attract as many highly capitalized auto or steel plants and railroad facilities as some other parts of the country. Because of the high fixed costs in these sectors, employers faced limited competition and could set, for a time at least, their own prices, passing wage hikes on to consumers. With these kinds of profit-making advantages, management didn't fight unions quite as hard. The South, however, eventually became home to textile mills, timber camps, and food processors—all fiercely competitive industries that relied on cutting costs, especially labor costs, to turn a profit. That emphasis on cheap kept southern employers outside the New Deal consensus and kept the overall rate of union membership low in the South. When the foundations of the global economy shifted in the 1970s and Keynesian policies fell out of favor, North Carolina and the states around it, with their competitive industries and growing number of anti-union employers, became the norm—not the exception.[38]

Even before the shift away from the New Deal, hostility toward labor got baked into the region's politics, especially in North Carolina. Tar Heel politicians tolerated, and even welcomed, anti-union industrialists.

They wanted their business. To get it, they passed anti-union legislation, looked the other way when law officers ripped through picket lines, and wrote the new script for the region, erasing the labor militancy of the past from the historical record and turning union men like Burnell McGirt and his Hamlet union brothers into quirky anomalies or dangerous renegades, not "true" sons of the Southland. Their collective efforts paid off and turned *union* into a dirty word. "North Carolina is guided by the belief that unions are an unnecessary disruption of the routine affairs of business and government," wrote North Carolina state house representative Paul Luebke, a Durham Democrat and University of North Carolina at Greensboro sociologist, in his 1990 book, *Tar Heel Politics*. Valerie Ervin, a battle-tested union organizer for the United Food and Commercial Workers Union, visited southern factories and small towns for much of the 1980s. But in North Carolina she discovered the real meaning of anti-unionism—it wasn't just ideology, it was force. "The toughest state I've ever worked in," Ervin said about the Tar Heel state. "People are afraid for us to come to their homes. They feel that there's going to be violence."[39]

While they treated the railroad and its unions as an exception, Richmond County employers and government officials were no more welcoming to unions than was the rest of North Carolina. Labor organizers like Ervin could expect to be greeted there with about as much warmth, to paraphrase a *Time* magazine reporter, as white Mississippians had extended to freedom riders coming into their state in the 1960s. The county's anti-unionism started at the top with the most powerful person around.[40]

In 1991, the *Charlotte Observer* called Richmond County's chief law officer, Raymond Goodman, "the last of the old-style sheriffs." Slim, balding, bespectacled, and slowed by a pair of heart attacks, Goodman might not have fit the role as well as he had in the past, but he still wore a big hat, rode shotgun in a champagne-colored Lincoln Continental, and chomped throughout the day on an unlit Garcia y Vega cigar. He let his deputies run around the county enforcing the law while he ate lunch at the Wendy's or the Holiday Inn and sat on a sofa just inside the front door of his furniture business in downtown Rockingham, right across the street from the county courthouse building. If he saw a politician or a reporter he wanted to talk with passing by, he sent one of his clerks out to chase him down and bring him into the store. Lawyers, judges, and shop owners stopped in to gossip with him about the comings and goings in Ellerbe and Hamlet or about who would win the next big race at the Rock— Rockingham Speedway, the massive one-mile oval NASCAR track on the northern edge of the county that was partly owned, some said, by the sheriff himself. Just behind him in the showroom, newlyweds peeked at the price tags hanging off bedroom sets and retired farmers picked out new La-Z-Boy chairs for their living rooms. Railway conductors and field hands asked the sheriff for favors, advice, and loans. It was politics and business the old-fashioned way. Goodman never forgot a name, a face, a family connection, or who owed him money or had done him wrong.[41]

In his first run for the Richmond County sheriff's office in 1946, Goodman lost. But he won in 1950 and never lost again. An unwavering Democrat with a pile of dependable votes in his pocket, beginning in the 1960s Goodman hosted a parade of candidates for statewide office who stopped by the furniture store and made small talk as they asked for his endorsement. This made him a player in the state capitol when his party was in office, and even when it wasn't. When Hamlet officials needed money to upgrade the city's water treatment facilities, they went to Goodman, and he marched a band of local leaders up to Raleigh to see the person in charge. They left with the money they needed. Even as the sheriff became a statewide power broker, he never took his eye off Richmond County or loosened his grip on the area.

Goodman didn't carry a gun, but people in Rockingham, Hamlet, Hoffman, Cordova, and the North Yard still feared him. "Raymond Goodman is the Godfather," reported a labor reformer after visiting the county. "Untouchable" was how another characterized his local standing. "Raymond Goodman, the Sheriff of Richmond County, has had people beaten and is crooked as a dog's hind leg," a local resident complained to Governor Jim Hunt, unaware perhaps of the alliance between the rough-and-tumble lawman and the upright Democratic politician. "But the people of Richmond County," he confided, are "scared to say anything of his actions."

According to some local observers, Goodman and his men stopped cracking heads in the 1960s and ran the county through a system of "accumulated favors." When his deputies brought a farmhand to jail on a drunk and disorderly charge, the sheriff might let him go the next morning, but if he did, Goodman expected his vote and his wife's vote and anyone else's vote living in that house in the next election and every one after that. He cut through red tape for local business owners and found jobs for the sons of supporters in his store, on county road crews, and on various maintenance details. He always took care of local preachers, donating money to help with an addition to the social hall or to fix a leaky sanctuary roof. On Christmas and Easter, he sent his deputies out on county time with fresh turkeys and tins of cookies to pass out to his customers as a thank-you for their business and their votes.[42]

When not many others did, Goodman courted the support of African Americans. To him, votes were like money; it didn't matter where you got them from, since they all counted the same at the final tally. When black railroad workers and farmhands couldn't take out loans at the bank, Goodman or one of his allies, someone like D.L. McDonald, gave them store credit and leaned on them at election time. The sheriff hired a few black deputies long before most small-town sheriffs dared to do so. Both on the streets and when it came to policing, African Americans generally considered Goodman "fair and impartial," even if they didn't completely trust him or the informers he kept on his payroll in their communities. A full decade before Congress signed the Voting Rights Act into law, Goodman made sure African Americans could register to vote in Richmond County. In 1972, he helped to make Maceo McEachern the first black man elected to the Richmond County Board of Education since Reconstruction. After McEachern moved up to the County Board of Commissioners, the two men clashed over a few key issues, and Goodman orchestrated McEachern's defeat in 1982. When racial tensions crested in Hamlet in 1975 after the local magistrate refused to issue an arrest warrant for Sergeant Bryant in the beating of Rhonda Scott, Goodman stepped in and personally arrested the lawman. Many African Americans repaid him for the loans, jobs, and political support he provided by voting for him in each of his election campaigns and supporting the candidates he supported. Others pointed to what he had done to McEachern and how Bryant's trial got postponed again and again. They said Goodman threw crumbs their way, not real jobs or real power. But still, until he retired in 1994, the sheriff was just about the only game in town.[43]

Goodman didn't learn politics at home. His father worked at a loom in a textile mill in Cordova, a short drive south from Rockingham. He cut hair on the side. He needed the extra money to put food on the table for Goodman and his fifteen brothers and sisters, who squeezed themselves into a rented mill house. Like most working-class southerners, the Goodmans didn't worship on Sundays in a fancy church with a college-educated preacher delivering the sermon. When Goodman's father died, he didn't leave his son a plot of land or a pile of money. Goodman had to make it on his own and without a lot of connections. He quit school long before the graduation ceremony and went to work in the mill. Most days when he finished his shift, he climbed into a truck and made deliveries for a local dry-cleaner. In 1938, a year after finishing a stint in the Navy and marrying Alice Smith from down the street in the mill village, Goodman took a job with a Rockingham furniture and hardware store. Eventually, he bought that business and renamed it R.W. Goodman. He expanded it over the years, adding a clothing store with fine suits and ties and buying up the buildings around it for showrooms and offices until he controlled almost an entire city block in downtown Rockingham.

By the 1970s, Goodman lived with his wife and children in a sprawling 3,300-square-foot home on one of Rockingham's fanciest, most elegant tree-lined streets. In addition to the furniture and clothing complex, he owned Richmond Yarns, Inc., a mill that employed 210 workers and was valued in 1975 at $2 million. His growing wealth came from his stores and factory and, it seems, according to some, from kickbacks on real estate deals and other ventures. "You didn't do business in Richmond County," explained William Morris, a former Imperial maintenance man, "without giving something to R.W." Again and again, state and county roads ended up running through property owned by Goodman and his closest associates. In order to finish their projects and thoroughfares, the government paid the sheriff and others top dollar to sell their land. Still, some said that Goodman made his real money overseeing the county's moonshining operations. At least, that's where the initial cash for his more legitimate enterprises may have come from. In 1957, law officers accused Goodman of stealing and then selling illegal liquor. He got off from those charges. But, after that, locals joked that the sheriff and his deputies were as much on the lookout for federal AFT agents as they were for thieves and shop-lifters. As ABC stores and restaurants serving beer and wine opened up in the county, some thought Goodman was changing with the times, scaling back his liquor business and orchestrating shakedowns and payoffs from the area's drug traffickers.[44]

When it came to business, whatever the business was, Goodman wanted to keep things the way they were. He wanted access to low-wage workers for his mills and retail operations and room to make deals without anyone poking around in his affairs. He didn't need rich people on his side; he needed people who needed loans and favors. It was one thing for the railroads to pay well—and do it over in Hamlet—but he didn't want that to become the county-wide norm. That's why, some said, he kept out other textile plants and why he tried to block Indiana-based Clark Equipment, a manufacturer of complex truck and bus transmissions, from purchasing an abandoned mill in Rockingham in the economically pressed mid-1970s. Even though the company was looking to escape from a union up north, some were convinced that the sheriff didn't want a rival firm coming into his county, setting a higher bar for wages and benefits. "He didn't want to pay these kinds of wages," Mike Quick heard some say. This was one time, though, at least in the short run, that Sheriff Goodman didn't get his way.[45]

Clark Equipment broke ground on a highly automated and massive plant on Highway 74, west of Rockingham, in September 1974. The company stayed in business there for a dozen years, providing one thousand dependable, well-paying jobs, jobs like the ones that used to exist on the railroads.[46]

In the early 1970s, as Clark searched for a new location in the area, Martin Quick returned from Vietnam hoping to work alongside his cousins and uncles on the railroad. Nothing opened up there, as Seaboard had just about stopped taking on new hires. Quick bounced from low-wage job to low-wage job. His frustrations mounted. But Quick caught a break when he got a position doing "gear work" with Clark Equipment.

Finally, he said, he "felt good. I could hold my head up." He opened a bank account at the credit union and made enough so that his wife, Mary Alice, could stay at home with the kids. It didn't last, however.

In 1986, citing the lower wages paid by its foreign competitors, Clark closed up shop in Richmond County. Some whispered that local workers lacked the skills and discipline needed for the plant's high-end manufacturing. Others pointed to a close union vote in 1979, when the United Steelworkers of America lost an election to represent Clark workers in Richmond County by less than ten votes out of almost eight hundred cast.[47] Still others pointed, again, to Goodman. Without Clark around, there would be less labor market competition, and he could pay his workers less and have greater control over others through credit and patronage.

Trying to make ends meet in the wake of Clark's departure, Martin Quick worked for a time at Imperial Food Products and then in construction; he was building prisons in 1991. None of these jobs paid enough to support his family, so his wife, Mary Alice, took a job working on the line at Imperial. In those same years of economic uncertainty, their marriage grew shakier.[48]

So did the Richmond County economy. After Clark's departure, average weekly manufacturing wages dropped in the area from $307.93 to $282.57 per week. That was closer to the cheap economy Sheriff Goodman wanted.[49]

Goodman liked unions about as much as he liked high-paying jobs and people who asked too many questions about his business operations and official duties.

Bob Hall of the Durham-based progressive and pro-labor Institute for Southern Studies chuckled when he recalled Goodman. He remembered the hat, the car, the cigar, and the sheriff's fierce anti-unionism. Years after the Hamlet fire, he recounted a story he had heard about a labor organizer at a local motel.

Early one afternoon, a representative from the textile workers' union checked into one of the motels on the highway cutting across the outer edges of Rockingham. By the time he set his bag down in his room, Goodman knew he was there. When the union man came back outside a little later with some buttons and brochures, a sheriff's cruiser was waiting for him, ready to escort him back across the county line.[50]

Years later, a local politician cracked that Goodman tried to keep everyone in the area "barefoot and backward."[51] At the very least, he wanted to make sure that wages stayed low and outsiders stayed out of his business. That sounded like the kind of place Emmett Roe was looking for as well, especially if it had an ample supply of cheap labor and civic leaders willing to look the other way.

2

SILENCE

Emmett Roe didn't stick out like Raymond Goodman did. He didn't drive a fancy car, wear a big hat, or smoke a fat cigar. And he didn't seem to care what people thought about him. He didn't care if they slammed him for not playing the part of a small-town southern business-man very well. He didn't care if people talked about his stocky frame, his throwback crew cut, or the white socks that always seemed to peek out from under his frayed and grease-stained work pants. He didn't mind if they joked about the rumpled jackets he wore to meetings with bankers and lawyers. He didn't care if they considered him gruff or belligerent or even vulgar, or if they whispered about his skipping church and Lion's Club meetings. "You would have been a bit embarrassed about him at lunch at the country club," chuckled Bill Sawyer, a die-hard Republican, ex-Marine, and representative of the Chamber of Commerce in Cum-ming, Georgia, where he occasionally encountered Roe, who owned a factory there, "He would have looked like he had just worked on your car." Yet, while Roe wasn't polished or a glad-handler or an operator like Goodman was, he still shared with the sheriff the fierce and determined commitment to have regulators, unions, and local, state, and federal lead-ers stay out of his business.[1]

Emmett Roe's business was food, mostly cheap food. By the time he bought the Mello-Buttercup Ice Cream plant on Bridges Street in Ham let in 1980, the fifty-three-year-old Roe, born in 1928, had been in the food business for more than thirty years. After leaving the Navy, where he had spent his time stateside, he got his start in his hometown of Troy, New York, selling butchered beef out of the back of his car. As he entered the second half of his twenties, he took a job with Empire Frozen Foods, which supplied restaurants, cafeterias, schools, and other commercial outlets with oversized boxes, bags, and blocks of processed foods.[2]

In the early 1960s, Empire offered Roe a chance to move up the corporate ladder, but it meant leaving Troy. However, at this point it wasn't a bad move for the married man and father of two sons and a daughter. By then, according to one local resident, Troy was a "town filled with hooligans and miscreants."[3] Once famed as the home of Uncle Sam and as an industrial hub churning out the nation's first machine-made collared shirts, the upstate New York city's glory days were long gone, and its downtown was crumbling. So, Roe said yes when Empire offered to promote him to executive vice president and put him in charge of a chicken-processing plant in Moosic, Pennsylvania, a town with five thousand residents, six miles south of Scranton.

In those early days, Roe ran the plant thinking, like many businesspeople did at the time, that labor and management could and should get along and that good relations would keep employees on the job and working steadily. At the time, the Scranton area still had a wide range of employment options, even for women, the target of Roe's labor recruitment efforts, so he couldn't dismiss their concerns. "He worked with us on the floor," recalled Betty Shotwell, who had a job on the Empire assembly line from 1965 to 1970, and then returned to the company in 1983 for five more years of processing chickens. "He boned and packed [chicken]. He worked with us as if he was another worker." Even though Roe could be a "screamer," sometimes angrily wagging his finger in workers' faces, each September he threw a big clambake for his employees at a lakeside picnic area not far from the plant.[4]

In 1970, Roe left Moosic for the opportunity to run a chain of fried chicken restaurants.[5] Three years later, that venture went bust, and Roe was back in Moosic. Using his house and other personal assets as collateral, he signed a five-year lease on the plant where he and Shotwell had worked. Later, he bought the 21,000-square-foot Empire factory outright for $200,000 and changed its name to Imperial Food Products Incorporated. Roe's new company started out small, with forty employees, but he beat the pavement and drummed up business, providing chicken products to grocery stores and food suppliers in eastern Pennsylvania and northern

New Jersey. By the end of the decade, the business had grown, and Imperial had a workforce of 120 employees.[6]

Roe launched Imperial at the very moment when doing business and making money in the United States was getting harder and more complicated. With profits on the wane just about everywhere, the 1970s brought increased taxes, added licensing fees, new regulations, stiffer competition, and renewed worker militancy. In response to the added pressures, Roe's managerial style changed. There were no more clambakes, and gone were the days when the owner filled in on the line or took a turn de-boning chickens. Most important, between the time when Roe had left Moosic to try his hand at the fast food business and when he returned in 1974, workers at the plant had voted in a union, Local 12 of the Amalgamated Meat Cutters and Retail Clerks.

A brochure put out by the Amalgamated in 1975 told workers that winning collective bargaining rights would provide them with an eight-hour day, higher wages, sick leave, additional holidays off and vacation time, life insurance, pensions, "paid clothes [and] changing time," and "many fringe benefits." In the end, the union vowed, "Your Dues Bring You a Better Life: Respect and Dignity."[7]

"He did not like unions," Shotwell remembered of Roe. "He just changed" after Local 12 came in. "He was more strict. He was very much down to business. He knew the union would be riding hard on him. This is what I think really changed him."[8]

Roe never spoke about Local 12 in public, but there seems to be little doubt that he loathed its presence in his plant. The idea that workers should have a say in pay rates or benefits or days off was, as the historian Erik Loomis put it, "an affront" to someone like Roe, who saw himself as a "maker," a doer, an asset to society providing jobs for others. Really, he saw employing people as a service. But in exchange for providing this social benefit, Roe, it seemed, thought he had the right to run his factory the way he wanted to, without question.[9]

Unwilling to share a seat at the table with a union representative or anyone else, Roe turned to his family to help him run the company. Even people who thought of Roe as coarse and callous acknowledged that he was a committed family man. "His life revolves around his family," a reporter concluded after interviewing several people who knew him. Roe's

only other passion was business. "He's a workaholic," observed Bill Sawyer of the Cumming Chamber of Commerce during his dealings with
him in the 1980s.[10] As the years passed, and his company grew and struggled, Roe trusted only family members to work hard enough, run his businesses the way he wanted them run, and keep things to themselves.

Emmett Roe's wife, Joan, worked as the company's secretary. His
daughter, Kelly, held the position of vice president for marketing and
sales. From the time they were teenagers, Roe's two sons, Emmett Jr. and
Bradford, spent summers and afternoons after school on the production
line and by their father's side. Both would go on to become company vice
presidents. After finishing college, Brad, as everyone called him, served
as the plant manager in Hamlet. Joan Roe's nephew, Edward Woncik,
worked in Moosic and later headed an ill-fated Alabama plant. Emmett Jr.'s father-in-law, James Neal Hair, worked alongside Brad as a manager and the number two in charge at the Hamlet plant.[11]

Beginning in the late 1970s, as his reliance on his family deepened,
Emmett Roe looked over his ledger sheets and began to think about moving part of Imperial's operations away from Moosic and Pennsylvania. He
started paging through trade magazines in search of newer, less expensive
locations. An advertisement from Mello-Buttercup, an ice cream manufacturer based in Wilson, North Carolina, listing a 33,000-square-foot
facility with ready access to transportation in Hamlet, North Carolina,
caught his eye. Roe's next step was to investigate the area's local history
and labor market.[12]

Louis A. Corning founded the Corning Quality Ice Cream Company as
the United States geared up for World War I. Originally from Elmira,
New York, Corning began his career as a pharmacist. On the side, he dab-
bled in vanilla, chocolate, and strawberry. His ice cream caught on with
locals, and in 1919 a larger firm scooped up his fledgling company. The
deal paid Corning well, but prohibited him from selling ice cream again
anywhere within 500 miles of Elmira. At the time, Corning was only in
his forties and was not ready to retire or go back to working behind the
pharmacy counter. "He picked up a map," Roland Corning, his grandson,
later a South Carolina politician, recalled, "and noticed all the railroad
connections in Hamlet." Eventually, his new company, Buttercup, set up

shop in a factory on Bridges Street. He bought his blueberries and peaches from local farmers. When trucks pulled up in front of the plant full of milk and butter, he paid local kids, often African American boys living in nearby houses and rental units, to unload the cargo. During the summer, he hired college students home from school to work inside the plant, and hot-shot pitchers and nimble shortstops to fill out the company's American Legion roster. Outside of work, Corning cruised up and down Main Street in a Pierce-Arrow coupe, the "swankest car in town." He socialized with the mayor and church leaders and brought five-gallon tubs of ice cream to dinner parties and bake sales.[13]

"It's FAMOUS because it's GOOD," Buttercup's slogan in the 1940s boasted. "Oh, they made good ice cream," Hamlet native Jane Mercer laughed. She remembered taking tours of the factory in grade school and getting to pick whatever flavor she wanted on the way out of the building. "People around here had a lot of pride in the Buttercup plant," said Barbara Thomas, whose husband, Richard, worked for a time as the manager. "Buttercup had a really good name. I felt like it was just a real part of Hamlet for so many years."[14]

Corning died in 1954, but family members maintained the business and its public presence for the next decade or so. Facing mounting competition from larger ice cream manufacturers, they sold Buttercup to the Coastal Dairy Company in 1969. For the next nine years, Coastal ran the business, now called Mello-Buttercup, as it had always been run, purchasing materials from nearby farmers, giving local kids jobs, and donating ice cream to church summer camps and end-of-the-season baseball banquets. But in 1977, the company shut down most of the Hamlet facility and consolidated its operations in Wilson, a slightly larger town one hundred miles away to the north and east of Hamlet.[15] The plant sat more or less idle until September 1980, when, according to Richmond County tax records, Emmett Roe paid $137,000 for the boarded-up factory.[16]

Before he signed the papers, Roe spent time studying Hamlet, the region, and the people who lived around the Buttercup site. Hamlet, he knew for starters, would bring him closer to his suppliers. Just outside of Rockingham was White's, a midsize chicken slaughterhouse. There were other processing plants in Moore and Union counties. In the areas to the west, around Wilkesboro and Morganton, farmers had taken to raising

chickens after World War II, while their wives and children took jobs
de-feathering and eviscerating the birds for weekly paychecks. Not far
away, in North Georgia, sprawling chicken plants cranked out boneless
breasts and leg and thigh parts by the millions on highly automated lines.
By 1980, when Roe bought the Buttercup plant, chicken had become the
South's largest agricultural product, bigger than tobacco in North Carolina, peanuts in Georgia, cotton in Mississippi, and all the crops combined in Alabama.[17] Roe, of course, knew about this transformation and
recognized that a plant in Hamlet would allow him to cut his shipping
costs. With a North Carolina location, he could buy frozen breast meat
from a southern supplier, process it in the South, and ship it to a Long
John Silver's fast-food outlet in the South for far less than it would cost
to move raw materials and finished product back and forth across the
Mason-Dixon Line.

Buying Buttercup cut Imperial's costs in other ways. As oil prices shot
up in the wake of Middle East wars and the formation of OPEC, the new
location would bring Roe closer to cheap power and a warmer climate
that required less electricity.

The real draw of the Hamlet location, though, was cheaper labor and
doing business in a region, state, and community where political leaders
felt like they had no choice but to keep costs down for industry by limiting business regulations. Roe felt like he didn't have a choice either. He
needed to make some changes to stay competitive.

The chicken industry, and the competition in it, set the price for his
raw materials and finished products. Given the relatively modest size of
his operations, there was nothing Roe could do about those factors. All
he could change were his variable costs, and the biggest variable for him
was labor. If he wanted to stay afloat and keep his family business going,
he felt he had to find cheaper workers, even if it meant moving all or part
of his factory and leaving behind some of the investments he had made in
equipment and capital improvements at the Moosic facility.[18]

When *Atlanta Constitution* editor Henry Grady and his followers first
sketched out a vision in the 1890s of a resurgent New South where industry replaced agriculture as the region's economic mainstay, they
imagined the states of the defeated Confederacy dotted with red brick

factories threaded together by husky train lines.[19] Bringing textile mills, furniture factories, steel plants, and railroads to Georgia, Alabama, and North Carolina involved more than dreaming, however. It required capital. Industrialists and investors, especially those in low-margin sectors of the economy like textiles and timber, were always on the lookout for lower costs, so southern boosters promised them an abundant supply of inexpensive labor to go with copious natural resources and raw materials. But even more important, Grady's followers pledged freedom—freedom to exploit waterways and forests and freedom from regulations and state intervention. Under these conditions, as the leading scholar of southern economic modernization, James C. Cobb, has explained, "industry could be its own boss." Every generation of southern boosters from the 1890s onward has renewed Henry Grady's call for more capital investment and more factories. Come south, they beckoned in the 1940s and again in the 1970s to prospective employers. When the industrialists moved in a little closer, the recruiters whispered, "We will leave you alone and let you run your businesses just the way you want."[20]

The eager men of the New South essentially pioneered a political economy that looked like a harbinger of the global phenomenon of neoliberalism, which is usually associated with a much later period. The region's early twentieth-century elected leaders, just like their counterparts a hundred years later in underdeveloped Bangladesh and Vietnam, let business leaders—who were feeling the heat of competitive pressures and shrinking profits in their current locations, wherever they were—know that they would keep taxes low and the government out of their affairs, giving them the freedom they sought to pursue the highest rates of profit possible through a combination of deregulation and benign neglect. Essentially, the men of the New South promised a social bargain at odds with the New Deal order and European social democracy, the reigning systems of governance in the mid-twentieth-century West. Instead, they built state structures that prioritized business growth and job creation ahead of protecting the vulnerable and providing social security.[21]

Roe knew what he wanted to hear from political leaders and government officials. When he first considered relocating to Hamlet, he might have been concerned about the state of North Carolina politics in the 1980s. As Roe weighed his options over where to move his operations, perhaps he read a speech from then governor James B. Hunt, a Democrat taking over the state's highest office from a Republican. Hearing the lawmaker's pitch for early education and racial reconciliation, Roe could have mistaken him for another New Deal liberal, pushing for the kind of safety-net seeking, regulatory government he wanted to avoid. But as he tuned in, he would have figured out that the young governor from Wilson County, a notch on the state's traditional tobacco belt running east from Raleigh to the coast, was an heir, above all else, to the region's pro-growth, New South tradition. He was the latest in a long line of North Carolina "business progressives"—men from both sides of the political aisle who imitated Henry Grady and ran the Tar Heel state for most of the twentieth century with a laser-like focus on boosting its economy by bringing in outside investors and businesses.[22]

Business progressives, like Hunt, followed the dictum that what's good for business is good for society. A better, more modern society meant moving away from agriculture and farming and the dominance of planters and cash crops. But, even more, it was about employment. "Southern businessmen," observed the historian LaGuana Gray, "focused on quantity of jobs over quality." More jobs, they insisted, translated into more money for lawmakers to spend on roads, schools, and prisons. The most effective government did what it could to attract more jobs, any jobs, even dirty and dangerous ones. "We all worship at the altar of jobs," one local development official confessed, "and don't differentiate between low and high wage jobs." Business progressives bet that the emphasis on jobs would pay off in the end with a steadier, more robust economy, and a wealthier citizenry, and they felt that getting those jobs, the foundation for moving forward, warranted making all kinds of deals with business owners and investors.[23]

In the 1970s, boosters and government officials took their faith in job creation as salvation on the road in search of a congregation. They targeted their message at firms located in union strongholds and in states with thick codebooks full of regulations. Anticipating Ronald Reagan and the larger break with the New Deal, North Carolina's industry hunters were not anti-government, not in the least; they instead wanted to redefine the role of government. To them, it was not first and foremost a protector of citizens or a watchdog of the economy. They saw it more as a banker, facilitator, and entrepreneur trying to sell what it had to offer in a competitive market to eager and savvy investors. Once businesses had settled into North Carolina, they imagined a government that was open to corporate leaders and steadfastly safeguarded the interests of job-creating industries by building roads and bridges, laying down water and sewer lines, keeping other costs and taxes down, and doing little else. "If business prospers," Hunt once said, summing up his governing philosophy, "so will workers." [24]

Jim Hunt was not the first southern governor to hit the road trying to lure jobs to his state. Convinced that Henry Grady's team of boosters and editorial writers couldn't get the job done on their own, in the 1930s Mississippi established a development board that was run by state officials and funded by the state treasury. The agency's goal was to sell the Magnolia State to outside investors. Over the next two decades, just about every other southern state imitated Mississippi and established a well-funded government agency to coordinate business recruitment schemes. In North Carolina, as in most other southern states, these boards had the backing of politicians from both parties and from every corner of the state, from the mountains in the west to the decaying plantation belt in the east. [25]

Few politicians, however, went hunting for businesses and for jobs with as much fervor as Jim Hunt did, and the times couldn't have been better for him and his message. As the 1970s revved up competition for businesses across the nation and, in fact, the world, numerous factory owners and investors, pressed by their own tightening circumstances, were on the lookout for cheaper options, and they were willing to move their operations to save money.

First elected in 1976, Hunt was known around the country, as the long-time *New York Times* columnist and Hamlet native Tom Wicker put it, as being "vigorous and active." He won acclaim from national Democrats and newspapers for investing in North Carolina's schools and building new water and sewage plants. But he was known even more, again in Wicker's words, as "a tireless pursuer of industry and economic growth." [26] To get the job done, Hunt cast himself as a "new" Democrat, not beholden to the racism of his region's past or his national party's longstanding connection to organized labor. "We should maintain our good business climate," Jim Hunt stated as he announced his re-reelection bid in 1980, just as Emmett

Roe was looking to relocate his factory.[27] The governor's message never varied. He never condemned unions outright, but he didn't support them or see them as part of the state's bigger plan for moving forward. He appointed officials with similar views to oversee business recruitment to the state. "North Carolinians are as bright as anyone else," Larry D. Cohick, Hunt's director for economic development, told a reporter. "I would guess that if they as a group wanted unions, the state would have them. If union leaders could demonstrate the need for unions, you would have them."[28] When the state's longshoremen pushed for a closed-shop agreement in the late 1970s, Hunt said no. Labor leaders pressed the governor to reconsider, and again he said no, this time more emphatically. Instead, he reiterated his support for the state's right-to-work law, a measure that made it difficult for unions to require membership and dues payments as conditions for employment at worksites covered by collective bargaining agreements.[29]

Hunt relied on more than pro-business speeches and anti-union gestures to bring new jobs to his state. By 1978, North Carolina had six full-time, well-paid industrial recruiters, each with a state-issued credit card and a generous expense account. Aided by his well-funded team of industry hunters and a beefed up, pro-business Department of Commerce, Hunt took to the road as soon he entered the governor's mansion and didn't stop moving until the end of his second term in 1984. He went from Pennsylvania to New York to Michigan trying, in his words, to convince audiences of "the enormous potential for growth and progress that this state has." He would tell audiences, "Our location is ideal; we have a perfect climate, unspoiled natural resources, our cities are still livable and manageable; our people are honest, thrifty, and hardworking."[30] Certainly he told them about the state's "pro-business climate," its right-to-work law, and the fact that North Carolina maintained the second lowest rate of unionization in the country. He told them that the state didn't have a whistleblower protection law on the books, that it had its own state-run OSHA department, and that it was one of only nine states where insurance companies could assign a doctor to examine an injured laborer in a worker's compensation case. When a deal needed closing, Hunt or one of his professional industry seekers would sweeten the bid by offering free access roads and sewer lines and breaks on industrial training, taxes, and salaries.[31] The efforts of Hunt's team delivered results.

They liked to brag that during Hunt's initial two terms in the office, the state attracted $41 billion in investment in new factories and industries. But the real focus was on jobs. In Hunt's first full year in office in 1978, the state of North Carolina created 42,000 new industrial jobs. What the governor didn't talk much about was the quality of these jobs or the rate of pay or the safety of the factories.[32]

By the 1980s, hunting for industry was not just a southern pastime, but increasingly a national one. Everyone, including Hunt, wanted to bag the biggest factories—the bigger the better. But Hunt didn't discriminate when it came to industrial recruitment. He wanted all the industries and all the jobs he could get, and he wanted them spread out across the map of the state, from mountains to the ocean, from the biggest cities to the most out-of-the-way counties. Following a North Carolina tradition pioneered in the 1950s by Governor Luther Hodges, he pushed to bring factories to small towns and whistle-stop junctions. Hodges believed that companies could be found that would "locate away from congestion and at the same time . . . draw upon a large and industrious labor supply that is mostly rural."[33] Hunt pushed to keep this tradition alive and, in the words of *New York Times* journalist John Herbers, to keep growth "scattered" and "away from cities and suburbs."[34]

Hunt's determination to turn North Carolina into a magnet for broadly dispersed new factories and relocated plants paid off, at least in the short run. By 1990, the state was, quite remarkably, the most industrialized state in the country, but by no means the most urban. That meant it had more industrial jobs per capita than Michigan, Ohio, Pennsylvania, or any other state. However, it also had the nation's lowest cost for worker's compensation insurance, the lowest average hourly wage, and, by then, the lowest rate of unionization. Neighboring South Carolina, just a stone's throw from Hamlet, had the second lowest rate. It, too, was attracting businesses at a rapid pace, and not just along its highways and interstates.[35]

Hunt didn't limit himself to the United States on his recruitment trips. In the spring of 1978, the governor, Richmond County sheriff Raymond Goodman, several aides, and a Raleigh television crew headed to Germany on a $30,000 junket paid for by North Carolina taxpayers in search of new private investment. Along the way, they stopped in Ahrensburg, not far from Hamburg, to announce that the BeA Fasteners Company—makers of industrial clasps for the furniture industry—would open a $1.3 million plant in Hamlet. Hans Hoewner, a member of the German company's board of directors, explained that his firm chose the location because of its "good transportation network and attractive industrial climate."[36] What he didn't say was that the state of North Carolina had agreed to pay half of his plant manager's salary for five years, or that the plant manager that he would hire was the same state industrial recruiter who had lured his company to Hamlet.[37]

Hunt kept quiet about the insider deal when he came to Hamlet in September 1978 for a blue ribbon–cutting ceremony. "I don't have to tell you what it means to Hamlet to have this plant here," the governor proclaimed. He continued, "Hamlet knows what it's like to have a booming economy, and then lose jobs. This plant is another step forward. By the end of the . . . expansion phase, there may be as many as 128 employees. That translates into more tax revenues for the county, more good paychecks, opportunities for advancement, and better lives for families." With BeA's arrival, he said, Hamlet got what it needed. "This is what we want for so many of the small towns in North Carolina," the governor asserted, "a chance to grow, yet retain the qualities that make them such good places to live and raise families in." Companies like BeA, Hunt declared, "are looking for a high quality of life, a welcome attitude on the part of local people, in addition to the transportation and other resources they need."[38]

In the heated, media-saturated days after the deadly Imperial fire, then-governor Jim Martin and other state officials insisted that no one had recruited Emmett Roe to come to North Carolina. No one from the Industrial Commission had taken him out for a steak dinner, and no one had promised to pay the salary of his plant manager. That was true, but that doesn't mean Roe hadn't heard Governor Hunt's business-first message or the business-first message of local leaders. Maybe Roe had seen one of the North Carolina Department of Economic and Community Development's advertisements in *Forbes* magazine in the 1980s, bragging about the state's "aggressive pro-business mind-set at all levels of government." "North Carolina takes great pride in the support government offers to businesses," said another state-produced recruitment brochure. "In regulatory matters," it continued, "North Carolina businesses find that they deal with Raleigh more often than Washington. North Carolina administers the Occupational Safety and Health Act, the Resource Conservation and Recovery Act, the National Pollutant Discharge System, the Clean Air Act, and most environmental regulations."[39] As Roe focused his search on the Buttercup factory, maybe he received a pamphlet from someone at Hamlet City Hall with the cover reading "Greetings from Progressive Hamlet: At the Crossroads of the Carolinas." As he flicked through the pages, he surely would have noticed the section with the heading "Climate and Farming" and read that "poultry was fast becoming an important fact of life in the area." The back cover touted Hamlet as "an attractive site for business" with clean water and a "labor potential" made up of "appealing people" from "the surrounding area," which it claimed was "populated with farm people who are native born."[40]

The last line was code. Businesspeople like Roe, explains the historian James Cobb, believed that growing up on a farm bred a brand of individualism that inoculated laborers against collective action. Like Hamlet officials, the Georgia Chamber of Commerce also used this widely held notion about farm families in its promotional literature, telling potential investors that the Peach State was filled with the kinds of people "who work closely together in their church and Sunday School."[41]

As Roe did more research on Hamlet, perhaps checking census records or reaching out to a professional human relations firm like Capital Associated Industries in Raleigh, he would have found out just what Governor Hunt meant when he said, "Hamlet knows what it's like to have a booming economy, and then lose jobs." Statistics told part of the story of Richmond County's economic decline. When Roe bought the ice cream plant in 1980, unemployment in North Carolina stood at 6.5 percent.[42] In Hamlet and Rockingham, the jobless rate in 1983, after peaking in the mid-1970s at almost 20 percent, still stood at 12.5 percent. By the end of the decade, after Clark Equipment and Carolina Paper Mills closed and textile mills cut their payrolls, unemployment leapt back up to 18.4 percent, making just about any job tolerable, if not desirable, even if it was a hot and filthy one that left your back and wrists throbbing. As Alfonso Anderson, whose wife, Peggy, died in the fire, put it, "Round Hamlet, things are slow and people are poor. They are thankful for any job they can get."[43]

Increased joblessness, Roe knew, meant increased competition for work at his plant, lower labor costs, and less room for open dissent. Plus, it meant he wouldn't need to build loyalty or listen to his laborers, as he'd had to do from time to time in Moosic. Hamlet was now a place with an abundance of workers, most of whom were without a lot of options. As Mack trucks moved more goods and the railroad shut down, union men had to work for less. At the same time, they had to compete with out-of-work textile workers for positions.[44] And in a pattern repeated across the United States in the 1970s, as men made less, families mobilized more of their resources. White women joined black women and entered the paid labor force in Hamlet in growing numbers, just like everywhere else in the United States. In 1970, 30 percent of women across the country with children under six years old held paying jobs; by 1985, more than half did.[45] Having more overall workers in the labor pool—a by-product of the collapse of the nation's primary industries like railroads, steel, and auto—drove down wage rates for semi-skilled workers, especially as regions and states started to openly compete with each other for industrial businesses. By the time Roe closed down his factory in Moosic, Pennsylvania, poultry workers there were paid 17 percent more than their North Carolina counterparts—an average of $322 per week, compared with $276, and he wouldn't have to pay quite that much in Hamlet.[46] Even if Roe didn't know the county's wage and unemployment statistics by heart, he knew from driving by the nearly shuttered depot and the empty storefronts on Main Street and Hamlet Avenue that the town's better days were behind it.

Abbie Covington, a Hamlet city councilperson in the early 1980s, whose father was once the mayor, an office she would later occupy, remembered being excited to have Imperial come to town "because of the jobs." A moderate Democrat in favor of growth, more employment, and an even-handed approach to local government, she had worried that "lots of companies wouldn't relocate to Hamlet."[47] Even as the railroad shed jobs, some investors, she'd heard, still shied away from her hometown, fearful that the lingering union allegiances of brakemen and mechanics somehow blew in the wind and could be stirred up at any time. Few people were likely more sensitive to the threat of a union than Roe was, but it seems he wasn't concerned about the community's collective-bargaining past. Nor was he interested in doing business the way Buttercup officials had done business, ingratiating themselves with city leaders and local citizens.

Roe didn't invite the mayor or the city council or the town manager over to the plant after he acquired it. He didn't show up at barbecue suppers at the American Legion Hall, bankroll Little League teams, or give away boxes of frozen tenders for middle school social events. He never moved to town and he never joined a church. The Imperial plant didn't even have a sign above its door. "It was a half mile from downtown," Mark Schultz, a labor safety advocate, remembered, "and you just got the sense that it was something that someone wanted to keep out of sight. Nothing about the place looked like a place where people went to work."[48] No balloons or ribbon-cutting ceremonies or photo ops accompanied Imperial's opening. Joseph W. Grimsley, president of Richmond Community College, was, like many locals, barely aware of the company's existence. "It really was a very self-contained operation," he recalled. "We invite people to various events," but "these people," he remarked about Emmett Roe and his family, "never showed up for anything we have done."[49] When the Richmond County United Way asked the Roes for permission to solicit contributions from Imperial workers, they said no. Other civic leaders got the same chilly reception. Donald V. McClain, executive director of the Richmond County Chamber of Commerce, visited the plant one day and asked Emmett Roe if he would join the organization. Roe said no. "It was like I was trying to get him to join the union," McClain remembered, "That's the type of response I got."[50]

"It was like a ghost operation," said Ron Niland, the Hamlet city manager through much of the 1980s and early 1990s. "As long as there weren't any problems and no one was getting hurt, no one paid any attention."[51]

No one paid much attention to Roe or his operation as he geared up for full-scale production at the plant beginning in 1980. It took time and money to turn the ice cream factory into a chicken-processing plant. Exits were moved. Additions were built. Coolers and fryers were brought in. However, architects didn't seem to be involved in any of the renovations. When Roe finished refitting the plant, it looked like a maze on the inside.[52] "They changed it so much I barely recognized it," said Richard Barnes, the president of Mello-Buttercup right before the company moved out of town. Each of these changes, seven in all, by law required permits. Yet Roe never applied for a single building permit as he expanded the plant from 21,300 square feet to 37,000 square feet. No one in Hamlet asked him for the paperwork, even as they surely heard the sound of walls coming down and delivery trucks grinding their gears as they hauled heavy equipment up the hill from the bottom of Bridges Street to the loading dock on the southern side of the plant.[53]

On November 1, 1980, just after Roe bought the building, a small fire broke out at the empty plant. Two and half years later, on May 27, 1983, another small but more intense fire erupted near Imperial's deep fat fryer. No one was hurt, but the blaze damaged a sprinkler system that Buttercup officials had installed a few years before.[54] Emmett Roe assured Hamlet fire officials that he would replace the damaged sprinkler with a new state-of-the-art one that turned on automatically. When asked years later if he had ever returned to the plant to see if Imperial had made the changes, Fire Chief David Fuller responded, "It wasn't our job."[55]

After that 1983 fire, Imperial did replace the roof over the main sections of the plant at a cost of $125,000. According to state laws on the books at the time, existing buildings did not have to meet newer, tougher code regulations unless they had been substantially renovated. Richmond County's building inspector, Jack Thompson, examined Roe's new roof in 1983 or 1984, but not the entire building. "I just figured," he said later, "the roof wouldn't be more than 50 percent of the property's value." When pressed about how he had calculated that, Thompson admitted that he had not checked the records and had only guessed at Imperial's worth. "I did look around, but as far as digging around looking to see what was holding the building up, I didn't do that. Didn't nothing stand out to me that wouldn't meet the code." Asked by a *Washington Post* reporter after the 1991 fire who was supposed to look into fire safety at the plant, Thompson said he thought that "OSHA would come around and check an industrial building like that."[56]

Turning chicken parts into chicken tenders required prodigious amounts of water and produced a steady flow of liquid waste, yet no one in Hamlet at the outset asked Emmett Roe if he had drawn up plans for water waste treatment or disposal. Over the course of the 1980s, members of the Imperial maintenance crew dug three—likely illegal—wells, one with a pump, inside the plant. This allowed the firm to take water from the city and have it processed as waste without paying the full charge. By one estimate, Roe paid about one-tenth of what he should have for water. For years, though, no one knocked on Imperial's door, so no one knew or wanted to know for sure about the rivers of water siphoned from the city.[57]

Even as Imperial expanded its operations and hired more people, the mayor and members of the city council never visited the factory. Neither did many other middle-class townspeople. Twenty years after the fire, residents of Hamlet said again and again that they didn't know much about the place or didn't even know it was there. When the plant exploded, some, especially on the white sides of town, still called it Buttercup. Town manager Ron Niland insisted it wasn't even up and running until a couple of years before the fire, when in actuality it had been operating for more than half a decade. It was like Roe and his operation were phantoms. But this, of course, was just what the plant owner wanted.[58]

Back in Moosic, though, Emmett Roe wasn't getting the anonymity he coveted. Another fire, this one described by the local fire chief as "pretty extensive," blew his cover. In August 1985, Helene Kosierowski, an Imperial employee in Pennsylvania, suffered second- and third-degree burns to her back and legs after getting sprayed by scalding hot cooking oil while working on the line. A local television station made the story public. That was how the federally administered Occupational Safety and Health Administration in Pennsylvania (OSHA) found out about the plant. When an inspector knocked on the door, Roe wouldn't let him in. Three months later, the inspector returned with a search warrant. After a painstaking examination of the plant, he cited the company for its lack of proper safety equipment, the presence of two electrical hazards, slippery floors, and failure to complete required forms that noted when workers were sick or injured. OSHA proposed $1,200 in fines. Imperial Food agreed to pay $800 and promised to fix the problems. It is not clear if there was ever a follow up visit to the factory.[59]

Two years later, in 1987, another Imperial employee in Moosic contacted OSHA complaining of unsafe working conditions. While examining Imperial's medical records, OSHA officials in Pennsylvania discovered that the plant's lost-workday injury rate was nearly four times the national average for manufacturing workers and twice the norm for food laborers. Inspectors wanted to go through the plant again. This time, Roe was even less receptive. Again, he refused to let the inspector inside the plant.

When the inspector returned the next month with another search warrant, Roe erupted. At first, he told the OSHA representative that he wouldn't let him inside while they were processing chicken. Then he refused to pull the plant's Local 12 shop steward off the production line to accompany the inspector on his rounds even though federal law required it. When he finally relented and called for the union agent over the company's crackling intercom system, Roe spat out a string of obscenities.

In his report issued in February 1987, Inspector E.F. Donnelly wrote that Roe displayed "utter contempt for OSHA." After combing through the Imperial plant, he found six violations, three of them "serious." (*Serious* was OSHA's term for issues that were noteworthy but not deemed immediately life threatening.[60]) Six months after Donnelly filed his report, OSHA was back at Imperial for a planned follow-up inspection. Investigators spent ninety-seven hours talking to employees and examining injury logs, checking on company safety procedures and policies, observing the way the assembly line and cooker operated, testing fire alarms, and opening and closing safety doors. By the time they had finished, they had uncovered thirty-three health and safety violations, fifteen of them serious, including slippery floors, the lack of first aid stations and clearly posted warnings about hazardous conditions, improperly shielded machines, unlit exit signs, blocked exit doors, and electrical cords lying in pools of water. One employee told the inspector that the plant was "an accident waiting to happen." This time, OSHA proposed a fine of $6,030. The company settled for $2,560 and agreed to fix the problems. A few months later, another fire broke out at the Moosic plant, causing $6,000 in damages. No one was injured, and it doesn't appear that OSHA came back to inspect the plant or to follow up on Donnelly's report.[61]

By now, though, Emmett Roe had had enough of Donnelly, the Amalgamated Meat Cutters and Retail Clerks Union, and the state prying into his business. Over the next few years, he shut down the Pennsylvania plant and moved his food business and as much of the equipment in his factory as he could get on a truck south. Somehow, Roe's woeful OSHA record of obstruction and safety violations didn't follow him. Though Donnelly scribbled at the bottom of his report a note about the Hamlet plant and the need to look into it, no one at OSHA's offices in Pennsylvania or in Washington, D.C., let OSHA officials in North Carolina know that a repeat safety offender had set up shop in their state.[62]

Roe didn't tell anyone either. North Carolina law required all new industrial enterprises to obtain a business license to operate in the state or face a fine. Roe never did register and he was not found out until after the fire. State law also required all new employers with eleven or more employees to register with OSHA and the Department of Labor in Raleigh. After that, the agency put each company into a lottery system. When its number came up, it would receive a surprise inspection at the facility. (Otherwise, a complaint would trigger an inspection, like it did in Moosic.) The chances of getting inspected in North Carolina or anywhere in the United States were not very high, but you never knew when the regulators might knock on your door. When people went looking through the Labor Department's records after the fire, they couldn't find any paperwork from Roe, leading them to conclude that he had never even filed the necessary forms with OSHA. Technically, this meant that Roe did not have the authorization to operate a business in North Carolina. That didn't stop him, though, from churning out cheap chicken products.[63]

Hamlet city officials continued to leave Roe alone, even as he moved more of his operations into town. Like so much else about Imperial, the plant owner's calculated silence only became clear after tragedy struck. Not long after the fire, Hamlet's tax collector, Susan Furr, dug through the files in her office. She found that the city had no listing for Imperial for personal property or inventory taxes, which accounted for the heavy machinery and other equipment in the plant. Furr went back to 1984 and still could not find a listing or payment for inventory taxes. Richmond County Tax Supervisor Amsey Boyd told a reporter that it was the property owner's responsibility to list his property for taxes. He said that he had been aware that inventory and personal property for Imperial had not been listed for years and had on a few occasions informed the company of its failure to comply, but no one from Bridges Street had ever replied. It did not seem like Boyd or anyone else from the county clerk's office or

City Hall had followed up on these findings or threatened to take away Imperial's business license—or even find out if they had one—or threatened to drag the company into court for failure to make payment.[64]

The state Department of Insurance reported, again, after the fire, that Imperial never obtained a building permit for the shed it built around the outdoor trash bin and dumpster where Loretta Goodwin and others got trapped during the fire. The door leading to that enclosure was locked from the outside at the time. Of course, this, too, was a violation of state codes.[65]

As he flaunted a number of laws without any repercussions, Emmett Roe must have sensed that no one in Raleigh or Richmond County or Hamlet would challenge him. By 1990, his company was one of the largest, if not the largest, private employer in Hamlet, a town that was starved for jobs. Local officials, according to city manager Ron Niland, practiced "benign neglect" when it came to Imperial and other job creators. This disregard continued as Roe ratcheted up production, adding more additions to the plant, starting a second shift, and hiring more people. The neglect continued, even after the small fires broke out at the plant in 1980 and 1983 and another one in 1987.[66] No officials came to the site, not even after South Hamlet residents complained about ghastly smells leaking from the factory. No one came when the city manager and others first noticed "cannonball sized" chunks of grease and fat in the city's water supply and figured out they had originated at Imperial. At one point, the city had to shut off its water supply for a few hours to clean things up. At that point, someone from City Hall came to talk to Roe, though one company official thought they treated the firm with kid gloves.[67]

A year before the 1991 fire, an exasperated Ron Niland finally confronted Brad Roe, by then the on-site, everyday manager at the plant, about wastewater problems. The recent college graduate promised to install pre-treatment facilities and put in place a plan to take care of the greasy waste generated by the production of chicken tenders and other chicken products. But he dragged his feet, challenging the city's water tests, cutting corners, and constantly pleading for more time. Through the first half of 1991, Niland wrote him ever more urgent and threatening letters. He even hauled Roe into City Hall at one point and demanded at a hearing that he show cause as to why officials shouldn't close down his plant. The result of the encounter was that the city gave Imperial yet another extension to fix things.[68] Eventually, Emmett Roe came to town to talk with Niland about the water and waste issues. During a break in the meeting, he leaned in close to the city manager, tapping him on the chest with his index finger. "I won't lie to you," the chicken plant owner promised, "but I will prevaricate." Over the next few weeks, Emmett Roe, along with Brad, Niland recalled, fought "tooth and nail" against making substantive changes to how the plant obtained and disposed of water. Emmett Roe, in particular, Niland concluded, "didn't want to spend any money." Eventually, the city gave Imperial thirty days to make the necessary adjustments. At the final hour, the company complied by doing the bare minimum.[69]

After the fire, Niland became convinced that Emmett Roe had stonewalled because he hadn't wanted anyone else to find out about the wells that had been dug in the plant's maintenance areas and the massive amounts of water that had been stolen over the years. The former city manager still wonders to this day what would have happened if he had gotten into the plant and if the city had followed through and shut Imperial down as it had threatened to do in the fall of 1991.[70]

The government agency with the most contact with the Roes in the late 1980s and early 1990s was the United States Department of Agriculture (USDA). Typically, Kenneth Booker, Charles Blumhardt, Grady Hussey, or another trained food inspector from the agency showed up at Imperial every day. "The . . . food safety inspector made sure the chicken [tenders] and marinated chicken breasts that left the plant were safe for consumers to eat," said Wayne Brooks, a USDA supervisor in Raleigh, the day after the fire. Looking out for consumers, Booker and Blumhardt—the two in the plant the most—usually started their day with a visit to the Imperial office. After that, they walked past the giant fryer, stuck a head in the blast freezers and coolers, checked the floors in the trim room for mouse and rat droppings, and peeked around the trash bins and compacter for insects. They made sure that workers scrubbed and disinfected the machines at the end of the day and kept rancid meat out of the tenders and fajitas. They noted when workers touched food products without washing their hands after using the bathroom or grabbed chicken that fell to the floor and put it back on the processing room conveyor belt, as some said Brad Roe ordered them to do when the USDA wasn't there to see them.[71]

Starting in 1989, the USDA sent Imperial a stream of notices about flies coming in from the areas near the loading dock and the dumpster. The Roes tried to get the government men off their backs by putting up flytraps and sending "five or six women," one supervisor recollected, "out there with fly swatters." But they couldn't contain the problem manually or cheaply. Flies kept sneaking into the plant from the exits on the southern end of the building because the door there wouldn't properly close and because workers going out for a smoke or to get something from their cars often left it open. In February 1991, Blumhardt found the "big roll-up door on receiving dock . . . wide open . . . [and] . . . no fly-fan." In July, inspectors again expressed concerns about the fly problem. Throughout the day, workers went out to the dumpster area to throw away empty chicken boxes and get a little fresh air. On July 2, Booker noted a "critical" deficiency. The door to the loading dock area was again not closing properly, "leaving [a] crack for flies to enter." "Flies," he wrote, "are in all departments. . . . A better program needs to be established to address the fly problem." The next day, Booker came back and found more flies. "Discussed fly problem with Brad Roe," he reported.

A couple of days later, Joseph R. Kelly, Imperial's night manager, laid out the company's response to the inspectors' most recent complaints about flies. "Outside door to this area," he explained in a note to the USDA, "will be locked at all times unless for an emergency." Over the next few weeks, Imperial built a shed, without a permit, around the trash compacter and dumpster where most of the flies came from. This structure featured, in Kelly's words, "a door on the inside and outside. Door on inside will be kept closed when not using dumpster and outside door will be kept locked." From inside the building, this door was an exit door. The USDA, nonetheless, seemed satisfied with Imperial's plan. As *Raleigh News and Observer* reporter Steve Riley wrote in his article breaking the news about the flies and the doors, Grady Hussey, a USDA inspector, "signed the report, verifying that corrective action had been taken." That brought an end to the matter of the flies. As a result, Emmett and Brad Roe avoided what they could least afford—a government shutdown of their chicken tender operations. "The only priority of management," Department of Labor investigators concluded after the fire, "was production and complying with USDA requirements."[72]

An exit door locked from the outside, however, violated just about every basic workplace safety rule on the books. "Are you kidding me?" Nellie Brown, a certified industrial hygienist and Cornell University professor of industrial and labor relations blurted out after hearing about Imperial's fly prevention plan. But the meat inspectors said nothing more, at least through official channels. They came and went on most days between July of 1991 and Labor Day of that year, vaguely aware, perhaps, that an exit door was locked, keeping the flies out and the workers in.[73]

When asked by Charlotte reporters why USDA inspectors did not object to the locked doors, Wilson Horne, the agency's Washington-based deputy administrator for inspections, explained, "We're strictly in there as food safety inspectors." Horne added that his men never filed reports regarding plant safety, not in Hamlet or anywhere else. "My thoughts are," he continued, "that a large plant having locked doors per se is not all that unusual. It's not something our inspectors are trained to look for. Our people are not trained to look for fire hazards." "We're terribly sorry about the accident, but it doesn't fall under our responsibility at all," Jim Greene, another USDA spokesperson, asserted. "It's not buck-passing," he continued, "but our job is to inspect meat and poultry products, and that's a full-time job itself. . . . We're not fire marshals, quite frankly. We're food inspectors, and that's our primary duty."[74]

Greene and Horne's logic was, according to Cornell professor Nellie Brown, that "people are expendable; the value is in the product."[75]

Tired of moving from base to base, one unfamiliar town to the next, William Morris left the military in the late 1980s and settled back in Richmond County, where he had grown up decades earlier and gone to high school. "Imperial," he remarked years later, "was just about the only job around." He put in an application and got hired to join the plant's maintenance crew. A few months after he took the job, Emmett Roe, he said, told him to put a latch and padlock on the door leading out to the dumpster. When he finished the job, he remembers walking into the small office across the street from the main entrance to the plant and handing the keys to Roe. They talked for a minute. Roe told him, Morris recounted in an interview twenty years later, that he had to lock the doors to stop his employees from stealing chickens.[76]

Like most workplaces, Imperial experienced some theft. Abbie Covington, the town's mayor at the time of the fire, said that a local restaurant owner once told her that he never bought chicken tenders from the Imperial plant; he just purchased them from one of Roe's employees. According to police records, officers caught an Imperial worker in March 1991 with $245 worth of boneless chicken breasts. Around that same time, the company fired a couple of other workers for stealing.

"I've heard the different stories that there was people stealing," a plant official told Department of Labor investigators, "But that, I mean, that's crazy." He added, "I know two or three people we caught, and . . . we didn't prosecute them." Seven years after the fire, Brad Roe talked to *Charlotte Observer* reporter Paige Williams and echoed the plant official's view of things. In the article, Williams stated that Roe said "he did not lock doors to keep employees from stealing chicken." "I processed 60,000 pounds of chicken a day," Roe insisted. "If a $30 box of chicken got thrown out that door out of $100,000 produced that day, that doesn't warrant a problem." Underscoring Roe's point, an Imperial supervisor told investigators after the fire that "there wasn't that much stealing going on there anyway." In the end, even though Emmett and Brad Roe fretted over the bottom line, they weren't, it seems, all that concerned about a few tenders going out a side door, not when they were buying frozen chicken breasts by the truckload. What Imperial, a "struggling company," in Brad Roe's words, couldn't let happen, though, was for the USDA to close the plant down because of a fly problem. That would cost them way more than a few boxes of stolen chicken would.[77]

Still, when Emmett Roe talked to William Morris about locking the doors, Morris remembers him spitting out a few choice words about stopping his "low-down" employees from thieving. Nothing was said about flies and the USDA. Maybe this was how the plant owner deflected attention away from the company and its actions toward workers. But it also might have said something about how he perceived, or wanted others to perceive, the community surrounding the building. Maybe it said something about how he saw the women on the line and the men unloading the trucks at the factory, and maybe how he imagined others saw them. Decades later, when talking about why the doors were locked, Morris, trying to explain what happened, called Emmett Roe a "stone-cold racist."[78]

"Emmett Roe," Imperial line worker Annette Zimmerman believed, "saw us as a group of niggers." She remembered a supervisor telling her on her first day on the job, "Don't ever talk to Emmett Roe. He says you are only good for two things, working his chicken and cleaning his house." "He thought we would steal," Zimmerman concluded. "It was prejudice." "He had that stereotype," she remarked twenty-plus years after the fire, "but all of us don't steal."[79]

When the State Bureau of Investigation went to talk to Hamlet Fire Chief David Fuller, a man considered by some around town to be a "good old boy," about the fire and the blocked exits, he told them, according to several people who were at the meeting, "that he was aware that the doors were locked, and that he knew if Imperial Foods didn't keep them locked, the employees would 'steal them blind.' "[80]

In later investigations, Fuller denied rumors that Emmett Roe had paid him and his fire crew off with boxes of tenders to leave his factory alone and ignore his company's disregard for worker safety.[81] Later, Fuller also denied rumors that he and other Hamlet firefighters knew about the locked doors or that they had a key to the door near the loading dock, the one that was locked from the outside and sent workers on the morning of the fire scurrying for cover as smoke filled the plant into the nearby cooler with the faulty door. Following the deaths at the plant, Kim Mangus, an Imperial maintenance supervisor, swore in a notarized statement that he had handed over a key to the door to Connie Crowley, one of Fuller's deputies. The firefighter told him, Mangus remembered, "as long as there were other exits where workers could get out and they had a key, that was all right." Based on this conversation, Mangus believed, "We'd covered the bases . . . as far as obtaining permission to have the lock on the door."[82]

Just days after the fire, Chief Fuller met with reporters and told a different story. He scoffed at the notion that he had signed off on a locked door. "That's ridiculous," he said. "Can you imagine us sorting through a big bunch of keys every time there's a fire? We're trained in forcible entry, and we carry bolt cutters on the trucks. We don't need to fool with keys."

Still, Fuller's denials did not fully put an end to the rumors, not in 1991 or years later, that he had okayed the locking of the back door to stop the theft of chickens and that he or someone in his department had had a key to that exit.[83]

A couple of months after the fire, L. Bradford Barringer also talked about exit doors, the character of Imperial workers, and theft. The owner of a Stanly County construction company and a member of the state OSHA advisory board, Barringer told *Raleigh News and Observer* reporter C.E. Yandle, "I imagine they stole chickens as fast as they could go. If there had been more honest employees the doors probably wouldn't have been locked." "Employers," he reasoned, "get frustrated."[84]

Even if Chief Fuller didn't justify, like Bradford Barringer did, the locking of the doors because of stealing (and the compromised integrity of Imperial employees), and even if he didn't have keys to the doors, he never practiced anything that could be mistaken for vigilant oversight to protect the lives of the men and women in the town's factories. The eight people in his department didn't regularly inspect Hamlet's industrial sites. Despite three fires at the Imperial plant in the 1980s, and chatter around the small town about the dangers inside the building, Fuller never knocked on the door with a pad and paper in hand ready to take notes and make recommendations. Some remember him in the factory, but none can recall him looking closely at the fryer, faulty wiring, or exit routes. And his department never drew up a firefighting plan for the building like the Rockingham Fire Department did with most industrial sites in its jurisdiction.[85]

On the day of the fire, Rockingham firefighter Frankie Moree arrived on the scene around 8:30 a.m. with the very first wave of firefighters and met with his Hamlet counterparts. To this day, he remains surprised, stunned even, that they didn't have a map of the plant to share with him and that they didn't know the location of the nearest water source. The Hamlet men were decent firefighters, Moree observed that day and on previous occasions working with them, but they weren't prepared for the fire. "We burned a couple of houses every week" for practice, he recalled. Northside, East Rockingham, and Cordova would send over their crews to join in the drills and talk about the best ways to suppress the fires. But, he said, "I never saw anyone from Hamlet come over."[86]

Even when the law instructed Fuller to conduct inspections, a loophole and budget matters kept him away from the town's industrial sites. During the 1991 legislative session, the North Carolina General Assembly passed a measure requiring all of the state's municipal and county governing units to appoint a fire inspector by July 1 of that year. The inspectors were expected to use the state's new uniform and comprehensive fire code to check every commercial building in their jurisdiction. But the state, operating on the cheap, didn't fund the program. By the summer deadline for compliance, only 257 of the state's 613 governmental units had named a fire inspector. Hamlet was one of those places that hadn't designated anyone for the job. "We can't afford it . . . I don't have the people to do it," maintained Chief Fuller. The city and the fire department insisted that they lacked the money to pay for inspections, so they didn't automatically inspect the commercial buildings and factories in their community. Local officials talked about having the Rockingham Fire Department conduct the inspections because it had the personnel, but the details never got worked out. In the end, no one ever walked through the Imperial plant long enough to notice the bolted door by the dumpster or the locked exit in the breakroom. No government official, except for the USDA men, ever made note in public or in writing that the Bridges Street factory lacked working sprinklers or that dangerous fluids sometimes leaked from connections perilously close to jets of gas flames. Again, no one said anything, perhaps because, as one local firefighter remarked, "You have two fires in this plant. Two. But no one gave a damn. No one." [87]

Yet the silence of local, state, and federal firefighters and inspectors wasn't enough for Emmett Roe. He kept on making more silence. In some ways, that was really what he and his son produced on Bridges Street. They processed silence as diligently and as aggressively as they processed chickens.

"I didn't know anybody who worked there," Hamlet's Ruth Land, the daughter of a railroad engineer and wife of a tractor-trailer dealer, told a reporter in 1991. "Just people you didn't know worked down there." Hiding the poor didn't just happen in Hamlet, or in places on the margins; it was, as the journalist Jonathan Kozol lamented, a national phenomenon in the years after 1980 as trade unionism and workplace activism waned against a backdrop of rising unemployment, swelling labor markets, and increased government efforts to attract new jobs. [88] If laborers and their representatives didn't speak up and their voices couldn't be heard, the government didn't have to spend money to listen to them, help them, or protect them. These were exactly the kinds of people Roe and his counterparts relocating to the American South and the Global South were looking for as employees—people easily replaced, easily silenced, and easily tucked away and out of sight.

Rockingham firefighter Moree, whose father had worked inside the Buttercup plant when only white people did, described the labor situation even more bluntly. "At that time," he said, some of the people in power in Hamlet "considered those workers just a bunch a damn niggers there [at Imperial], and no one cared." [89]

Over the years, the Roes relied on the clerks at the government-run employment services offices in Hamlet, Rockingham, and other nearby towns to funnel the kind of workers no one cared about to their doorstep. The agency sent them single women with children, often from the projects in South Hamlet near Bridges Street or from one of the shotgun shacks in the North Yard on the other side of town. They sent high school dropouts. They sent those discarded by the textile mills and by Clark Equipment after it left the county in the late 1980s. After cycling through the local reserve army of the underemployed and undereducated, the Roes cast a wider net. They employed women and men from Bennettsville, South Carolina, and Gibson, North Carolina, whistle-stop towns even more economically depleted than Hamlet was, who were willing to drive twenty and thirty minutes each way by car for a low-paying job in a dank chicken plant. These, too, were people invisible to Ruth Land and local officials. [90]

Hamlet resident O'Neal Patrick lived close enough to the Imperial plant to hear the screams of the women and men trapped inside on the morning of the fire. A few days later, he told a reporter from National Public Radio that "jobs are so hard to come by in Hamlet that even if the workers didn't like the conditions at the plant, they were afraid to quit. There's no place you can get a job around here. And the poultry plant is about . . . the only . . . place you can get a job and they treat you like dirt when you're there. They care more about their chicken than they do a human." [91]

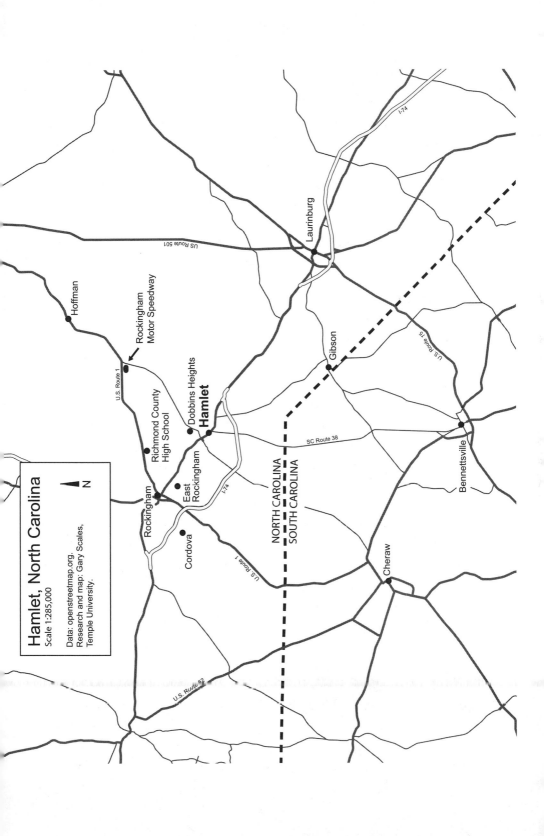

Hamlet, North Carolina

Scale 1:285,000

Data: openstreetmap.org.
Research and map: Gary Scales,
Temple University.

N

"You couldn't complain, you couldn't say anything," Imperial line worker Loretta Goodwin remembered. If you did, "you were out of there." But the problem was that, as Annette Zimmerman explained twenty years after the fire while thinking about the local labor market, "there was nothing . . . to do, and this," she remarked, pointing in the direction of the Imperial site, "was just about it."

The lack of employment options reinforced workers' silence. Maggie Brown said that although she and her co-workers talked on breaks and on their way home from work about the lack of fire drills, slippery floors, exposed electrical wires, and locked doors, she knew of no one who complained to the Roes or the supervisors. "We weren't allowed to speak to Emmett Roe," recalled Lorrie Boyle. "They were afraid that if they did" say anything, added onetime packing room worker Mary Ann Primus-Darien, "they would get fired." [92]

"The managers didn't talk to anyone like they was human," Mary Pouncey said about Imperial. "But we managed. When you got three or four children, and that is all you have, you can put aside what he says." So she stayed quiet about the popping sounds she heard coming from the fryer and about the plant's unmarked exits. "They never had a drill, at least while I was working there," Pouncey told a documentary film crew in 1992. "There was no sprinkler system. There was a lot that you knew that wasn't right, but if you complained about it, you got fired." [93]

Line workers sometimes fashioned their own silences. Ada Blanchard grew up outside of Rockingham on a sandy patch of land her father worked as a sharecropper. In her teens, she ran off to Allentown, Pennsylvania, and then to Philadelphia. A failed marriage brought her back to North Carolina in the mid-1980s. Years after the fire, she said that she had learned to speak up for herself up North. She called herself a "loud mouth." When she first started working at Imperial, she complained all the time about the lack of fire drills and the flash fires breaking out near the gigantic fryer. She wanted to say something to the bosses, but her co-workers stopped her. Every time she was about to point out some shortcoming, they reminded her of the realities of both her life and the local political economy. They told her what she already knew: there weren't many jobs in Richmond County that paid above minimum wage, especially if you were a black woman with kids like Blanchard and 70 to 75 percent of her co-workers in the trim room, packing room, and processing room were. You just had to keep quiet and keep your thoughts to yourself and your friends. Working in a small town in North Carolina and holding on to a job meant keeping your mouth shut and keeping the secrets of the plant secret.[94]

Emmett Roe was never going to be the first to talk. Even after the fire, he maintained a terse, sometimes belligerent silence. Based then in an Atlanta suburb, he arrived in Hamlet within twenty-four hours of the fire breaking out. When a radio reporter asked him about the locked doors, he shrugged and said he didn't know anything about them. When two reporters from the *Charlotte Observer* tried to slip into Imperial's office across the road from the charred plant, Roe told them to leave and slammed the door in their faces. Asked to confirm that he was, in fact, Emmett Roe, he shot back, "Never mind who I am. It's not important." When one of the reporters persisted, Roe gave him the finger.[95]

Roe took a softer approach a few days later. Several people who saw him after the fire said he was crushed. Mayor Covington remembers him weeping on the phone. Another associate saw him with his chin buried in his chest.[96] In a letter to "All Employees," typed out in all capital letters, he wrote, "THERE IS NO QUESTION BUT THAT THIS HAS BEEN A TRAGEDY FOR THE FAMILY MEMBERS OF ALL IMPERIAL EMPLOYEES, PARTICULARLY OF THOSE WHO LOST THEIR LIVES OR WERE INJURED." Concluding his five-sentence note, he got as emotional as he would get in public, yet he did not take any responsibility for the tragedy, saying, "OUR HEARTS, OUR THOUGHTS, AND OUR PRAYERS ARE WITH ALL THOSE IN THE COMMUNITY WHO ARE SUFFERING A LOSS AS A RESULT OF THE ACCIDENT."[97]

After that, Emmett Roe went quiet again, never explaining what he meant when he called the fire an accident. He never spoke at length with city officials. He never sent the families of the dead or injured get well notes or sympathy cards. Even as "Wanted for Murder" posters with his picture on them started to pop up in union halls and churches across the United States, he said nothing.[98]

3

CHICKEN

It was more sticky than hot on Labor Day in 1991 along North Carolina's roadways. Not even having the air-conditioning cranked up all the way in a car could blunt the humidity or cool down the black vinyl seats. Some families were, no doubt, looking to break up the ride. Get something cold to drink, a burger, perhaps some chicken strips, and an ice cream cone to finish the meal. When they reached the top of a ramp leading off just about any highway in the Tar Heel state, there was a McDonald's, and a Hardees a little farther down the road, and maybe a Bojangles or a Kentucky Fried Chicken. Shoney's sometimes sat across the median from the McDonald's. Getting something to eat at the casual, medium-priced restaurant chain would take a few minutes longer than at the fast food places, but it would be cooler in there, and it wouldn't hurt, some parents surely thought, to sit for a while and relax before getting started back on the road and getting sweaty all over again.

Once Shoney's customers had settled into their booth, a server would come over and fill up tall plastic glasses with sweet tea and water. She would pass the adults laminated tablets that unfolded like an accordion into sixteen pages of burgers, Salisbury steaks, and marinated chicken and rice dishes. The kids' menus made out of paper featured games of Tic Tac Toe next to cartoon pictures of the smiling Berenstain Bears family. This time of year the menus doubled as book covers. On one side of the menu, there were instructions for how to turn it into a protective shield for the history or science textbooks that teachers would hand out on the first day of school a few days later. Along the sides, the menu offered educational advice. "Writing," it coached, "teaches us to think more clearly and make our ideas known to others." And history "is the story of what we did and where we went!"

Food choices filled the other side of the menu. Everything for the kids was cheap. Shoney's charged just 99 cents for spaghetti. The "Junior All-American" with two burgers and fries cost $2.47. Shoney's sold a "Kid's Chicken Dinner" with "fried chicken fillets," french fries, and a "slice of dinner bread" for $1.99.

Of course, the Shoney's menu didn't say where the fillets came from, though if that highway ran through North Carolina, the chicken products probably came from the Imperial Food Products plant in Hamlet. But it didn't say that, nor did it say anything about the powerful forces that allowed Imperial to supply those chicken products so cheaply. Still, some families at Shoney's that weekend probably commented on what a good deal they got when they ordered the chicken dinner from the kids' menu or even from the adult one. Maybe one of them even noted how chicken prices in general seemed to going down while just about everything else seemed to cost more.[1]

A watershed moment in the history of American eating took place in 1992.[2] That was the year that per capita chicken consumption surpassed per capita beef consumption in the United States, turning the nation, in the words of one cook, from a "beef country to a chicken country."[3] The defeat of steak and hamburger stemmed from nothing more complicated than "simple economics," the pop economist Daniel Gross contended years later. By that, he meant price.[4] While the cost of beef steadily rose during the postwar years even as warnings about the health risks associated with red meat aired on television and flashed across newspapers headlines, chicken got cheaper and cheaper. In fact, in 1987, chicken cost the same in real dollars as it had in 1923.[5]

But there was nothing simple about the making of cheap chicken. Each bird, each leg and thigh part, each skinless, boneless breast, and each nugget and golden fried fillet served at Shoney's was a product of what might best be called poultry capitalism, a tightly wound economic system that generated relentless competition among producers and manufacturers; the ceaseless exploitation of farmers and slaughterhouse and processing plant workers; the industrialization of animals themselves; the constant innovation of biologists, marketers, and flavor specialists; and, in the end, lower consumer prices hiding a host of unseen and unaccounted-for external costs.[6]

Imperial Food Products was a small, even marginal, player in the system of poultry capitalism that emerged in postwar America. Each week in 1991, the company bought somewhere in the neighborhood of 144,000 skinless, boneless chicken breasts from, among other places, Georgia-based Cagle's, a company bigger than Imperial but a fraction of the size of the big multi-state and multi-national players, Perdue, Tyson, and Holly Farms. They were the kings of growing, slaughtering, and processing chicken and making it the cheapest source of meat-based protein in the United States in the last decade of the twentieth century.

During the early part of the century, the poultry industry in the United States operated on a relatively small scale. Rural women, with the help of their children, raised from a handful to a few dozen chickens for eggs and the occasional holiday supper. The animals roamed around the farmhouse, pecking at seeds and leftovers thrown in their direction. Living off discarded scraps, the birds remained thin and gaunt. Some families, like the Cagles, started to purchase a few extra bags of feed or some leftover corn and began to experiment with more intensive chicken growing, raising scores of chicks in low-slung wood coops, selling live hens to local grocers to earn some extra cash, and trading eggs for bacon and help with a broken tractor. Even this slightly larger, but still small-scale, cultivation made good economic and biological sense given the well-known fact that chickens easily passed along viruses and other illnesses. Because of this, it didn't pay to raise too many of the animals at once in the same place, but this also limited output and kept poultry prices relatively high.[7]

But George L. Cagle, like others in the changing world of chicken, had bigger ambitions than a chicken coop or two in the countryside. In 1940, he used $8,000 from his savings to open a poultry retail shop in Atlanta's bustling Five Points section. Some of the chickens in the store came from his farm, but most came from other growers scattered around northern Georgia. Cagle's business took off, and the family started to sell thousands of pounds of meat each week. With the outbreak of World War II, the government rationed beef, so families could only buy a few pounds of steak or hamburger each month for their dinners and Sunday suppers after church.[8] Demand for chicken soared as poultry suddenly had to fill the void for many American families who couldn't imagine a proper meal without a meat-based protein dish on the center of the plate. War workers on their way home from production jobs and housekeepers doing the shopping for their families would stop by the Cagle store to pick up a whole chicken. They would point to the bird they wanted and wait while Cagle or his teenaged son, Douglas, plucked the feathers and cut off the head. The neck and feet were still on when the customer walked out the door. Soon, restaurants, hotels, and hospitals called on Cagle for chickens. They, too, faced beef cutbacks because of rationing. While the company grew, it remained dependent on a slew of small and medium-size chicken growers for its main product. But this supply chain would have to change if Cagle wanted to expand his business and make more money.

Like much of America, Atlanta boomed after World War II. It was a time when new ideas found new opportunities. In the early 1950s, Douglas Cagle took over the company and began to turn it into a consolidator, or a vertically integrated business in the world of poultry capitalism. Between 1953 and 1963, he bought a number of slaughterhouses and a feed mill. He merged his firm with other regional chicken producers. After that, Cagle's—as the company started to be called—added a hatchery, a fleet of trucks, and several more processing facilities to its physical plant. By 1980, the company had amassed $139 million in assets as it captured, slaughtered, and dismembered 1.5 million chickens a week. It then sold plastic-wrapped packages of cut-up birds to supermarkets and boneless breasts and other products to further processors, the name the poultry industry gave to outfits like the Roes' Hamlet operation that took already processed chicken parts and leftover scraps and changed their shape and form by adding ingredients like salt, fillers, and breading to them before cooking them.[9]

Unlike the slaughterhouses and feed plants in its portfolio, Cagle's didn't own the land or the facilities where growers raised broilers (chicken bred to yield meat, instead of eggs, primarily) from chicks to full-size birds. Instead, beginning in the 1940s and 1950s, they searched the foothills of Georgia and the Sandhills of the Carolinas looking for partners. Company representatives drove up to small farmhouses. Surely, they stepped out of their cars with a bit of wariness and concern. They knew they were calling on people well known for their hair-trigger tempers, fierce independence, and willingness to protect what was theirs with fists, knives, and guns.[10]

Making a living in these parts had never been easy for small farmers. For decades, they planted row after row of cotton and tobacco, unsure of the price they would get at the end of the season. Hoping to increase their yield, they used bag after bag of fertilizers until they leached the red clay and flinty soil of all nutrients. Some families had already weighed their economic prospects in the countryside and packed up their stuff and moved to the closest mill village. Others had invested in small trucks and drove each morning into town to lay track, bag groceries, or fix cars. The holdouts who didn't want to leave their farms, no matter what, were ones who listened to Douglas Cagle and his associates. Cagle reminded the farmers of the unpredictability of crop prices and the sorry state of their land. He told them that they could make a steady living raising animals rather than crops while still anchoring their lives in the countryside.

Cagle offered farm families a contract modeled along the lines of the "grow out" system first pioneered by fellow Georgian and poultry consolidator Jesse D. Jewell. "We furnish the baby chicks and the feed," Jewell explained about the grow-out system. "[Farmers] furnish the house, the equipment, and the labor, heat, and we pay them according to the number of pounds of chicken they get out of the number of pounds of feed they use." Not that different from sharecropping, Jewell's system offered farmers a chance to grow someone else's crop on borrowed capital. To get into the business, farmers had to revamp their operations and build coops for the chickens. Often, they needed to take out loans to do so. At first the banks didn't ask many questions, especially when white landowners— who made up by far the majority of the chicken growers in the South— came in to borrow money. Sometimes a Cagle's representative co-signed on the loans to make sure they went through smoothly.[11]

To the farmers who signed these early contracts, the windowless wooden poultry houses, as they called the coops, represented hope the hope of staying on the land and making it. But for many, that optimism quickly faded. Throughout the 1950s and 1960s, competition in the poultry industry stiffened. In response, companies like Cagle's, as well as Perdue and Tyson, pressed growers for more. They wanted bigger birds that were grown faster. They pushed the growers to take on more debt and modernize their poultry houses. They wanted them longer and wider and made from aluminum with huge exhaust fans at either end, complex feeding machines running down the middle, and intricate lighting systems above. In essence, the company demanded that they turn their farms into animal factories. By this point, farmers who had taken the leap into poultry capitalism and remained in the system couldn't say no.

"Contracts," as the investigative journalist Christopher Leonard noted in 2015, could be "canceled for nothing more than refusing to toe the company line." [12] If a farmer's broilers did not get big enough fast enough, or as fast as a neighbor's did, the family lost its contract. If they didn't modernize their facilities, the company could break the contract. Each demand for capital improvements pushed farmers deeper and deeper in debt. If farmers resisted taking out another bank loan or tried to do things their own way, they got no chicks. If they had no chicks, they couldn't raise broilers. If they couldn't raise broilers, they couldn't pay their loans. Then they lost their farms. The key to the system was that there was nowhere else to turn. In yet another hallmark of the world of cheap, despite worshipful talk of markets and freedom, the chicken consolidators sought monopolies over competition, and they found this power on the margins, in economically pressed rural hinterlands, in country crossroads even smaller than Hamlet, places far from cities where people had few options.

As the contract system spread in the years after World War II and gathered more momentum in the 1960s and 1970s, the chicken industry's center of gravity continued to move southward from New York and Delaware. By the time Emmett Roe bought the Buttercup plant in the early 1980s, the United States led the world in poultry production, and the South led the nation. Ten years after that, North Carolina emerged as the fourth largest poultry-producing state in the country behind Georgia, Alabama, and Arkansas, and chicken overtook tobacco as the state's number one agricultural commodity, generating over $1.5 billion in business each year. [13] This transformation could not have taken place without the further intensification of the contract system and the mounting dependence of growers on consolidators like Cagle's and, of course, the much bigger players like Perdue and Tyson. Locked in their own competitive battles, these companies demanded more investment from growers and oversaw the doubling and tripling in the size of both the southern poultry houses and the overall output of chicken in the region.[14]

Over time, the modest chicken houses perched along tobacco roads mushroomed into concentrated animal feeding operations (CAFOs). As long and as wide as a football field, these highly modern, highly productive animal factories churned out tens of millions of broilers in coops, applying the industrial logic of efficiency to the feeding and growing of chickens.[15] They became every bit as productive as the colossal factories at River Rouge and Bethlehem Steel were in their day. Just like those famed industrial sites, the chicken factories of the Southland encouraged endless technical and scientific innovation. Yet while auto- and steelworkers generally shared some of the gains of their industries, the growers rarely got their piece of the pie. Over time, raising bigger broilers faster didn't necessarily make the growers richer or more financially stable. Some still had to work a second job hauling timber or managing a McDonald's outlet. Most stayed up late worrying about bills. Because of the strictures of the contract system, and because of the endless demand for more investment and debt, and because increased production by the chicken growers led to downward pressure on prices and usually to more production and another wave of price cuts, few farmers got rich or even gained a toehold into the middle class.

"In reality," writes a historian of the Maryland chicken industry, Solomon Iyobosa Omo-Osagie II, "a grower, did not really 'own' the business." He or she was "operating the business" on behalf of Jesse Jewell or Cagle's or Gold Kist.[16] In many ways, the farmers had been turned, as one journalist described it, into "serfs with a mortgage." Many who decided to get into poultry to hold on to their rural roots and independence instead found themselves trapped in an endless cycle of debt and near poverty, in a system not that different from the sharecropping regime that had exploited many of their parents and grandparents for decades before. Consumers, though, benefited from the growers' unseen pain as they paid less for chicken at Food Lion and Shoney's.[17]

Contract farmers and chicken consolidators weren't the only forces pushing poultry prices down for consumers.

In 1946, one of the nation's first true supermarket chains, A&P, spon-
sored a "Chicken of Tomorrow" contest. The company awarded a prize to
the person who bred the biggest bird with the biggest breasts. Noting the
American preference for white meat over dark meat—not dissimilar from
the nation's choice of white bread over wheat bread—farmers and poultry breeders figured out how to engineer top-heavy chickens that looked
more like a Barbie doll than like the skinny, scrappy barnyard chickens
that had roamed the Cagle family yard and poultry houses in the years
before World War II. A&P held more contests over the next decade, and
each one delivered weightier, even more top-heavy designer chickens.[18]

By this point, food scientists, not rural tinkerers, had taken over the
process of managing and manipulating biology. Like their agricultural
school colleagues working on corn and soybeans, during the 1950s and
1960s researchers in poultry science departments at North Carolina State
University, the University of Georgia, and Cornell University developed
endless ways to "accelerate the biological productivity" of broiler chickens.
(Again, hens generally laid eggs, while broilers were raised for their meat.)
Using new building materials and lighting, they outlined more efficient
models for CAFOs, figuring out how to confine chickens longer, feed
them more carbohydrate-rich foods faster, and use vitamins and chemicals
to curtail the spread of disease as best they could in swelling coops. Following the lead of the Chicken of Tomorrow contestants, other scientists
focused on genetics and breeding. They engineered chickens that grew to
full weight faster, eating less along the way. Essentially they turned broilers, explains the historian William Boyd, into "highly efficient machines
for converting feed grain into cheap animal flesh protein."[19]

In 1928, it took 112 days to raise a 2.8-pound chicken that ate roughly
12.5 pounds of food as it grew to maturity. Forty years later, it took half
that time for the grow-out, the industry term for the amount of time it
takes for a chick to reach its full weight as a broiler. Ten years after that,
broilers raised on animal farms were 25 percent bigger than their prede-
cessors were and ate only half as much feed. In 1995, the average industrial chicken hit the scales at six-plus pounds. It took forty-seven days
for the animals to get that big, and, along the way, they consumed only
ten pounds of feed. If, as the trade journal *Poultry Science* marveled, a
newborn six-and-a-half-pound baby grew at the pace of these chickens

of tomorrow, it would tip the scales at six hundred pounds by its second month alive.[20]

The new miracle breeds of broilers, with names like Vantress and Cyprus C, that Imperial bought from Cagle's to make its tenders, fillets, and nuggets got bigger, faster, while consuming less feed. When these puffed-up creatures tried to walk, they could barely go more than a step or two without wobbling and toppling over. To get them to this size, the growers turned the overhead fluorescent lights in the chicken houses on for twenty to twenty-two hours a day because they wanted their chickens to eat like pigs, and they knew that these birds were biologically hard-wired not to eat in the dark. So the animals lived in artificial light and ate almost around the clock, even if it made them sick.[21] Many became so agitated in these bright, closed quarters that they attacked the birds next to them and sometimes tried to peck themselves to death. Protecting their investments and pushed by the contractors, growers would de-beak the broilers, sometimes with an instrument that resembled a blowtorch and usually without administering any anesthesia. The system wouldn't allow for any unnecessary expenses. The growers did, though, turn to a pharmacy of other drugs for other reasons—all economic. Anxious birds didn't eat. When they didn't eat, they didn't grow to their full weight in a flash of time. Jumpy birds also tended to yield tougher meat. By the 1980s, in response, some growers started to lace their chicken feed with Benadryl to settle the nerves of the cooped-up birds and keep them on the fast-growing track. Others dropped traces of caffeine into the feeding machines so the birds would stay awake and keep eating. Perdue apparently added xanthophyll to its feed mix, a dye found in alfalfa and marigold petals that turned the skin of broilers an artificial shade of golden yellow. Birds living so close together easily passed germs and diseases to one another, so farmers put penicillin, tetracycline, chlortetracycline, and oxytetracycline in their foods. Over time, as a result, broilers inevitably became resistant to some of these antibiotics, starting another round of chemical solutions and producing a range of possibly dangerous food-borne illnesses for chicken eaters.[22]

In 1986, a group of radical activists calling themselves London Greenpeace—they had no formal relationship with the more famous and well-known global environmental organization, Greenpeace—began passing out a six-sided leaflet along the city's high streets entitled "What's Wrong with McDonald's?: Everything You Don't Want to Know." The rather plain-looking black-and-white broadsheet accused the fast food giant of economic imperialism, false advertising, environmental destruction, the systematic exploitation of workers, and the "torture and murder" of millions of animals each year. The American-based company responded to the charges by secretly infiltrating the group and later by suing it for libel. The British press dubbed the ensuing trial, which began in 1994, "the McLibel Case." [23]

As it wound through the courts, the McLibel case became the longest-running civil trial in British history. In his initial 1997 decision, a technical victory for McDonald's that would be appealed and argued over for almost a decade afterward, the judge, who had pored through mountains of documents detailing the company's business practices, wrote a detailed section about the treatment of the industrially produced animals the firm used for its nuggets. "Broiler chickens," he had learned, "spend the last few days of their lives with very little room to move. The severe restrictions of movement of those last few days is cruel." [24] As the chickens exploded in size, he explained, their living spaces shrank. They could hardly turn to the right or left or spread their wings. Their naturally skinny legs were often snapped in half by the weight of their not-so-natural oversized, genetically engineered breasts. Crippled from hip and leg deformities, these chickens couldn't drag themselves to water or food, so many died of dehydration and starvation. Others collapsed because their lungs and hearts couldn't keep pace with their swelling upper bodies. Veterinarians knew that barnyard chickens didn't naturally die of heart failure, but factory birds, they told the McLibel judge, perished this way all the time from what poultry companies rather innocuously called "flip over syndrome." [25]

Like the poultry consolidators used by McDonald's in England and around the world, Cagle's dropped baby chicks off at the farms it had under contract at regular intervals. Forty-two to forty-seven days later, a crew returned to pick up the broilers. A chicken catcher, as he was called, waded into the pens and grabbed the now six-plus-pound animals by their feet and shoved them into crates, often with such force that as many as 30 percent of them arrived at the slaughterhouse, their next stop in the process, with broken bones. Cagle's employees stacked the crates of captured chickens, one on top of the other, on trucks headed to plants in Macon and Pine Mountain, Georgia, and Collinsville, Alabama. During the ride, urine and feces soaked the animals from top to bottom. Once they were unloaded, the broilers, many now lame, were hung up by their feet and dragged through an electrified saltwater bath so that they wouldn't flap their wings when workers slit their throats. When the process ran the way it was designed to run, the charged water rendered the chickens unconscious so that they felt next to nothing through the rest of the killing process. But because Cagle's executives, like others in the poultry business, feared that too much of an electrical jolt would taint the meat with a slightly burnt taste, animals often remained fully conscious when their throats got cut. [26]

Terrified and disoriented, many birds defecated on themselves as they were being killed. Covered in feces, the now dead or nearly dead broilers were then dragged through a chemical-filled and scalding hot bath to help ease the removal of their feathers in the next stage of the disassembly process. But all of the excrement on the birds went into the water and seeped inside them through the bedsores many had developed from sitting too long in the animal factories because their spindly legs couldn't support their bloated bodies. After that, machines ripped the intestinal tracts out of the bodies of the dead birds. As they did, fecal matter sprayed onto the machines, the tables, and workers' hands and then it came into contact with the bird's muscles, tissue, and organs, providing multiple opportunities for contamination.[27]

Cheap government added to the toxic mix stirring in the chicken slaughterhouses of the United States. In 1978, the Carter administration's Department of Agriculture, eager to jump-start one section of the nation's stagnant economy, approved a measure that allowed for the washing of broilers in chemical baths instead of the more labor-intensive process of cutting and cleaning fecal matter and other disease-carrying materials off the birds one at a time. The eviscerated carcasses would now sit for an hour or so in a tub of chlorinated ice water, almost marinating in germs, bacteria, and diseases that could make consumers down the line sick to their stomachs. This stage of production, as one health writer explained a number of years after the fire, "is where the main contamination with feces takes place. Feces left on the meat from the disemboweling process mixes with the water in the tank, contaminating all the other birds with possible harmful bacteria and bird pooh. That's why it's called the fecal soup." The Carter administration's ruling not only cooked up this awful mess, it also permitted processors to ratchet up their assembly lines, going from around seventy birds per minute to as many as one hundred birds per minute. More chickens going through plants, and through the fecal soups in them, translated into cheaper chickens both in the supermarket and in fast food outlets. But it also meant more chances for consumers to get sick. And finally, the new speed of production also meant that more of the cruelties practiced on animals would be inflicted on workers.[28]

Curious about the triumph of chicken in the South, in 1989 *New York Times* reporter Peter Applebome headed to the broiler belt, a swath of counties that overlapped quite closely with the Bible Belt. He watched the blur of birds get disassembled in a violent flash and heard firsthand about the impact of the slaughterhouse speed-up. At a Cagle's processing plant in Macon, Georgia, where chickens on their way to places like Imperial Food Products went by line workers at a rate of nearly one hundred per minute, Applebome met Betty Harpe.

"I'm in pain the whole time at work and at home," Harpe told him. Reaching up to the line, deboning chicken breasts, and cutting chunks of meat with heavy scissors strained the tendons in her hands and wrists, producing tendonitis and carpal tunnel syndrome, a painful nerve disorder caused by repetitive motions and capable of producing permanent damage. Harpe was not alone in her discomfort. A 1989 North Carolina Department of Labor study calculated that twenty-five out of every one hundred poultry workers in the state suffered from some kind of occupational injury. That added up to three times the rate for all private-sector workers across the country. Later that same year, the Institute for Southern Studies, a North Carolina–based nonprofit research and advocacy group, estimated that two thirds of employees in the state's chicken plants suffered from a cumulative trauma disorder to their hands, wrists, and backs as a result of repetitive motions.[29]

Applebome collected more anecdotal evidence at the Cagle's plant on workplace injuries from Jessie Lee Moss, a nine-year employee of the company. Most nights, sharp pains raced up her arms and chased her out of bed. To make the stinging go away, she ran water over her wrists. When she couldn't take the sleepless nights anymore, she opted for costly surgery. She showed Applebome the scars on her wrists.[30]

As workers and animals suffered from injuries, restaurants and cafeterias featured more chicken products, with consumers paying less for the items. Between 1950 and 1999, chicken production in the United States, led by gains in the South, increased on average by 7 percent each year. As it did, the price of chicken dropped, and then dropped again. By 1990, it cost one-ninth of what steak cost and 20 percent less than pork, though this gap would close in the years to come as pork production, in the words of one investigative journalist, became "chickenized." "It's the cheapest protein out there," a hotel chef noted about chicken as he searched for more recipes to put on his menu and cut his costs.[31] Looking for a deal and maybe a little less fat, shoppers tossed chicken products into their shopping carts or ordered them from fast food outlets without much thought or knowledge about where the birds came from, how they got from the farms to their kitchen counters, or how they ended up on their plates as salt-filled marinated chicken breasts or battered and fried chicken tenders. Poultry capitalism, like the beef capitalism of Upton Sinclair's *The Jungle* and most other modern food capitalisms, discouraged knowing.

While consumers, at least in the short run, benefited from the drop in chicken prices and the downward pressure that it eventually put on pork prices and other commodities, Cagle's and other broiler producers found themselves locked in a vicious cycle of destructive competition. Making money in poultry capitalism meant pushing growers, workers, and animals to do more, and make more, with less. But it also meant finding new ways to add value and profit to raw materials, and that meant paying more attention to consumer budgets, eating habits, and tastes—especially tastes, because making cheaper, bigger chickens with inexpensive, chemically laced feed meant making blander chickens with less flavor in each bite.

"Man, this shit is right, yo," beams Wallace, one of the fresh-faced drug dealers from the first season of the HBO show *The Wire*, as his friend Poot dips a McDonald's Chicken McNugget into a small plastic container of honey mustard sauce. Reaching for another piece of deep-fried, breaded chicken and filler product, he pauses for a moment to think, and then launches into a tribute to the inventor of his favorite food.

"Got the bone all the way out of the damn chicken," Wallace tells his associates, Poot and D'Angelo, who are sitting with him on an orange couch in the courtyard of a low-rise Baltimore housing project. "Till he come along they be chewing on drumsticks getting their fingers all greasy." As just compensation for the foresight and genius it took to pull off this impressive feat of extraction, Wallace guesses that the McNugget's inventor must be "richer than a motherfucker."

That's when D'Angelo, the twenty-something, just out of prison, crew leader, who in a later episode will offer an insightful reading of *The Great Gatsby*, stops him. In a voice dripping with distain at his partner's naiveté about the way that markets and the larger economy of capitalism work, he tells him, "The man who invented them things is just some sad ass down at the basement of McDonald's, thinking of some shit to make some money for the real players." [32]

Robert C. Baker was that guy in the basement who invented the chicken nugget sometime around 1963, nearly twenty years before it first appeared on a McDonald's menu. But he didn't work for the fast food giant. His laboratory sat in Bruckner Hall, home to the Institute of Food Science and Marketing, on the Cornell University campus. And Baker wasn't some sad ass. He was a well-liked, hardworking, and widely respected professor. Even now, Cornell cafeterias still use his vinegar-based recipe for barbeque chicken. As a tribute to Baker's lifelong work with chickens, the American Poultry Institute named him to its Hall of Fame in 2001. When Baker died a few years later, the *New York Times* ran an obituary that stretched over two columns and called him "something of a chicken Edison." [33]

Like the Wizard of Menlo Park, Baker was an inventor, an innovator, a researcher, and a popularizer. While Baker wasn't the easily duped fool that D'Angelo imagined, he did work closely with the chicken industry, helping it conquer beef for protein supremacy in the United States in the early 1990s, and his office was, for a time, in a basement. [34]

"He was a very practical, very applied guy," Joe Regenstein, one of Baker's Cornell colleagues, recalled. Born in 1921 in Newark, New York, a town a little smaller than Hamlet that was located eighty miles south of Lake Ontario, Baker grew up on a farm. His family tended to apple orchards and the chickens roaming around the house. They started the day by collecting the eggs laid by the hens. On special Sundays, Baker's mother sent him out into the yard to grab a chicken. She told him which one to pick—usually the oldest one and the one who had stopped producing eggs. Once he caught the chicken, he wrung its neck, cut its throat, hung it upside down to bleed it out, and then brought it to his mom. She put it in boiling water, and then Baker helped her pull off all of the feathers and the yellow fuzz on the skin. Once they finished cleaning the outside, they cut off the feet and head and gutted the inside. His mom then cooked the chicken and served it to the family, Baker warmly recalled, with buttery homemade biscuits. This wasn't just a family tradition. This was how many Americans ate chicken in the 1930s.[35]

As the Great Depression waned, Baker left Newark to study pomology, the science of fruit cultivation, at Cornell. After finishing his training, he got a job working for Cornell Extension Services traveling around the Finger Lakes area teaching best practices to local farmers. After a few years riding the bumpy backroads, Baker returned to the lecture halls and seminar rooms, shifting the focus of his studies and earning a master's degree in marketing at Pennsylvania State University and then a PhD in animal science at Purdue University. In 1947, Baker returned to Ithaca to help expand Cornell's fledgling poultry science program. The study of chickens as an academic field had only just begun in the early years of the twentieth century, but it intensified and flourished in the postwar era. This was when Baker and his colleagues started to garner support to study consumer tastes and how to better market and manipulate the biology and genetics of egg-laying hens and meat-rich broilers.

"He really believed in using the total material," Regenstein remembered. "He was opposed to waste." Tightening up the system, Baker thought, could shore up profits for chicken processors and offer solutions to problems of hunger and starvation in an increasingly overpopulated, underdeveloped world. Carrying these values with him into the lab and into the field, he tried to devise ways to use leftover poultry parts and unused scraps in new and novel ways. Though he wrote hundreds of reports and research papers, Baker wasn't an academic in the most common sense of how scholars operated then or now. He didn't just apply for grants from the National Science Foundation and other scholarly organizations. He focused on product development and market testing for industry, mostly the chicken industry, with some side work devoted to fish companies. He specialized in, and virtually invented, the field of further-processed chicken, the market niche that Imperial would later operate in.[36]

Robert Baker's unstated job at Cornell was to resolve the contradictions of poultry capitalism by searching for ways to sell the glut of chicken churned out by Cagle's and other highly efficient producers. Selling chicken in postwar America, though, was not all that different from selling dish soap, blue jeans, or sports cars. It wasn't about manipulating consumers, but rather was about making products that fit the circumstances of people's lives, whatever they were. Understanding the 1970s in the United States meant, in particular, recognizing the deep impact of inflation and declining wages. Both factors combined to shrink the purchasing power of working people and the poor at Shoney's, supermarkets, and corner stores. It made them dependent on cheap meat and cheap calories. Even though overall food prices dropped somewhat during the 1970s because of the impressive efficiencies and massive output of industries like poultry and corn, the poorest of the poor still spent close to 30 percent of their income on food, while the working poor spent between 15 and 20 percent and the upper-middle-class families spent less than 10 percent of what they made on feeding themselves and their families.[37]

Food, however, remained one of the few "fudgeable" items in the family budget. Poultry plant operatives and fast food and service workers—the vanguard of the new working class of the 1970s and beyond—couldn't cut back on rent, car insurance, or weekly loan payments for bedroom sets and washing machines. For them, these were fixed expenses. Food, however, provided some wiggle room. You could buy less meat and make soups and stews if you had the time or owned a slow cooker. You could replace beef with chicken. You could watch out for sales, clip coupons, and pick up boxes of generic cereal and macaroni and cheese. A few dollars here and there might stop the power company from cutting off the electricity or the phone line from going dead. Cheap supermarket goods became, then, a necessity much more than they were a target of bargain-hunting adventures. As steady blue-collar work disappeared, like those positions at

Clark Equipment and on the railroad, and rates of unionization dipped, families started to depend on cheap food to make ends meet. Soon, they came to expect food items to be cheap; their budgets demanded it.

Looking for bargains, consumers in the 1970s began to toss more packages of cut-up chicken into their shopping carts. That's because by this point chicken was the cheapest meat in the store. Further-processed chicken cost a little more than whole birds or pieces did, but it too remained relatively inexpensive and was easy to prepare.

The trade-off between time and money was another thing on the minds of working-class shoppers in the 1970s. By the time the Watergate hearings made it onto TV and the oil-producing countries of the Middle East formed OPEC, convenience trumped flavor in the kitchens of many Americans. This development was part of a long and complicated process. Food makers had pushed canned goods and cake mixes since the early days of the twentieth century. Along the way, they helped to transform American tastes and habits. Mostly, though, they made convenience a factor in every family's cooking calculations, with the balance in the postwar years tipping heavily toward quick and easy. By the 1970s, Americans had, according to one food researcher, "gotten into the hurry up mode."[38] Easy to make. Easy to eat. Easy to clean up. That's what sold in America, with its increasing numbers of mothers and married women working outside the home for pay. Families mobilized female labor for a slew of reasons, none more important than coping with the long-term drop in blue-collar wages that began in the 1970s, the same drop that made cheap food not a choice but a necessity. Yet, despite the feminist stirring for equality reflected by the formation of the National Organization of Women (NOW), the near bra burnings at the Miss America Pageant in Atlantic City, and the appearance of magazine feature stories about caring men, like Alan Alda, chipping in at home, in most American households, going to the grocery store and making dinner remained women's work no matter how many hours they sat in an office or stood along an assembly line. So too did cleaning, laundry, and getting the kids to baseball practice, Bible study, and 4-H meetings. In single-parent homes, the fastest growing kind of home in poor communities across rural and urban America from the 1970s forward, it didn't matter because there was no one else around but the mom, usually, to do all of the things that needed to be done.[39]

When it came to cooking, many women looked to cut down the time they spent over the stove or in front of the oven. Few women, of course, stopped cooking altogether. They just needed some easy alternatives for weekday meals in order to balance all of the tasks on their to-do lists. The push for less kitchen time translated into less cooking from scratch and a heavier reliance on processed and hyper-processed foods like hot dogs, instant mashed potatoes, and chicken nuggets and tenders.

In 1960, the average cook, almost always a woman, spent two hours a day in the kitchen. Three decades later, a very different average American domestic manager, who by then most likely had a job outside the home, commuted to work, and was maybe the only parent in the house full-time, spent, on average, less than thirty minutes in the kitchen each day, the lowest amount among the world's thirty-four industrial nations.[40]

As convenience began to dictate food choices, the very notion of cooking changed. This could be seen in cakes and casseroles and in recipes for chicken and side dishes. By the time the Imperial plant opened in Hamlet, cooking a chicken no longer meant roasting a whole bird for hours on end or simmering it with cut-up vegetables for even longer, let alone catching it, killing it, and cleaning it. Maybe it meant dredging pieces of pre-cut chicken in peppery flour and frying them in a heavy, well-seasoned skillet a couple of breasts or thighs at a time. For some, it meant barbequing on a grill or tossing a boneless chicken breast in a pan. But, by the 1980s, that chicken breast might come pre-seasoned and portioned out. Chicken for dinner could also mean "Shake and Bake" with Stove Top Stuffing or Minute Rice and a can of corn. But when time was really short, chicken meant zapping chicken nuggets and other further-processed chicken(ish) products in the microwave, itself a product of the less-is-more ethos of cheap.

In 1978, less than 10 percent of American households had a microwave. Twenty years later, just about every kitchen, office, and lunchroom had one, and the machines, usually made in factories in faraway places in the developing world, cost about as much as a meal for a family of four did at a mid-priced restaurant like Red Lobster or Shoney's. With food ready in a jiffy, families feasted on dishes made of newly processed foods and old foods processed in new ways.[41] When microwaving would take too long or entail too much work, families and individuals went out and ordered from value menus at fast food outlets.

In 1940, Americans spent 15 percent of their food budgets on eating outside the home. Thirty years later, this number had climbed to 28 percent. By 1987, it had jumped to 35 percent. Most of the visits, if not most of the money, especially for working people, went to buying processed burgers and further-processed chicken nuggets, often priced at a dollar each or on sale in two-for-one specials, at McDonald's or Burger King or Hardee's. This quickly added up in terms of both dollars and calories. By 1990, Americans consumed 15 to 20 percent of their total caloric intake at fast food chains.[42]

Marketers encouraged the consumption of convenience foods. They portrayed cooking as a slog, as something that no one would do if they didn't have to. Some ad men went a step further, labeling microwave meals and eating out as a sign of freedom. "Don't cook, just eat," implored one advertisement. McDonald's urged families in the 1980s to give "Mom a Day Off." Going a step further, Kentucky Fried Chicken ran a spot showing a bucket of its secret recipe fried chicken under the banner "Women's Liberation."[43]

As fast food restaurants multiplied and freezers stuffed with highly processed meals stretched over several supermarket aisles, the idea of food, including chicken, changed. Food as a concept drifted further and further away from its natural form as a plant or an animal. "I grew up on a farm," remembered Robert Baker, as he explained how he would chop the head off a chicken and "then we'd scoop it into a pail and it would lie in the house a bit before my mother would get around to cooking it." During the war and afterward, city dwellers stopped by a place like Cagle's and left with a whole bird. By the 1960s, consumers purchased cut-up pieces of chicken. That way they got what they wanted, which was always part of the promise of modern buying. If they wanted just legs, that's what they got. Same with breasts and thighs. By the 1970s, the skin came off (for health reasons) and the bone came out of the breasts (for convenience). From there, the chicken men, like Baker, tried to figure out the bird's next incarnation.

Even in the early 1990s, at that crucial moment when chicken overtook beef in the battle for national meat supremacy, sales of chicken lagged behind production. While chicken consumption in 1990 climbed 6 percent, overall production jumped 10 percent. Because of these sideways numbers, chicken never really had a chance to celebrate its historic victory over cows. Even in its moment of triumph, the industry saw a ceiling building over its head. It had to figure out how to knock through that to get to another level or it would risk a long, unpredictable run of overproduction, underconsumption, and uncertain profits.[44]

Part of the problem was chicken itself. While chicken became cheaper in the 1970s and 1980s at the very moment when prices started to matter more to inflation-rattled consumers, it lacked the different cuts and varied textures and tastes found with beef and pork. There were no savory ribs or smoked bacon or buttery tenderloins. Big jumps in output that were dependent on an endless diet of corn and additives, moreover, produced mild, flavorless chickens. The renowned chef James Beard joked as early as 1962 that industrial chickens "looked beautiful, but taste like absolutely nothing."[45] With consumers constrained by the simple choice between bland dark meat and blander white meat, marketers detected, in this age of endless variation, a new problem for the broiler industry: "chicken fatigue."[46]

Robert Baker spent much of his career battling "chicken fatigue." All the better, he believed, if he could come up with convenient options that used leftover parts and pieces of the bird. Better still if the items' hidden qualities hooked customers and kept them coming back for more. Between 1960 and 1980, Baker helped to create more than fifty further-processed chicken-based foods in his Cornell lab.

The site is important here. Food in postwar America increasingly came from labs, not fields. Scientists working with marketers tried to come up with new and alluring products made from cheap ingredients. Many of Baker's creations were like the drinks that recovering alcoholics concoct in their kitchen sinks. They looked like the real thing and sometimes tasted a little like the real thing, but they weren't quite the real thing. In Baker's case, the "real thing" was beef or pork. Over the years, he developed chicken baloney, chicken steak, chicken salami, chicken chili, chicken hash, and chicken pastrami. Another of his inventions was chicken loaf. "That's like meat loaf," Baker said. Chic-A-Links "looks and tastes like pork sausage." And as for Chickalona: "That's chicken baloney that's white."[47]

But Baker's most famous and lasting invention was the chicken nugget. He drew his inspiration from the fish stick. Already by the start of the 1960s a staple of frozen food aisles, this early convenience food turned leftover parts and bits into something saleable. Using all of the chicken became even more important as poultry companies looked for added revenues in the feverishly competitive, supermarket-driven market where profit margins were constantly getting squeezed by each and every new merger, productivity gain, and big store opening.

Initially, Baker tried to imitate the fish stick made famous by Gorton's.[48] Creating a thin, two-inch-long, rectangular chicken product with white-colored meat on the inside surrounded by a crunchy golden crust presented two food engineering challenges for Baker and his student collaborator on the project, Joseph Marshall. First, they had to devise a way to meld the meat extracted, scraped, or sucked off chicken carcasses along with ground-up feet, skin, and other parts of the bird as well as the fillers together without using a thin outer skin like the one on the outside of a hot dog. Second, they had to figure out how to make sure that the batter stayed attached to the meat despite the inevitable shrinkage caused by the heat from a fryer and the cold from a freezer used to preserve the food. "They solved the first problem," explains the food writer Maryn McKenna, "by grinding raw chicken with salt and vinegar to draw out moisture, and then adding a binder of powdered milk and pulverized grains." The end result resembled moist white clay, malleable enough to shape but dense enough to hold its form. Baker and Marshall added sodium phosphate to the mix to cover up off notes, or sour and bitter tastes. The salty additive also ensured that the chicken sticks would have a longer shelf life, another key to further-processed supermarket foods. Baker and Marshall cracked the second problem by shaping the clay-like food into narrow strips, coating them in a batter of eggs and cornflake crumbs, and then freezing them before they heated them up. After cooking, the food scientists cooled their product a second time in a blast freezer set at minus ten degrees. That way, the nugget-sticks were already partially cooked and could easily be reheated at home in an oven or microwave or in a fryer at a fast food restaurant. This allowed marketers to pitch the further-processed chicken pieces as an easy-to-make, timesaving, freedom-delivering convenience food.[49]

Baker knew enough about the psycho-biology of food to know that the texture of the chicken sticks combined with the fat and salt that he loaded into them would get eaters coming back for more. When one of his co-workers was asked whether Baker understood this almost addictive dynamic, he answered, "Yes, for sure."[50] The fat in nuggets rewarded the brain with instant feelings of pleasure. The salt had a similar effect. Baker added just the right bit of texture and crunch to the give the product a satisfying mouth feel. At the same time, the nuggets, like most of the foods he favored, had a broad, and never too strong, taste appeal. Like most food scientists, Baker knew that sharp and distinct flavors overwhelm the brain and depress the desire for more, so he made sure that his mainstream chicken concoctions had a pleasing but not overriding taste.[51]

Once the chemical and technical problems with the nuggets got sorted out, Baker and his team designed a label and shipped boxes of the chicken product off to five local supermarkets and grocery stores, where they seemingly had connections and where the items would find a place in the frozen food aisle near the Swanson TV dinners and Gorton's fish sticks. In their first six weeks in stores, Baker and his team sold more than 1,200 boxes of these precursors to the chicken nugget. Within six months, they had sold out. But they didn't make any more once the last packs left the stores. Baker and Marshall and the others in the lab moved on to the next chicken product. The nugget, it seems, remained a secret of upstate New York for more than a decade.[52]

By the 1970s, McDonald's, apparently unaware of Baker's experiments with chicken sticks, began to search for its own car-friendly, easy-to-eat chicken alternative to hamburgers. With the price of poultry falling with each new efficiency gain in the animal factories in the fields and the slaughterhouses, and with warnings about the health risks associated with beef popping up in news articles more frequently, the fast food giant needed a chicken option on its menu. Company officials also worried about the "veto factor," when someone in a lunch party, for instance, rejected a trip to McDonald's because they didn't see any healthy choices on the overhead menu.[53] In these early days of red meat fears, chicken, and anything called chicken, fell under the wide umbrella of "good for you." To meet the new demand, the senior chairman of the company, Roy Kroc, suggested as a possibility chicken potpies similar to the firm's handy and successful hot apple pies. The product flopped in taste tests. McDonald's experiments with not so healthy KFC-style fried chicken didn't go much better.

Around this time, in that laboratory that D'Angelo from *The Wire* imagined, Rene Arend, McDonald's European-trained executive chef, was tinkering with a new side product he called Onion McNuggets, bite-sized chunks of fried onions. Frustrated because he couldn't get real onions to conform to the company's industrial standards of utterly predictable taste, he abandoned the project. "But Rene," a colleague asked not long after the chicken pies and fried pieces of onion failed to catch on, "why not try chicken nuggets instead?"[54]

Within days, Arend came up with a prototype of the Chicken Mc-Nugget, breaded and fried pieces of chicken meats and parts encased in a crunchy crust. Over the next few years, he and his co-workers in the Mc-Donald's kitchens confronted the same challenges Baker had faced years before—how to extract moisture from the meat and get the breading to stick to the mixture of meat pieces, parts, and filler. By 1979, they had figured out the problems on their own without Baker's advice or knowledge.

Without much advance advertising, in March 1980, McDonald's debuted the McNuggets, cooked at the time like its fries, in beef tallow, at fifteen outlets in Knoxville, Tennessee. They couldn't keep the boxes of McNuggets in the heating trays, as the new chicken product set sales records at just about every outlet. "Word of the new product's magic," writes *Salon*'s Maryn McKenna, "spread quickly among franchisees." Store managers from Spartanburg to Spokane wanted the new item. They didn't get them right away because the fast food company couldn't make enough of them. To meet the soaring demand, Tyson Foods hastily developed and patented a new breed of broiler chickens especially for McNuggets and dedicated an entire Arkansas factory to producing the new fast food sensation. By 1983, McNuggets got rolled out nationally, and just a few years later, McDonald's became the world's second-largest consumer of chickens; only Colonel Sanders's Kentucky Fried Chicken bought more birds.[55]

McNuggets weren't just a hit at McDonald's stores; they changed the American way of eating chicken. By the 1990s, less than 15 percent of slaughtered broilers were sold as whole birds. At the supermarket, some consumers still chose parts wrapped in see-through plastic, which were branded as fresh and wholesome in endless Tyson and Perdue television advertisements. By this time, though, shoppers were becoming more likely to purchase further-processed chicken. Most of it would be shaped into something that didn't look like chicken, and it would be soaked in salt and fried in fat. So much for chicken as a healthy alternative to beef, but perception and reality took a while to match up on this score, especially with helpful nutritional information hard to come by.[56]

McNuggets were a nearly perfect industrial food, at least in the short term and from the producers' perspective. They started with cheap, essentially leftover ingredients, stray pieces of chicken and bits stuck to the bone as well as unused skin and other parts. From there, the manufacturers added corn-based filler and a corn-based coating. Corn, of course, was the incredibly cheap, highly subsidized agricultural wonder of the postwar era and, as a result, it often cost food-processing companies less then it cost farmers to grow and harvest the crop. Salt, another main ingredient, was even cheaper, selling for less than ten cents a pound and delivering a wallop of flavor and the promise of a longer shelf life. Water was the cheapest, and probably most highly subsidized of all of the ingredients in nuggets. In some cases, it made up as much as 15 percent of the foodstuff. "The more water you can add to your nuggets," observed the food writer Mark Schatzker, "the greater the profit." The finished product could be zapped in a microwave and eaten on the go. Nuggets required neither a fork nor a plate. That meant no cleanup. This was a tailor-made convenience food for hard-working, wage-stagnant, inflation-wrecked America.[57]

But it was the dipping sauces that powered the nuggets' success. Almost single-handedly, they warded off chicken blandness and chicken fatigue. "We like foods that have an identifiable strong flavor, but we tire of them very quickly," explains the taste scholar Michael Moss. Yet, accompanied by small plastic trays filled with sweet, high fructose corn syrup–infused (and therefore inexpensive because of subsidies) ketchup, honey mustard, and barbeque sauce, nuggets could change all the time, even between bites. This malleability maximized the appeal and everyday (or every other day) eat-ability of McNuggets and the many knockoffs they inspired.[58]

Adults liked Chicken McNuggets and their imitators, but kids, it seemed, couldn't get enough of them. They wanted nuggets at McDonald's, Burger King, Red Lobster, Shoney's, and every other restaurant. They wanted them at school and at home. They got them on metal trays with applesauce in the cafeteria and in microwave-ready containers with fries in the frozen food section of the supermarket. They got them shaped like cartoon characters, trucks, trains, and dinosaurs. Because of their popularity and ubiquity, chicken nuggets were crowned the "hot dog of the 1990s." [59]

Looking for new ideas and information on the latest food trends, Emmett Roe occasionally flipped through the pages of the trade journal *Restaurant News*. It didn't take him long to learn about nuggets after their debut in the early 1980s and the new markets they opened up for chicken parts and leftover pieces. He wanted in.[60] By the time he made his move, however, nuggets, even low-quality ones made with lots of filler and dark meat remnants, had already become an incredibly competitive and risky slice of poultry capitalism.[61] As factory farms and slaughterhouses added to their capacities and killed increasingly bloated chickens at faster and faster rates, the broiler industry endured wave after wave of overproduction, followed by another round of aggressive cost-cutting. In this tight market, further-processed products presented potential new revenue streams and additional sources of profit—and new bouts of competition. Not long after the McNuggets' astonishing debut, Tyson, Perdue, and the other industry giants pounced. Using their size and ability to invest in new highly automated machinery for their factories to their advantage, they grabbed hold of the massive fast food and supermarket business for salty and fatty breaded and fried chicken products. They weren't letting go of this money-making sector. That left a tiny corner of the market, the specialty niche, for smaller companies like Imperial Food Products.[62]

Shut out of the mass market for nuggets, Roe manufactured in Hamlet further-processed and customized chicken products made mostly from already cut up frozen boneless breasts. He sold them to small and medium-size restaurant chains in the South. He used discarded meat to make generic nuggets that his traveling salesmen marketed to schools and other companies, which sometimes sold them under their own labels. But, like a shark, Roe had to keep moving or die in the unforgiving waters of the

1980s poultry industry, where the choices for smaller players, like Imperial, were always pretty narrow.

To position his company in this tight market, Emmett Roe—and later Brad—enlisted Imperial in the fight against "chicken fatigue" and, even more immediately in the mid- to late 1980s, against the quickly emerging phenomenon of nugget fatigue, especially for grown-ups. Many adults wanted less breading and more meat with their chicken. One option was the tender, typically a two-inch strip of white meat pulled from a chicken breast or a fillet of white meat cut from the breast. Companies like Shoney's and Long John Silver's served these items battered and fried. Pitted against the nugget, tenders were bigger and had a wider surface area, which could lap up more sauce. Even though they were usually served fried, some consumers still regarded tenders as a wise and healthy fast food choice. Unlike the 1980s-era McNuggets and other chicken nugget products made from a little of this and a little of that and fried in saturated fats, tenders were pulled from or cut from chicken breasts and often were prepared in 100 percent vegetable or soy oil. They seemed meatier and more chickeny, which, in turn, gave them a hint of healthiness or at least less of a sense of unhealthiness.[63]

For another segment of the quickly changing chicken-eating market, fried tenders weren't healthy enough. Looking to capture part of this niche, product designers in the late 1980s came up with an array of roasted, broiled, grilled, boneless, and skinless chicken items. Better yet if these new foodstuffs were convenient and easy to prepare—and loaded with heaps of unseen salt and high fructose corn syrup to keep costs down, deliver a blast of flavor, and leave them on the shelves for as long as possible without spoiling.[64] Roe and the small restaurant and fast food chains he worked with paid close attention to fluctuating consumer demands, and they picked up on slight, but still significant, shifts in chicken preferences, designing their products to meet these changes.

Monica McDougald worked at Imperial in the months leading up to the fire. She usually spent a part of her day laying pieces of Cagle's chicken breasts, dipped in sweet and salty lemon, barbecue, and teriyaki sauces, on the conveyor belt. Other times, like the morning of the blast, she shredded meat for chicken fajitas, another item on the company's ever-changing product list.[65] Still, in 1991, Imperial's mainstay remained battered, fried, and salted chicken tenders. It sent these to the southern outlets of Long John Silver's, Red Lobster, Captain D's, and, of course, Shoney's.

Despite the niches in poultry capitalism they had carved out for themselves, Emmett and Brad Roe couldn't insulate their firm or their family from the relentless competition and predatory practices of other companies. Knowing that they held the upper hand, fast food chains and schools demanded to pay later and pay less when they did write checks. Emmett Roe responded to business pressures by cutting costs wherever he could and getting as much out of his labor force as possible. Leading up to the fire, he and Brad and his plant management in Hamlet continued to demand that workers wear smocks and caps on the job, but now they made them pay for the gear. He started to charge them for a larger portion of their health insurance as well. He got his supervisors, including Brad, to ride the women on the line to make sure they limited their bathroom breaks, stayed busy during their time on the clock, and, it seems, processed tainted meat when the USDA men weren't looking.[66]

One day, Imperial worker Thomas Oates picked up a piece of chicken off the floor and started to carry it over to the "inedible room" when Brad Roe spotted him.

"Where are you going with that damn chicken?" Roe asked, according to what Oates told a journalist in the late fall of 1991. "I want the [expletive] chicken picked up and put in the box."

Oates replied that he was following "the USDA man's instructions."

"I ain't the USDA man," Roe shot back, Oates recounted. "I own this place."

Another time, Oates said, he told Brad Roe that some of the chicken in the cooler smelled so bad it would "send a buzzard running for a gas mask." Roe, he claimed, brushed off the warning and let him know, "As long as it's not green, go ahead and run it."[67]

But the boldest and most significant way that Roe and his father tried to protect themselves against the pressures that poultry capitalism exerted on smaller players was to become a bigger player. From 1987 to 1990, they opened three new plants and moved in new business directions, all in the hopes of limiting their exposure to the fluctuations of the cheap chicken market. Yet the opposite happened. With each new plant and each new investment came new vulnerabilities, more debt, and greater pressure on the bottom line, which must have seemed to the Roes like it was always moving down in the late 1980s and early 1990s. In some ways, the Roes were a lot like the growers that Cagle's bought its chickens from; they were at the mercy of bigger forces, stuck in an economy in which they had only a limited number of possible customers and therefore had little control over their own economic fate. In order to survive in this world, the Roes built systems based on debt and uncertainty, speed and terror, cruelty and compulsion, repressed voices and official neglect. But even this danger-ous and risky combination of tactics wasn't enough to overcome the larger system of cheap.

In 1987, with an eye toward diversifying, Emmett Roe bought a Colo-rado meat-processing plant that did some work with beef. The next year, Roe made his biggest and riskiest move ever. Putting down his business and personal assets as collateral, he took out a loan from Northwestern Bank in Pennsylvania for $5 million. He dumped some of the money into the Hamlet plant. He used the rest, along with some capital from his nephew Edward Woncik, to buy Haverpride Farms from Northern Pride, a British-based corporation. Located in Tarrant, Alabama, just a few miles northeast of Birmingham, Haverpride Farms specialized in mak-ing chicken nuggets and patties. Though sales had lagged at the sprawling facility, Roe thought he could turn the oversize operation around, or per-haps he thought that expanding his enterprises represented the only way for his company to survive in the cutthroat world of further-processed chicken and compete with the economies of scale and branding efforts of the biggest players in the market.

In 1989, a couple of years after the Haverpride acquisition, Emmett Roe bought another factory, acquiring the abandoned Mrs. Kinser's facil-ity just off Main Street in Cumming, Georgia, for $725,000.[68] Before it became part of Imperial, the plant made pimento cheese spread and cole-slaw packaged in plastic tubs for picnics and backyard barbeques. Around the time he opened the Cumming branch, Roe shut down the Moosic plant for good and moved with his wife into a three-thousand-square-foot townhouse in Dunwoody, Georgia, a prosperous north Atlanta suburb. That put him within a day's drive of most of the satellites in his burgeon-ing, yet debt-strapped, chicken empire.[69]

Things fell apart in a hurry for Roe. The Colorado business never really got going. Far from Roe's home base and outside the reach of his Rolodex of chicken contacts, the plant struggled. It mostly made products for a single buyer, but by the late 1980s that buyer had pulled out. Soon, the plant ran below capacity, opening just a couple of days a week.

Meanwhile, just as the Cumming plant started to crank out chicken nuggets and other chicken products, a fire caused by an electrical malfunction broke out there on Christmas Day 1989.[70] As inspectors combed through the scorched sections of the plant, they found broken sprinklers, a faulty ventilation system, and a couple of poorly marked exits. The bill for the damages added up to $1.2 million, more than the factory cost in the first place. Roe temporarily moved equipment and production to a nearby facility. Fire or no fire, he had to pay his bank note, so he couldn't stop making nuggets and tenders. Not long after getting the Cumming site back up and running, in December 1990 another fire broke out. This one was smaller and less intense than the previous one. Yet despite the setbacks in Georgia and Colorado, Roe's biggest problems were in the rambling plant in Tarrant, Alabama.[71]

Shortly after purchasing the Haverpride facility, Roe shook hands on a multi-year deal worth as much as $20 million to supply generic nuggets to Lyle Farms, Inc. The Roswell, Georgia–based food brokerage planned to sell Roe's further-processed microwavable chicken products to supermarket chains and other outlets under the Big Top, Shur-Fine, and Jewell labels. Almost as soon as the nuggets hit the freezer aisles and gas station warming trays, Lyle officials claimed that they started to receive complaints. "Where's the chicken?" customers supposedly asked. Lyle accused Roe's company of using rancid meat and of cutting costs and corners by concocting nuggets full of more than the usual amount of filler, breading, and water. Perhaps this was the only way Emmett Roe, the firm's chief decision maker, could service his mounting debts or deal with the razor-thin margins in big food. Or perhaps Lyle was flexing its muscles and shaking down a smaller player in the pecking order of poultry capitalism.[72]

By March 1990, Lyle had allegedly reneged on its deal with Roe's company. Yet it kept, according to one inside source, as much as a million dollars' worth of unpaid-for chicken products. This was money that Roe didn't have.[73] By then, the only contract the hulking Haverpride plant still had left was to supply nuggets to an Alabama school district for lunches. This deal was set to expire when classes ended late that spring. That didn't give Haverpride enough cash to cover its bills and keep the factory running. And there was no extra money from any of the other parts of Roe's shaky chicken empire to bail out the Alabama branch. By this point, Roe hadn't paid in full the finance corporation he relied on for debt relief or his chicken suppliers in months. His companies in Georgia and North Carolina owed thousands in back taxes, and the Alabama outlet fell so far behind on its electric bill that the power company turned off the lights. Even before Haverpride went dark, Roe reportedly stopped paying his share of his employees' health care coverage, though he apparently continued to draw deductions for this expense out of their paychecks, using the funds, it seems, to cover other costs and keep the plant open and their jobs still going. Haverpride operatives only found out about the owner's moves when they went to the doctor's office and discovered that they had no insurance.[74]

When Emmett Roe closed the plant in Alabama in 1990, he didn't tell anyone ahead of time. He left without giving workers a sixty-day notice as federal law required. More than a hundred Haverpride employees sued Roe and Imperial Food Products. The United States District Court in Birmingham awarded them more than $250,000 in severance pay. But when the fire broke out in Hamlet the next year, none of the Haverpride laborers had yet received any money, and many were still looking for work.[75]

Following the setbacks in Alabama, Colorado, and Georgia, Emmett Roe focused his energies on Hamlet. Workers recalled seeing him around the plant more. He and Brad ratcheted up production on Bridges Street after the Haverpride closure, steadily running a second shift and speeding up the lines. They needed the Hamlet plant to help turn the family company's fortunes around. It was at this point, as Imperial cranked up production, that the Hamlet city manager, Ron Niland, started to notice those "cannonball"-size chunks of grease in the local water supply.[76]

Still, the bank notes and creditors hung over the Roes' heads and the heads of their workers, even if they didn't know it yet.[77] When repairs needed to be made in Hamlet, Brad Roe, the person usually on the scene, ordered the mechanics to move as quickly as possible. He told them to use the parts they had, even if they weren't the exact right ones. A little clamp or an extra screw could get the job done. Usually, the maintenance crew didn't turn off the gigantic three-hundred-gallon fryer when they worked around it. It would take an hour to get it heated back up again, and that would waste money and leave workers sitting around the breakroom or outside on company time. Nothing ran at Imperial without the fryer, explained former employee Martin Quick. Roe could not have people waiting around. This same money-saving logic persuaded him to lock the breakroom and side doors at the Hamlet plant. When workers got caught sneaking out for a smoke, or when a few of them lifted a box or two of tenders, it cost the company money. More important, they locked the doors because it satisfied the USDA inspectors by keeping the flies out and the factory open. At this point, there was no way Imperial could afford to have another one of its factories shut down.[78]

Persevering was never about fairness or equity. It was about dealing with the risks of poultry capitalism. In 1991, every part of Emmett and Brad Roe's business was exposed to risk, and they were trying the best they could to stabilize things and keep going. Yet eliminating risks for management meant multiplying risks for animals, for workers, and for the city of Hamlet. This persistent precariousness was woven into every corner and every venture in the risky business of cheap chickens.[79]

4

LABOR

Even with her three daughters standing behind her, Georgia Quick seemed alone, lost in solitude. Maybe the memories of the sinister smoke and impenetrable darkness at the Imperial Food Products factory that day in 1991 set her apart. Or perhaps it was her past that made her seem so isolated, or maybe it was the people who weren't there that made her come off as somewhat detached.[1]

Georgia Ann Foster was born in Chesterfield, South Carolina, at the tail end of the baby boom, on April 4, 1960. Her father didn't stay around long—at least not long enough for Georgia to get to know him. Unsure if she could make it on her own, Georgia's mother took Georgia and her sister across the state line to live with a relative in Gibson, North Carolina, a speck on a highway map eleven miles south of Hamlet and a stone's throw from the South Carolina border.

Not long after moving, her mother met and married another man. Georgia's stepfather took one look at his new daughter's high cheekbones, light skin, and faint freckles and said "no way." He wasn't having a white man's child live in his house. Georgia never met her biological father, so she couldn't say for sure whether she was part white or maybe part Native American or part something else. Her mother didn't provide many details about the family tree either. Years later, Georgia looked for her dad, hoping to sit down in the same room with him and study his face and hear his stories, but she didn't get to him before he died.

With her mom starting a new life with her new husband, an aunt raised Georgia and her sister in rural Scotland County, North Carolina. The family never owned any land. They worked as sharecroppers and day laborers, picking cotton and peaches and doing all kinds of other jobs to get by. Georgia grew up doing what farm girls do. When she wasn't at school or in the fields, she fed chickens in the yard and did a list of chores. She cleaned pots and dusted, but no one really taught her how to cook.

Country life did, though, teach her the significance of the seasons. Early fall was for picking cotton, spring for planting and getting the fields ready, and mid-summer represented the lay-by time to take it easy and tidy up the house, mend fences, and fix the tractor. Even though she missed a day of school here and there to work in the fields, Georgia still managed to graduate from high school, earning her diploma from Scotland County High School in Laurinburg in 1979.

As Georgia got older, the seasons started to lose some of their meaning. County and state workers poured hot tar over gravel paths and made the nearby towns an easy drive away. The mills, lumberyards, railroads, government offices, and hardware stores enticed more men with promises of work not subject to the ups and downs of distant commodities markets or the whims of the weather. Some of these jobs paid enough money to buy a beat-up car and packets of hot dogs that went in new refrigerators bought on credit and paid for with cash each week. It didn't matter so much anymore how many kids you had or how much land you owned or rented or what kind of deal you struck with the landlord and the merchant for seeds and fertilizer. What mattered in this changing rural world was a good, steady job—a job that could lift a man without a high school education and his family into the upper ranks of the working class or the bottom ranks of the middle class. A job that paid a man enough so that his wife could stay at home and cook and clean and tend to a vegetable garden and a yard full of hens and roosters, even if she did have to work outside the home every once in a while when illness, injury, or a leaky transmission pushed the family budget to the brink.

By the time she was in her late teens, Georgia wanted to get out of her aunt's house and "be on her own." Garry Quick seemed like the way to do that. He had a decent job at a nearby cotton gin. When farmers brought their crops in from the fields, he unloaded the bags of raw cotton and then loaded up the bales of processed fleece. He made sure the machines ran smoothly and fixed them when they jammed with rocks and sticks. The rhythms of cotton growing still mattered to him. His wallet was full between January and July, and a little lighter in between. When farmers weren't bringing in their crops, Quick did odd jobs for his boss and others in town. For the most part, the white man who owned the cotton gin treated him well. He paid him on time and let him live in the house next to the gin rent free. Garry could afford a few Christmas presents and an occasional night on the town. That job and the somewhat steady paycheck that came with it made the slightly older Garry Quick attractive to nineteen-year-old Georgia Foster.

Georgia and Garry got married within weeks of Georgia's high school graduation, on June 20, 1979. She packed up her stuff from her aunt's house and moved into the home next to the cotton gin. "I had to learn to cook," she remembers. Pretty soon, she could cut up a chicken on her own and put three meals a day on the table. A few years later, Georgia and Garry's daughter, Alicia, was born. For a while, things went pretty smoothly for the young Quick family, but the sweeping forces of history and economic change had them in their sights.

Cotton's kingdom crumbled in postwar North Carolina. In 1980, the state's cotton output matched what it had been in 1840, and that amounted to just one-sixth of the total harvested in 1926.[2] With overhead costs rising, global competition stiffening, and crop prices fluctuating, some farmers gambled on animal crops, a gamble that paid off only for a few. Others gave up on the land, except for tending to a garden, and joined the exodus into town for work. Others tried their luck up north or in the cities of the South. For Garry Quick, fewer cotton farmers meant less cotton to process at the gin, and this wasn't good for him. By the mid-1980s, his somewhat steady job became even less steady. Instead of nearly year-round work, he started to get a few months here and a few months there. To make up for the shortfall, he mowed lawns and picked fruit. As money came in fits and spurts, emotions ebbed and flowed in the Quick household.[3]

Georgia didn't like waiting for Garry to give her a few dollars to pay the phone company or buy groceries or cleaning supplies. She needed money, her own money, even if getting a job outside the home did run the risk of driving another wedge between her and her husband.

"I wasn't interested in the factory," Georgia remembered about the start of her job search in the 1980s. With this in mind, she didn't fill out an application at White's Poultry or Perdue, slaughterhouses in and around Rockingham, or at any of the textile mills in Richmond County, not that they were hiring anyway. She wanted what people who lived in the country called "a clean job," one that was inside and not too hot or messy. She got one that paid minimum wage as a cashier at Roses, a Henderson-based discount department store. She left that job to work at Family Dollar, another, though slightly more down-market, North Carolina–based retail chain. They hired her as an assistant manager, and promised her a promotion if she worked hard and followed the rules.

"At the time," Georgia commented, "You didn't see many blacks as managers."

Not long after she got the position, however, Georgia's store started to experience what her bosses labeled as significant "shrinkage," or theft. No one accused her directly of any wrongdoing, but a supervisor ordered her to take a polygraph test. Nervous, perhaps, about sitting in a room with all of those wires and with a white man in a tie, she apparently didn't pass. Now, she was out of a job, and out of an opportunity to climb out of the rut of small-town, low-paid, dead-end labor.[4]

By this time, Georgia had car payments to make every month on top of everything else. Needing a job right away, she headed to the employment bureau; they sent her to Marley's Engineering Products, a firm specializing in heating and cooling parts, located in Bennettsville, South Carolina, twelve miles away from her house. There, as she put it, she "separated threads for minimum wage." One of her co-workers there told her about Imperial Food Products. The company paid $5.50 per hour, and that, Quick recalled, "caught my attention." She also heard that the plant offered benefits, holiday bonuses, and a few paid vacation days each year. Her friend told her that, in addition, the company sometimes had overtime work available and paid time and a half for the extra hours. "The reason I went to Imperial," Quick said, "was it was paying more than anywhere."

During her job interview, if you can call it that, Imperial officials didn't ask Georgia too many questions, though they probably did ask her if she had ever felt any tingling in her wrists and hands. As one supervisor explained, the company had one essential criteria for employment. It tried not to hire line workers with a history of repetitive-motion injuries.[5]

Quick must have told them that she felt okay and didn't have any nagging aches or pains. She got hired at Imperial on Valentine's Day 1989. "This," she declared years later, "was the best a black woman with a little education could get."

Georgia Quick started at Imperial on the second shift. By the late 1980s, Emmett and Brad Roe extended production in Hamlet as they tried to expand their business, and later in order to recover from their bracing financial setbacks in Colorado and Alabama. On her first day, Quick pulled into the company's gravel parking lot. She walked to the wood-framed office across the street from the unmarked front door of the red brick factory. The company's only human resources person met her and gave her a rundown on the job. He told her she needed to be on time for work and that if she came late she would get written up. Five mistakes and she would be out of a job. When they went over to the plant, the first thing that hit Quick was the smell. She would later say it reeked of day-old chicken. Trying not to think about it, she turned her attention back to the company official showing her around. He pointed out the time clocks in the marinating and cutting room and showed her how to stamp her card, then he told her that she needed to punch in in the afternoon and out at midnight. He showed her the breakroom with the lockers, long tables, and vending machines.

Nearby were the bathrooms. The company guide laid down the rules: a ten-minute break two hours into her shift, a half hour for lunch (or a meal) midway through, and one more ten-minute break after that. Use the bathroom during those times, he told her. If you have to go at another time, don't take more than five minutes when you do or you will be written up. Five write-ups, he reminded her again, and she would be out of a job.[6]

Quick would get paid every week. If she wanted health insurance, she could get it for herself and her family beginning 90 days after she started the job. The company would take $10–15 out of her check for each person covered by the plan.

Every once in a while, he continued, confirming what she had heard before she took the job, the company would ask her to work overtime. She would be paid for time and half when she did, and she best show up, if she knew what was good for her, on those Saturdays when they asked her to be there. Maybe he told her, too, about the Christmas party. There would be sandwiches and soda, but only workers would be invited. No spouses to dance with.[7]

A foreman told Georgia she couldn't wear heels or open-toed shoes, not that she would have wanted to after seeing the grease and water that puddled up on the concrete floors. If she had a few extra dollars, he suggested, she should go to K-Mart and buy a pair of shoes with grippers on the bottoms. They would make it easier for her to move across the slick surfaces that covered the plant. She couldn't wear rings, earrings, or necklaces. No chewing gum while on the line either. No eating except in the breakroom. The last two were USDA rules. He told her to avoid loose-fitting clothing, because the sleeves could get caught in the machinery. He walked her over to where she could find the blue smocks and mesh hairnets she needed to wear on the job. He told her she would have to clean these at home herself. Later, Quick learned that this was a new policy, one only recently implemented. Previously, the company had paid for laundry. He told her to wear gloves and explained that she could buy them for fifty cents a pair over at the office. The company didn't provide those anymore either. And he told her that if he or anyone else caught her stealing chicken pieces, she would be fired on the spot and hauled down to the police station.[8]

The company official didn't say anything to Quick about what to do in the event of a fire or an emergency. He didn't offer instructions about how to operate the fire extinguishers. He didn't say anything about exits or which doors were locked and which were not. He didn't mention anything about the company's evacuation plans. He didn't say one word about safety meetings set for the next week or next month or ever.

After watching another line worker for an hour or so, Quick's training period was over. Before the whistle blew for the first break, she stood on the line, pulling apart pieces of marinated chicken and laying them flat on a conveyor belt before they went into the flash freezer. The chicken pieces came fast. She struggled to keep up. It got easier after a few weeks on the job, but it was always hard to keep up with the pace of the line.

Again and again, however, Imperial's derelict equipment saved the day for Quick. The belts often stopped moving. "The fryer," remembered another worker, "would break down at least twice a week." When the equipment faltered, Quick and the others on the line got unscheduled breaks.

As Imperial Foods revved up the work in Hamlet, adding shifts and more overtime, mechanics constantly had to "nigger rig" the overtaxed machinery, in the words of one white worker. But they couldn't fix everything right away, and Imperial laborers, white and black, came to count on the malfunctions to give them a chance to catch their breath, massage their wrists, rub some Bengay into their backs, and sit outside and get some fresh air.[9]

No one at Imperial, certainly not "the line ladies," as the women who loaded the conveyor belts were called, had a job set in stone. "We move the people around daily in the plant from room to room," a foreman explained. "It was almost like an everyday thing." The company shifted workers to where they needed them the most. The strategy of shuffling employees from station to station, from the trim room to the processing room, had an added advantage, managers believed. It kept the workers from breaking down. "After we started . . . changin' 'em around on jobs," one foremen recalled, "we had less problems with peoples' wrists or backs or things like that."[10]

Most nights, Quick stood in pools of water in the trim room, pulling at tough white tendons, cutting out stray pieces of bone, and scraping fat from chicken pieces that sometimes felt slimy or smelled sour. "I hated this job," she recalled. "It was cold and wet." No matter what it was like outside, it always felt like a frozen tundra in there—the temperature never climbed too far above freezing. After an hour in the trim room, Quick would be soaked from the waist down, shaking off drops of water as she walked. The cold seeped inside her. She wore two, sometimes three, pairs of gloves to keep her hands warm and fingers moving, but nothing really helped. No matter how many pairs of socks she put on or the shoes she wore, her feet felt like icicles all night long. She tried wrapping them in plastic bags as some of her co-workers did, but this still didn't keep out the cold. Nothing helped but getting home and pulling off her wet socks and taking a few minutes, if she had them, to rub her hands and warm up her toes and feel them move again before she had to start to cook and clean.[11]

Sometimes, as the clock inched toward midnight, Quick would start to drift off, thinking about her daughter and the piles of laundry back home. She never got very far away, though. "Get to work," the foreman would bark in her direction, asking, "What did you come to work for . . . just to stand around?"

The second shift, Quick remembered, had fewer supervisors and managers than the first shift did. That gave it a looser feel than daytime. The workers tended to be younger, unmarried and without kids, and rowdier. They goofed around more, smoked dope on breaks, and kicked frozen chicken parts around like hockey pucks. "Still," Georgia pointed out with a shot of pride, "we got the work done."

Quick worried all the time about child care. Who could watch her daughter? How much would it cost? Most nights, Quick's aunt took care of her. But not long after Quick started at Imperial, her daughter began to struggle somewhat in school. Quick thought it would help if she were home after classes ended, so she asked the foreman for a transfer to the first shift.

By that point, a year into the job, Quick had already lasted longer than most of the women and men who went through Imperial's first day of orientation and training. Theresa White lived in the public housing project down the street from the plant. A few days after the fire, she stood next to a loose stream of yellow police tape surrounding the perimeter of the mangled building. She looked up and said to a reporter, "I worked in there for eight days once. . . . Then I quit. Slavery time's been over. I couldn't do it anymore." [12]

Some didn't even last a week. Imperial consistently registered high turnover rates. That's one reason the company didn't invest much time in training and didn't make health insurance available to new workers for three months. (New laborers not used to the work usually got hurt during their first ninety days on the job.) "It was like a revolving door in there," Quick's co-worker, Ada Blanchard, recalled. It didn't take some people long to realize that standing on a soggy concrete floor for eight hours a day with their hands buried in ice-cold buckets of chicken wasn't for them. The promise of a Christmas dinner and $60 holiday bonus wouldn't get the smell of grease out of their hair or the taste of raw chicken out of their mouths, so they quit. For others, it was the nagging pains. Shorter workers strained their shoulders reaching up all day, while taller ones wrenched their backs bending down. For others, it was the relentless pace of the line. They couldn't keep up with the chicken pieces zipping along the conveyor belts, so they quit. Still others couldn't take the constant haranguing from the foremen and supervisors and the endless warnings of write-ups for infractions of company rules. "They had a real attitude problem," one woman thought of management. "They treated the workers like children."[13]

Some hated the constant surveillance, especially the monitoring of bathroom trips with stopwatches. Others didn't like the threats. If you talked back, you would be fired. If you missed a couple of days, even if it was to take care of a sick child or an ailing parent, you could be fired.

Gingerly navigating the slick tile floors wasn't easy either, especially with a foreman telling you that if you fell three times you would be fired. Some suspected that this rule was in place because the company wanted to find a cheaper worker's compensation provider, and reporting injuries would make it harder to qualify for the lower rate. Sometimes Imperial reimbursed employees for hospital visits and the money spent on splints and Ace bandages as a way to deal with repetitive motion injuries and to discourage workers from filing insurance claims.[14]

Others just couldn't handle the logistics of the job, getting a ride to the plant before daybreak every day, and finding someone to watch the children and get them home from school. As one manager commented, trying to explain why Imperial experienced so much turnover, "The attendance policy being too tough on them, transportation, baby-sitting, another job closer to home; reasons like that." Others just couldn't see working so hard and putting up with the freezing cold and sour smells for only a little more than minimum wage, even if it ranked among the best paying jobs around. Once they left Imperial, some got another low-wage, low-skill job, while others signed up for public assistance and food stamps.[15]

Even though the first shift meant more supervisors, more rules, and less downtime because the rickety conveyor belt and sputtering fryer got fixed faster, Quick liked working during the daytime better than in the evening. It put her more on her daughter's schedule. Plus, she had more in common with her co-workers on this shift. Most were single mothers or women with underemployed husbands. A number of them were older and, like Gail Campbell, didn't drink, smoke, or swear. On Sundays, they put on flowery dresses and matching hats and headed off to church. On the job, they sang gospel hymns and chatted about Bible passages.[16]

Over many months and years, first-shift workers transformed the songs and conversations into an alternative social security system. "Everyone looked out for everyone else," Quick said. They shared tips on how to stay warm and deal with the foremen, Brad Roe, and, to a lesser extent, Emmett Roe. They lent each other hairnets, gloves, Tylenol, and sometimes small amounts of money. On payday, Quick and a few of her friends raced down Bridges Street during their lunch break to a local grill and treated themselves, she remembered with a smile, to bags filled with hot hamburgers wrapped in grease-stained paper. On most mornings, she carpooled with other women to save on gas. "After a while," Quick explained, "it was like a family." [17]

The warmth and trust between workers didn't change the fact that Quick, like Ada Blanchard, "didn't like how we were treated by management." [18] "They didn't care anything about how you felt, who you were," Mary Bryant remembered, voicing a complaint common to Imperial workers. "All they wanted was for you to run the chicken." [19]

A number of Imperial workers associated the relentless, chicken-first mind-set with Brad Roe. After finishing his studies at the University of Scranton, a Jesuit school near Moosic, Roe, then in his early twenties, moved to North Carolina to manage the Imperial plant. This was about the same time that Georgia Quick started to work there. As tall and thin as his dad was thick and pudgy, Brad had shaggy hair and a full mustache. He was chattier than his father. He could be quick with a joke and even quicker with a sports report, skills that he would put to good use after the fire when he made a living as a bartender. Like his father, though, he worked hard and put in long hours. While some of the line ladies and maintenance crew liked Brad and thought he played fair and by the rules, others resented him and bristled at his sometimes hot-tempered managerial style. A few saw him as a spoiled child or as a kid who couldn't, or wouldn't, stand up to his domineering father. They remember him answering just about any question that involved personnel or money by saying, "Let me ask my dad." [20]

Georgia Quick saw him as a young man—a young white man—without a wrinkle on his face or a gray hair on his head telling women, most of whom were African American and who had worked at the plant since he was a teenager, what to do, and not always doing so in a kind or polite way.

Quick and her co-workers also thought Brad Roe, or maybe his father, had ordered the supervisors to rule the shop floor, especially in the second half of 1991, with an "iron fist." "Don't be lenient," they reportedly instructed. "Show no mercy."[21]

"Sometimes he would be friendly; sometimes he wasn't," Quick remarked about Brad. He had a nice side, but he had another side, she recalled, that was "nasty," "mean," and "obnoxious." He would yell at workers to stop goofing off and get back to the job. He yelled if anyone raised a question about faulty equipment or a concern about rancid chicken, reminding them of their disposability. "If you don't like the job," Quick recalled him hollering, "leave, and don't let the door hit you on the way out." He pushed the maintenance men to hurry up and fix machines as quickly as possible to get the line back up and running before anyone had time to take an unscheduled break. All he cared about, one of Quick's male co-workers concluded, "was the product, getting it out."[22]

But for Quick and the other first-shift women, liking the job or liking Brad Roe was never really the issue. They needed a job, one that didn't require a lot of training, education, or experience. They needed to make money for their families, and they would absorb the pain, abuse, and petty rules because to complain was to risk getting fired, and then there was nothing.

That was Georgia Quick's story. With her husband gone much of the time now that his work at the cotton gin wasn't as predictable as it used to be, Quick needed a steady paycheck. For someone living in a small town with a high school education and a resume filled with a string of low-wage jobs, there weren't a lot of options available.

Kate Nicholson worked alongside Georgia Quick on the first shift, and they had followed similar paths to get there. In 1991, Nicholson was a thirty-eight-year-old mother of two with a tenth grade education. When her husband lost his job at a Richmond County textile mill, she went to work at Imperial. "I needed a job," she explained to a reporter after the fire without elaborating, because there was nothing else to say.[23]

Years before the fire, Elizabeth Bellamy finished high school and en-rolled in a few college classes. She hankered for something beyond a farm girl's life. That hunger put her on a Greyhound bus one day, tracing the well-worn path of the Great Migration that had taken two generations of African Americans from the South to the North in search of freedom and opportunity. In New York City, she met a carpenter with a steady job, and they had two kids together. But the crack epidemic spreading across the country in the 1980s caught up with Bellamy's family. Drugs weren't new to the city, but crack was something different. One hit and many were hooked.

Bellamy's husband couldn't escape crack's pull and ended up in prison on drug charges, another new American reality. For a while Bellamy stayed behind, a single mom living in a distressed, underserved corner of the city, but she couldn't deal with the pop of gunfire coming from the park across the street day and night, night and day. Worried that her daughters would get caught in the crossfire, she joined the reverse migra-tion of black southerners back to the South in the 1980s.[24]

Returning to South Carolina, Bellamy hoped to buy a house and get a second chance at the American Dream. But first she needed a job, and the only one she could find was at Imperial Food Products, a twenty-five-minute drive from her parents' home in Bennettsville. Her nineteen-year-old daughter, Felicia Odom, went to work with her.[25]

"I feel like I am carrying the weight of the world on my shoulders," Mattie Fairley admitted, saying what a lot of her co-workers must have felt. A high school dropout, she became a mom at seventeen and a grand-mother at thirty-seven. A string of low-wage jobs picking peaches and cutting apart chickens at a nearby slaughterhouse pushed her in the di-rection of the Imperial plant. Making $5.50 an hour, she was the main breadwinner in her family, with a stack of bills to pay and a pack of people to feed. "Sometimes," she said, "I feel like giving up." But she didn't. She showed up at Imperial on September 3, 1991, after a long weekend and said good morning to her co-workers, stowed her stuff in her locker, and got ready for the shift ahead.[26]

At the same time as Georgia Quick's husband's paycheck from the cot-ton gin started to shrink, newspapers and television stations declared a "farm crisis" in the United States. Celebrities and commentators took notice. Willie Nelson and Neil Young put on Caterpillar baseball hats and sang anthems to sturdy rural folks at Farm Aid telethons broadcast on MTV. *Time* and *Newsweek* let their readers know about the economic catastrophe with emotional cover stories. The singers and magazine pieces portrayed the farm crisis as a Midwestern phenomenon, as a threat to the family farm and the hardy souls who ran them and were trying to tough it out on the plains against heartless bankers, faceless agribusinesses, and wild swings in international crop markets. But the farm crisis was really much bigger and broader. It was a crisis of small towns all across the country that were dependent on the incomes of farmers, yes, but also on rural, largely male, industrial laborers with good jobs buying groceries, fence posts, baseball gloves, and legal and accounting advice. As interest rates jumped, crop prices sagged, and factory jobs vanished in response to inflation and the rising global competition of the 1970s, retail sales shrank in these towns where the interstate never went and Starbucks would never open. Businesses closed. Unemployment claims rose. New companies, paying less than the companies they replaced, came in and dangled much-needed jobs in front of fearful workers and beleaguered local officials. The drug trade took off, while U-Hauls pulling trailers, driven by the top students in their high school classes, headed out of town in the direction of cities and suburbs, often in the glimmering and glowing Sun Belt. "Anyone who can move out of town will go," observed the rural sociologist Michael Jacobson. "There's nothing left there—no jobs, few stores, and no community services."[27]

In Hamlet and other dots on the map between the nation's cities and oceans, the stories were the same. Statistics sketched the plotlines of decline. The numbers told of joblessness and falling hourly wages, population loss and store closings. By 1990, 40 percent of North Carolina's rural families lived below the poverty line. The percentages were even higher for African American families. Fewer than one in six black men in the old railroad towns and county seats held white collar jobs.[28] By the 1970s, many of the best paid in the black community worked in factories, at rail yards, and on the docks. Yet, just like on the Southside of Chicago, in North Philadelphia, and in soot-covered Bessemer outside of Birmingham, rural areas hemorrhaged these kinds of blue-collar positions, like the one that Georgia Quick's husband held that had allowed him and those like him to support a family and play the role of a "decent daddy," as the urban ethnographer Elijah Anderson has called it.[29] These were husbands who made enough money, and earned the social respect that went with it, to take care of most of the financial needs of their wives and children with a little left over for a night at the movies and even some to put away as a buffer against hard times.

But decent-paying options for working-class men, especially African American working men, were drying up across North Carolina and the rest of rural America. As the mills, foundries, and machine shops closed their doors and the empty storefronts and vacant windows along Main Streets multiplied, working people like Garry and Georgia Quick saw their options dwindle and their prospects dim. With so many avenues of opportunity closing down for so many, places like Gibson, Bennettsville, and Hamlet became, in the words of the journalist Osha Gray Davidson, "rural ghettos."[30]

The mid- to late 1980s marked the height of the Reagan-era boom on Wall Street and across much of the Sun Belt. But Hamlet didn't share in the economic resurgence. As the CSX railroad cut back, eliminating the best and safest jobs for miles around, unemployment in Richmond County jumped to 9.7 percent, lower than it was during the 1970s, but more than 3 percentage points above the state average and double the rate for the urban centers of Charlotte, Greensboro, and Raleigh. For African Americans, joblessness reached well above double digits. That number would go up again before the end of the 1980s as Clark Equipment closed and the county's textile mills scaled back.[31] With work disappearing, to borrow sociologist William Julius Wilson's phrase for what had plunged the nation's inner cities into despair and dislocation in the 1970s and 1980s, wages evaporated and the lack of spending trickled down throughout the small-town community. Hamlet Hospital, along with local banks, churches, shoe stores, and greasy spoons, closed or scaled back. Rates of depression, suicide, child abuse, and domestic violence spiked. Some took to the bottle; others fell into the darkness of crack and meth.[32]

With drugs came crime followed by more aggressive policing. In the months on either side of the Imperial fire, the local paper, the *Richmond County Daily Journal*, chronicled a litany of break-ins, robberies, and drug busts. Someone held up a Hamlet Christian bookstore at gunpoint in broad daylight in 1991. Over a three-day span in the fall, police nabbed Cedric Hester and charged him with possession of twenty-two grams of cocaine; they arrested Ronald David Buck and Wilbur Alphonso Dockery on charges of intent to distribute cocaine. A few months earlier, the paper had reported on a rash of "strong-armed burglaries" in Hamlet. Just weeks before the fire, a drug deal, or maybe a same-sex prostitution deal, gone bad, two people disappeared from The Pantry, a convenience store known for illicit activities, not far from the Imperial plant. They were later found dead in the woods. That followed another double murder four months earlier. "It seems like maybe drugs and violence have just reached the saturation point in the big cities," speculated Hamlet police chief Terry Moore in 1991. "It's beginning to spread to the countryside." [33]

Cordelia Steele, a social worker in the area who was educated at Bennett College in Greensboro, a historically African American liberal arts college for women, had another take on the community's budding drug and social problems. "If you are poor, if you are minority," she observed in her decades of work on the ground in Richmond County, "you may not know how to get social services and may distrust mental health services." Without access to these options, Steele observed, many people pressed by economic and family pressures started "to self-medicate, and before you know it, you are physically addicted." [34]

Widespread unemployment and drug use created mounting demands for social services. Faced with cuts from both Washington and Raleigh, local governments around Hamlet could not keep pace with the swelling need for drug treatment, family counseling, and job training. Schools didn't seem to be responding to the developing crisis either. In 1980, almost half of Richmond County residents over twenty-five years old hadn't graduated from high school. In an economy that increasingly valued education over muscle and college degrees over union cards, local students scored on average seventy points below the state's average on the SAT, and even further behind their counterparts living in metropolitan areas. [35]

The Reverend Harold Miller detected a sense of "social restlessness among young people" when he got to Hamlet in 1988. If you didn't have an education, he said, "nothing was happening. There was little opportunity."

Miller also noticed what others noticed, that those who could—those with a diploma and enough money to pay for moving costs and a deposit on an apartment—got out of the area and disappeared into the twisting streets of the suburbs of Charlotte, Columbia, and Atlanta. Without their best and brightest, small towns couldn't make up for their subpar schools and couldn't compete for the high-wage industries that might have helped to pull their communities out of the doldrums.[36]

The brain drain stretched across Hamlet's racial and class divides. Josh Newton grew up "upper lower class," as he called it, in a white railroad family. They went out for a fast food dinner once a month and to Jimmy's Seafood in Rockingham once a year. He hadn't been much farther than Southern Pines, twenty miles north of town up Route 1, before he went to college. But once he left for Belmont-Abbey College in 1983, he never moved back to Hamlet to live. Neither did many of his more ambitious high school classmates. "Few came back," Newton recalled, "except one guy who opened a small law firm."[37]

African Americans joined their white classmates in the flight out of town. The gains of the civil rights movement certainly didn't end segregation in Hamlet, but they did provide some with the chance to move up, often by moving out. Allen Mask Sr., an African American school administrator, raised two sons in Hamlet, both of whom would become doctors. Neither came back home after medical school. "Ain't nothing to come back to," Mask lamented. "Really, they would come back if there was something to come back to."[38]

One thing to come back for was Friday night football games under the lights. By the 1970s, Richmond County had only one high school. Students, parents, alumni—just about everyone, black and white, in the area—filled the stadium to watch the Raiders race up and down the field. More often than not, the games ended with a drink and a victory celebration before the fans went their separate ways back to their homes and neighborhoods that were still divided by class and race. In the years on either side of the fire, the county's African American community, Hamlet's especially, produced a startling collection of top-tier football and baseball players. Some credited American Legion coach and railway worker George Whitfield for the development of the local talent; others said it was coincidence or fierce ambition born out of desperation to get out of their fading hometown and county any way they could. In the mid-1980s, the "Fantastic Four"—Louis Breeden, Mike Quick, Franklin Stubbs, and Perry Williams—all starred at Richmond Senior High School. After that, they played for big-time universities and then with the Los Angeles Dodgers, New York Giants, Philadelphia Eagles, and Cincinnati Bengals. None of them, though, settled back in Hamlet or spent the off-season there training or living near their parents and relatives.[39]

Most working people, however, stayed put in Richmond County. Mike Quick's cousin, Martin Quick, the husband of Mary Alice Quick, who was killed in the fire, wanted to get out of Hamlet in the 1980s, but he couldn't do it. He didn't think he had enough education and because of that, he said, he was "afraid" that he "couldn't make it in a city or up North."[40]

Mattie Fairley couldn't escape either. Born and raised in Hamlet, she lived with her husband and children in a rented duplex a short walk from the Imperial plant. When Maurice lost his construction job in the 1980s, "they talked about going somewhere." But they never left, and she went to work for the Roes. "I can't get out of Hamlet," Mattie told a reporter from the *Washington Post* after the deaths of many of her friends at Imperial.[41]

Larry Lee knew people like Mattie Fairley and Martin Quick. For most of the 1980s, Lee worked as the executive director of a seven-county regional planning commission in northern Alabama and traveled from one rural ghetto to another pushing for adult education as a way to drag people out of poverty. He watched the downward spiral of places like Florence, Alabama, a place like Hamlet, where the loss of good, well-paying jobs was followed by poverty, crime, and surging rates of incarceration leading to fractured families and often increased numbers of single moms in search of work, any kind of work. That's how it went across the rural South. Lots of people and lots of places were hungry for investment and employment opportunities. Enter the new company coming into a small town to play the part of the savior. Rarely, though, did the new enterprise bring salvation. More often, it came to seize a monopoly over a local labor market flooded with job seekers and run its operations just the way it wanted without local officials putting up much of a fuss. That was the tale of the rural ghetto that Lee observed again and again. The changes left people "hungry" and "vulnerable," especially, he noted, women "with no husband or a husband without a job and a couple of children who would need a job."[42]

By 1990, Georgia Quick lived in one of those places, and she was on her way to becoming that kind of woman. Her husband's job was not as secure as it once was, and neither, it seems, was their marriage. There were arguments about bills and about what to do. Nerves got frayed. Words were exchanged. Tenderness turned to bitterness. Garry stayed away more and more. As paychecks shrank and good jobs continued to disappear, so too did men—North and South, white and black, in cities, in company towns, and in the countryside. In an economically rational response to work for men drying up, women and teens went looking for jobs in larger numbers, creating even greater downward pressure on wages and leaving employers with a newfound surplus of people to exploit and get rid of if they couldn't keep up with the pace of work or follow all the rules or complained about the conditions.

The pressures of the rural ghetto, just like those of the urban one, weighed the heaviest on African Americans. Often, they were the last hired and the first fired. Calling the years after 1973 "black folks' worst nightmare," the well-regarded *St. Petersburg Times* pointed to a massive jump in African American poverty and unemployment rates across the country during the Carter and Reagan years.[43] According to the paper's extensive research, the key factor was the restructuring of the economy and the resulting disappearance of steady jobs for undereducated men as unionized factory operatives, machinists, longshoremen, and painters and handymen for schools and hospitals. At the same time, federal budget cuts reduced the number of state and municipal posts and chopped construction, plumbing, and carpentry payrolls. The loss of all of these jobs hit male laborers hard, especially in the African American community. Systematically denied a decent education by segregation, the funneling of black students into vocational courses, and outright racism, a smaller percentage of black men than white men spent enough time in the classroom to move into professional and high-tech jobs. That meant that African

Americans for decades depended disproportionately on blue-collar work for their wages and avenues out of poverty. According to one study, well into the 1970s, more than 70 percent of all black men in cities and surrounding areas held blue-collar jobs. In a stunning turnaround, by 1987 the industrial employment of black men had plummeted to 28 percent. The sharp reduction in public services, stemming from Reagan-era cuts, meant that once the jobs left, little was done to bring them back or to train unemployed laborers for new opportunities.[44] With the New Deal on the wane and the tone of the nation's politics changing, there was no Marshall Plan for the nation's urban or rural ghettos nor was there an updated version of the WPA. Only more spending cuts, attacks on welfare, and a racially targeted war on drugs followed the mass layoffs.

Detroit, of course, was the nation's onetime arsenal of democracy and a postwar industrial juggernaut. But the forces of deindustrialization slammed the city and especially its black communities. By 1980, half of Detroit's adult male population, by then the majority of whom were African American, worked sporadically or not at all. This turned out to be more than just a Detroit problem. Black men in Watts, in Greensboro, and in Richmond County, North Carolina, struggled under the weight of massive joblessness. So, too, did working-class white men, but they didn't have to deal, like black men did at the same time, with the meanness of the American past, lingering discrimination, new(ish) policing and prison regimes, and the everyday injuries of racism.[45]

In their book *American Apartheid*, sociologists Douglas Massey and Mary Denton try to make sense of the changes taking place in the African American community from the 1970s forward in the United States. "Ghetto blacks," they note, "face very different neighborhood conditions created by residential segregation." "A large share," they continue, "live in geographically isolated and racially homogenous neighborhoods where poverty is endemic, joblessness is rife, schools are poor, and even high school graduates are unlikely to speak Standard English with any facility." When employment opportunities dried up in the Carter years, black men in these walled-off areas, they further explain, generally lacked connections to employers in new and emerging industries. They remained stuck, then, in places from which work kept disappearing. As a result, Massey and Denton contend, "young men coming of age in ghetto areas are relatively unlikely to find jobs capable of supporting a wife and children."[46]

Sitting in a church social hall around the corner from the Imperial site twenty-four years after the fire, Annette Zimmerman thought about the job market in the area in the 1980s. Black men in largely segregated South Hamlet, she recalled, didn't have many options. "There just wasn't nothing," she said, shaking her head. Without job opportunities, men started to vanish to, as Zimmerman remarked, "who knows where." That left behind a lot of single moms, Zimmerman included. Some opted for public assistance. But most southern states paid so little into welfare that AFDC (Aid to Families with Dependent Children) and food stamps together barely added up to half of what was needed to cross the poverty line. Perhaps this explains why North Carolina and South Carolina had two of the lowest percentages of families receiving welfare in the country. These statistics weren't about a lack of need; they were about the logic of cheap. State governments in the Carolinas kept taxes low for businesses and services lower for those in need. In the 1980s, with New Deal thinking in retreat, lawmakers drained federal and state budget lines aimed at the poor. These cuts in welfare spending, in turn, added additional workers to the labor pool, making the women and men in it, yet again, even more vulnerable targets for companies like Imperial.[47]

"My husband wasn't doing what he should have been doing," explained a southern woman about to take a job in a poultry plant in the 1980s, "so I went over there to make up the money not in my household." This mirrored what was going on in the lives of Georgia Quick, Annette Zimmerman, Loretta Goodwin, and so many of the other women on the line at Imperial. Most didn't *want* to be there; they *had* to be there.[48] With men making less, more women entered the paid labor force and stayed in it longer, adding, yet again, to the glut of workers in the labor markets, which in turn pushed down wages and muted, one more time, the voice of labor. But what other choices were out there?

"Women who'd grown up with the expectation that they'd have partners to help them raise their children" found themselves in the 1980s and beyond "with none," remarked the award-winning memoirist Jesmyn Ward, who grew up in Mississippi's rural ghettos. Her father bounced from job to job, household to household. He never left for good, but he wasn't a constant presence at her house either. He had "relationships with other women and married them and left them also." "Perhaps," Ward speculated, her father and his friends were looking for "a sense of power that being a Black man in the South denied them." And perhaps they were looking for an economy that had left them, too.[49]

The family that Ward's father intermittently left became, for some, a statistic. But it was also a social fact. By 1980, single-parent homes were on the rise, especially in households where the parent still there, usually a woman, had a high school–level education or less, and this was especially true in the African American community. By 1990, women headed fully 40 percent of the nation's black families. Richmond County followed the national trend. In Hamlet, women headed 34 percent of black families. As this number rose, in the South and elsewhere, poverty rates climbed. By 2000, women headed two-thirds of the nation's poor families.[50] It made brutal economic sense why single-parent households lagged behind two-parent households. With overall workforce participation rising and jobs in manufacturing plants and on the railroad disappearing, wages for working people in the United States fell across the board. One income, or one welfare check, simply wasn't enough to support a family.

Given the absence of well-paying, steady jobs for men, women, observed Jesmyn Ward, "worked like men then, and raised their children the best they could." That became, she thought, their "burden to bear." "She could not leave," Ward wrote of her mother, so "she worked and set about the business of raising her children."[51]

Ward's mother may have worked like a man, but the jobs she got cleaning homes and processing catfish didn't pay like railroad work or work in an auto plant. As a result, her family, like so many families in the rural ghettos and other places where industrial work and union jobs disappeared, had to make ends meet on one salary, a salary pushed downward by a job market swelling with underskilled, undertrained, and systematically undereducated women of all races.[52]

Twenty-five people died in the Hamlet fire. Eighteen were women. Twelve of the plant employees who died were African American and twelve were white. The fire's twenty-fifth victim was Philip Dawkins, the white truck driver for the Lance vending company, the one recognized by his firefighter son at the scene. This quick demographic profile of fire victims points to yet another dynamic of the rural ghettos of the 1980s. Twenty years after the protests in Birmingham and Selma, race still mattered in Hamlet and just about everywhere else in the United States. African Americans remained poorer than whites, and African American women remained concentrated at the bottom of the labor market. Most still cooked and prepared food, though not so much in other people's homes as they had in the past. Now they were doing so in the small food-processing plants and slaughterhouses popping up along state and county roads across the Carolinas and other rural sections of the nation. At Imperial, somewhere around 75 percent of the line ladies were African American. But in every part of the factory white and black women worked side by side. The plant was, perhaps, one of the most integrated spaces in Hamlet. But while African Americans could get a job at Imperial and Family Dollar and go to the county high school and play football and baseball and attend formerly all-white universities in Chapel Hill and Raleigh, what's clear is that many of the economic advantages of the post–civil rights era went to employers.

Imperial Food Products didn't have to discriminate when it came to exploiting the vulnerable. Segregation had produced a divided labor market. Custom and law reserved some jobs, especially industrial jobs, for whites, and other positions, usually dirtier, lower paying work, for African Americans. As segregation-era statutes came off the books in North Carolina, poor whites, poor blacks, and poor Native Americans—Latinos had yet to move into the state in large numbers by 1991—now competed, quite often, for the same jobs.

In similar ways, the women's movement added to the labor pool. Beginning in the 1970s, more women entered the workforce and they could apply for a broader range of jobs than ever before. But this progress also allowed a company like Imperial to equally underpay white and black women. To the Roes and those in their human relations department, anyone who filled out an application was, by definition, part of a cheap, easily disposable, and interchangeable labor supply. In other words, they were ideal workers to process chicken parts at fast speeds in dangerous conditions and keep quiet about it.[53]

———————

When they took a job on Bridges Street, working outside the home was not new for Georgia Quick or Ada Blanchard or Lorrie Boyle. But without a husband around or a steady flow of money coming into their households from a second income, they had no choice but to take the highest-paying job available. They didn't have the luxury of looking for clean work or getting paid less while they waited for a promotion. It didn't really matter whether they liked what they did or not—it was a bonus when they did. They couldn't pick a job based on safe working conditions; they simply hoped that employers valued their bodies and lives, but knew better and didn't count on having anyone to protect them. With so few jobs available in their area, they couldn't choose their boss or make him treat them right.

Work, of course, bled into home life. Imperial's employees tried not to worry if they missed a parent-teacher conference or if they had to rely on the television as a babysitter after school and during the summer—they had to go to work. Even though most surely understood that preschool would benefit their children, they couldn't afford any extra costs. This, of course, meant that their kids didn't always enter kindergarten ready to learn, and that put them at greater risk, as a 1990s study by the Anne E. Casey Foundation revealed, "to experience academic failure and to drop out." If that happened, the children joined the stream of cheap labor gathering in rural areas, helping to hold down their own wage rates and those of their moms and neighbors. As teens, the children of the working poor were more likely to get pregnant or run afoul of the law, getting caught in the grinding wheels of the emerging prison-industrial complex. If they did graduate from high school, they were less likely to go to college. Like poor kids everywhere, the least and moderately educated in rural towns faced long odds of economic success as adults.[54]

Imperial's floor ladies saw the roads to poverty around them in every direction. But what choice did they have? As single moms relying on wages, not welfare, they couldn't stop working, they couldn't rest, and they couldn't complain. It was hard to organize on the job, and most national unions bypassed people like Georgia Quick and places like Imperial in states like North Carolina because the odds of winning a contract didn't make it worth the investment. Quick couldn't quit or protest with her feet—not without a backup plan. Being a single mom, and that's where Quick was headed, made choice an extravagance, muffled her voice, and cut her freedoms in half and then some. This combination of circumstances is what made Quick and her "super-exploitable" co-workers valuable—essential, really—commodities in the economy of cheap.[55]

The facts of cheap stared back at Quick every morning as she got up for work. She had to have a paycheck and she had to keep going, even if it meant trudging through pools of freezing water and enduring the insults and tirades of nasty foremen and the boss's son.

Georgia Quick's paycheck didn't give her much of an upper hand over the welfare-reliant, and it didn't insulate her or her daughter from risk. It didn't protect her if her car broke down or if she twisted her ankle. It was, though, how she coped with the world of cheap.

Still, every paycheck came with possibilities. Georgia Quick and her co-workers Lillie Davis, Loretta Goodwin, and Annette Zimmerman brought home somewhere between $175 and $200 each week, more if they worked overtime on Saturdays and less if their hands hurt so bad that they couldn't tie their shoes in the morning or if they had to rush one of their children to the emergency room and miss part of a shift. Yet their pay envelopes represented more than cash for boxes of cornmeal mix and paying down the electric bill. They purchased these women a sliver of independence.

Unlike many of her co-workers, Lillie Davis was married to a man with a decent job. He didn't want his wife working at Imperial or anywhere else, but she insisted. She wanted money that was hers so that she had a say over what she picked up at the grocery store and the presents she bought at Christmas.[56]

For Georgia Quick, a paycheck meant that she didn't have to wait around the house to get money from her husband to buy a winter coat or pay the heating bill.

For Annette Zimmerman, the job represented a ticket out of the projects and away from the prying eyes of meddlesome caseworkers. During her years in public housing, government officials had come knocking on her door, grilling her about her wages and personal life. When she started to earn more money, working overtime and collecting time and half for these extra shifts, they had means-tested her and jacked up her rent. If someone spent more than two nights on her couch, they had wanted to know his name so they could put him on the lease. The whole complex where she lived had started to feel to her like a prison, especially after maintenance crews put up spotlights in the back and cameras in the front of the buildings. Working on the line at the Imperial plant provided Zimmerman with just enough money to rent a place of her own and gain a measure of privacy.[57]

Feelings of independence, however, never lasted long. Every paycheck also served as a reminder of the precariousness of the lives of Quick and Zimmerman and, to a lesser extent, Davis. A job for them did not mean financial security. It meant endless, unresolvable budgeting.

On average, Imperial workers allocated their weekly paychecks of $175 to $200 in roughly the following manner:

Housing	25%
Transportation	20%
Food	16%
Telephone	13%
Utilities	12%

For most, that left about $30 a week for health care and medicine, clothing, child care, toiletries, cleaning materials, pencils, notebooks and other school supplies, furniture, appliances, cable television, and going out to a movie and a meal at Hardee's. Everyone had a strategy for getting by, but their plans inevitably revolved less around choices than around doing without and playing a perpetual game of catch up.[58]

When Georgia Quick started at Imperial, she was still married. As long as her husband kept his job, they lived rent-free in that house next to the cotton gin. Without help with housing, making ends meet proved difficult.

Elizabeth Bellamy built her family budget around rent-free living as well. After her husband ended up in a New York prison, she and her daughters crowded into her parents' house in Bennettsville. What she saved on rent she paid in car payments and gasoline for commuting to work. And fuel prices, of course, were on the rise through the 1980s in response to ongoing tensions in the Middle East and the formation of OPEC.

Ada Blanchard had her own way of making ends meet. She put up with the monitoring from caseworkers and lived with several of her children in a non–air conditioned one-story, low-slung brick unit in a Rockingham public housing project. The father of her children paid no formal child support. She did, though, get about $80 each month in food stamps. According to state government tables, she earned too much to qualify for Medicaid. Imperial's health care plan was an option, but in the months before the fire, Imperial, by then sagging under piles of debt from the Haverpride debacle and other missteps, cut its health care contributions. By the summer of 1991, "our insurance," remembered one worker, "was $13.75 a week, and if you have children and wanted to put them on it, it was $73 a week."[59] "I didn't have the extra money for that," Blanchard explained years later about these health care costs that added up to a third of her paycheck. Without insurance, she couldn't always immunize her children and had to pay for asthma medicine out of her own pocket. Mostly, health care for her amounted to praying every day that no one in her family got sick or hurt.[60]

Making a little less than $200 a week meant that it was impossible for Ada Blanchard or Georgia Quick to get ahead. Neither of them could put money away for a down payment on a house, afford to go back to school, or get the vocational training they needed to get a cleaner, healthier, better-paying job in a changing economy. It wasn't easy when they hit a bump in the road. A sick child and a little extra for the doctor could easily bring the repo man to their door to collect the sofa or the car. The end of each month was the hardest. Sometimes the children's father or another family member would help out, but sometimes no one had anything extra to pitch in. In their careful and extensive study of single women and low-wage work, sociologists Kathryn Edin and Laura Lein discovered that roughly a quarter of the people they surveyed, including people who processed and prepared foods for a living, went without a meal at some point during the year. Most mothers reported putting less on their plates so that their kids could have enough to eat. Ten percent said that they regularly experienced hunger. A third had their phones cut off, and more than half had no health insurance. Under these financial constraints, they often re-acted to circumstances rather than planned ahead, and, all too often, this meant paying fees on late bills and bounced checks or skipping preventive maintenance on their houses or their heath that cost more in the long run and put them further behind.[61]

Most Imperial workers couldn't afford to miss work, not even for a day or an afternoon, if it meant no pay. Yet it was hard to avoid mishaps. Imperial wasn't one of those neat, modern, orderly factories where every-thing had a place. It was more like a cluttered and chaotic maze. Stuff was stacked and piled everywhere. Annette Zimmerman fell one day and twisted her knee trying to sidestep a sack of flour on the slick and greasy concrete floors. A co-worker took her to the breakroom. The plant didn't employ a full-time nurse. The general manager, James Hair, met her and gave her a few aspirin and an Ace bandage and asked her if she was ready to go back on the line.

"No," she said, "it hurts too much."

It must have, because Zimmerman went to the hospital to have it ex-amined. The doctor gave her crutches and told her to stay off her bad leg for a couple of weeks.

Fearful of losing her job, within days Zimmerman hobbled back to the line. She complained that her knee still hurt, but not to Hair or any of the other supervisors. Her co-workers listened and nodded their heads. They didn't have to ask. They knew why she was there. "I needed a job," Zim-merman said, "and there wasn't another plant to go to."[62]

"At the end," Georgia Quick recalled, thinking about the months and weeks before the fire, "it got really worse. It was awful."

She thought she could detect a change in Brad Roe's face and move-ments and hear it in his voice. As the summer of 1991 drew to a close, he seemed to burst into the factory every afternoon, hollering about one thing or another. To Quick he seemed "volatile," like he was coming apart at the seams. He yelled and cursed, she remembered, at everyone, includ-ing the foreman and maintenance crew. Some Imperial workers thought he was unhinged. Georgia wasn't sure what the cause was, but she felt cer-tain something wasn't right with Brad.

The equipment wasn't in much better shape than Emmett Roe's son.

"Things started to fall apart," Quick noted. The maintenance men and mechanics had a "heavy load" at that time. She watched as they patched the machines together and rushed around trying to keep the line up and running. She sympathized with them and the pressures they were under.[63]

Quick dreamed about quitting. She wanted to leave the slimy floors, foul-smelling chicken, and yelling behind, but she couldn't afford to make the move. By 1991, she and her husband had essentially separated. She was twelve weeks pregnant and living in a run-down trailer.[64] "I was scared to leave," Quick admitted, "because where else would I go? To me, this was a lot of money."

The money coaxed Quick out of bed at daybreak on the Tuesday after Labor Day in 1991. "I really didn't want to go to work," she remembered. "This was strange." She thought about taking the day off, something she almost never did, but she didn't want to leave Alberta McRae, a co-worker and carpool companion, without a ride. "If I didn't go, Alberta had no way to go." And both of them, of course, needed the money. Money for rent, money for food, money for electricity, and money for doctors' bills.

After their usual twenty-minute drive, Quick and McRae pulled up to the Imperial plant. They walked in the front door, punched their time cards, and headed to the breakroom. They sat down, like they always did, to eat breakfast before the start of their shift. Danny Pate, one of the supervisors, came in and told them to report to the processing room, not their usual spots. The fryer, he explained, had been down all weekend and had just gotten back up and running. They needed to get caught up there. The mechanics were still milling around and tinkering with things when Quick and McRae got there and started to process chicken.

Twenty minutes later, Georgia Quick heard a loud bang, screams of fire, and then everything went "pitch dark."

5

BODIES

An archivist for the state of North Carolina tucked the death certificates for the victims of the Imperial Food Products fire away in an ordinary-looking government building in Raleigh, not far from the state house and the governor's mansion. The records are contained in a single gray folder. The only place to sit and go through them is at a clunky, heavy metal desk in a windowless room.

The names of the dead are listed one per page. Each report contains the information you would expect to find on a death certificate. Each lists the last known address. Each notes their age, marital status, how much schooling they had, and the time, place, and cause of death.

Though filled with dispassionate, clinical language and terminology, these records possess an eerie intimacy. They include a glossy headshot of the victim and a generic sketch pinpointing the spot of every scrape, pock mark, bruise, burn, and soot stain found on each body. The examiners discovered and noted needle marks running up and down both arms of one of the dead. He tried to hide his habit from his co-workers with bandages.

The medical examiners listed in detail what the victims wore on their bodies at the time of their deaths.

Brenda Gail Kelly had on a blue shirt, white jeans, and white shoes. She had a bow in her hair.

Michael Allen Morris had on rubber boots and a black T-shirt with the words "I Survived Hugo"—a hurricane that blew through the Carolinas in 1989 killing dozens of people and causing billions of dollars in damages—written across the front.

At the time of the fire, Donald Brice Rich had on blue denim over-alls and a dark T-shirt proclaiming his allegiance to the holy trinity of "Women, Wine, and Overtime." Underneath his clothes, he had a col-lection of tattoos on his arms and shoulders depicting a skull and dagger, a grim reaper, a lightning bolt, and a cobra riding on flaming wheels that said MARY.

Scotland County's Rose Lynette Wilkins had a rose tattoo and noth-ing in her pockets.

Many of the dead still had on their blue smocks and white aprons. Some wore rings and watches, and several of the women had painted their finger- and toenails, bright red in one case.

Medical examiners dug through the pockets of Josephine Barrington, whose son went back into the fire to save her from the smoke and flames only to perish with her. Emptying her pants, they found bifocals, red hair clips, nail clippers, scissors, a small tin of Tylenol, a coin purse with three five-dollar bills, three one-dollar bills, ninety-one cents in change, a ring with seven keys, and a few sticks of chewing gum.

Doing their jobs with characteristic thoroughness, the medical person-nel jotted down the color and material of the bras and underwear the vic-tims wore. They recorded whether or not they were circumcised and if their teeth were fully intact or they relied on dentures.

Before returning them to undertakers in their hometowns of Ellerbe, Laurinburg, Rockingham, and Hamlet, the examiners measured the pre-cise length and exact weight of the naked bodies. They wrote down the numbers in the designated boxes on the death certificates.

If the height and weight data for the victims were plugged into a for-mula measuring body types, eighteen of the twenty-five who died on Sep-tember 3, 1991, at the Imperial Food Products plant would be considered overweight. By this same rough gauge, five would be deemed "grossly over-weight." Several of the death certificates added brief descriptions about the body types and shapes of the dead. "Overweight," said one. "Large woman," recorded another.

The bodies of the Imperial victims were not just personal stories of in-dividual choices about what to wear on the outside and underneath and what messages to have written on their arms and shoulders. They were also facts and numbers. But these bodies, like all bodies, were at the same time products of history. They were reflections of the nation's way of eating, of particular ways of measuring things and people, of the narrowing of American politics, of the triumph of business interests over everyday economic security, and of the growing indifference toward the lives of the poor and the vulnerable.

Just like Hamlet's local labor market and just like the chicken tenders made at the plant, the bodies of Imperial workers were also not exceptions. Rather, they represented the mainstreaming of cheap.[1]

After holding steady for three decades after World War II—an era tagged by the food historian Harvey Levenstein as "the golden age of food processing" and marked by the surge in McDonald's outlets, the triumph of french fries over baked potatoes as a side dish, and the widespread appearance of vending machines that spat out bottles of sugary Coke and Pepsi for pocket change—the nation's obesity rate started to climb in the 1970s, slowly at first, but then faster and faster. In the 1960s, the Centers for Disease Control (CDC) estimated that 13.5 percent of Americans were obese or had a body mass index (BMI) above 30, the numeric line, according to experts, separating healthiness and unhealthiness.[2] (BMI is a widely used, and sometimes criticized, measure of obesity that derives its quotient by dividing a person's weight by his or her height squared.) This number started to jump in the 1970s. Twenty percent of Americans had a BMI of over 30 in 1980. The percentage rose to 30 percent a decade later. By 2000, nearly 60 percent of all Americans were either overweight or obese by this measure. Children were especially vulnerable, with the number of overweight kids doubling in the 1980s. In poorer, more rural communities, like Hamlet and Bennettsville, the numbers were even higher. By 1995, public health officials declared that weight gain had developed into a full-fledged epidemic in the United States.[3]

As the nation's waistline grew, commentators began to add up the costs of a heftier republic. Researchers at the prestigious Children's Hospital of Philadelphia blamed over 100,000 deaths each year across the country on obesity. According to health officials, overweight individuals faced a higher risk for heart disease, high blood pressure, diabetes—especially type 2 diabetes—joint problems, respiratory issues, and even breast, colon, and gallbladder cancer. Overweight adults experienced disrupted sleep and tended to get sick more often and underperform at work. One study even linked dementia to weight gain. More than 66 percent of people with arthritis, according to another study, could be considered overweight or obese. Like adults, heavier kids confronted problems with their hips, knees, and joints.[4] They were more likely to get bullied, skip school, do worse in class, and, some contended, suffer from low self-esteem and body shaming and discrimination. Several researchers even framed weight gain as a national security issue. "Between 1995 and 2008," one scholar noted, "the military was forced to reject more than 140,000 recruits because they were overweight."[5]

"Obesity costs lots of money," insisted Kelly Brownell, the one-time director of Yale's Rudd Center for Food Policy and Obesity. "The costs," he added, "are incurred by individuals, businesses, the country, and the world." Overweight individuals spend twice as much on health care and medication than do their less heavy neighbors. Health economists estimated in 2003 that the direct and indirect costs of obesity, of early death, of weight-related illnesses, and of lost productivity reached between $117 and $239 billion annually. According to another assessment, health expenditures resulting from obesity cost every single family in the United States $1,470 per year.[6]

As early as 1977, the Select Committee on Nutrition and Human Needs told the United States Senate that the country faced a looming public health and fiscal crisis. "The over-consumption of food in general has become a major public health problem," testified Dr. Theodore Cooper, assistant secretary for health in the Department of Health, Education, and Welfare. He estimated that, at the time, about 20 percent of all adults in the United States were "overweight to a degree that may interfere with optimal health and longevity." The secretary and others, including South Dakota Senator George McGovern, drew a comparison between overeating and smoking. "These dietary changes," warned the 1972 Democratic presidential candidate, "represent as great a threat to public health as smoking."[7]

McGovern's reference to smoking was a telling one. For much of the 1960s, smoking represented the nation's number one public health threat and expense. After discovering a definite link between smoking and cancer in the 1950s, Dr. Alton Oschner of Tulane University had declared an all-out war on smoking. He targeted smokers in his fight. In his popular book *Smoking: Your Choice Between Life and Death*, he tagged smokers again and again as "selfish" and called smoking the "most selfish habit anyone can have." While Oschner pushed for government warnings on cigarette packs and talked of lawsuits against the nation's tobacco giants, he stressed the individual act of quitting as the initial line of defense in the battle against smoking. If smokers stopped smoking, the problem would go away. He recognized that it wouldn't be easy, but he insisted that if smokers exercised greater self-control and made the right choices for themselves, for those around them, and for the entire nation, the problem would disappear.[8]

As more and more experts and policy makers drew a parallel between smoking and overeating, personal choice started to frame the discussion around obesity. Applying Oschner's approach to cigarettes and public health to the issue of obesity, experts began to link weight gain to poor and selfish eating decisions. Americans grew heavier, they said, because they were too lazy to cook at home. They ate out too often and ate too much at fast food restaurants. Lisa Mancino, a food economist for the United States Department of Agriculture, calculated that just one meal a week away from home can translate into two extra pounds of weight gain a year for the average consumer.[9] According to this math and this way of thinking, the solution was to eat somewhere else and make better choices at home. Researchers for the *New England Journal of Medicine* estimated that Americans gained on average 3.35 pounds per person per year between 1986 and 1990.[10] Several researchers argued that too much television and not enough exercise were the causes for the jump. Yet a majority of commentators as well as scholars kept the analysis simple and pointed to the obese as the cause of obesity. They got big because they chose the wrong foods. They put chips, cookies, and beer in their shopping carts instead of peas, carrots, and Florida orange juice. On top of that, they drank too much soda. But, mostly, Americans were fat because they consumed too much of the wrong things. It was that simple. They needed to eat less and make better choices.[11]

Early in the twenty-first century, President George W. Bush summed up mainstream thinking in the country and showed just how deeply ideas about choice were baked into discussions about weight gain. "Good foods and regular exercise," the president insisted, would reverse the upward trend in BMI rates and "save our country a lot of money—but, more importantly, save lives." A letter to the editor of the *Atlanta Journal Constitution* echoed the president's remarks: "Choice is what is to blame for obesity. Americans have the freedom to choose. That is our flaw, we are free to do what we want and most humans chose the easy way—fast food instead of a salad and liposuction instead of exercising." [12]

Just as in the battle over smoking, the political and social realities of class, race, and gender threaded through remarks about weight. Obesity rates were not evenly distributed across America. Because of their almost complete dependence on cars to get from place to place, rural folks walked less and tended to be heavier than urban dwellers. The poor, people of color, and single moms grew larger at double the rate of white middle- and upper-middle-class men and women.[13] As reporters and commentators cited these numbers, they repeated the arguments of anti-smoking advocates, welfare opponents, and promoters of less government (for some) that dominated American politics in the 1980s. The poor were poor because they made bad choices, like "choosing" welfare over work and having more kids over thrift and abstinence. The overweight were overweight because they lacked willpower and compounded their bad decision making. They were the problem, and their bodies showed it. Rather than saving their money, they went out to McDonald's or Shoney's. They passed up spinach for french fries and grilled chicken breasts (in the late 1980s, falsely assumed to be automatically healthy) for fried tenders. They cooked too little, used the microwave instead of the stovetop, and bypassed tap water in favor of oversize bottles of Coke, Pepsi, and Sprite and, worse still, twelve-packs of beer and jugs of fortified purple wine. They didn't exercise enough either. Commentators talked about obese people skipping the gym in favor of sitting in front of the television snacking on a supersize bag of Doritos filled with shocking amounts of fat and salt. And they kept making these choices day after day. As George Bush suggested, their bad decisions cost taxpayers billions of dollars and weakened the nation.[14]

This kind of thinking turned the obese into not just people with problem bodies but also into irresponsible citizens. As irresponsible citizens, they didn't deserve the state's largesse and support. This perception both reflected and shaped public policy. After heated debate, in 1978, the Democratic-led Congress approved the Humphrey-Hawkins Act, calling for full employment and stable consumer prices. The measure was more symbolic than anything else. It had little teeth to it and even less funding behind it. In retrospect, it was, it seems, a last and final gasp of the New Deal order, a tribute to the nation's passing faith in the broad benefits of high wages and widespread buying.[15] By the early 1980s, policy discussions in the United States had changed and changed dramatically. The ideas of cheap rose to the fore, influencing ideas about government and its role in the economy and every daily life, including school food policies, which quickly seemed as emblematic of their era as the Humphrey-Hawkins Act was of an earlier moment in time. Reduced tax revenues due to business losses and jumps in unemployment led to government cuts at the federal and state levels, which in turn reduced support for school nutrition and exercise programs. Faced with persistent shortfalls and narrow choices between an extra science or reading class and physical education or home economics, educational administrators often chose biology and English over gym and cooking courses. To cover up the growing holes in their budgets, they cut down on visits from nurses and slashed funding for teacher's aides. Often these were the people who oversaw non-academic activities, like going outside to play and taking time for lunch. According to a 2001 study by the Clearinghouse on Early Adult Education and Parenting, almost 40 percent of the nation's school districts had cut or eliminated recess because of a lack of funding. With money in short supply, more and more new school buildings went up in cities and towns without costly playgrounds or gyms.[16] Some school districts cut back on their sports programs while others entered into dubious privatization deals. They let Coke and Pepsi line their halls with vending machines stocked with high-calorie foods and drinks in exchange for money for new scoreboards for the baseball field and helmets for the football team.[17]

The Reagan administration, looking for more money with which to pay for the Contras and several colossal new aircraft carriers, cut support for the school lunch and food stamps programs. Famously, officials in Washington tried to reclassify ketchup as a vegetable on school lunch trays to save money as well.[18] Distrustful of the decision making of the poor and the not thin, some lawmakers proposed limiting what recipients could purchase with federal and state funds. While the nation's growing legions of the working poor were told they couldn't buy wine or beer or some prepared foods with government-issued food stamps, they could still use them to purchase cookies, chips, and soda. Big food and big agriculture celebrated choice as well, it seems. When a number of lawmakers suggested restrictions on sugary drinks and salty snacks, industry representatives rolled out the flag and complained that any limits on consumer choice amounted to an alarming loss of cherished freedoms. Few congressional representatives wanted to vote against American rights or forgo campaign contributions from big donors, so it remained okay to buy chips and soda with government funds.[19]

But policy makers didn't cut food subsidies altogether; they just redistributed the benefits of government action and spending so that more of it flowed toward industry and industrial farmers. Between 1975 and 1990, the United States government wrote checks worth billions of dollars to wheat, soybean, and corn growers. As these policies made these commodities cheaper, food scientists figured out ways to insert inexpensive goods into more and more links in the food chain. Corn went into chicken feed, and it went into the batter that coated nuggets and tenders, into the filler, and into the high fructose corn syrup (HFCS) that sweetened the dipping sauces.[20] Between 1997 and 2005, according to calculations done by researchers at the Global Development and Environment Institute at Tufts University, animal farms, slaughterhouses, and processors in the United States saved $3.9 billion annually because of government subsidies to corn and soybean growers. The broiler industry alone saved as much as $1.25 billion over this period as a result of the same subsidies programs. In terms of total operating expenses, this amounted to, according to the Tufts scholars, a 13 percent reduction in costs for broiler and egg producers with nothing put aside for growers of healthier fruits and vegetables. These policies, then, artificially made healthier food items look more expensive.[21]

Corn subsidies, in particular, helped to make fat-filled calories cheaper and more accessible. "Humans aren't the only ones who are fatter than they used to be," the sociologist Michael Carolan remarked in his 2011 study of cheap food. During the 1960s, a 3.5-ounce piece of chicken, he explained, contained just under 4 grams of fat. By 1970, that number had risen to 8.6 grams, and, by 2004, industrial chickens fed a steady diet of cheap, corn-fortified foods arrived at stores and fast food outlets packed with more than twenty grams of fat in each serving. As Michael Crawford of London's Institute of Brain Chemistry and Human Nutrition observed, "While chicken was at one time a lean, low-fat food, it is no longer." He wondered, "Does eating obesity cause obesity in the consumer?"[22]

Eating chicken nuggets and tenders made by Imperial and Cagle's meant eating another dose or two of fat added from the further processing and cooking of the items. For most of the 1970s and 1980s, American eaters still chose chicken because the industry's efficiencies lowered the price, but also because they thought poultry was healthier than red meat no matter what. That's what newscasters, reporters, and ad men told them. Based on the headlines and commercials, most consumers associated chicken with good, sensible food choices. The word *chicken* in chicken nuggets and chicken tenders implied that there was actually chicken and some healthiness to be found inside the crust of these items. This, of course, was in the years before the author Michael Pollan led a food movement urging the close and painstaking reading of labels.

Of course, chicken nuggets were never a smart food choice. To begin with, there was never very much chicken in the nuggets, as most people understood the idea of "chicken." Twenty-plus years after the fire, a pair of Mississippi-based food scientists decided to do an "autopsy" on a chicken nugget. The name *chicken nugget* was, they concluded, "a misnomer." It implied that the meat inside was chicken meat, but the main components they discovered were chicken skin and chicken fat.[23] In fact, six chicken nuggets, weighing about 3.4 ounces, contained almost twice as many grams of saturated fat as a regular 3.2-ounce McDonald's hamburger.[24] They contained as much salt as well. While salt itself isn't fattening, it can lead to bloating and weight gain as well as to an increased risk of high blood pressure, strokes, kidney stones, and stomach cancer. Plus, it definitely makes you thirsty, and in many instances this means reaching for the nearest, tallest cup of Coke or Dr. Pepper and all of the liquid calories found inside such drinks.[25]

Still, well into the 1990s parents continued to think, based on news reports and advertising about the evils of red meat, that the chicken in nuggets and tenders made them a healthier choice than hamburgers or steak. With cost, convenience, and the well-being of their kids in mind, mothers and fathers fed cheap chicken(ish) products to their children. As they did, they unknowingly provided their sons and daughters with a kind of gateway drug to a life of fast food and meals built on a pleasant mouth feel, explosive flavors, and immediate satisfaction. After that first bite through the crust and the crunch, the fat and salt in the nuggets took over, and that's why kids, teens, and grown-ups came back to them again and again. "Salt, sugar, and fat are what psychologists call reinforcers," explains the food researcher and journalist Mark Schatzker. "They trigger bursts of potent neurotransmitters and activate the same brain circuitry as heroin and cocaine." Dr. Gene-Jack Wang, a neuroscientist at the Brookhaven National Laboratory, wasn't surprised about the similar effects of junk food consumption and drug use. "We make our food very similar to cocaine now," he remarked. "We purify [it]. Our ancestors ate whole grains, but we're eating white bread. American Indians ate corn; we eat corn syrup."[26]

When the Imperial plant caught fire in 1991, it had been four years since that watershed moment in American eating when chicken passed beef as the nation's number one source for meat-based protein. By then, the nugget had triumphed within the world of poultry capitalism. Half of all the chicken eaten in the United States in 1991 resembled the addictive and intensely adulterated foods that Schatzker and Wang commented on. Kind of like crack, they were ubiquitous, cheap, further processed, and hard to give up. The larger transition from home-prepared chicken to industrial-made fried chicken products marked what the historian Steve Striffler has called the "dangerous transformation of America's favorite food."[27]

Richmond County, North Carolina, witnessed the same sort of weight gain as the rest of the country did. In 2001, the obesity rate for the towns, crossroads, and small cities surrounding Hamlet had jumped up above 33 percent, almost 3 points higher than the state average and 12 percent higher than the rate registered in Orange County, home to the University of North Carolina at Chapel Hill and statistically the thinnest county in the state.[28] Over the next few years, the numbers would continue to rise, along with poverty rates. A 2006 study of public health in North Carolina reported that between 60 and 65 percent of Richmond Country residents were either overweight or obese.[29]

One week after the Imperial plant caught fire, the *Richmond County Daily Journal* ran a national story on its back pages about childhood obesity. The article contained the usual data on the costs of weight gain and the usual list of recommendations to solve the problem. The experts interviewed for the piece asserted that Americans needed to get far fewer of their calories from fat, especially saturated fats. They needed to consume less sodium and exercise more. They suggested fewer fast food meals and more home-cooked dinners. They urged people to add more whole grains and additional servings of leafy green and dark yellow vegetables to their diets. Parents needed to find out more about what their kids ate for school lunch and afterschool snacks. All of this was sound advice, but most of the choices outlined in the paper stood outside the reach of the poor and working poor who had labored on the line at Imperial and in other low-wage positions in the county.[30]

Knowing exactly what was in a chicken nugget or on a school lunch tray wasn't easy or convenient. "Ultimately," writes Ann Vileisis, in her book *Kitchen Literacy*, "we have ended up in the absurd situation today that most of us, as consumers, know very little about what we eat; and, sensing a 'dark side' to our foods' production, many of us don't even want to know."[31] This "covenant of ignorance," as Vileisis calls it, allowed chicken producers, just like it did beef and pork processors, to hide much of the story of how cheap chicken tenders made their way from the farms to the slaughterhouse to the Imperial plant and onto Shoney's tables and into the school cafeterias. Pictures on the menus didn't, of course, depict the suffering of spindly-legged broilers. There were no glossy images of urine pouring down on birds or of stunned animals getting dragged through vats of fecal soup. There were no snapshots of workers trying to shake off the pains in their wrists and fingers. Food labels were almost as hard to find as these kinds of disturbing images were. When Imperial exploded, most lunchrooms didn't have breakdowns of the caloric, salt, and fat content of their menu items. Supermarket labels weren't much better, with unrealistic portion sizes and vague ingredient lists. Most eaters, as

Vileisis sensed, rarely volunteered to learn this information. Knowing was a lot of work, and in the short term it wasn't likely to change what an underpaid worker making $5.50 an hour fed her son or daughter or whether they signed up for the school lunch program or not.

In his book *Cooked*, the food writer Michael Pollan cited a 2003 study by a group of Harvard economists that linked the increase in obesity in America to the decline of home cooking. The Ivy League researchers determined that housekeepers across the nation spent on average just twenty-seven minutes a day fixing their meals. The road back to a thinner and healthier nation, Pollan insisted along with others, ran through the kitchen and the preparation of fresh foods. What Pollan didn't acknowledge in his book or in his well-paid and attended addresses to college audiences was that poor women, the most statistically vulnerable group to obesity, never really stopped making food and eating at home.[32] In fact, North Carolinians earning less than $15,000 a year consumed five times as many meals at home as their wealthier neighbors did. Given what they got paid on the job and collected from public assistance, they couldn't even afford a few items off the Hardee's value menu except on special occasions. But at the same time, highly processed fast foods were creeping into their homes and changing their ideas about cooking, especially as already prepared food often cost just about the same as uncooked food. Given the physical and emotional rigors of low-paid factory and service work, these items were hard to pass on, even if they weren't all that healthy.[33]

"My hands would swell up," Imperial worker Ada Blanchard explained years later, sitting in the yard by her trailer outside of Rockingham. "I couldn't cook for my kids." Like many of her co-workers, she knew how to make a meal from scratch, and that's what she did when she had the time and feeling in her fingers, like on the weekends and holidays. But during the week, when another shift was only a few hours away, she made dinners that were quick and easy, things like canned spaghetti and chicken tenders.[34] Writer J.D. Vance grew up among the white working class in a small town in Ohio. In high school, he got a job as a supermarket cashier, a position he said turned him into an "amateur sociologist," closely studying the contents of shopping carts. He quickly learned to recognize the choices made by people like Ada Blanchard. "Some folks," he noted, "purchased a lot of canned and frozen food, while others consistently arrived at the checkout counter with carts piled high with fresh produce." "The more harried a customer," he observed, "the more they purchased pre-cooked or frozen food, the more likely they were to be poor." [35]

Around the same time that Vance started to study shopping patterns and Blanchard reflected on her cooking, journalist Tracie McMillan went undercover to find out about the "American way of eating." After a few months cutting garlic in California's Central Valley and stocking the produce sections of a Walmart store, she started to make the same choices Blanchard made and for the same reasons. Work in the world of cheap was painful and exhausting. "We didn't cook much," McMillan wrote about herself and her mostly female co-workers. "We were too busy. All of this—the chore of finding food, the lack of time to do anything with it when we did, the indifference to our meals—was familiar." [36]

Over time, the indifference that McMillan documented led to a drop in culinary knowledge that, in turn, heightened families' dependence on pre-made, further-processed foods. In the past, daughters (and some sons) generally learned how to cook at home from their mothers, aunts, and grandmothers. As women, who still were usually in charge of food in most households, worked more hours outside the home and spent less time in the kitchen, children sat through fewer informal lessons on how to make meatloaf or fresh green beans or chicken soup from scratch. Budget cuts, at the same time, led to sharp drops in spending on home economics classes in public schools. Unable to cook for themselves or too busy to learn on their own, many, and especially the working poor, allowed the companies that churned out cheap foods, like Kraft, Campbell's, General Mills, and Imperial—often companies that they themselves worked for—to do most of cooking for them. Few saw the danger in this kind of voluntary deskilling, at least not at first. [37]

Even those with the time, knowledge, and inclination to cook would have found it hard to follow the recommendations made in that *Richmond County Daily Journal* article. Finding fresh, whole-grain foods year-round in Hamlet's foodscape would not have been easy. At first glance, the town and areas around it didn't look like food deserts or toxic food environments, but up close and for those with thin paychecks, that's how they operated. At Hamlet's mini marts, the racks were filled with chips, pork rinds, Twinkies, and Little Debbie cakes. At the Piggly Wiggly and the Food Lion, there were a few rows of fresh fruits and vegetables. But these sections were never as big or as full as the ones at the Harris Teeter or Kroger's in the sprawl-lands of Charlotte and Raleigh. No doubt, it wasn't easy to find brown rice or brown bread in Richmond County in the 1980s. If these health(ier) food items did make it onto the shelves, they were rarely cheap, or cheap enough, not when every penny and every minute counted. If an Imperial worker wanted to treat her family or herself to a break from cooking, the only restaurants in Hamlet or in Rockingham that working people could afford served burgers and fries or chicken nuggets and fries or fried fish and fries, or endless helpings at a steakhouse salad bar loaded with bite-size fried shrimp, fatty cheeses, creamy dressings, salty croutons, bacon bits, syrupy pineapple chunks, and sugary custards. None of this food, of course, was good for you.

Margaret Banks, Sandra McPhaul, and dozens of other Imperial workers commuted on backcountry roads twenty to thirty miles each way to the job. They might have had some land circling their homes, but the long, painful days on the line gave them little time for a garden. As soon as they opened the door after coming home from their shift, hungry kids peppered them with questions: "When are we eating? What's for dinner?" Many were too tired to plan dinner, or maybe they didn't know how to prepare fresh vegetables or couldn't find affordable, healthy options in the supermarket. So, when it came time for dinner, working mothers popped some tenders into the oven or microwave with mac and cheese on the side and turned on the television. Everyone was happy—or quiet, at least. Most mornings during the school year, line ladies on the first shift left the house before the kids were up. That meant, as Annette Zimmerman explained, something quick—knock-off cornflakes, Pop Tarts, or Eggos— for breakfast. All were easy to make and easy to eat, and all had some of the same addictive qualities found in nuggets and tenders.[38]

Every study on the rise of obesity rates in the United States recommended more exercise. According to the reports, the poor spent far too little of their leisure time walking, running, or doing aerobics. Maybe that was because there weren't many low-cost gyms or walking trails in Bennettsville, South Carolina, or the North Yard community outside of Hamlet, and there were no plans to build them in the years after 1980 when North Carolina legislators from both parties competed to see who could slash the deepest into the parts of the state budget that had nothing to do with road building or industrial recruitment. There weren't a lot of gyms open to the public to begin with, and investors weren't lining up to put a Gold's Gym in one of Hamlet's abandoned storefronts or near Rockingham's housing projects. Not many, if any, Imperial workers had money for a gym membership on $5.50 per hour anyway. Riding a stationary bike while the kids were at home, with piles of laundry on the floor and shopping lists to fill, probably didn't make much sense to most working women. How would you manage to pay for one of those bikes in the first place when you had a stack of bills, and where would you put it a house filled with kids and relatives?

Really, the article in the *Richmond County Daily Journal* and most of the other reports on obesity in the 1980s and 1990s missed the key issue behind the timing of the tipping of the nation's scales. More than supersize meals, more than subsidies for corn and soft drinks, more than government cuts in support for recess and healthy school lunches, more than chicken pieces loaded with fat, salt, and sugar, the jump in obesity in poor communities turned on income. In fact, across the country, bodies got bigger as pay envelopes shrunk. This represented a massive, almost schizophrenic, historic shift. For more time than anyone could possibly count, poor people starved. They starved during the Roman Empire and the Renaissance, and during Charles Dickens, George Orwell, and Upton Sinclair's days. Novelists and commentators read their thin, gaunt, and emaciated bodies as sure signs of poverty, just as they read girth, plumpness, and softness as indicators of wealth. All of a sudden, the cultural codes reversed themselves. "Thinness" became a sign of righteousness and success; "fatness" an emblem of poverty and failure.

The American diet was filled with danger long before the spike in obesity in the 1970s. Coke machines appeared at bus stations and crossroads gas stations after World War II. At the same time, boxes of sugary Betty Crocker cake mixes began to line supermarket aisles. McDonald's opened its first franchises in the mid 1950s, about the same time that Swanson's began selling TV dinners, followed two decades later by its larger, more caloric and fat-filled Hungry-Man meals. Imperial workers, single moms with jobs, unemployed railroad men, and farm laborers without crops to pick didn't suddenly choose to eat at Hardee's—one of Hamlet's only fast food joints—because they liked the food better than healthier options. Women who pulled pieces of marinated chicken out of vats on Bridges Street all day long didn't microwave pre-made burgers and sausage biscuits because they thought they were the best food for them and their kids. They didn't serve fries instead of broccoli because they didn't know the value of vegetables. They chose foods that tasted good and that their sons and daughters liked because they really didn't have a choice, even as commentators constantly talked about choices. They ate what they could afford in terms of price and time.

The early 1970s marked a critical turning point not just in foodways and the making of American bodies, but also, more importantly, in the real wages and overall incomes earned by the vast majority of the nation's workers. Beginning after World War II, laborers and their families saw their take-home pay steadily climb year after year. For most people in the United States and specifically in Hamlet, this rise defined the postwar experience. But beginning in the early years of the 1970s, interest rates and prices for many household items—excluding chicken and other processed foods—started to rise. Double-digit inflation cut into people's buying power. But some income was better than none. As global competition heated up in the early 1970s, in what should by now be a familiar tale, millions of Americans, especially men in high-paying union positions, lost their jobs. Nationally, unemployment nearly doubled from 1973 to 1975, reaching 8.3 percent, before it fell back and then peaked again at 9.5 percent in 1982. For manufacturing workers, the numbers were worse. From Maine to California, hundreds of factories closed and thousands of jobs disappeared. To track the era's economic devastation, statisticians combined the rates of unemployment and inflation to come up with what they called the Misery Index. According to this grim yardstick, 17 percent of the nation lived in economic agony in the mid-1970s. The number jumped to 21 percent in 1980.[39]

For many, the mobilization of more family members, especially women, blunted the decline in real wages and buying power. By swelling the labor market, however, the new entrants into the workforce put downward pressure on wages. None of this helped single moms in small towns or cities. They still had to take care of everything at home on one paycheck—one that was shrinking because of rising inflation and job competition. That made cheap necessities more valuable than ever before.

Workers in small-town North Carolina faced their own additional miseries in the 1980s. Governor Jim Hunt and his successors' efforts at industrial recruitment had paid off and brought thousands of new positions to the state. The Tar Heel economy did especially well in attracting to its rural counties industrial bottom feeders looking for the cheapest labor available anywhere. Not many of these jobs, located far from the highways, paid well. As a result, while incomes in all of the southeastern states rose by two percentage points in the late 1970s to 86 percent of the national average, North Carolina's rate of pay fell two points behind the rest of the region.[40] By the middle of the 1970s, the state ranked dead last in the country in industrial wages. Each week, North Carolina laborers made $52.53 less on average than their counterparts made in other parts of the United States.[41]

Workers in meatpacking and food processing faced added challenges. Through much of the 1970s and 1980s, larger and larger companies were taking over more and more of the plants where cows and chickens were disassembled and transformed into burgers and tenders. Like Emmett Roe did when he moved from Pennsylvania to North Carolina, these firms fought back against unions and government regulations by shifting their operations farther from the urban cores into small towns and rural ghettos filled with economically vulnerable and desperate laborers. They didn't worry about turnover rates, because the jobs were easy to learn and there always seemed to be another person waiting to take a turn on the line. Operating under these conditions, employers had few incentives to raise wages.[42]

The simultaneous fall in wages and drop in the price of further-processed foods wasn't just about efficiencies, subsidies, and relentless economies. It was about the cheapening, once more, of the American social contract. In 1914, Henry Ford had set a new wage standard for the country. Looking to reduce turnover rates, dull the appeal of radicalism, and swell the market of buyers for his mass-produced Model Ts, Ford famously paid his workers an astounding five dollars a day, doubling the going rate. Other companies followed Ford's lead. In tight labor markets, they had no choice if they wanted to hire workers. With the advent of the New Deal and the industrial mobilization for World War II, Fordism—and the idea of seeing laborers not solely as a cost to employers but also as vital consumers critical to growing aggregate demand and sustaining the overall health of the nation's economy—became central to corporate and government policy.[43]

The idea of *more* as a social good got carried into the postwar era and made it, in the words of the historian Jefferson Cowie, "an extraordinarily good time to be a worker." For the very first time in United States history, the nation's largest businesses and the federal government recognized unions and collective bargaining as legitimate aspects of American life. But even more important, they saw working-class prosperity as a key indicator of economic health. As a result, Cowie writes in *The Great Exception: The New Deal and the Limits of American Politics*, "more income, more equality, more optimism, more leisure, more consumer goods, more travel, more entertainment, more expansive homes, and more education were all available to regular people than at any other time in world history."[44]

Beginning in the 1970s, this notion of *more* got turned on its head. The link between wages and consumption remained intact, but it began to operate in a different direction. The Ford worker, the standard bearer of American labor—buying a new car every other year and packing the family up for an annual vacation to Cedar Park or Disneyland or Yellowstone—was replaced after 1975 by an Imperial worker counting the loose change and crumpled dollar bills in her pocket as she headed into the supermarket to get a low-cost package of chicken nuggets or a bag of tenders to feed her family for dinner.

Cheap food stood at the heart of the inversion of Fordism. As family incomes shrank, the regular people that Cowie talked about became dependent on paying less. Inexpensive, industrially produced chicken products and mass-manufactured fries meant they could still put plenty of food on the table. Their families wouldn't go hungry. They could even afford cake, packets of chocolate chip cookies, and MoonPies full of HFCS that cost a quarter in 1991 in the Lance vending machines in the Imperial breakroom.

———

As poultry capitalism and the larger "chickenization"—to borrow journalist Christopher Leonard's phrase—of the food industry pushed down the incomes of farmers and workers, they created a ballooning group of consumers who had no choice but to buy the cheap necessities they made and sold.[45] The economy of falling paychecks channeled people toward a dangerous eating routine of chicken tenders and hot dogs, frozen fries and boxes of macaroni and cheese, toward a diet marked by convenience and easy preparation and filled with fat and salt, a diet marked by the absence of whole grains and costly fruits and vegetables. This did, in fact, turn out to be a matter of choice, a matter of rational economic choice.

In the years before the Imperial fire, the prices of healthy and unhealthy foods moved in sharply opposite directions. "If you look at the relative price of fruits and vegetables," the writer, academic, and food activist Marion Nestle pointed out, "it has gone up by 40 percent since the 1980s, when the obesity epidemic first began. In contrast, the relative price of processed foods has gone down by about 40 percent. So if you only have a limited amount of money, you are going to spend it on the cheapest calories you can get."[46]

Imperial worker Annette Zimmerman knew just what Nestle was talking about. Every once in a while, she explained, she would stop by a small grocery in Hamlet run by Mr. Turner because he carried fresh produce and "gave credit." Usually she went for what was cheap. And fruit, she said, "back then cost way more than processed food." With money short, she got chips instead of grapes and fish sticks instead of fresh fish. The kids ate sugary cereal for breakfast and popped something in the microwave for dinner a few nights a week when her arms and wrists hurt too much to cook.[47]

When they qualified for them, Annette Zimmerman and many of her colleagues relied on food stamps to help them feed their families. Yet, in some ways, the Great Society program unintentionally added to the problem of too much of the wrong kinds of calories. Working families received their food stamp allocation once a month, so they tended to buy in bulk, and that meant purchasing long-lasting, often salty, HFCS-infused further-processed foods.[48]

A steady diet of further-processed foods didn't *make* people sick or overweight, but it did make it harder for them to get and stay healthy.

According to the documentary film *A Place at the Table*, three dollars' worth of fruit adds up to 307 calories. That same three dollars can buy as many as 3,767 calories of processed foods. Over time, the utterly rational choice of purchasing more calories for less money left an imprint on people's bodies, especially bodies without time for exercise, access to parks or jogging trails, or jobs an easy walk down a well-maintained sidewalk from their homes. The comparative cost of cheap calories, combined with the nearly addictive qualities of the main ingredients of cheap food—fat, sugar, and salt—explains better than any other factor or set of factors the jump in weight gain in the 1980s in the United States. The cycle started with thinning pay envelopes and the limited choices that this economic fact left for low-paid workers when they thought about their meals and snacks.[49]

Because the dangers in the American diet were linked to income, they were, like so much of life in the United States since the downfall of the New Deal and Fordist pay standards, not evenly distributed. That made low-paid Imperial workers doubly vulnerable at the supermarket and at work. Most, of course, took the highest-paying jobs available to them in Hamlet, and for many that meant working at Imperial and still not having much money to spend on basic necessities. Foremost, a tight budget meant limited food options. According to researchers at the Children's Hospital of Philadelphia (CHOP), "There is a strong relationship between economic status and obesity, especially among women." Poor women, the numbers show, are six times more likely to be obese than are women from middle- and upper-middle-class homes. Children whose parents rely on welfare and low-wage work to get by are particularly vulnerable to both the short-term and the long-term health risks associated with dangerous diets and weight gain.[50]

In post-1970s America, an alarming paradox of plenty came into play. The poorer you were, the more likely you were to suffer from the ill effects of weight gain. That's because dangerous foods fit the tightest time and money budgets. The most vulnerable chose cheap food because they had to. The person who crunched these numbers the hardest was the head of the household, often in poor families a single mom without much education. She stood at the bottom of the nation's wage pyramid. Low pay mixed with conditions at America's supermarkets and restaurants pushed these women and their children into places of food insecurity. It also left them vulnerable to new forms of discrimination. Studies have shown that people seen as heavy are often passed over for better jobs and housing opportunities, leaving them stuck in a cycle of poverty and impoverished food choices.[51]

Despite working in a dangerous environment and living in a dangerous foodscape, Imperial workers rarely made enough to afford their own health care coverage. The costs and consequences of poultry capitalism got passed on to local teachers tasked with handling inattentive students, to parents dealings with their children's asthma and joint problems, to health care workers with nothing left in their budgets trying to help their clients cope with weight gain, to everyone, it seems, except for the companies behind the system of cheap. Imperial and Cagle's didn't pay for the outcomes of their choices. They didn't clean up the environmental messes caused by the pools of urine and piles of feces left standing on the land and leaking into water systems, messes produced by animal factories contracted to them. They didn't compensate homeowners who watched the values of their properties plummet when one of their animal factories opened down the road and released noxious fumes into the country air. Imperial workers, too, paid with their broken bodies. They didn't get much in the way of compensation from the company when they pulled a muscle in their backs or tweaked their wrists. When line ladies complained, foremen and supervisors told them that they had a mild form of arthritis or some other injury caused by gardening or sewing away from the job, not an ailment associated with repetitive motions at work. In the end, it didn't cost the company one extra penny when workers quit because they couldn't move their hands and went on public assistance. When that happened, it was the taxpayers (and to a certain extent, workers themselves) who absorbed the costs of cheap further-processed chicken.

Neither Imperial nor Cagle's kicked in to help offset the costs of obesity either. No fast food company in the 1990s paid a premium or social tax for making poorly labeled food like substances, things like chicken tenders and fried apple pies, that made people susceptible to weight gain. The government, in turn, underwrote the costs for companies like Imperial, Cagle's, and McDonald's with road building, low-interest loans to growers to expand their animal factories, agricultural research, and corn and soy subsidies. With its tuition support and grants to poultry science programs, it helped to pay for product development for big chicken companies and high-energy feeds for chicken consolidators. With more government aid, food companies like Monsanto and Kraft, Imperial and Cagle's, turned the cheap goods around them into dangerous calories. Yet they weren't taxed or penalized for doing this. In fact, the only regulations anyone came up with, and these were proposed years after the fire, were to tax Happy Meals and bottled soda. However, many of the same people who accepted seat-belt mandates and helmet laws dismissed these measures as the unnecessary overreaching of an obtrusive nanny state. All the while, the United States government refused to underwrite the distribution of healthier, locally made foods. This absence of support, in turn, made these foods seem to cost more in the supermarket than corn-based products and other mass-produced, highly processed food-like goods that benefited from subsidies and the blind eyes turned toward both the environment and worker safety.

At the same time, the most vulnerable—those on public assistance, the working poor, and especially single moms with kids—didn't have adequate health care coverage. They put off seeing a doctor or used the emergency room for well-care and advice about a cold or allergies or asthma or diabetes. Of course, this was, in the long run, the most expensive way to take care of themselves and their children. But what choice did they have? Adding insult to injury, right there in the hospital, even at a place like the Children's Hospital of Philadelphia, an institution that documented the dangerous spread of weight gain and its class-based implications on its web page, there was, for years, a McDonald's selling all kinds of risk behind the welcoming face of Ronald McDonald.[52]

Imperial workers and their bodies were locked into this system of false choices. They got paid little and had few realistic options for supporting themselves and their families. That, in turn, limited their food choices and essentially doomed them to consume the generic foods they made at work, or foods just like them in terms of price and empty calories. Eating tenders, fries, and soda for lunch and dinner put them at risk and made them and their bodies appear costly to congressmen and commentators newly alarmed, beginning in the 1980s, over the high costs of the so-called obesity epidemic. The madness of the system made them and their bodies look like a problem, a momentous financial burden that threatened the republic and its more disciplined citizens. It made them seem like they had made an endless series of bad choices. But really, they had been rational consumers. Choice, in the sense of what to eat, was a luxury that they didn't really have. They ate cheap foods because they had to on the wages they made, even if the consequences proved dangerous and costly. No real alternative existed, not with the government operating most often in the interests of business and trying to drum up jobs and tax revenues by underwriting the entire system of cheap and dangerous food.[53]

"It's the reverse of industrial development," Bob Hall of the Institute of Southern Studies commented years later when thinking about the fire at Imperial. In the 1980s, places like Hamlet, with its boarded-up businesses along Main Street, cheered when a company like Imperial came to town. They called men like Emmett Roe job creators. But the jobs they offered and products they sold took healthy people and turned them into physical wrecks. Scores of sturdy women and men raised on peach farms and cotton patches building fences and picking crops in the hot sun broke down after a year or two on the chicken-processing line. Many were bloated and bruised. Some ended up disabled and unemployed at a cost to everyone, it seemed, except for the companies that were supposed to be doing the industrial development. Busy moms fed the cheap foods they made at work to their kids for dinner and got them hooked on the taste and short-term high of heavy doses of fat, sugar, and salt. And they fed them the same things the next day and the day after that, until their bodies and their families' bodies appeared, just by looking at them, as part of the problem.[54]

6

DEREGULATION

Reporters flocked to Hamlet after the fire. Journalists tracked down survivors on the street and knocked on the doors of grieving spouses, aunts, uncles, and friends. They camped outside of the fire station just off Main Street waiting to ask Chief David Fuller about sprinklers, locked doors, and the absence of lighted exits with panic bars in the plant. Journalists from all over the state and country crowded into City Hall news conferences, peppering Mayor Abbie Covington with questions about the factory, the Roes, and the town. Photographers snapped pictures of orphaned children riding their bikes back and forth in front of the crumbled plant. Television crews interviewed grief-stricken parents and snuck into church memorial services. They filmed workers as they picked up their last paychecks and spouses as they gathered up the belongings left behind by wives and husbands who perished in the fire.

Back in the newsrooms in Raleigh and Charlotte, Baltimore and New York, journalists dug into Emmett Roe's past and learned about the company's shaky finances and mounting debts. They researched the explosive growth of southern poultry capitalism, and they looked closely at the Occupational Safety and Health Administration in North Carolina. They quickly discovered that even though federally run branches of the agency had scrutinized Roe's Pennsylvania operations, and even though the Imperial plant had caught fire three times between 1980 and 1987, no safety inspector had ever stepped foot inside the factory. But that wasn't the biggest surprise. With a bit more digging, the journalists found out that North Carolina, and its state-operated OSHA program, had the lowest ratio of factory inspectors to workplaces in the entire county. With the number of safety officials it had on the job in 1991, each of the state's 180,000 factories, eateries, and mills could expect a random inspection of its facilities once every seventy-five years.[1]

Businesspeople knew all about North Carolina's limited enforcement of workplace safety. It had been no secret when Emmett Roe moved to the state in the 1980s, and it was no secret in the summer of 1991. Government officials knew as well. Six months before the fire, the federal Department of Labor criticized North Carolina's worker safety program, saying that the state jeopardized the health and well-being of tens of thousands of working people by not inspecting enough workplaces or unearthing enough serious violations in its factories and plants. The report sat on the desks of bureaucrats in Washington and Raleigh, and nothing was done about its troubling observations.[2]

"Now," NBC reporter Robert Hager gravely pronounced on the network's nightly newscast on September 4, 1991, "it's too late."[3]

Hager expected more from OSHA and more from the government. He expected it to protect Hamlet workers, but by 1991, the ethos of cheap, the push to reverse Fordism, and the faith in business as the answer to the nation's economic woes had worn thin the law's protective shield and most people's belief that it could help them.

Richard Nixon signed the Occupational Safety and Health Administration Act (OSHA) into law in 1970 over stern objections from the Chamber of Commerce and other business concerns. For decades before, American courts generally did not hold employers accountable for the safety of their workers. The burden fell, instead, on the workers themselves. Legal precedents established that once a person accepted a job, she or he accepted the stated, and often unstated, risks of the position. OSHA, however, promised an expansion of the social contract. "So far as possible," the law read, "every working man and woman in the nation [shall have] safe and healthful working conditions . . . free from recognized hazards that are causing or likely to cause death or serious physical harm." To back up the pledge, the law granted the United States secretary of labor broad powers to conduct unannounced inspections of private workplaces with more than eleven employees, formulate necessary regulations to ensure safety, require employers to keep detailed on-site logs of work-related injuries and illnesses, and issue citations and impose and publicize civil penalties for serious violations.[4]

I.W. Abel, the president of the United Food and Commercial Workers Union, called OSHA a "giant step forward."[5] He compared the law to the Wagner Act, the landmark legislation signed into law by President Franklin Roosevelt in 1935 that protected the rights of workers to strike, organize, and collectively bargain. But OSHA did more than give workers new rights; it seemed to require new responsibilities for employers, obligating them to reduce the risks of illness and injury on the job regardless of the cost. In addition, it gave the Department of Labor the power to make sure that employers complied. OSHA, wrote the presidential historian H.W. Brands, summing up the potential impact of the law, "put . . . the federal government's nose into the offices of nearly every employer in the country."[6]

Few American politicians were more calculating than Richard Nixon was. At first glance, OSHA looked like an impressive extension of the New Deal and a noteworthy case of a Republican bolstering the regulatory state and expanding the powers of the federal government. To be sure, Nixon never belonged to the staunchly anti–New Deal wing of his party. He didn't shy away from government solutions to problems, nor did he consistently deliver long speeches on the virtues of the free market. But Nixon never stopped scheming or adding up votes, and he never thought an election was in the bag, even when he held double-digit leads in the polls. In the early 1970s, as he got ready for his re-election run in 1972, Nixon wanted the support of the growing Goldwater wing of his party. He wanted them to think he was one of them. Looking to connect with the burgeoning conservative movements stirring within the GOP across the country, the president talked about the need to restore authority to the states. He called his plan New Federalism and promised to direct money and power away from the federal bureaucracy and "back" to states, counties, and municipalities. The plan struck a chord with traditionalists, especially hardline segregationists in the South—another group close to Goldwater that Nixon wanted to bring into his fold—clinging to notions of states' rights in the face of civil rights gains and the movement of African Americans into the Democratic Party.

A key section of the original OSHA law embodied Nixon's New

Federalist promise. Under this provision, individual states were allowed to form their own state-run worker safety agencies. While these agencies were supposed to uphold federal standards, they remained in the hands of state officials, who could stipulate their own fines and punishments.[7] A few states, like California, opted to do more for their workers than the federally mandated plan called for, so they set up their own state-managed workplace safety agencies. Most states that adopted the state-run plans, like North Carolina and its southern neighbors, set up their programs to do less for laborers. Less, they were convinced, would keep them competitive in the never-ending industrial sweepstakes and allow them to lure factory owners, like Emmett Roe, dogged by federally employed OSHA regulators in Pennsylvania, to their borders. The New Federalist sections of the OSHA law explain, in part, how North Carolina slipped to last in the country in its ratio of safety inspectors to workplaces by 1991 without penalty and how this lapse would, in turn, put pressure on other states to cut safety corners so they could lure new businesses to their towns and cities in yet another rotation of the cycle of cheap.

In the 1972 campaign, Nixon wasn't only pursuing the votes of Goldwaterites and southern state's rights advocates. He had an even larger ambition. He wanted to pull white workers, union men in hard hats and steel-toed boots—the same men captured in famous photographs using flags to battle against anti-Vietnam protesters in New York City—away from the Democratic Party. He began courting them in 1968 with promises of law and order and opposition to "forced" busing. OSHA represented another part of that pursuit, a political gift to laborers. But Nixon's appeal to construction workers and plumbers proved, probably not surprisingly, to be more show than substance.

From the very start, OSHA never got the funding it needed, so it never became a vigorous regulatory presence on the shop floor. It remained vulnerable to budget cuts and the political whims and attacks from business interests and supporters of cheap government. But, at the same time, it did serve as a promise—a promise of government-guaranteed workplace safety, and many in labor circles after 1970 went about holding employers and state and federal agencies to the letter of the law.

————

Germans call the rules and careful balance between abiding by the law and punishment for transgressions *ordnung*, or order. For OSHA to work, it needed *ordnung*, the same kind of *ordnung* that allowed for the smooth operation of German subways, buses, and trams. There are no ticket takers, tokens, or swipe cards on Berlin, Munich, or Frankfurt public transportation. Yet, because inspections are random and unannounced, most adult customers pay to ride from one part of a city to another. If officials catch someone without a ticket, they remove him or her from the train, sometimes in full view of others. Usually, they issue warnings when they nab a non-paying passenger the first, and even the second, time. After that, it becomes a criminal offense. Violators can end up in court and face stiff fines and, in extreme cases, prison sentences. Even more crucially, most Germans acknowledge the value of their transport networks. They understand the need to comply, pay their fares, and help to underwrite the system as a contribution to the larger public good.

Unannounced inspections maintain order by keeping would-be slackers on their toes and playing by the rules. The same idea underscored OSHA. Inspections would determine whether OSHA really did stick the government's nose into business operations and decision making. For the law to work, inspectors had to be on the front lines. There had to be enough of them, and they had to threaten employers with enough surprise visits so that managers and bosses didn't know when they were coming. When they did come, they had to have the authority to punish lawbreakers with stinging fines and even jail sentences.

Across the country in 1991, however, OSHA employed a mere 1,300 inspectors for 7 million workplaces. That translated into one inspector for every 4,666 job sites. If every safety official knocked on the door of one business every day, it would take him twenty years to visit every supermarket, slaughterhouse, machine shop, and factory in his portfolio. In North Carolina, as the NBC journalist Robert Hager and others learned after the fire, the ratio of industrial sites to inspectors was three and half times the national average. That told Emmett and Brad Roe and other businesspeople in the state that the system posed only the faintest threat to their prerogatives to run their factories any way they saw fit.[8]

When OSHA officials did issue a fine, it didn't cost employers much, in monetary terms, inconvenience, or social standing. Nationally for the period from 1972 to 1990, the median fine collected in accidents that killed or injured workers on the job was less than $500. The original law that allowed states to establish their own OSHA operations also allowed them to set their own penalties. That's why, over the same time span, the median fine in 470 cases investigated in North Carolina was $395, the eleventh lowest in the country. By contrast, in Pennsylvania, where Imperial operated for much of the 1970s, the median fine reached $640. But even that didn't amount to much more than a rap on the knuckles for firms that ordered steel by the ton and chicken parts by the truckload.[9]

Worst of all for worker safety, OSHA suffered from the start from a case of bad economic and ideological timing. President Nixon rolled out the program in the waning days of the American Century as the United States economy ended two and half decades of robust and broadly shared growth. No one, not even the experts, saw the end coming. In fact, most mainstream economists and policy makers said what happened couldn't happen. "Prevailing Keynesian economic thinking," writes the historian Michael Stewart Foley, "suggested that unemployment and inflation would never rise simultaneously, but in the early 1970s they did, and a new phenomenon—'stagflation'—appeared."[10] The impact was immediate. Foreign competition jumped. Companies cut wages, laid off workers, and shut down hulking and aging industrial plants, especially in union strongholds. At the same time, the price of goods, led, of course, by oil and gasoline, rose steadily and kept rising faster than most people's by then sluggish wages. After accounting for inflation and taking out taxes, in July 1981 the average American had 9.7 percent less to spend than a decade earlier.[11]

Presidents Nixon, Ford, and Carter promised to curb inflation and restore well-paying jobs and lost income. For a time, each pursued a variation on the theme of New Deal–inspired spending solutions, mostly wage supports and price controls. Nothing seemed to work. Business profits kept falling. Tax revenues waned. Inflation and unemployment remained alarmingly high. The failure to push wages and employment rates back up to their postwar levels made cheap consumer goods and foodstuffs, and the ideas behind a reversal of Fordism, more valuable, appealing, and necessary than ever before. But, even more, the persistence of economic uncertainty opened the door for new ideas about the scope of government activity and the basic social contract.[12]

The inability of presidents and lawmakers to quickly reverse the course of stagflation eroded faith in government as a credible problem solver, a faith that had already been rattled by the lies of Vietnam and the deceptions of Watergate. As more and more Americans faced reduced wages and surging inflation, Republicans and moderate Democrats started to listen to traditional conservative critiques of New Deal thinking and deficit spending. Struggling to keep small businesses going and make mortgage payments, many became increasingly receptive to the notion that government wasn't the best or only solution to pressing social and economic problems and might, in fact, be part of the problem, and that raising aggregate consumer demand wasn't the answer, but cutting costs and taxes (their taxes) might be. Many became convinced that the government no longer facilitated growth but rather held back the economy by taking too much out of the paychecks of hardworking people and putting it into the wrong hands. More business, less regulation, and fewer unions, they started to think, could decrease prices, create more jobs, and cure the country's economic ills. "This argument," explains the historian Rick Perlstein, "was precisely the opposite of Keynesianism," which is that higher wages and more government protections benefited everyone. It wasn't just businesspeople or policy wonks at conservative think tanks in California or free market economists at the University of Chicago who were thinking this way. Throughout the mid-1970s, store owners, small manufacturers, farmers, and independent truck drivers came to similar conclusions on their own, even before they heard Jimmy Carter and Ronald Reagan groan about red tape, union bosses, runaway inflation, and government interference.[13]

Because of its direct costs to employers and its role in workplaces across the country, OSHA turned out to be critical in changing the minds of many Americans about the larger issues of regulation and government involvement in the economy. "Over the decade of the 1970s, OSHA, along with the EPA—Environmental Protection Agency, which was also signed into law by Nixon during his first term in office—came to symbolize the evils of big government," James Smith, an official with the United

Steelworkers of America, told a reporter in 1981. "This, in turn," he contended, "made the agency a prime target for the regulatory reform that will somehow make our country great again."[14] As early as 1972, an official from the National Association of Manufacturers complained about OSHA's "massive regulations." "It impinges," he contended, "on almost every aspect of day to day operations of business to a greater extent probably than any other law on the statute books." The conservative publication *Human Events* labeled it "the chief federal harassment agency," claiming that its rules made it nearly impossible for small businesses to function and hire new workers. OSHA has become, a Harvard economist remarked, "perhaps the most prominent symbol of mis-guided regulation." The costs of OSHA, maintained a New York City consultant, added up to "about 10% of our income." "It is about time," he concluded, "that the fool regulations and meddling by government should stop."[15]

From the start, corporate interests had opposed OSHA. But new resistance stirred by the latter half of the 1970s and into the 1980s. According to the historian of "the businessmen's crusade against the New Deal," Kim Phillips-Fein, the mounting opposition to OSHA represented "a first step in a broader campaign to challenge the system of government regulations." Pushing back against the agency turned scores of middle-class Americans, and not just employers, into converts to the idea that a pro-business government could grow the economy, create new jobs, and keep prices down for everyone, and that this represented a better course of action than extending the New Deal or the Great Society. Increasingly, OSHA's opponents defined worker safety not as a right, as labor leaders had tried to make it since the 1960s, but as a factor in a cost-benefit equation that had to be balanced against the freedom of the market and its ability to deliver cheap goods, ample jobs, and steady profits. If a regulation absorbed business profits, by this way of thinking, it needed to come off the books because the most essential role of government was to clear the path for economic growth, not to create social security or protect ordinary Americans. Business became, in a sense, the new voice of the public interest, but in its 1970s incarnation it no longer stressed the relatively high wages that it paid to workers. Instead, it highlighted the bargains it provided to shoppers. In this way of thinking, OSHA became an enemy not just to industry, but to everyone concerned with kick-starting economic growth and providing consumers with cheap essential goods.[16]

The pushback against OSHA came just as the American labor movement began its long, slow retreat in the South and everywhere else in the country. Union membership in the United States peaked in the 1950s at 35 percent of nonagricultural workers and then held steady at around 30 percent for the next two decades. In 1971, unions represented 27 percent of the nation's workers. The collapse of manufacturing, rising competition, and the expanding geography of cheap—where companies relocated to out-of-the-way places like Hamlet with swelling pools of labor and limited employment options—cut deep into the American trade union movement. At the same time, inflation jarred mainstream social thinking. For much of the postwar period, unions and the burgeoning middle class stood together in favor of higher wages. But the government's inability to control inflation led shop owners and office workers to adopt new ways of thinking. Many started to blame unions for the sharp rise in prices, which was fueled, they argued, by bloated paychecks for blue-collar workers along with generous pensions and health benefits. As most people pointed to unions as a problem, they started to look to business to address the nation's economic challenges.[17]

As business got assigned the role of the nation's chief economic engine and therefore a force for social good, organized labor got framed as a special interest. Ronald Reagan, the former president of the Screen Actors Guild, hammered the point home in his first days in office. When the country's air traffic controllers defied a court order and went out on strike protesting low wages and unsafe working conditions, he fired them, telling the media, "There is no right to strike against the public safety by anybody, anywhere, at any time."[18] From that moment on, labor fell back on its heels, increasingly unable to check the ideological surge in favor of less government and lower prices that eroded support for decent pay and worker safety. By 1991, unions represented only 15 percent of the nation's workforce. Only a fraction of that number of laborers were in the South and West, where industries rushed to relocate in the postwar years and take advantage of access to cheaper labor and cheaper raw materials.[19]

Weaker unions meant a weaker voice for labor on the shop floor and in the public debate over wages, regulations, and worker safety.

Middle-class North Carolinians joined the grassroots pushback against OSHA, unions, and the larger commitment to a government-built and -maintained safety net. Rocky Mount businessman Michael Amstray complained in the mid-1970s about OSHA's "Gestapo powers." He asked Governor James Hunt, the state's leading pro-business Democrat, to abolish the regulatory agency and bring an end to its "ineffective and unnecessary reign." A cardboard box manufacturer from a nearby town called OSHA "nit picking and counter-productive." Stephen Vickery of Morehead City added that OSHA and its fines threatened to put his feed mill out of business and his employees out of work, making them a drain on the local economy. That put him squarely on the side of deregulation, the same side as James Larkee, an Arden resident who called OSHA "a direct violation of the constitution" that placed "unreasonable financial burdens on the business and industry of our country." [20]

Charlotte lawyer and Republican Party activist Hugh Joseph Beard Jr. described OSHA as "the capricious power of a runaway, oppressive bureaucracy" that "victimized" business owners and their employees. Endless paperwork and rough interrogations, he said, turned mill owners and shopkeepers into "second class citizens." Vowing to fight for the "individual freedom and liberty" of those oppressed groups, in 1978, Beard initiated litigation challenging the North Carolina OSHA law. He told supporters that the agency's "unwarranted inspections" violated the rights of employers and constituted "unlawful government activity." [21]

As Beard built his case against North Carolina OSHA, he reached out to leaders of the American Conservative Union (ACU). A year before the Charlotte lawyer went to court, the ACU had launched a larger national Stop-OSHA campaign. Railing against the agency's "overweening power," the conservative umbrella organization founded in 1964 by William F. Buckley and dedicated to the principles of personal responsibility, a strong national defense, and the idea that "capitalism is the only economic system of our time that is compatible with political liberty" sought to "abolish OSHA or dramatically overhaul it." Searching for recruits for its deregulatory counter-insurgency, the ACU assembled a list of business owners fined by OSHA, addressing its letters to them, "Dear Victim of OSHA." [22]

As a stopgap strategy until it managed to get the law off the books, the ACU published a pamphlet, advising employers on what to do "When OSHA Knocks at Your Door." Emmett Roe seemed to have followed the conservative group's advice in Moosic in the 1980s. The ACU urged business owners to stop OSHA inspectors from entering their plants without a warrant. While the inspector went to court to get the proper documents, the company could quickly address any possible safety violations. Once the inspectors got inside in the building, the ACU advised non-cooperation and foot-dragging. "It is important to remember," the group reminded supporters, "that the smallest victory may provide the key that finally puts an end to the bureaucratic nightmare that OSHA has brought on this country."[23]

It didn't take long for politicians from both parties to pick up on the grassroots rumblings about OSHA. Still, historians of recent America almost always depict Ronald Reagan's election in 1980 as a breaking point with the New Deal regulatory past. No doubt this makes schematic sense, but the insistence on critical elections like 1980 and on sharp turning points obscures some key continuities from the American past, like Jimmy Carter's mixed message on workplace safety, government regulation, and the broader social contract.

On the campaign trail in 1976, the Georgia peanut farmer talked about increasing the minimum wage and strengthening OSHA.[24] He hit at his Republican opponent, President Gerald Ford, for adopting "only three new sets of [safety] standards" while in office. He hinted that Ford had watered down health and safety protections in exchange for hefty donations from large corporations. Carter promised, in contrast, to guarantee "each and every American the right to a safe and healthy place of work." "Our occupational and safety efforts," he pledged, "must continue until our working citizens are safe in their jobs."[25]

Once he entered the White House, Carter followed through on several of his pro-labor promises. He appointed Dr. Eula Bingham, a University of Cincinnati professor of environmental health, to run federal OSHA. Although she had never belonged to a union or worked for one, Bingham brought to the post a long record of support for government action to create safer workplaces. Her academic research focused on the deleterious effects of pollution and chemical carcinogens on the environment and on laborers and dovetailed with her advocacy. Leading up to her appointment as the OSHA head, she served on a number of government commissions and safety boards, including as a scientific and policy advisor for the National Institute for Occupational Safety and Health from 1972 to 1976.

During her term at OSHA's helm, Bingham set new workplace standards, guaranteeing workers' "right to know" about exposure to lead, arsenic, cotton dust, and other dangerous substances. Under her leadership, OSHA inspected more establishments and levied more fines than the previous administration had. In addition, it referred twenty-eight cases to the Justice Department for criminal action.[26] Early in her tenure, she took a shot at Nixon's concept of New Federalism and asserted the power of the national government. She reminded the state OSHAs, like North Carolina's—"not very politely," according to one source—that federal OSHA and federal standards remained preeminent.[27] Mark Schultz, who headed a North Carolina–based worker safety group, called Bingham "a real health and safety advocate."[28]

Yet only months into his administration, plagued by inflation and a sharp downward slide in his approval ratings, Carter and his aides started to chip away at OSHA, increasingly letting the marketplace rather than health mandates determine safety standards. In 1978, the President's Council on Wage and Price Stability called on OSHA to reevaluate its methods of dealing with noise in the workplace and search for the most cost-effective, though not necessarily the healthiest, solutions. The acting director of the council, William Lilley, stated: "While the Council certainly supports the goal of improved worker health, it is important that any regulation . . . be noninflationary by designing them to be as efficient and as effective as possible." He continued, "The council is very concerned that these regulations, by dictating the method companies must use to protect workers and by mandating uniform standards and solutions on every company in every part of the country, will necessarily impose costs on the economy which far exceed the benefits which might result."[29] Carter's leading economic advisors repeatedly counseled him to do something about OSHA specifically, calling it "the leading national symbol of overregulation." "To not act decisively," they insisted, "would be perceived outside the labor movement as a retreat from your commitment to major regulatory reform . . . [and] your anti-inflation program."[30]

"It is a major goal of my administration," Carter declared midway through his presidency, "to free the American people from the burden of over-regulation."[31] Reflecting the growing faith in cheap in Washington, the president's anti-inflation program pointed right at OSHA, saying it needed to "seek to minimize . . . costs." Regulations, it further contended, must "achieve their goals at the lowest possible cost."[32] In a sign of how quickly the center of gravity had shifted away from New Deal thinking about the utility of higher wagers to trigger greater demand toward the idea of providing cheap goods as a solution to declining incomes, Carter spoke during the 1980 election of deregulation as one of his "greatest achievements." "We believe," he said on the campaign trail, anticipating Ronald Reagan's first inaugural address and promoting the presumed social value of cheap, "we ought to get the Government's nose out of the private enterprise of this country . . . so that the customers get a better deal and the business community gets a better deal as well."[33]

Unlike his predecessor, Ronald Reagan didn't send any mixed signals when it came to OSHA or deregulation or the virtues of low prices and the power of the market to fix economic problems. In 1976, the Californian told the television news magazine *60 Minutes*, "Right now business is regulated in America by government more than it is in any other country in the world." In the very next breath, he quipped that OSHA seemed determined to "make a worker completely safe by taking away his job."[34] Campaigning against Carter four years later, he promised to "review . . . thousands and thousands of regulations," eliminating all that were unnecessary and burdensome "to the shopkeepers and the farmers . . . as well as to business and industry." OSHA ranked at the top of Reagan's hit list of "meddlesome" agencies. Without saying a word about the need for workplace safety, he repeatedly complained that OSHA harassed employers with costly inspections and cumbersome regulations. At one point in 1980, he "seriously questioned" the need for OSHA. In another speech, he advocated sending OSHA, in its entirety, back to the states to administer. Though he never mentioned specifics, Reagan made it clear that he thought worker safety rules did more harm than good by "shackl[ing] the economy."[35]

After defeating Jimmy Carter, Ronald Reagan attacked government regulations, in the words of the *New York Times*, with a "meat cleaver."[36]

In his inaugural address, he promised to curb the federal bureaucracy and stressed the market as the surest remedy to the country's economic ills. Within days, he appointed his vice president, George H.W. Bush, to head the carefully named Task Force on Regulatory Relief.[37] He tagged devoted deregulators to head key regulatory agencies. Reagan put Mark Fuller, a leading free market advocate, in charge of the Federal Communications Commission. James Watt, the president's choice to oversee the Environmental Protection Agency, pledged to tear down any obstacles in the way of economic growth, promising supporters that under his watch the country would "mine more, drill more, [and] cut more timber."[38]

The Reagan administration brought the same approach to OSHA. The president named Raymond Donovan, a New Jersey construction executive, to head the Department of Labor. In the years leading up to his appointment, OSHA had cited Donovan's firm for code violations 138 times. Inspectors classified fifty-eight of these infractions as "serious," which according to OSHA's definition meant there was "a substantial probability that death or serious physical harm could result." Further setting the tone, in 1981 the administration's deputy assistant secretary of labor argued that "in recent years OSHA has brought to a new height the adversarial relationship between government and business." "OSHA has performed as a policeman in the past," he commented, pledging a more cooperative relationship with business that would, in turn, allow the economy to grow, create jobs, and deliver cheap goods to consumers.[39]

To run OSHA itself, Reagan appointed another construction industry executive, Thorne G. Auchter. The first director of the workplace safety agency to come from the ranks of business, the thirty-five-year-old Jacksonville, Florida, resident occupied the vice president's office of his family-owned business, the Auchter Company, one of Florida's largest commercial, institutional, and industrial construction companies. In 1980, the firm held over $100 million in contracts. Civic-minded, in a business sort of way, Auchter served on the board of directors of the Northeast Florida Association of General Contractors and as the vice chairman of the Jacksonville Economic Development Council. He brought with him to his new post not just connections but also, like Donovan, a wealth of experience with OSHA. In the eight years prior to his selection, government regulators had inspected his company's work sites fourteen times, charging it with six serious violations and forty-two lesser ones, for a total of $1,200 in penalties. Auchter's background and experience with OSHA, *Industry Week* reported, had "some in business . . . smiling while labor was frowning." *Newsweek* called the businessman-turned-government-official a "front-line soldier in . . . the war on deregulation."[40]

During his stint in government, Auchter promised to battle against what he called OSHA's longstanding "bias" against business, replacing it with what he described as a more neutral stance. Within days of taking charge, the construction executive, who had handled special events for Reagan's 1980 Florida campaign, made it clear what he meant by an even-handed approach when he recalled half a million dollars' worth of OSHA-produced brochures on the hazards of brown lung—a crippling respiratory disease triggered by breathing cotton dust that could be prevented by the installation into the mills of expensive filtration equipment. He labeled the training manuals "offensive" and "obviously favorable" to labor, even though he admitted to one reporter that he hadn't read them very closely. His gripe seemed to be with the cover, which pictured a thin and weary-faced worker and evoked the political aesthetics of Farm Security Administration photographs from the Great Depression era. According to Auchter, the image generated pro-labor sentiments. Eventually, the booklet found its way back into circulation without the front page. The repackaging cost the Department of Labor $15,000. It also cost it a number of seasoned employees. Within a couple of months of what labor leaders called Auchter's "book burning," a California factory inspector quit his job, saying he "couldn't function in that type of environment."[41]

Following Reagan's as well as Carter's leads, Auchter ordered the implementation of cost-benefit analysis as the key criteria for workplace safety measures. Under this scheme, regulations had to show that their benefits didn't just protect workers but also were worth it, that the costs did not pose a threat to ongoing profits. If there was a cheaper way to fix a safety problem, like disposable masks in dusty factories rather than expensive ventilators or earplugs in noisy machine shops as opposed to putting up sound-deafening enclosures, then that was the director's first choice.[42]

There was another aspect to Auchter's "neutral" approach: business interests came first. He believed only business could solve the nation's economic problems. Mirroring the thinking of Jim Hunt and other North

Carolina business progressives, he thought that the government's role was to make that happen and then get out of the way.

During Auchter's OSHA tenure, he told the United States Chamber of Commerce and the National Association of Manufacturers that he preferred voluntary compliance over federally mandated regulations. He wanted industry to monitor itself. This would cost less and work better. If business regulated itself, down the line, perhaps, there would be no need for OSHA. The quicker this happened, the better, Auchter seemed to think. Perhaps this explains why he stood by without raising his voice while Congress repeatedly cut his agency's budget. During his stint in Washington, federal support for OSHA, adjusted for inflation, fell by 39.1 percent. Staff positions and the number of field inspectors were cut, even as the number of factories, often in out-of-the-way and difficult to regulate places, rose across the country. With its stripped-down personnel, OSHA responded promptly only to "imminent danger" complaints—those likely to cause immediate death or injury. OSHA no longer automatically inspected a plant accused by workers of committing safety or health violations. Instead, it sent the employer a letter, like it would to Imperial in 1987, and waited for a response. Follow-up inspections fell by 82 percent. Between 1980 and 1984, "serious" citations issued by the agency dropped by 50 percent, the total dollar amount of fines plunged by 80 percent, and the average penalty paid per violation declined as well.[43] During this same period, the number of fatalities in American workplaces dipped, in part because of the larger economic restructuring going on and the disappearance of so many jobs in construction, railroads, and heavy manufacturing. But during these same years of the Auchter reign, the number of injuries and lost workdays for all laborers increased, suggesting a deterioration in overall workplace safety.[44]

Workers and their battered unions sensed the changes. Between 1980 and 1982, inspections initiated by complaints from employees fell by 58 percent. Women and men on the shop floor felt the weight of the government's silence and feared losing a job in a contracting economy, so they kept quiet.

But union leaders, staunch liberals, and health and safety advocates did not keep quiet about Auchter and his business-first regime. "The Reagan Administration," charged the leaders of AFL-CIO, "has substituted dollar costs for human values in the administration of occupational safety and health laws. No longer is the safety and health of workers the prime concern, but rather the protection of management from being requested to shoulder its obligations to provide a safe and healthful workplace for America's working men and women."[45] Ralph Nader charged Auchter with "shackling" OSHA. His ally, Philip J. Simon of the Center for the Study of Responsive Law, felt like a witness to the "unraveling of the health and safety net." Others accused Auchter of avoiding a full-on frontal assault on OSHA that surely would have stirred organized labor's ire, opting instead for a quieter plan of a "thousand cuts," each compromising just a little bit more the safety of workers. Alarmed by the changes, Auchter's predecessor, Eula Bingham, complained in 1981, "The trend is to stop protecting workers and let the free marketplace determine safety standards. I thought the country decided 10 years ago (with OSHA's establishment) that that doesn't work."[46]

The attacks on Auchter were, nonetheless, slightly misplaced. It wasn't that they were wrong about him or his faith in cheap, free market solutions, but they exaggerated the commitment to worker safety in the initial law and even under the Carter administration. Still, they captured Reagan and his allies' hostility toward OSHA. Perhaps most important, they sensed that the cuts combined with the public attacks on the regulatory state emboldened employers, encouraging them to see workplace safety as a negotiable item, as a luxury of prosperity and steady profitability, but little more than an afterthought in an age of inflation and rising competition.[47]

The OSHA budget cuts at the national level seeped down to North Carolina. In part, this reflected changing federal budget priorities. But, at the same time, the emerging consensus taking shape in Washington around having less government was also happening in Raleigh. North Carolina Democrats and Republicans joined the crusade to reduce taxes and pare down the spending in all areas except for roads, prison and school construction, and industrial recruitment.[48] The rat-a-tat of fire against regulation and against OSHA delegitimized the notion of worker safety as a right and made it difficult to defend it against the zeal for budget cuts. It turned advocates of safe factories into special interests—selfish, privileged voices who placed parochial concerns ahead of creating jobs and lifting the country and the state out of their inflation-blasted financial hole. This was already the long-held position of North Carolina's business progressives in both parties. For decades, they had focused on jobs ahead of wages and deemed industrial recruitment a competitive sport, a way to top the North in something other than football or basketball. They never intended for worker safety to get in the way. By the mid-1980s, they didn't have to, not any more than some of the state's best college teams had to worry about NCAA sanctions in those days when recruiting a star quarterback or point guard often involved an envelope stuffed with cash or the keys to a brand-new car.

When the fire broke out in Hamlet, John Brooks headed the state's Department of Labor. By then, he had held this elected office since 1977. In fact, Brooks was, at the time, the longest-serving labor commissioner in the state's history. Despite his success at the ballot box, Brooks didn't fit the mold of a typical North Carolina politician. He wasn't a banker in a Brooks Brothers suit with a buttery accent and country club connections or a small-town lawyer with a disarming and stunning recall of the articles of the Constitution. He wasn't quick to quote the Bible or reel off the results from the latest NASCAR race at Wilkesboro or Rockingham. He wasn't a backslapper or one of those guys who held court at a Raleigh hotel bar when the legislature was in session. His critics thought of him as tireless yet abrasive and often tone-deaf. A graduate of the University of Chicago and former aide to the Democratic governor and one-time presidential candidate Terry Stanford, Brooks wore thick glasses and off-the-rack gray suits, making him look more like a nerdy economics professor than "the bad boy of state politics," as a leading business periodical once dubbed him.[49] He earned this nickname because of his reputation as a quiet pro-labor voice in a steadfastly anti-union state. While in office, Brooks expanded job training, made sure amusement rides and elevators got inspected, and stepped up minimum wage and maximum hour protections. Despite his standing as a friend to workers, Brooks remained a cautious advocate of labor; he never pushed back hard against the state's pro-growth, business political interests, and he never questioned the state-run status of North Carolina OSHA. Even if he had, it probably wouldn't have changed the balance of power very much. That's in part because the commissioner of labor never had a lot of power to begin with or much of a statewide profile. At the same time, Brooks stayed close to the North Carolina consensus on labor and OSHA because he wanted to keep his position, and this was one of those jobs that was, once you had it, relatively easy to hold on to if you didn't rock the boat or get blindsided by tragedy.[50]

At the start of each legislative session in what would become an annual ritual of futility, Brooks called on the governor and leading members of the General Assembly. He asked for more money for the Department of Labor so it could hire additional administrators, statisticians, and inspectors. He wanted more experts in the Raleigh office and more staff in the field. At one point, he pushed for a workplace safety commissioner in each of the state's one hundred counties. He was, as usual, rebuffed. The neglect was starting to take its toll—not so much on Brooks as on the state's workers.[51]

In the decade leading up to the Hamlet fire, the state's inspectorate was on the decline and enforcement was waning. In 1980, North Carolina had 1.9 million workers and forty-seven safety and health inspectors. Ten years later, after adding a record-setting 700,000 new jobs, many of them in dangerous industries like meat packing and small-scale manufacturing, North Carolina had only forty-two inspectors, or just 34 percent of the minimum required by the Department of Labor's relatively lax national standards—not that any federal officials moved to punish the state for its deficient numbers. But even that number didn't tell the whole story. Only twenty-seven or twenty-eight of the state's inspectors were fully qualified to conduct workplace safety inspections. (The others performed health inspections.) That gave the state the worst ratio of inspectors to industrial sites in the entire nation. But it wasn't like North Carolina was opposed in principle to hiring people to oversee various aspects of daily life. In 1991, the state employed 400 agricultural agents to check on its declining farm sector and another 203 wildlife officers to enforce hunting and fishing laws. The point was that the state refused to make a similar investment in workplace safety, no matter how many times Brooks or the head of the state AFL-CIO asked.[52]

With a dwindling OSHA inspectorate, North Carolina workers faced riskier conditions. Between 1983 and 1985, according to data from the North Carolina Occupational Safety and Health Project, laborers in the state were "getting hurt more often" and the "injuries [were] more disabling." During this small window of time, North Carolina experienced a 9 percent increase in the total rate of work-related injuries and illnesses, a 20 percent increase in the rate of lost workdays, and a 20 percent increase in the number of workers injured on the job. Between 1985 and 1986, one out of every fourteen private-sector workers in North Carolina suffered, at some point, from a job-related injury or illness.[53] While injuries rose, surprise inspections, the most effective way to keep employers on their toes and adhering to the law, dropped. In 1989, unannounced factory visits, as opposed to visits scheduled in advance, comprised 69 percent of the total inspections in North Carolina. A year later, that number fell to 54 percent, compared to a national average of 67 percent. A year after that, unannounced inspections dropped to one-third of all inspections in North Carolina.[54]

Even when it did agree to look into a case, the North Carolina Department of Labor acted so slowly, it seemed to be always dragging its feet. By the time of the fire, the agency had a backlog of sixty-one "serious" complaints, all of them waiting for an investigation. Some of the cases dated back as far as 1984. "A large backlog," noted a federal OSHA investigator in the summer of 1991, "is an indication that resources aren't being used efficiently or that more resources are needed." Despite the troubling signs, Washington didn't force North Carolina to spend more to protect its burgeoning workforce.[55]

Commissioner John Brooks tried to force the state's hand. Just months before the fire, he requested $17.5 million from the General Assembly to hire 292 new staffers, including an additional 108 inspectors. The increase would have brought the state in line with federal standards. Governor James Martin, the state's Republican chief executive, dedicated to cutting taxes and continuing to attract new businesses to the state, countered with a recommendation to spend $500,000 to hire thirteen new inspectors. Struggling to deal with a budget shortfall, the legislature, with bipartisan support, rejected both proposals and *cut* five of the Department of Labor's positions while, again, taking almost nothing away from allocations for the highway department or the agency in charge of industrial recruitment.[56]

In the press and in the halls of the General Assembly, Brooks fumed about the cuts. None of his protests, however, won him any new allies.

Maybe because of his brusque manner or because his plans could hurt the state's competitive advantage in luring new firms, Brooks was never a favorite with lawmakers, not even those from his own party. But even as he asked for more funding, he never spent all the monies he had, something he had a difficult time explaining after the fire. In the fourteen years before the Hamlet tragedy, Brooks returned $7 million in unspent funds to federal and state authorities. In 1991, the Department of Labor had five open and unfilled inspector positions, yet it still gave $453,000 in unused money back to Washington.[57] That money could have paid for additional factory visits or moved along the state's backlog of investigations, including a six-month inquiry into carpal tunnel syndrome at a Perdue poultry plant that kept two department agents busy full-time without yielding a decisive ruling one way or the other. Brooks claimed that the state government's low pay scales, another element of cheap, made it tough for him to hire and retain well-trained and qualified inspectors. Critics accused Brooks of micromanaging the agency and dithering when it came to making choices. "There is no one more brilliant in the state," a friend told a reporter. "But sometimes John will sit on his ass until the Nina, the Pinta, and the Santa Maria get back before he'll make a decision."[58]

Maybe if Brooks had acted faster, the agency he ran could have used some of the money it had to purchase new informational posters. The state's OSHA law required employers to hang signs in their plants with the number to call to report safety violations. Three-quarters of the signs in North Carolina in 1991, however, listed a phone number that had been disconnected. When a caller dialed it, she didn't even get a forwarding number.[59]

Imperial workers couldn't even see the wrong number. According to several reports, the plant's time clocks blocked the OSHA sign that someone had once hung up on the wall.[60]

After the fire, Brooks took a lot of heat for his managerial style, but the problems were bigger than him. The system in North Carolina and around the country had its limits, and bending them to accommodate the interests of labor didn't seem like one of the ways that they could go. "Even good, well-intentioned labor laws are no protection," asserted Albert Shanker, the head of the American Federation of Teachers, in an essay in the *New Republic* in 1992, if the government, at both the state and federal levels, won't impose the measures and won't issue fines that cost employers more than the price of a few boxes of frozen chicken tenders. Effective workplace laws can't be self-enforced if employees have no voice. How many workers, desperate to hold on to a job at an out-of-the-way plant in a community with a labor surplus, were willing to pick up a phone to call in a safety violation, especially when the first number they dialed was disconnected? How many knew that the OSHA law even existed when they had never seen an OSHA inspector? The inspectors they did see, like the USDA men, hung out in the office and seemed, in the words of one worker, to be "chummy" with management and they also seemed to be much more interested in the meat and in shooing away flies than workplace safety issues.[61]

When an Imperial worker did approach a USDA official sometime around 1990 to tell him about safety concerns, the meat inspector answered, "I had no jurisdiction over that."[62] Without the government on the ground or a union backing them up, how many workers had the gumption to challenge their employers? Without the threat of a challenge, what held worker safety laws in place? Why would employers, especially financially strapped employers in competitive industries with razor-thin profit margins, abide by the laws and update and maintain their plants when they knew they couldn't get caught? Who wouldn't cut a few corners in the face of mounting economic pressures? Why would employers buck the trend and volunteer to sacrifice profits when the public debate pointed to regulations as the cause of economic stagnation? Who would spend the money needed on safety when politicians sang the praises of business and derided government action?[63]

"An employer doesn't have to be an Einstein," Tony Mazzocchi of the Oil, Chemical, and Atomic Workers International Union said in 1990, "to figure out you probably aren't going to get inspected." Without "dead bodies," Jim Moran, a Philadelphia health and safety expert grimly joked a few years before the fire, the agency wouldn't inspect a factory. The Reagan administration's systematic cuts to OSHA did more than just eliminate the chance of a knock at the factory door; they also made it easier for employers to run their plants to meet the imperatives of cheap and deliver low-cost goods to consumers, including their own workers.[64] Emmett and

Brad Roe seemed to make a similar economic and social assessment. At Imperial, managers jacked up line speeds, skimped on preventive maintenance, and put off replacing outdated equipment.[65] Why pay for new machines or new protections or follow every safety rule or suggestion in a manual when labor was cheap and easily replaced? Why abide by the rules when no one was going to enforce them, not OSHA inspectors or unions or line workers? If a company like Imperial wanted to follow the letter of the law on worker safety, it essentially handicapped itself. As David Bell, who calculated economic impacts for OSHA, explained, "When a competitor can cut costs by cutting corners on safety, (other) company officials don't like being placed at a competitive disadvantage." Often it wasn't simply a matter of liking it or not; it was a matter of staying in business, not getting undercut by a competitor, and making enough money to pay off outstanding bank notes.[66]

Workers felt a similar sense of risk, and, as it was with businesspeople, this sense of peril shaped their attitudes toward government. According to one estimate, the economic restructuring of the 1970s and 1980s erased 15 million jobs. Fearing that enforcing OSHA standards would cause their creaky, outdated, and often isolated factories to close, laborers begged their union representatives and co-workers to back off and look the other way in the face of asbestos in the air, gas smells, leaky connections, and much-needed plant repairs. "For many today," observed the *New York Times'* influential labor correspondent William Serrin in the 1980s, "job safety is far less important than simply work—any work."[67]

An activist, a reformer, and later an academic, Mark Schultz worked in the 1980s for the Wisconsin Occupational Safety and Health Project, a private, nonprofit organization of workers, union locals, and health and legal professionals. In this job, he lobbied Badger State legislators to enact more stringent safety measures, counseled union members on how to spot violations, and led workplace seminars on how to avoid injury. In 1990, he took a similar position with the Durham-based and newly established North Carolina Occupational Safety and Health Project.

Schultz quickly learned that he wasn't in Wisconsin anymore. For starters, he didn't develop extensive union contacts in North Carolina. The political climate was different as well. He couldn't find more than a handful of General Assembly members willing to listen to his push for more inspectors and increased investment in factory safety. When he tried to get something done about the alarming rise in cases of carpal tunnel syndrome in the state's slaughterhouses and poultry-processing plants, lawmakers nodded their heads and then urged caution. "We need to maintain a good business climate," they repeatedly counseled Schultz as they brushed aside his suggestions.

North Carolina workers sensed, Schultz believed, the state's indifference to their safety. They knew that their jobs came with risks and that the line speeds in many plants led to repetitive motion injuries and threatened their limbs and fingers. They knew that some factory owners thought about safety second and churning out the product first. But they also knew the cost of breaking the silence that businesspeople like Emmett Roe coveted. As bad as conditions were at Imperial Food Products or at a poultry slaughterhouse in Siler City or at a hog factory in Smithfield, the line workers at these places at least had a job and drew a weekly paycheck. Some sensed the dynamics of a competitive industry without speaking the language of boardrooms and trading floors. If they complained too much, if their co-workers raised their voices too loudly, there was always the chance that the factories would disappear and never come back. That's what happened to the railroads in Hamlet and to Clark Equipment in Rockingham, wasn't it? They closed down—in the case of Clark, after a close union vote—and took their jobs with them.[68]

Even if a line worker at Imperial did decide to say something about the conditions at the plant, she probably didn't know where to turn. Several times during the 1980s, OSHA inspectors reached the doorstep of the Bridges Street factory but never made it inside. For a number of years after they sold the factory, Mello-Buttercup officials leased back a small section of the plant from Emmett Roe. They employed three people there to store and distribute ice cream throughout Richmond County and the surrounding areas. For some reason, state inspectors kept returning to this tiny corporate footprint. In October 1981, an OSHA official found three minor violations there and issued no fines. He returned in May 1984 and found three more non-serious problems and again issued no fines. Five months later, as Imperial cranked out batches of fried chicken parts, he conducted another follow-up investigation to make sure that

Mello-Buttercup had addressed his agency's safety concerns. Three times, then, an OSHA inspector was only a wall away from the Imperial shop floor, but he might as well have been in another county. Even if he had smelled gas or rotten chicken, he couldn't just knock on the door. By law, OSHA officials weren't allowed to decide on their own to drop by a plant that hadn't been selected for inspection by the Department of Labor in Raleigh. Court decisions held that regulators could only launch a safety visit in response to a complaint or random selection.[69]

When an Imperial employee in Hamlet wrote to OSHA in October 1987 about maggots in the breakroom and filth and lice in the women's bathroom, Max Avery, an OSHA review officer, wrote the company a letter and asked for a response. The factory's general manager, James Hair, answered each of the charges with a curt dismissal:

"Description of Alleged Violations," he wrote, continuing:

Item #1: Body lice in women's bathroom. These were not body lice, but someone had combed hair in sink, leaving head lice. We immediately called in the pest control company and had them go through the women's bathroom even though we knew it was head lice.

Item #2: Maggots have been seen in the canteen (eating area.) This could not have been because we clean the area three times a day and it is scrubbed down every night completely.

Item #3: Women's bathroom is very dirty. This could not possibly be. We have someone pick up after the morning break, lunch break, and afternoon break. The facilities are also scrubbed and sanitized every night.

No one from OSHA visited the plant to follow up, and no one responded to Hair. His word was enough to close the case.[70]

In June 1991, just months before the fire, several South Hamlet residents complained to the city council that tractor-trailers dropping off frozen chicken breasts and picking up tenders blocked Bridges Street, sometimes for hours at a time. One council member declared this a safety issue that warranted OSHA's attention. Another suggested writing a letter to the Roes. That's where the matter ended, it seems.[71]

Imperial worker Conester Williams wanted someone to inspect the plant. Years later, she remembered calling up the local employment bureau—the agency that often acted as Imperial's labor recruiter in Hamlet and Rockingham—to talk to someone about the unsafe and dangerous conditions at the factory and to urge them to stop sending out-of-work women and men, as they had for years, over to Bridges Street until something was done. She never heard back from anyone at the office, and the flow of workers just kept coming.[72]

One company official said he had a copy of OSHA standards in his office desk. "I couldn't understand a whole lot of it," he admitted to investigators after the fire. Another remembered glancing at the thick book of rules and regulations once. "'Course," he commented, "you got to have a B.A. degree to read the darn thing." After that, the rules stayed in his desk.[73]

The bigger problem was that the ethos of cheap eroded Imperial workers' faith in the government. It certainly didn't seem to be functioning in their interests. This was a serious, and perhaps purposeful, side effect of the business-first politics that had flipped the New Deal and Fordism on their heads. Deregulation tended to erode support for state action among those who needed it most. Imperial workers almost never spotted a local firefighter or city official in the plant, and this came on top of years of experience for African Americans away from the job with Jim Crow policing and uneven schooling and government services in their parts of town. Most days, though, employees did see the USDA men in the factory. They saw them check the floors and freezers, search for mice droppings, and shoo away flies. And, of course, they saw them inspect the meat. They also watched as chicken breasts spotted with mold and fungus got dipped into batter and packed into boxes. Just about every day, USDA officials walked across Imperial's slippery floors as gas fumes wafted through the plant. These officials saw the mechanics struggling with the fryer and the conveyor belts. But the USDA inspectors never said anything. Workers saw that USDA men walked in and out of the plant the same as always, even after the doors near the dumpster were locked, one of them from the outside. And they saw the USDA men in the office, sipping Cokes and chatting with Brad Roe as if they might be friends.[74]

Reporting unsafe conditions to the USDA men must have seemed to Imperial workers like a risky strategy. At the same time, few knew that they could pick up a phone and report violations to unseen OSHA officials (if they got through to the right number). Not many would have trusted that their complaints would go undetected by the Roes. And who could take this risk? Who could risk that Brad Roe, with his fiery temper, might find out that they were the one who had blown the whistle? What they saw inside Imperial every day didn't inspire much confidence in federal, state, or local oversight.[75]

Imperial workers weren't the only ones keeping quiet or worried about choosing between "risking jobs and risking their lives."[76] The changing tenor at OSHA under Reagan muzzled workers everywhere. Ken Silver, a Massachusetts health and safety activist, reported that factory laborers in his state doubted that the agency would address safety problems. "They just don't feel OSHA can help them any longer," he said.[77] As a result, another layer of silence hung over the Imperial plant and places like it across the country. Saying nothing was the best way to keep a job during a time when finding a job was hard enough and the economic winds were blowing hard in the wrong direction. In some ways, working people cheapened themselves, concluding based on all the information around them that they had a choice between safety and work, and just about everyone chose work.

James Martin occupied the Victorian-era governor's mansion in Raleigh when the fire broke out at Imperial. A Princeton PhD and former chemistry professor at Davidson College, the Mecklenburg County Republican looked the part of a North Carolina politician just about as much as John Brooks *didn't* fit the role. Tall and square-jawed, with a deep voice and a thick mat of black hair, he could smile for the camera and talk to donors. His academic smarts, political experience as a six-term United States congressman, and good looks helped to make him just the second member of his party to hold the state's highest office since the last days of Reconstruction. Party registration and his opposition to abortion rights and the Martin Luther King Jr. holiday aside, Martin did not represent a sharp break from the past. His pro-business, limited-regulation politics overlapped with those of his Democratic predecessor, Jim Hunt, more than they did with those of the state's other leading Republican at the time, the force behind the anti-communist, evangelically fueled, surging New Right, Senator Jesse Helms.

Both Martin and Hunt believed, as a matter of faith, that job creation and industrial recruitment signaled economic health and benefited society, while taxes, red tape, and regulations cut into corporate profits and held down the economy. "We want jobs," Martin told a reporter. "Which of those [jobs] don't you want?" Like Hunt, he saw the point of government as helping businesses succeed and prosper by keeping labor costs down, unions at bay, and the state's roads as straight, smooth, and far reaching as possible. That way they could deliver affordable everyday goods. A few new prisons and a couple of nationally recognized universities couldn't hurt matters either.[78]

Martin reacted to the fire, at first, as a business progressive would. Within hours of the blaze, the governor told a pack of reporters that he wasn't sure that the state needed more factory inspectors or any other kind of dramatic change to its labor and workplace rules. But Martin had enough of the politician's gift—that skill that Brooks seemed to lack—to know when to make a quick pivot and bounce away from an unpopular stance. Sensing the gathering outrage at the locked doors and lack of OSHA oversight, Martin quietly shifted his position. When pressed, he pushed blame onto Brooks. If the head of the state's Department of Labor had done a better job, maybe, the governor suggested, things could have turned out different. At the same time, he distanced the state from the Roes, telling reporters that no one in Raleigh had ever recruited Imperial or offered the chicken processors any special favors to relocate to Hamlet. Knowing that the public wanted to see some changes, within days of the blast, Martin pledged funds for two dozen new factory inspectors, called for the establishment of a state fire inspection division, urged the USDA to cross-train its staff to recognize safety problems while performing their regular duties, and pressed for the establishment of a worker safety hotline that laborers could call anytime, day or night, to anonymously report locked doors, leaking chemicals, and other hazardous conditions. True to his faith in more business and limited regulation, Martin rejected demands from the state AFL-CIO to turn North Carolina's OSHA program over to the Department of Labor in Washington. He called that "federal intrusion."[79]

Still, the fire and the public reaction to it worried the state's pro-business, anti-regulation forces. Less than a week after firefighters pulled all of those bodies out of the Imperial plant, Courtney Roberts, the director of a Charlotte-based construction industry trade group, expressed his sorrow for the loss of life in Hamlet. He quickly added, though, that he thought that current OSHA standards did the job. "I think there's going to be an overreaction," Roberts feared. "Then," he continued, "there will be new rules that will result in problems for business and industry. . . . That's inevitable."[80]

The inevitable did happen. First, OSHA moved on the Roes' Georgia operations, closing down the Cumming factory when it found out that employees there had not received fire training and that the plant lacked an automatic fire suppression system and did not have visibly marked fire exits.[81] More important, in the spring of 1992 voters in the North Carolina Democratic Party's primary swept John Brooks out of office and replaced him on the ticket with Harry Payne. On the stump, the six-term, liberal-leaning, well-regarded state representative from New Hanover County chided Brooks for his ineffective, top-heavy managerial style and promised to beef up the state's Department of Labor.[82] After prevailing in the primary and then in the general election, Payne took office ready to seize the moment and press for key workplace safety reforms. In 1992, the North Carolina General Assembly would follow his lead and pass a slate of new laws aimed at making its workplaces safer.

But, by then, most of the reporters had stopped shining a spotlight on the deeper causes of the fire, and they even stopped coming to Hamlet, except for the few who returned sometimes in early September to check in on the anniversary of the fire. The rest of the time the town was just like it was before the hydraulic hose burst and started to spew flammable fluid in every direction. Quiet. Out of the way. Except there was just about no place in Hamlet to work anymore that paid even a dollar above minimum wage. On the ground things really weren't much better for working people.

7

ENDINGS

F ive minutes. That's how long it would have taken the members of the Dobbins Heights Fire Department to drive a truck with lights flashing and sirens blaring from their station house to the Imperial Food Products plant on Bridges Street in Hamlet. Yet they were never called on the morning of September 3, 1991, leaving some—especially in the black community—to wonder why.

Before Dobbins Heights was Dobbins Heights, it was the North Yard, and for most of the twentieth century this small, almost entirely African American community of less than a thousand residents remained, in administrative terms, an unincorporated section of Richmond County. That meant it didn't have its own local services or its own direct representatives. While residents paid taxes to Hamlet (sometimes) and Richmond County (more often), they didn't get much in return. In the middle of the 1960s, a local minister spearheaded the formation of the North Yard Improvement Association, and the group raised money to install streetlights along a couple of its main thoroughfares. Yet when Emmett Roe bought the Imperial plant almost twenty years later, some North Yard streets remained unpaved and potholed. Few had sidewalks. The sewers backed up when it rained, and area residents joked that the gurgling water system remained so faulty and inadequate that two people on the same street couldn't take a shower at the same time and have enough pressure to rinse off the soap.[1]

But one of the main reasons that North Yard residents got organized was to deal with fire safety. In the mid-1970s, community members alleged that if they called the dispatcher in Hamlet, he would ask them for

their address, and when he found out where they lived, he would press
them to find out if they had insurance or $300 in cash. If they didn't
have of either of these things, or couldn't convince the person at the other
end of the line that they did, the trucks didn't come their way. The only
sure way for North Yard residents to put out a fire, then, was to start their
own fire company.[2]

Two years after the founding of the North Yard Volunteer Fire Company, local community leaders sought annexation by Hamlet. It seemed
like the right time. Hamlet was about to enter a growth spurt. Between
1980 and 1990, it would add hundreds of acres of new territory and 1,200
new residents, largely through annexation. But Hamlet officials turned
down the request from the North Yard to be part of the city, telling reporters that they couldn't afford the cost of taking on an economically
distressed community. North Yard residents felt sure that race, along with
need, figured into their neighbors' calculations.

Following Hamlet's rejection, North Yard leaders began to push for
incorporation so that the community could become a town with elected
leaders, a budget, and municipal services. Around this time, some residents started to call the neighborhood Dobbins Heights, named after
Pastor Jim Dobbins, who in the 1930s had owned a big chunk of the area's
land.[3]

On May 8, 1984, local officials held a referendum on incorporation.
The measure passed, though just barely, and only after a recount following the discovery by poll watchers that several corpses had risen from the
dead to vote. The shaky start of Dobbins Heights, as it was now officially
called, was soon forgotten as the town's African American mayor and all–
African American city council secured state and federal grants to pave
streets, lay down sidewalks, fix up and fence in a park, and purchase new
fire equipment—fire equipment they were ready to use on the morning of
September 3, 1991.[4]

At 8:24 a.m. on the day of the fire, Captain Calvin White of the Hamlet
Fire Department jumped into his truck and raced to the site of the Imperial plant. As he turned down Spear Street, he saw out of the corner of his
eye the crown of a woman's head sticking out from an opening between
the wall by the trash compactor and the loading dock. When he made a

left onto Bridges Street, he knew right away by looking at the density of the smoke that this was, in his words, "a horrific fire." He immediately put a mutual aid call into Rockingham, sending out word that he needed every available firefighter in the area to come at once. Somehow, that message never got to Dobbins Heights.[5]

As soon as Ernest Cannon, the Dobbins Heights fire chief and a Vietnam veteran, got to the station on the morning of September 3, he called over to Hamlet and let them know that his men were ready to help. By then, most of the community's volunteer firefighters—and that was all there was in Dobbins Heights in 1991—had already heard about the fire. All of them knew someone who worked at the plant. Some, like Johnny Reddick, had family—his wife, Cleo—inside the building.

Stay ready, Hamlet Fire Chief David Fuller, now in charge of the operation, told Cannon, adding that he would call back when he needed help from Dobbins Heights. The phone never rang. Cannon reached out to the Hamlet Fire Department two more times that morning. Finally, he drove over to the Imperial factory. He got the same message in person. Stay ready. We may need you here, Fuller told him, or we may need you to put out a house fire or take care of some other problem in Hamlet while our men are occupied. Stand by.

As Cannon and his men remained on standby, the East Rockingham Fire Department and the Rockingham Fire Department rushed to Bridges Street. Fuller and his men reached out to the Cordova Fire Department, eight and half miles away, because, as the chief later said, the firefighters there had experience with large and tricky fires. The Hamlet Fire Department asked the Northside Fire Department, also eight miles away, to hurry over with its equipment truck that was able to refill the oxygen-filled air packs that firefighters depended on to breathe as they crawled through the smoke-filled building trying to put out the fire and locate missing bodies. Fuller requested additional assistance from Richmond County Emergency Medical Services and rescue squads from Ellerbe and Hoffman. All that day the Dobbins Heights Fire Department remained on standby status.[6]

Rockingham City firefighter Frankie Moree was one of the first on the scene at Imperial. He was also among the first to enter the building. Without a map of the plant, something he couldn't believe that Hamlet firefighters didn't have, the fire suppression team headed for the processing room, but they had to withdraw because of the heat and smoke. They relaunched their attack through the equipment room and, by 10:00 a.m., they had gotten the fire under control. Search and rescue operations started around 8:45 a.m., with the final victim, maintenance man John Gagnon, being pulled out of the building shortly after 12:20 p.m. Thinking back on this nasty and tricky fire, Moree felt certain that the Dobbins Heights volunteers, whom he had worked with a couple of times before on house fires, were "underqualified" to handle something this big and complicated. So, while Moree didn't think much of David Fuller, his pre-fire planning, or his leadership of the Hamlet Fire Department, he did think he made the right call to keep the Dobbins Heights crew out of the building that morning, though he thought that they could have pitched in with first aid and other relief efforts outside the plant.[7]

"You can get too much help," Fuller explained to a local reporter when asked why he didn't call in the Dobbins Heights Fire Company. Asked another time about why he never picked up the phone, he questioned the qualifications of the firefighters from the nearby town. On yet another occasion, Fuller told reporters that these men should have felt "honored" just to be on standby.[8]

A few months after the fire, Ernest Cannon put on a suit jacket, crisp white shirt, and thickly knotted tie for an interview with a documentary filmmaker who was working on a project about the Hamlet fire. He looked straight into the camera and read, in verse, his answer to Fuller's declaration about honor and standby status:

"I'm honored to be unable to save my wife's life.

I'm honored to be unable to save my cousin's life.

I'm honored to be unable to save my neighbor's life."

"Why do you think you were turned down?" Cannon was asked by the filmmaker.

Cannon took a deep breath before answering. "Well," he said, "I can't say." But then he did say: "Personally, I believe that racial decisions had a lot to do with it. And the town I live in is predominately black . . . the only (one like it) in the area."[9]

"We could have saved at least one life," a "pissed off" Cannon told a journalist who asked him about the fire and his company's standby status on another occasion. "We could have got some of them doors unlocked. We could have assisted the first responders. . . . They didn't have enough man power." [10]

But his company wasn't called and, as he explained, to yet another reporter, "It was a racial thing. We are just as qualified as his volunteers." "I know they're prejudiced," Cannon charged, talking about Chief Fuller and some of his men, "Hamlet has always looked at Dobbins Heights that way." [11]

Cannon based his suspicions about racial bias, he said, on his familiarity with the Hamlet Fire Department. They had trained his men, and the two companies had worked together on a few fires. But these weren't his only experiences with his counterparts. A few months before the Imperial explosion, the Dobbins Heights Fire Department, Cannon explained, had purchased new radio equipment. Almost as soon as it was up and running in mid-August, Cannon's company started to receive daily threats that their station would be blown up and its firefighters attacked. One time, he claimed to have heard someone on the other end of the radio snarl, "Nigger, get off the airwaves." He was convinced that he recognized the voices. They sounded to him like several Hamlet firefighters he knew. [12]

Fuller had a different explanation. He scoffed at charges that his department shunned the Dobbins Heights firefighters because they were black. Calvin White, the Hamlet Fire Department captain, was (and is) black; same with Wayne Covington, a Rockingham firefighter, who was on the scene that day. "I had every sex and race involved in the fire and rescue," Fuller rightly noted. "The fire departments that were called to the scene are also racially mixed. That is obviously not any consideration I would have." Fuller based his decisions, he said, on competency, not skin color. Dobbins Heights wasn't called, Fuller insisted, because it did not have "experienced personnel and leadership." Summing up, Fuller declared, "I was looking for good, seasoned firefighters and their leaders." [13]

Hearing Fuller's explanation didn't change Cannon's mind. It just made him madder. He wouldn't let anyone, he fumed, "slander the reputation of this station." He insisted that some of the firefighters at the scene were "no better than we are." No matter what Fuller or Moree said or how many other black firefighters were there that day, he remained convinced that race lay behind the snub. He wasn't alone in his suspicions or his distrust of those running the Hamlet Fire Department or the town itself.[14]

The same film crew that Cannon had spoken to about being put on standby status interviewed a rail-thin, unnamed, twenty-something African American man from Hamlet. With the burnt factory in the background, he told them a story about a woman, he said, who was pulled from the plant during the fire but was not given any oxygen for twenty minutes. Without prompting, he said, "she was black." To him that was the most salient detail about her.

Most of the firemen, he added, again without prompting, were white.

"They were trying to help," he said, "but I guess there weren't that many."

Before the interviewer could get out a follow-up question, the man continued, "They got a black fire department over here, they didn't even call . . . it's all black, they didn't even call. . . . That was on the news."

"The fire chief said they didn't have enough experience," he went on, talking about Hamlet's David Fuller.

"The way I see it, if they didn't have experience they won't be firemen at all. They had to have training and stuff."

"As a matter of fact, they were the closest ones. The ones in Dobbins Heights."[15]

He left it at that.

Ruth DeRosa, a white researcher from Duke University, who came to town to study the after-effects of the Imperial tragedy picked on what that African American man told that film crew. In her conversations with locals in the winter and spring of 1992, she noted a surge in "racial tensions," as she called them, swirling through Hamlet, Dobbins Heights, and the nearby communities. As she listened to African American laborers and their families reflect on their lives, she heard them mention again and again the "fire house incident." To the people she talked with, this wasn't a decision about competence—it was about race.[16] The supposed brushoff of this fire crew shaped how black people made sense of what happened that September morning in 1991, what truths they believed and which ones they didn't, and how they would live with the fire and its deadly consequences. Mostly, though, the supposed snub of Ernest Cannon's men rekindled a sense of distrust in Dobbins Heights' and Hamlet's black communities, where faith in government and city officials was always in short supply and was running especially low in an age of cheap where some lives seemed to matter more than others.

In the first days and weeks after the fire, Hamlet seemed to come together as one community. The city council declared a thirty-day period of mourning and flags in town were flown at half-staff. Mayor Abbie Covington worked day and night to cope with relief, the media, and what to do next.[17] Local businesses and community groups chipped in where they could. The City Limits nightclub in South Hamlet held a pig pickin' to benefit survivors. Members of the American Legion put together a free quasi-taxi service, driving Imperial families from their homes in Hamlet and Bennettsville to supermarkets, funeral homes, and hospitals. The Salvation Army distributed clothes and toys, while the Red Cross and the United Way handed out bags of groceries and coupons for meals at local Chinese and barbecue restaurants.[18] Florists donated funeral floral arrangements, church members baked sheet cakes for wakes, and beauticians did the hair of mourners without charge.[19] CSX, Coors, and Pepsi donated money for relief. The Masonic Lodge #532 of Hamlet and the Women's Aglow Chapter of Rockingham made contributions. Local churches stepped in as well. During the first three months after the fire, the Hamlet Ministerial Alliance raised and dispersed more than $58,000 to victims. They bought new beds for orphaned children and paid outstanding utility bills. They helped others with money for car payments, rent, and taking care of the mortgage. They provided travel expenses to families visiting wives, sons, and daughters in intensive care units in Charlotte, Durham, and Chapel Hill. As Berry Barbour, the pastor at the downtown United Methodist Church, remembers it, Imperial workers would come in and ask for something and they left with a check, "no questions asked."[20]

Outsiders pitched in as well. In December 1991, the City of Hamlet, with the help of the Lost Santa Project from Raleigh, held a Christmas party and passed out gifts wrapped in colorful paper and decorated with bright bows to children whose parents were killed or hurt in the fire. Stanley Tools of Charlotte canceled its annual picnic and gave the money it would have spent on the event to Imperial families. The White Oak Grove Baptist Church of Greensboro adopted a few local kids and sent them money for food and clothes. Churches from Lenoir, Pittsboro, and Pineville sent checks and good wishes. Handmade condolence cards and small contributions came to Hamlet City Hall from schoolkids and their parents in Logan, Utah; Lancaster, South Carolina; and Shippensburg, Pennsylvania, as well as Pittsboro, Raleigh, and Roanoke, North Carolina.[21]

"The people were lucky it happened here," Mayor Abbie Covington said more than twenty years after the blaze. "People wrapped their arms around them. The community cared. I have never seen so much caring in my life."[22]

State worker Martha Barr came to share Covington's assessment of the generosity of Hamlet residents. Two decades before the Imperial plant went up in flames, the Baltimore native and graduate of Mary Baldwin College in Virginia moved to Raleigh. Over the next twenty years, she became a specialist in worker's compensation administration, holding jobs on different occasions for lawyers on both sides of the issue. In 1990, she took a position with the North Carolina Industrial Commission, the agency that oversaw the state's worker's compensation program. Twenty-four hours after the fire, she rode in a car with her bosses, commission head Judge James Booker and safety director Ned Vaughn-Lloyd, as they headed south from Raleigh to Hamlet.

Prior to opening its North Carolina plant, Imperial had compiled such a woeful and shaky safety record in Pennsylvania and Alabama that it couldn't find an insurance company willing to write it a worker's compensation policy, which it had to have in order to do business in the state. That put the company in what was called the assigned risk pool. In order to write worker's compensation policies in North Carolina for stable and safe companies, insurers had to pick up a few of the risky firms that no one else would to take on. As Martha Barr explained it, "No one would willingly go into assigned risk. Your premiums would be higher." But Imperial's past cheapness gave it no choice, so it ended up in the assigned risk pool. Liberty Mutual Insurance Company didn't have a choice either. In order to get other worker's compensation business in the state, the firm got some business it had never solicited or wanted, Emmett Roe's included.

Not long after Martha Barr and her bosses got to town, they ran into the adjusters from Liberty Mutual at the factory site. The insurance company representatives were trying, with somewhat mixed success, to get the information they required from Imperial officials and city leaders so they could fill out the forms that survivors and their families needed in order to qualify for worker's compensation benefits. The adjusters assured Barr that they would get the information and that their company would honor all claims. Barr promised them, in turn, that she would do whatever she could to help.[23]

Barr also learned that other state officials and Hamlet city leaders planned to open a Victim's Assistance Center at the city library to help Imperial families get the support they were entitled to and the advice they needed on Monday, September 9. Once she heard the date, she remembered right away that this was the first day of Rosh Hashanah. Barr hesitated for a moment about returning to Hamlet and missing services on one of the holiest days on the Jewish calendar. But she decided that coming to the aid of the anguished town and its grieving people was the right thing to do, an act that honored both her faith and the holiday.

Barr stayed in Hamlet from early Monday until late Thursday of that next week. She tried, as she later recalled, "to cut every bit of red tape." She laid out for families the state's worker's compensation rules and showed them what boxes to check and where to sign so they could get some money to help pay their rent and not fall behind on their car notes. Barr explained to husbands, wives, and children of the victims that they would be eligible for a death benefit equal to two-thirds of the deceased's weekly pay for four hundred weeks. She let them know that they were entitled to a $2,000 burial benefit as well. When the survivors, burned and bruised in the fire, approached her table, she let them know that they would receive two-thirds of their weekly pay as long as they were medically disabled and that the state would help with the bills from their doctors and psychologists.[24] Each day she was there, she didn't leave the Industrial Commission table until she answered every last question and made sure every one of the people who came by filled out all of the forms correctly. On her way out of Hamlet, Imperial workers thanked Barr; they blessed her and held her tight in their arms. They hadn't expected this much from a government official, and while they knew that two-thirds of their paycheck plus a little more from donations and Social Security wasn't much, it was better than nothing, and maybe it was just enough to get by on until the plant reopened or other work became available.

Those four days in Hamlet, the "bravery" of the town's people, and those teary-eyed thank-yous, stayed with Barr. She identified with their struggles so much that she developed, as she put it years later, "my own grief." She dealt with it by writing. During the first winter after the fire, she composed a cassette tape's worth of songs about Hamlet and its people. She celebrated the spirit of collectivity generated by the fire that to her melted away divisions in the town. In "A Love Song to Hamlet," Barr described Hamlet as "Just a southern town that's sleepy." "What really showed what Hamlet was made [of] and all about," she wrote, was how "friends and neighbors help each other" and how "the folks" of "this dear town rallied to give aid and succor to people who were down." "No one," she proclaimed, "went hungry or was homeless. To this the folks of Hamlet saw." [25]

Ruth DeRosa arrived in Hamlet for the first time several months after Martha Barr made her initial visit to town. At the time, the Nashville native was enrolled in Duke University's PhD program in psychology. Her supervisor, Susan Roth, specialized in post-traumatic stress disorder (PTSD). Teaming up with colleagues at the Triangle Research Institute, well known for its work with Vietnam veterans, and the University of North Carolina, Roth applied for and received a grant from the National Institute for Mental Health to study the fire's trauma impact. Juesta Caddell of the Triangle Research Institute coordinated the adult portion of the study while Lisa Amaya-Jackson of UNC oversaw the child study. The project team hired DeRosa as a research assistant and sent her to town to collect data in the field, data she later drew on for her dissertation. [26]

For the next twenty weeks, DeRosa traveled to Richmond County just about every weekend, usually staying at the same Rockingham motel, often in the same first-floor room. She came and went with such regularity that one of the night clerks assumed that she was having an affair with a local married man, not interviewing fire survivors and their spouses in their homes or at the project's rented office not far from Hamlet's Main Street.

While conducting her research on the impact of the fire, DeRosa met countless Imperial workers and their widowed wives and husbands and orphaned children still haunted by the sights, smells, and sounds of September 3, 1991. Recalling the smoke, the sound of those terror-filled calls for help and divine intervention, and the noxious odors of burning chicken fat and hydraulic oil, some felt alternatively jumpy and detached. Many couldn't sleep. Others couldn't get out of bed in the morning. Almost everyone touched by the tragedy experienced some combination of sudden flashbacks, recurring nightmares, and other symptoms from mild to severe associated with post-traumatic stress disorder.

For months after the fire, Pearlie Gagnon, maintenance supervisor John Gagnon's widow, didn't feel like eating and she couldn't sleep. One afternoon, unable to hold her head up for another minute, she dozed off, only to be woken up by nightmares. She dreamed that someone was redoing her yard by digging a huge hole in the middle of it. At the bottom of the pit, there was someone screaming over and over again, "Let me out." [27]

The boom of thunderstorms and the crack of lightning frightened others. Fall brought the familiar smell of burning leaves and triggered new anxieties. So did the sticky waves of heat that rolled through the southernmost parts of North Carolina in summer.

Many survivors and family members avoided small rooms and tight spaces, including cars. In a place like Hamlet without any public transportation, this turned them into virtual shut-ins. Before the fire, nineteen-year-old Teresa Ellerbee had planned to go to college. Just a few months later, she had given up on that dream and rarely left the house. "I can't work now," she whispered to a reporter. "It's too hard." [28] "The fire has taken my peace of mind," lamented another former first-shift worker, "Since the fire I don't want to go anywhere." [29]

A number of survivors and family members got hooked on painkillers and prescription drugs. Some drank too much. Some overate. A few overspent on funerals, cars, and going out, and faced (new) financial challenges.

Some felt shame. They hated the way the papers portrayed them as chicken thieves. "When it first happened I felt dirty, nasty," one Imperial worker told Ruth DeRosa. Another added, "I don't want to tell anyone I worked there because a lot of people said it was the employees' fault because they should have reported the doors being locked to the board." Others battled with survivor's guilt. One woman would down a few drinks, get into her car, push the pedal to the floor, and try to crash. "I was mad at the Lord for not taking my life," she said. "I've had a real problem with faith," a former Imperial worker confessed to DeRosa. "I've been calling my minister . . . about why they got killed and I didn't."[30]

Some couldn't explain their behavior, even to themselves. A few months after the tragedy, one woman was doing her laundry when her iron caught fire. "I just stood there," she said. Another woman won't bring anything flammable near her house. Another constantly checked the locks to her doors, fearful that something might happen to her children. Yet another survivor scorched the lawn in front of his home because he worried that the grass might catch fire and burn the place down.[31]

It wasn't just the survivors or their widows who were hurting. On the morning of the fire, neighborhood children had heard the blare of sirens and scurried over to the plant. They had watched as rescue workers carried soot-covered and lifeless bodies out of the building. Afterward, they, too, couldn't shake the event out of their heads. One Hamlet teen told a member of Ruth DeRosa's research team that when he closed his eyes he saw his aunt sitting crouched and shivering in the cooler before her death. When he shut them even tighter, trying to make her go away, she was still there. Some kids felt guilty. One elementary school student worried that his mom had almost died because he didn't eat his cereal that morning. Mary Alice Quick's twelve-year-old son, Terrell, got kicked off the school bus and then suspended from classes. "My momma is dead," he announced. "I don't have to listen to anyone."

"The hardest thing for me," explained a Hamlet teacher, "is to get them in studying mode. I want them to know that life goes on and you need an education."[32]

A few neighborhood kids took their anger out on the building. After dark, starting the night of the blast, teenagers chucked bottles at the Imperial plant and set random fires on the grounds, revenge, perhaps, for what had been done to their parents, aunts, and cousins.[33]

As Rosa DeRosa and other psychologists noted, a lack of trust can trigger some of the anxieties and behaviors associated with PTSD. Rightly or wrongly, fire victims and their families felt betrayed by the Roes, government officials, and the refusal, as they saw it, of local leaders to mobilize all available resources on their behalf on the day of the explosion, as symbolized by holding the Dobbins Heights Fire Department on standby. Many felt sharp pains and constant aches for months and then years after the tragedy and wondered if the doctors at Hamlet Hospital and at Duke and UNC, where airlifts had taken some of the hurt and injured the day of the fire, had given them the correct treatments and medications. They worried if they would ever be able to trust their bodies and their minds again. Some felt abandoned by God and even by their husbands, wives, and children who were consumed by the fire's deadly fumes. Many felt numb, isolated, and alone. They couldn't connect with people and so they avoided the emotional and physical intimacy on which trust depends and can be built anew.

"My boyfriend tells me I'm totally different," Gloria Malachi told a reporter in December 1991, "like I'm trying to push him away or don't want to be bothered."

You're "grouchy," Malachi's boyfriend told her.[34]

Family members didn't always understand the daily, unexpected traumas fire victims experienced. Spouses and children encountered the sometimes chilly emotional distance of their partners and parents and felt rejected. Some lost their patience. Others tried tough love. They told their wives and daughters, sons and neighbors to snap out of it. But this only made the dread, the shame, and the survivor's guilt worse. And it kept trust, that key to recovery, at a distance.

Black and white foremen, line workers, and fire and rescue personnel all mourned and grieved and experienced trauma after the fire. But the pain may have been more intense for some in the African American community. Members of Ruth DeRosa's Duke University–Triangle Research Institute–UNC team discovered that the African American children and adolescents of Imperial employees registered higher levels of posttraumatic stress than did their white peers.[35] Maybe this had to do with trust—that crucial factor in recovering from PTSD. Maybe the wariness started with the first time they heard a racial slur thrown their way or the first snub they felt at a store. Maybe it began on Hamlet's athletic fields, where black students got steered away from playing tennis and from the quarterback position. Maybe it had something to do with tensions on the street and a distrust of the sheriff's office and of local police and the fire department. Or maybe it had to do with how relief workers treated their parents and relatives. Some African American survivors felt like white workers received larger relief funds than they did. When they attended job fairs for unemployed Imperial workers, some felt like white co-workers got interviews for office jobs and factory positions, while they got steered toward domestic help and restaurant work. "As a black woman," Annette Zimmerman believed, "they only thought I could cook or clean."[36]

Reverend Harold Miller preached at one of the black churches on the southern side of Hamlet. He didn't grow up there, so he had a kind of critical distance about the place. In the months after the fire, he noted a sharp rise in the level of distrust—and that is the word he used—among his congregants toward white city leaders, state representatives, and members of the local fire department. This feeling wasn't entirely new, as the race riot and fire bombings that took place in Hamlet in 1975 revealed. Well before Imperial exploded, many African Americans had no doubt heard stories about the Hamlet Fire Department, about Fuller being a "good old boy" and hiring a few of his own kind, and about his department sometimes refusing to come into their neighborhoods to put out house fires. Some in the black community wondered if their families and friends had been sacrificed the morning of the fire because of hard-boiled racism. If this could be true, and if what Annette Zimmerman believed about relief officials was true, many African Americans had to wonder how they could trust elected leaders and other public representatives going forward. Without that trust, it was hard to imagine recovering from the fire and investing in the town's future.

Hamlet's racial geography only added to the already festering distrust that, in turn, exacerbated PTSD symptoms. Much of black life in Hamlet, especially working-class black life, was centered in South Hamlet, and there was almost no way to get there without going down Bridges Street. That meant going by the Imperial site and the charred and twisted remains of the factory, still standing there with the yellow police tape fluttering in the wind, one year after the fire, around the time that Ruth DeRosa wrapped up her research in town.

State worker and songwriter Martha Barr traveled back to Hamlet on a bright, warm September morning to mark the fire's one-year anniversary. She joined two hundred others gathered around the still waters of City Lake, a park with geese, ducks, picnic tables, and benches just below the town's Main Street. Fanning themselves with paper programs to keep away the heat and mosquitos, the largely white crowd, dressed in short-sleeved shirts and gingham sundresses, stayed quiet as the Reverend James Bailey of the Hamlet Ministerial Alliance delivered a short and solemn opening prayer. When he finished, he called to the podium "our beloved Mayor Abbie Covington." Applause from the audience. Covington, her voice shaky with emotion, thanked the city's elected officials and employees for their efforts to keep the town together in the days and weeks after the fire. Reverend Harold Miller followed the mayor and urged Hamlet citizens to "turn to God . . . to help bear each other's burdens." When he finished, Martha Barr walked up the rostrum. Slowly, in alphabetical order, she read the names of each of the twenty-five women and men who had perished in the fire. After she said each name, a silver bell chimed. When Barr came to the end of the list, Reverend Bailey brought up Catherine and Amy Dawkins, the widow and pre-teen daughter of the Lance deliveryman who had died in the blaze. They unveiled a granite memorial inscribed with the names of each of the victims. Another prayer, and the ceremony ended.

"I haven't been able to alleviate the suffering," Abbie Covington told a Raleigh television reporter after the lakeside service, "but we have shared it."[37]

The spirit of togetherness invoked by Covington, Barr, Bailey, and Miller wasn't the only emotion swirling through Hamlet that anniversary day. At Saint Peter United Methodist Church, located a few blocks from the lake and less than a quarter of a mile down Bridges Street from the Imperial site, another memorial service took place. "This one," explained a newsman, "was a little more lively, a little more angry, and a lot more black."[38]

Reverend Jesse Jackson was the featured speaker at Saint Peter. He was accompanied by Sheriff Raymond Goodman and members of Citizens Against Repulsive Environments (CARE), a local environmental group trying to stop the dumping of PCBs and other toxins in largely poor, African American areas in Richmond County. When they entered the church, the packed and sweaty crowd jumped to its feet and roared, "Jesse, Jesse" over and over again. With "Amen" punctuating nearly every line of his address, Jackson, a formidable candidate for the Democratic presidential nomination in 1988, did what he usually did, firing up a crowd with a mix of Biblical quotes, black pride slogans, and call-and-response alliteration. He closed, like Covington had earlier in the day, with a rousing, though class-tinged, call for unity. "Here workers sit in this church," Jackson intoned, "black and white together, bound by this tragedy. We'll either live together as brothers and sisters or perish apart as fools."[39]

Most everyone in the pews at Saint Peter knew that Mayor Covington and other city officials had blocked Jackson from speaking at the "official" City Lake service. They also knew that this wasn't the head of the Rainbow Coalition's first visit to Hamlet. A week or so after the fire, he went to see injured Imperial workers at the Carolina Medical Center in Charlotte. From there, he traveled two hours east to meet with families, clergy, and city officials from both Hamlet and Dobbins Heights.[40]

Mayor Abbie Covington knew that Jackson could be a polarizing force, especially in the white community. "I don't want people to get upset," she said about his initial visit to Hamlet in the fall of 1991. Somewhat reluctantly, she agreed to join him that time for an assembly at a local school, a march down Main Street, and a visit to a pantry distributing food to Imperial families. Covington came away from the encounter with a bad impression of Jackson. She felt like he came to Hamlet to exploit the town's tragedy for his own public relations gain, a common reading of the itinerant activist and "parachute politician" both locally and nationally in the 1990s.[41] "Jesse Jackson," Covington remarked years later, "came down, handed out baskets, got his picture taken, and left." From there, the relationship between Covington and Jackson soured. Undoubtedly, the hardworking and civic-minded mayor, who felt the losses at Imperial in her own deep and personal way, didn't like it when Jackson, while weighing another run at the presidency, told crowds around the country, "We have to go to Hamlet." He was using the town she represented and the tragedy that had taken place there as examples of callous neglect in his rallying cry against deregulation and union busting. Jackson even compared town leaders to "slave masters."[42]

More than anything, though, Covington blamed Jackson for injecting race into the legacy of the fire, a place, she said, it didn't belong. After all, Covington would say, more than half of the fire victims, thirteen out of the twenty-five, were white. The mayor wasn't alone in blaming the civil rights leader for fueling racial tensions in Hamlet. Martha Barr agreed, saying that Jackson "caused a great alienation that never had to exist." "When Jesse Jackson came to town," Ruth DeRosa remembers, with a hint of apology, mentioning her own liberal politics, "it got worse." Instead of bringing people together, his visits, she thought, stirred up suspicions and tensions. Jackson's presence in town terrified some whites, another health care provider recalled. A few feared that he would rouse their black neighbors and stir a second race riot in town.[43]

Months later, when local African American leaders asked Mayor Covington to include Jackson in Hamlet's official one-year commemoration of the fire, she wouldn't hear of it. "Several . . . individuals were anxious to have him speak," Covington remembered. "We didn't feel it was appropriate." "We wanted," she said, "to keep it on the plane of community healing." Hamlet's all-white city council backed her up and voted not to invite Jackson to appear at the memorial service. City manager Lee Matthews said, "Mr. Jackson stood for political forces, organized labor forces, and we didn't want it to be a political rally." Covington agreed, telling a reporter that Jackson would inject "politics" into the event, but mostly, she said, "It was our tragedy."[44]

That wasn't how the overwhelmingly black crowd crammed into Saint Peter in South Hamlet saw it. Some whispered that Reverend Harold Miller, the black preacher who participated in the official ceremony at City Lake, had "sold out his people."[45] Others spoke up loud and clear. "Why," fire survivor Conester Williams fumed, "should anybody try to take away our freedom of speech?" "When the smoke cleared," Sam Breeden observed, "it was 'that' group versus 'this' group." Ada Blanchard thought that the two memorial services revealed quite clearly the "separation here in this city between the citizens and the mayor." Covington never sought, Blanchard believed, "our input." Her friend and co-worker, Annette Zimmerman, agreed. "They should have been thinking about us, not Jesse Jackson," she maintained, "He was leaving, we were still here."[46]

The racial divisions on display that day, Zimmerman said, weren't new. Rather, they reflected the racial divide that had always existed in Richmond County. The lines of separation were just "more visible," she noted, one year after the fire, and they would remain in full view, Zimmerman insisted, for years to come.[47]

At both of the memorial services on the one-year anniversary of the fire, co-workers who hadn't seen each for a while asked about their kids and spouses, sore backs, seared lungs, and everyday anxieties and struggles. But, as one news reporter overheard, mostly they talked about the "the progress of lawsuits that have been filed on their behalf."[48]

That's what Ruth DeRosa and her team of trauma researchers heard as well—unending talk of attorneys, lawsuits, and settlements. Behind this talk was something deeper.

"There was so much anger," recalled child and adolescent psychiatrist Lisa Amaya-Jackson, who worked with DeRosa. She wasn't surprised by this emotion. The books on her shelves and the articles in the file cabinet at her UNC office taught her that when humans cause trauma through neglect or malice or even by accident, those left dealing with the consequences often feel anger, dismay, and rage. In response, they tend to formulate "revenge fantasies." "The victim can feel good," explains another trauma expert, "by planning vengeance and may experience pleasure at imagining the suffering of the target and pride at being on the side of some spiritual primal justice." Imperial survivors certainly experienced a similar rush of feelings. Maybe that was why a few people vandalized the plant and others spray-painted "KILLERS DIE, 25 LIVES" across the walls of the abandoned offices. Or maybe that explains the behavior of the son of one of the fire victims. Police found him one night standing in front of a Rockingham store holding a can of gasoline and a lighter. Down the street, two other businesses were in flames.[49]

As Amaya-Jackson remembers it, many of the Imperial victims were "focused . . . on revenge against the Roes." While some shared their "revenge fantasies" about hurting the owners, sending them to prison, and making them feel the kind of pain that they themselves had felt, most looked not for actual physical vengeance, but rather for some sort of moral justice. When they did, they looked largely to the courts to provide it, opting for litigation over legislation as the prime form of redress.[50] They wanted the Roes to *pay*—that's the word they used—for what they had done. They wanted them behind bars. And given how much, in the eyes of workers and their families, Emmett and Brad Roe seemed to care, to the point of obsession, about making money and "getting out the product," they wanted them to feel it financially.[51]

Clinical psychologist Juesta Caddell would come back from her interviews with Imperial workers and tell her colleague, Amaya-Jackson, what she heard in the field. With strained and edgy voices, victims and family members would say, "When I get my money, that's when justice will be served." "We'll get justice," another said, "in the courts." "They will pay," another added, "and then they will have nothing." Once they saw the Roes carted off to prison in handcuffs, once they got a check signed by the Roes (at least symbolically), then, and only then, some victims believed would justice be done. With it, many hoped, would come an end to the nightmares, flashbacks, jitters, and fears.[52]

Faith—faith in God and community as well as faith in justice, legal justice—sustained many in the years after the fire. But this faith in the courts had a dangerous side effect. If, as Amaya-Jackson worried at the time, the trials got delayed or clients didn't completely understand or believe their lawyers, or if the sentences handed down by judges didn't seem to fit the crime, the trauma for fire survivors and family members could get worse.[53] More distrust of officials. More sleepless nights. More racing hearts and cold sweats. More reckless spending. More need for pills and booze to dull the pain. More revenge fantasies. And a greater and more pressing need to do something to stop the voices in their heads and the pain in their hearts.

As early as September 11, 1991, representatives from the district attorney's office that covered Richmond County told reporters that they were considering filing serious charges against Emmett and Brad Roe and several others. At one point, the state labor commissioner, John Brooks, urged prosecutors to seek murder charges against the owners. The labor and activist group Black Workers for Justice, which began to organize in Hamlet after the fire, issued its own call to arrest Emmett Roe and put him on trial for murder. Then for months there was no word from the DA's office. Finally, in March 1992, it was announced that a grand jury had handed down indictments on twenty-five counts of involuntary manslaughter to Emmett Roe, Brad Roe, and James Hair. District Attorney Carroll Lowder explained to the press, somewhat vaguely, the thinking in his office. "The evidence is all about workplace safety," he said. "That's what the evidence supports in my opinion." Each charge carried a maximum sentence of ten years.[54]

Some Imperial workers and their families grumbled about the "involuntary" label. Others did the math and calculated that the Roes and Hair could each serve 250 years in prison—life and then some. To a number of them, this seemed "just."[55]

Emmett Roe hired Joseph B. Cheshire V to represent him. Many considered the forty-four-year-old Raleigh man to be the best criminal defense attorney in the entire state of North Carolina. Willing to fight like a "cornered dog" for his clients, he didn't know at first what sort of case he had with Roe.[56] For months on end, the press had pounded the factory owner. Story after story talked about the broken lives of Imperial workers and the locked doors that plunged the rural community into grief. Still, Cheshire knew that the key to a murder case in a small town in North Carolina was not so much what the newspapers and television reports said but what the prosecutor thought. If the district attorney valued the lives of the victims, Cheshire had learned over the years, then he stood at a distinct disadvantage. But, if he didn't, there was room to make a deal, and that sort of negotiation was another of Cheshire's talents as a lawyer. A profile in the *Raleigh News and Observer*, in fact, called the curly-haired, not quite buttoned-down Groton prep school graduate "The Deal Maker."

To get a sense of what would be on the table in Roe's case, Cheshire drove south from the capital to Matthews in 1992 to the offices of Carroll Lowder, the DA for the district covering Hamlet and Rockingham and several surrounding counties. Short, stout, and balding, Lowder, first elected in 1971, had built a reputation over the years as someone who could sway juries and put people behind bars. As a local reporter noted, he rarely "lost." He also had a reputation as a "good old boy." This meant that he talked with a southern accent and could glide through the courthouse crowd of lawyers, clerks, and law enforcement officers telling jokes and slapping backs. But in this case, it also carried with it, it seems, some troubling echoes of the region's painful racial history.[57]

A few years after the Imperial fire, the ACLU filed a motion on behalf of a black man charged with murder in Lowder's district. Research by the liberal organization uncovered some disquieting patterns. In this white-majority area, fifteen men had in recent years been given the death penalty. All but one of them was African American, and all too often they were convicted by all-white juries. On the other hand, they discovered that Lowder's office regularly extended non-capital plea bargains to defendants in cases involving black victims while insisting on capital penalties in white victims' cases. Digging for more evidence, the ACLU looked into the case of David Junior Brown, a black man convicted in Lowder's jurisdiction of murdering a white woman and her daughter. He was sentenced to death. In the trial notes, they found a piece of paper with the word "nigger" scrawled across it.[58]

When Cheshire got to Lowder's office, they talked for a few minutes about the weather and people they knew in common. As the conversation turned to Emmett Roe's case, the defense lawyer pretty quickly figured out where things stood. They didn't discuss much about the charges of neglect against his client or the 2,500 pages of evidence on the fire complied by the State Bureau of Investigation. Cheshire remembers Lowder, instead, talking about stolen chickens. "That's what these people do," he recalled him saying. Finishing his thoughts on the character of the men and women who worked at Imperial and died there, Lowder added, again according to Cheshire, "They were just a bunch of low-down black folks anyway."[59]

Cheshire got back in his car and headed home to Raleigh, knowing that the DA clearly didn't value the victims in the case and that there was a good chance he could strike a deal for Roe that would keep him away from a jury trial and lifelong prison sentence. "Sometimes beneficial plea offers fell in your lap," Cheshire said years later, "and you could not say, 'I am not going to accept that gift for my client because of your bigotry,' you accepted it and moved on." That, Cheshire added, "is one of the conundrums of the criminal defense lawyer."[60]

In September 1992, a little more than a year after the fire, the *New York Times* announced "a surprise plea agreement" in the Imperial case.[61] Avoiding a criminal trial, Emmett Roe pled guilty to twenty-five counts of involuntary manslaughter. As part of the settlement, the state dropped all charges against Brad Roe and James Hair. Emmett Roe was sentenced to nineteen years and eleven months in a minimum-security facility, with parole possible in less than five years.

After he formally entered his plea in court, Roe was taken to jail. He didn't make a statement to the press, though Cheshire described his client to the media as a "nonviolent" person who struck a deal to "save his family." [62]

Assistant District Attorney David Graham also spoke to the press. He painted a different picture of Roe. "Our investigation did show that Emmett Roe ran the plant as a dictator," he explained. "He personally made the decision to padlock the door." Insisting that justice had been served, he concluded, "I'm confident the person who is responsible . . . is in prison." [63]

Reporters tracked down Imperial survivors and the families of the victims to get their reactions. "Someone asked me what I thought was fair punishment for them," Catherine Dawkins, the widow of the Lance delivery man, remarked, "and I said, 'I don't think the electric chair would be as bad as what Phil went through the last few minutes of his life.'" [64] Line worker Dolores Gail Pouncey couldn't believe that Brad Roe had gotten off without punishment. He was "the worst," she said. "It was a set up," declared Mary Alice Quick's sister, Martina. Emmett Roe, she insisted, should "have to [do] the whole 250 years." "I don't think it's fair," proclaimed Lula Smith, whose daughter, Cynthia Ratliff, died at Imperial, "He's responsible for the fire. That's like murder." [65]

Fire survivor Conester Williams felt a mix of anger and disappointment. "Those were twenty-five of my best friends who died in that fire. I feel like he deserved more time." Still, she held out hope for justice: "I feel in my heart God is going to punish him in prison." [66]

Frustrations with the criminal justice system didn't stop Imperial workers from looking for revenge, for justice, and for money in civil court. An army of lawyers arrived in Hamlet on September 3, 1991, just behind the fire trucks and the news vans. Some came from up the road or had offices near the courthouse in Rockingham. Others flew in from Washington, D.C., or drove down from Durham. Hospital workers found lawyers wandering the corridors of ICU units looking for victims and family members. A few days later, "ambulance chasers" stalked the Victims Assistance Center. There were so many of them there that the city called in extra police officers to keep them away. Funeral directors heard late-night knocks on their doors. So did preachers. Several Imperial workers belonged to Reverend Miller's First Baptist Church. While he prepared to bury his parishioners and minister to the needs of the living, his phone rang. A lawyer on the other end of the line introduced himself and promised him a handsome finder's fee or a hefty church donation if he steered clients in his direction.[67]

Some of the meetings between lawyers and Imperial families produced mismatches. Well-educated and confident attorneys sweet-talked anguished and undereducated poor families. They promised justice in the form of financial windfalls. Just sign on the dotted line. Some told the bereaved that the cases would be hard, that testifying in court could dredge up painful memories and stir up raw emotions. They urged caution, explaining to them how hard it was to predict how juries and judges would react to evidence. It was harder still, some explained, to guess the size of settlements. Some victims and family members took note of the guarded tone and remained cautious. Others heard what they wanted to hear. They dreamed of roomy new homes out in the country and gleaming Cadillacs parked in the driveway. One local car dealer, in fact, offered loans to Imperial workers, saying they could drive their new vehicles off the lots right away and pay off the notes—with, of course, high interest—when they got their money. For others, it was simple. "We got bills to pay," was how Ada Blanchard, who couldn't go back to work yet and was trying to get by on worker's compensation and unemployment benefits, explained her reasoning for hiring a lawyer.[68]

By the first Christmas after the fire, just about everyone who had worked on the first shift at Imperial and their families had lawyered up, some with local attorneys and others with out-of-town solicitors.

In fact, nine days after the fire, the estate of Mary Lillian Wall, who got trapped behind the padlocked door near the dumpster and couldn't get out before the poisonous gases lurking in the plant killed her, filed the first lawsuit. Her lawyer alleged that Emmett and Brad Roe had removed evidence from the plant and, even more seriously, that they had showed "willful and wanton misconduct" with the locked and bolted doors. Despite the serious accusations, her attorney asked for the very modest sum of $10,000 in damages.[69]

Three weeks later, on October 2, 1991, Woody Gunter, a steady and thoughtful Rockingham lawyer representing Mildred Lassiter Moates and Gladys Faye Nolan, filed a civil suit charging the Roes with negligence and deliberately eliminating "effective interior barriers" that could have prevented the "spread of fire." Trying to find an escape, the filing claimed, Moates fell down and was trampled by her frightened co-workers, themselves running in the dark. She lost much of her eyesight and suffered permanent brain damage as a result of her injuries. A doctor pronounced her "neurologically unresponsive." Gladys Faye Nolan commuted to Imperial from Wallace, South Carolina, a town a third of the size of Hamlet. She fell unconscious during the blaze and suffered afterward from respiratory problems and severe burns on her arms. Worse were the flashbacks and nightmares that had her reliving the blaze from morning to night each day. Gunter raised the stakes on the lawsuits and asked for hundreds of thousands of dollars in damages for his clients.[70]

On October 18, 1991, John P. Coale, a high-profile Washington lawyer and the husband of Greta Van Susteren, later a Fox News personality, filed a sixth lawsuit, accusing Imperial Food Products of cutting back on maintenance at the plant to maximize profits. The plaintiffs included thirteen people injured in the fire and the relatives of ten people who died. Two weeks before he showed up at the U.S. District Court in Greensboro, Coale had been charged with illegally soliciting clients in Hamlet, though a warrant against him was never served. As he walked out of the courthouse the day of the filing, he told reporters that his clients stood to collect "hundreds of millions of dollars" from the company and its insurers. "This can hardly be called an accident," he said in a statement, "Roe and his subordinates guaranteed that a disaster of this magnitude would occur."[71]

Over the next several months, other fire victims and their families filed dozens of additional wrongful-death suits and more than fifty personal injury cases. The suits accused Emmett and Brad Roe and plant management of repeated acts of "gross, willful, and wanton" negligence, failure to provide proper fire suppression, and purposefully blocking exits and locking doors. By the start of 1992, Imperial Food Products and the Roes faced more than one hundred different lawsuits from dozens of lawyers and law firms all around the Southeast and mid-Atlantic.[72]

Most Imperial families dreamed rather modest dreams of paying off debts to funeral homes and furniture stores and escaping unscrupulous landlords and drafty tar-paper-covered shotgun houses. Some, stoked by the boasts of Coale and a few other lawyers, dreamed bigger dreams filled with tall houses, long boats, and flashy cars.[73] Most of them still wanted the Roes to suffer in some way, but this would get complicated.

Following a two-month investigation, the North Carolina Department of Labor cited Imperial Food Products for eighty-three violations of OSHA standards, many of them "willful." The agency fined the company a record-setting $808,150.[74] Emmett Roe called the ruling "simply absurd" and suggested that the fine was a politically motivated attempt by the state's workplace safety agency to stay out of federal hands.[75] Softening his pitch, if not his parenting style, the head of Imperial Food Products explained in a letter contesting the penalties, "My knowledge of the operation led me to believe it was a safe place to work. The fact that I ordered my son, Brad, to work in the plant . . . should, to reasonable people, dispel any notion that Imperial willfully violated anything which had any likelihood of causing death or serious bodily injury."[76] Still, Roe told state officials a month after the Labor Department's ruling that he was "financially unable to pay even one dollar of any fine you have assessed."[77]

The Department of Labor wasn't the only group knocking on the doors of Imperial Food Products' suburban Atlanta headquarters. Northwestern Bank of Pennsylvania in Wilkes-Barre wanted its loans paid back. Crown Credit, Credit Alliance, Dana Commercial Credit, Fleet Credit Incorporation, Hyster Credit, Orix Credit Alliance, and Rivera Finance were all looking for payments. In the fall of 1991, Imperial owed Cagle's tens of thousands of dollars for frozen chicken parts. The company hadn't paid all of its taxes or its water, utility, and phone bills in Cumming or Hamlet in full. And it had outstanding bills from Kikkoman International of San Francisco, Dixie Janitorial Services of Hamlet, the Sparks Belting Company of Grand Rapids, Michigan, L & L Welding of Rockingham, and Multi Spice from Tupelo, Mississippi.[78]

By August 1992, Emmett Roe ended up in bankruptcy court, though he showed up in the Greensboro chambers without a lawyer, acting confused and befuddled. "I don't know where I am," he whispered to Judge James Wolfe. "I have no assets." Claiming that banks removed $600,000 from his accounts the day after the fire to pay back the money he owed them, Roe declared, "I'm broke."[79] In a court filing, he said he had no cash, no savings, no furs or jewelry, and no auto, video, or computer equipment of any value. Over the next year or so, creditors, court officers, and forensic accountants found out that Emmett Roe wasn't lying, though some of the victims still believed he was hiding money and other assets.[80]

With Imperial Food Products out of money, lawyers turned their attention to the firm's three insurers: the American International Group, U.S. Fire Insurance Company, and the Liberty Mutual Insurance Company. For months after the fire, these companies balked at paying fire victims, though Liberty did honor worker's compensation claims. They argued that the conditions at Imperial were so bad, and so systematically unsafe, that they shouldn't have to pay the claims. Yet, by December 1992, the insurance companies had abandoned this argument and agreed to pay $16.1 million, the maximum coverage held by Imperial, to the 101 individuals and families who had filed claims in the names of dead, injured, and emotionally scarred victims. Based on a formula that factored in future income and the severity of injuries, a formula hammered out by the judge and insurance company representatives—the lawyers for the families had little say in the matter—payouts in the wrongful-death cases ranged from $175,000 to $1 million. Settlements in the seventy-seven injury cases began at $2,500 and went up to $1,138,000.70 for Mildred Moates, who remained a year after the fire permanently injured and in need of nonstop care.[81]

In 1993, lawyers for Imperial victims and their families filed another lawsuit, charging "reckless misconduct" against forty-one different companies for contributing to the disaster. They accused parts makers of selling shoddy products and oil companies of hawking dangerously flammable fluids. The suit named Stein, the manufacturer of the industrial fryer at the center of the processing room, as a defendant. It charged Kemlite, the maker of the drop tiles that hung over the fryer, with marketing a product that ignited too easily and released, when it sparked, hazardous levels of carbon monoxide that blinded, disabled, and disoriented people.[82] The multifaceted case turned out to be incredibly complicated and involved dozens of lawyers across multiple state lines. Expenses piled up as attorneys turned to teams of costly experts, scientists, and professional videographers. Eventually, after years of motions and counter-motions, the judge awarded the plaintiffs $24 million in damages. After covering all of the overhead costs and paying all of the lawyers' fees, Imperial workers settled their cases for between $35,000 and $70,000 each. They used the money to pay more bills and settle some debts, buy new trailers and cars, and purchase clothes for their kids and grandkids.[83]

Other lawsuits took aim at local and state governments. Several plaintiffs blamed the city of Hamlet, in particular the fire department, for negligence. They argued that the department's failure to inspect the plant and its alleged delay in entering the building on the morning of September 3 contributed to the death toll. After talking with Fire Chief David Fuller several times, the insurance company's claims supervisor Gary Johnson recommended a negotiated settlement. He didn't think the chief would make a credible and compelling witness on the stand if asked about the locked doors or allegations that he had a key to at least of one of them or rumors that the Roes paid off his department with chicken tenders. When Johnson pressed Fuller about these charges, the chief denied them, but he didn't get incensed. He didn't say, as Johnson expected him to, "That's a damn lie and I challenge any son of bitch who thinks it to say it to my face." With the backing of the town's elected council, its insurer, Harleysville Insurance Company, paid out between $250,000 and $500,000 to fire victims, and the case went away.[84] Another suit was filed against the state's Department of Labor for failure to inspect enough workplaces, but it didn't yield a settlement of any kind. Under North Carolina's Tort Claims Act, a person injured by the state's negligence could, in principle, collect up to $100,000. By a 5–2 decision, however, the North Carolina Supreme Court held that the labor department's failure to inspect the Hamlet factory, "while neglectful, is not the kind of negligence for which damages can be collected." From there, an appeal, *Stone III v. the North Carolina Department of Labor*, went to the United States Supreme Court, but the justices voted against hearing the case without comment.[85]

For some, the lawsuits created more disappointment, distrust, and trauma rather than a clear sense of justice. Unanswered questions surrounding the legal maneuvering of lawyers and how the settlements in their cases were determined acted for some as yet another set of triggers, especially when added to lingering questions about why Dobbins Heights firefighters were left on standby and why Hamlet officials said nothing about the locked doors. Unable to trust local leaders, the state Department of Labor, the fire department, the legal system, and their lawyers generated all-too-familiar—especially for people battling PTSD—feelings of helplessness, vulnerability, and dread. Some didn't even trust family members after sons and husbands stole from them and distant kin showed up asking for money. The uncertainties and tensions around the settlements negated the larger imagined moral mission of the lawsuits: justice.

The money burned a hole in some pockets. Lisa Amaya-Jackson remembered one woman who bought a new car for herself, one for her mom, and another for her dad. Pretty soon, she ran out of money, but not before her back pain, problems breathing, and frequent nightmares ended. Maybe she was thinking of Evelyn Wall, who received a six-figure settlement check.[86] "I never put any of it in the bank," she told *Washington Post* reporter Wil Haygood. Ten years after the fire, she was broke, her body so busted she couldn't sweep her kitchen floor without losing her breath and her mind so rattled with trauma that she couldn't tolerate crowds, even family gatherings. And she couldn't get through the day without a combination of antidepressants and high-blood-pressure pills. She felt like people in Hamlet looked right through her; maybe she reminded them of what they wanted to forget. It's like we "aren't human," she said.[87]

Drugs took over the lives of a few survivors. Sober and not so sober family members asked victims for gifts and interest-free loans, saying that they deserved this or that for taking care of the kids in the past and providing years of meals and housing. Georgia Quick couldn't remember the last time she saw her mother before she showed up at Duke University Hospital, where a number of injured workers ended up after the fire. Pretty soon, Quick knew why she was there. She wanted money. So did a few other family members, leaving her to wonder whom she could trust.[88]

Most felt like they didn't get what they were owed. "They didn't do us right," Ada Blanchard said about her lawyers and the judges after getting her settlement. "No," another survivor declared in 2015, "I don't think I got a fair settlement. No one did." Many were convinced, as one put it, that the lawyers "stole from us." The ones who seemed to cope the best with the tragedy were the ones who got treatment for their PTSD symptoms and were represented by lawyers they trusted, like Woody Gunter. Still, many wondered why they got what they got and why someone else, with less severe injuries or emotional pain, in their estimation, ended up with more. What was fair about that, they wondered? How did the lawyers end up with so much of the money? They weren't the one who suffered, were they? Some, as Stephen Frye, the psychologist who treated a number of the survivors, observed, were even competitive about the lawsuits. With new money creating new tensions, friends and family members, in some cases, turned against each other in the most vicious of ways.[89]

Frye told a story of an Imperial worker who picked sweet potatoes as a child, gave birth while still in her teens, and spent years battling with an abusive husband before she finally got him out of the house. For weeks after the fire, she sat almost motionless, not saying a word. Slowly, she got back on her feet and hired a lawyer, who then filed suit against the Roes and other plant managers. With her first settlement check, she put a down payment on a trailer and took in one of her sons, an out-of-work and troubled Gulf War veteran. Over the next few years, he allegedly drained his mother's accounts, and the bank foreclosed on her home. With her second settlement, she bought another home. Not long after, she went to church one day like she usually did and died there. Apparently, she had never drawn up a proper will, so her husband, who she had not officially divorced and who supposedly hit her while they were still together, got everything she had.[90]

Elaine Griffin's family life unraveled after the fire as well. Four years before the explosion, she started to work at Imperial. Some of her co-workers envied her. She had married the love of her life, Albert. He often came by the factory with greeting cards and flowers and they would walk to the parking lot holding hands.

Griffin escaped from the deadly smoke out the front door with singed lungs and burns on her legs and arms. When she went to sleep sometimes, she had nightmares about returning to the plant. "In [one] dream," she said, "I went back to work. I could visualize what it would be like. Those footprints on the door."[91] The first few months after the fire were hard on her and her family financially. Without work, they worried about paying their bills and buying Christmas presents for the kids.

Like most of her co-workers, Griffin hired a lawyer. Eventually, she got a settlement check of $30,638.48—not as big as some, but that was, in part, because she didn't suffer from extensive or debilitating injuries,

according to medical and court records. She got some more money from
the second settlement.

Sometime between the fire and that second settlement, Albert started
to smoke crack, and he couldn't stop. Arguments between Elaine and Albert, as reporter Wil Haygood heard from Griffin's friends and neighbors,
"kept erupting . . . over money."

"If she got $100, he didn't want $50," Elaine's onetime co-worker Annette Zimmerman recalled, "he wanted the whole $100." [92]

By 1997, according to some who knew her, Elaine was fed up. She
had cut Albert off from her bank accounts and her worker's compensation checks. She may have even taken up with another man. He lashed
out. In April of that year, police came to the couple's trailer and arrested
Albert for assault to inflict serious harm. A little more than a year later,
on May 27, 1998, Police Captain Jay Childers returned to the trailer at
2:40 in the morning. He found Elaine slumped over the couch with blood
coming out of a hole in her head. The couple's grade-school son told investigators that his parents had been fighting. A Jennings Model 32-caliber
automatic pistol and a few spent shell casings lay on the floor. At first,
Albert insisted that his wife had killed herself. More than a year later, he
waived his right to a trial and pled guilty to second-degree murder. The
judge sentenced him to 191 months in prison with 426 days credit for
time spent in custody. [93]

The trauma of the fire didn't end for Philip Dawkins Jr. the day of the
fire, that day when someone handed the volunteer fireman his father's
lifeless body.

Before the fire, Philip Jr. liked to ride off-road vehicles through muddy
trails and along the backroads of Richmond County. But afterward, he
became, according to a friend, withdrawn and quiet, and rarely left his
house. [94]

In April 1995, Philip Jr.'s wife, Wendy, by then lost in a haze of crack,
went missing. Her husband joined the search for her until her bruised
and beaten body, wrapped in a trash bag and blanket, was found floating
in Blewett Falls Lake, a reservoir known for bass fishing a short distance
from Hamlet. Somehow, the circular weights and anchor attached to her
didn't keep her at the bottom of the water. It turned out that Philip had
killed her. According to the evidence, he had shot her in the back of the

head at the home they shared together with their infant son before loading her into a boat and dumping her into the water.[95]

Not every story, of course, ended in gun blasts, bloodshed, and addiction, though far too many did. And far too many fire victims and survivors, for far too long, continued to feel a mixture of dismay and distrust.

For weeks after the fire, Georgia Quick lay in a hospital bed at Duke University. Estranged from her husband, far from her daughter, and unable to talk because of her injuries, she felt alone and isolated. The nurses on her floor became the most constant and warming presence in her life. They took care of her wounds and brought her food. Even more, they inspired her. A few years after getting out of the hospital, she went back to school and became a certified nurse's aide.

Quick couldn't have moved into her new, cleaner, and steadier career without the help of her lawyer, Woody Gunter—"He went out of his way for me," Quick noted—and without the help of Dr. Stephen Frye. Forty-six at the time of the fire, the Charlotte-based psychologist had spent years working with Vietnam veterans and teaching them how to cope with sudden flashbacks, pressing anxieties, and other PTSD symptoms. Representatives for Liberty Mutual Insurance, Imperial's worker's compensation carrier, contacted Frye while Quick was still in the hospital after they realized that the survivors' psychological injuries were as bad as, if not worse than, their physical ailments. He made his first trip to Hamlet in October 1991 and met twelve rattled women and men in a room with folding chairs in City Hall. After that meeting and a few others, "people would come up to me privately, almost in a fearful way," Frye recounted, "and ask if I could come back and see them individually. I thought it was wonderful that they could ask." Over the next eight years, Frye estimated that he made the same seventy mile drive from Charlotte to Hamlet more than seven hundred times, eventually offering counseling to thirty-five victims of the Imperial fire, including Georgia Quick, in group and individual sessions.[96]

"When I started to see Dr. Frye," Quick recalled years after the fire, "that's when I started to feel better."

The same was true for Lillie Bell Davis. Within weeks of the fire, she began working with Dr. Frye. He helped her understand that she wasn't alone and that she needed to explore her pain, grief, and loss in order to reclaim her life. Frye was still going back and forth from Charlotte to Hamlet when Davis got a settlement check for $60,000. In Richmond County's anemic real estate market, that was more than enough, as she wrote in her self-published memoir—the writing was itself part of her therapy—"to buy the home we always dreamed of." She and her husband moved from the place where they raised their children to a place where they "could have something better" and where her new piano, another part of her therapy, "would fit real nice."

Moving out of town might have been, in part, what saved Davis and allowed her to launch what she called "a new beginning."[97]

As the one-year anniversary of the fire approached, Ruth DeRosa wrapped up her field research. The weekend trips to the Rockingham motel and the raised eyebrows from the front desk ended. As she packed up her interview notes, she knew that some fire survivors still suffered from PTSD symptoms. A major contributing factor, she determined, was the charred and mangled Imperial building. It was still there, looking almost exactly like it did the morning of the blaze. Marks from the investigation still remained spray-painted on the doors. Crumpled plastic trays used to package chicken products rested in random piles on the sides of the building. When it rained, some said, they could still get a whiff of fried tenders lingering in the air.

Stephen Frye and other psychologists who worked with Imperial survivors also saw the plant as a trigger.[98] When their patients went by the site, their breathing picked up, their hearts started to pound, their muscles tensed, their eyes teared, and they broke out into a cold sweat. But to Ruth DeRosa, the burnt factory shell surrounded by patches of weeds and piles of broken glass was more than just a trigger—it was a "form of terror."[99]

Like most Hamlet residents, the town's mayor, Abbie Covington, wanted the plant torn down. "It reminds me of a tomb," she said. But she didn't necessarily want to turn the site into a memorial—not at first, at least—as some of the survivors and their supporters insisted on doing. Concerned about the lack of jobs and tax revenues in town, she, a few city council members, and a number of businesspeople hoped to get another factory onto the prime industrial spot with its easily accessible railroad spur. Still, whenever Covington could she avoided the plant, what she called the "the ever present reminder" of the Imperial tragedy, by driving the other way or taking the long way home, if she had to, rather than turn down Bridges Street.[100]

Yet African Americans, especially working-class African Americans, couldn't so easily avoid the wreckage. They couldn't just walk the other way or go down another street. The Imperial plant stood squarely on the black side of Hamlet's persistent residential racial divide. One month after the fire, two months after the fire, a year after the fire, the plant was still there. If Dobbins Heights' Johnny Reddick or Rockingham's Elaine Griffin or Hamlet's Annette Zimmerman wanted to go to Saint Peter United Methodist or the Prayer and Faith Temple Church of God in Christ, or to the City Limits nightclub or to the Buttercup Park with their kids, they had to pass the factory's burned-out remains. When they drove to see friends who lived in the Leroy Hubbard Homes housing project, they could see through the broken windows into the plant. When the leaves had fallen, they could see the plant from Main Street. Coming the other way, they could still see the loading dock where the truck was parked the morning of the fire as well as the door that had trapped Loretta Goodwin inside. If they looked hard enough, they could even still see the boot prints left by maintenance man Bobby Quick when he kicked down the breakroom door on the morning of September 3, 1991.[101]

Bobby Quick's strong legs helped to save Gloria "Tootsie" Malachi's life. A year later, though, Malachi's back still throbbed, and she still suffered from chronic headaches. The physical ailments were easier to deal with than the mental anguish, the paralyzing fears and never-ending anxiety. From the front windows of her house, just a few doors down from the plant, she could see, first thing every morning and last thing every night, the building's burnt and twisted remains. "I get scared when I go by the plant," she told a reporter. "This affects my mind. Sometimes, I feel like I don't have a future."[102]

With Malachi and her neighbors in mind, Hamlet's African American leaders started to press city officials to get rid of the mangled structure. Determining the building's precise legal status presented some tough legal challenges, especially when no one on the all-white city council or in the city manager's office was eager to pay for lawyers' fees out of the city's already tight budget for something that wouldn't generate additional revenues. At least, that's what the people living near the factory came to believe. "There were accusations about the city regime," recalled Reverend Miller, "about their indifference." Inaction on the building, coupled with talk that won't die down about the "fire house incident," as locals referred to keeping the Dobbins Heights Fire Department on standby on September 3, 1991, created a perception that the city's white political leadership put money ahead of people, especially black people. This, in turn, Miller observed, stirred up more distrust and "fueled a growing racial divide." [103]

A few years after the fire, the city ordered Imperial Foods to clear the site, but neither Emmett Roe nor Brad Roe responded. They were trying to put Hamlet behind them. Emmett Roe was embroiled in his own legal battles, and Brad Roe was trying to patch together a new life. Not long after the fire, he got married and moved to Charlotte and then to Atlanta. In both places, he worked as a bartender. Complicating matters, Imperial Food Products was locked in bankruptcy proceedings. Even if the town had the money and wanted to tear down the plant, local officials couldn't do so without a judge's approval or a clear deed to the property. Hamlet didn't have either of these things, though it didn't seem to some like town leaders pursued either of these avenues very aggressively. Several lawyers for the victims and their families didn't want the building gone. They still needed it to construct their cases. The building made up part of the physical evidence. [104]

So the plant stayed there past the second anniversary of the fire. It was there when the first lawsuits were filed. It was there when Joe Cheshire went to see Carroll Lowder. It was still there when the first settlement checks arrived, and it was there when Emmett Roe went to prison and when he got out. It was there when Elaine Griffin was shot dead and Wendy Dawkins's limp body was plunged into a lake. It was there when Lillie Bell Davis moved out of town.

Allen Mask Sr. had once served as the principal of the Monroe Avenue Elementary School. Like most well-educated African Americans in the area, he didn't live in Dobbins Heights or in South Hamlet near the plant and the projects. But he still felt the burnt and kudzu-draped building's presence in his community. In 1998, he wrote to Jim Hunt, who was at the time beginning his second stint in the governor's office, about the fire and the state of his hometown. That tragedy, he told the state's Democratic chief executive, has left "an indelible scar on the members of this community." But would you believe, he asked him, that seven years after the fire, "the carcass of that tragic building still stands in its ruins . . . as a reminder of this tragic loss still to this day?"[105]

Reverend Tommy Legrand joined forces with Mask to get the building torn down and removed. Years before the fire, he had been living and working in Philadelphia. One day, as Legrand explained it, he had a vision. The Lord called him to rural North Carolina. Within weeks, he stood on the back of a pickup truck, preaching the gospel to anyone who would listen in Dobbins Heights and the African American sections of Hamlet. He kept at it, and his following grew. Eventually, he secured a small patch of land at the corner of Thomas Street and Buttercup Avenue in South Hamlet and founded the Prayer and Faith Temple Church of God in Christ. In the early days, the congregation met in a simple structure with wood benches and no running water or electricity. Over time, Legrand built, largely with his own hands, a plain, low-slung brick sanctuary and then a food pantry, both of which stood across the street from the swings and basketball court at Buttercup Park, a stone's throw away from the Hubbard housing project and the Imperial factory site.[106]

By the 1980s, Legrand had extended his ministry out into the community. He belonged to a local group pushing for better schools and the recognition of Martin Luther King Jr.'s birthday as a local and state holiday. Some called him a "hot head," others a "rabble rouser," but Legrand felt like he couldn't attend to his mostly poor and working class congregation's spiritual needs without dealing with the cloud of "hopelessness" he saw hanging over the area around his church.[107]

"My aim," Legrand declared, "was to upgrade the community, to instill hope."

"The building was an ugly site," he remarked. "It stole hope."

A year after Mask wrote to Governor Hunt about the building, eight years after the fire, Legrand addressed Hamlet's city council. By this time, the Hamlet preacher and doctor, representing the two sides of the economic divide in the town's black community, were working together. With Mask in attendance, Legrand told the elected officials that the abandoned Imperial site served as "a constant reminder of the tragedy." Healing could only come to the community around his church when the industrial ruins were cleared away and replaced by a memorial, not developed for future commercial use, as several council members were urging.[108]

"It is our feeling," Mask explained in a letter to Jesse Jackson in 1999, "that if it [Imperial] had been in another neighborhood, by now, some means would have been found to get rid of this building, and build a park, [or] center or something positive could have come from this tragedy."[109]

"It's given us a black eye," Hamlet City Manager Lee Matthews admitted in 2000 about the fire and the factory shell still standing. Yet, again and again, the city and the state balked at doing anything. There were liens, judgments, and budgets to worry about, they said, and not disingenuously, but African American residents remained convinced that what was lacking was the will and concern for fire victims and the people of color living around the building.

State Senator Wayne Goodwin heard Mask and Legrand. The white Democrat from Hamlet asked for help from his colleagues in the General Assembly to clear the Imperial site. He told them that "many of the survivors lived within 100 yards of the structure" and that it had a "psychological effect" on them. Few of his fellow lawmakers, though, jumped at the chance to pitch in. Some questioned if this was, in fact, the state's responsibility. Others threw up their hands and said that there wasn't enough money in an already tight budget for tearing down and removing the wreckage of burnt factories. Rebuffed at first, Goodwin kept pushing in Raleigh.[110]

Reverend Legrand kept battling away in Hamlet as well. Around the time of his city council appearance in 1998, the South Hamlet religious leader struck up a relationship with his congressional representative, Robin Hayes, a first-term Republican from Concord. Not many from Hayes's party got elected in these parts of North Carolina, not even in the era of Ronald Reagan, and especially not in Richmond County where Sheriff Raymond Goodman, a staunch Democrat, kept things under tight control even after he stepped down from power in 1994. Desperate to see the Imperial building gone, Legrand vowed to work with anyone who would listen, and Hayes, an economic and social conservative, heard him. He heard him when he told him how hard it was for local residents to drive by the plant on their way to the grocery store or gas station or a Little League game. When Hayes had a chance, he cornered the House majority whip, Tom DeLay, and majority leader, Dick Armey. He told them about the burned-out factory and how it brought "back a flood of bad memories every time someone looks out their front door." Trying to help their colleague from a majority Democratic district, the Republican house leaders approved a $50,000 grant to the city of Hamlet to get rid of the building as part of a $11.3 billion federal relief package to deal with damages stemming from Hurricane Hugo.[111]

By this point, almost ten years after the fire, the factory site was in a treacherous state. Torn pieces of paper and shards of glass littered the ground. Beams poked out. Walls listed to the right and left. Neighborhood kids climbed through holes in the perimeter fence to explore the wreckage. Teenagers hid behind the vacant site, smoking joints and drinking cans of beer and bottles of vodka. Locals feared another round of tragedy caused by neglect. What if the structurally compromised building collapsed on a kid? What if a piece of glass ripped through someone's shirt or shoe? Rumor had it that there were barrels of toxic chemicals and noxious liquids buried in the rumble. What if a young boy or girl swallowed something poisonous? What about all that asbestos supposedly in the plant?

Still, city leaders turned down the $50,000 secured by Representative Hayes, saying that it wasn't enough to do the job the right way and pay for a full and necessary environmental impact study. In page after page of precise lawyerly detail, city attorney Stephan Futrell advised local officials against accepting the grant because of "unresolved liability issues." Ten years and counting after the fire, the building remained up on Bridges Street, part of South Hamlet's landscape of hopelessness.[112]

African Americans in Hamlet didn't fully believe the budgetary or legal reasons for the town's inaction. Some suspected that local white Democrats were playing politics with their part of town. They thought that the majority-white city council might have turned down the funding from Congress because its members didn't want to help an embattled

Republican. Others repeated rumors that local leaders didn't want the Imperial site cleared for a memorial. This tension and mistrust in the black community was further evidenced by the fact that Loretta Goodwin swore that she heard that Mayor Abbie Covington and her family owned the property and that they wanted to sell it to another industrial firm and make a hefty profit, a rumor that, even if it was repeated, was entirely unfounded.[113] For others, especially African Americans, the only explanation for the building's still being there revolved around issues of race and class. "I honestly thought if it had been in an upscale neighborhood," Annette Zimmerman said, "it won't have taken so long." "If this would have been in another neighborhood," Allen Mask argued along similar lines, "it wouldn't have been there that long, that's for sure." If Hamlet city leaders had wanted to build a new fire department on this location or something that the white community needed, there was no question, Mask maintained, that the "city . . . would find a way to get it built."[114]

Finally, in August 2002, state senator Goodwin, with the help of PTSD researcher Lisa Amaya-Jackson, got the state's health director, H. Dennis McBride, to declare the Imperial site "a public nuisance." Once that label got officially pasted onto the property, lawmakers in Raleigh came up with a $78,000 grant to Hamlet to tear down the building.

"There [is] a great sense of gratitude that it [is] finally happening," declared Reverend Legrand. "There [is] excitement for the victims. I hope it brings some healing for them."[115]

Later that year, Congressman Hayes joined Reverend Legrand for a service at his church. After reciting prayers and singing songs, the congregation marched behind Legrand, armed with a sledgehammer, over to the Imperial site. Legrand and Hayes each took a whack at the building and then stepped aside as a backhoe started to claw at the plant's remains. It took months to bust through the tangle of weeds and layers of concrete and steel and get everything removed.[116]

Hamlet is a small town, so it shouldn't be surprising or ironic that one of the men who worked on the removal was fire survivor Annette Zimmerman's husband.

Today, the property is cleared. It is a flat field of thick blades of grass mixed with batches of weeds and a few random bare spots. At one end, near where the loading dock once stood, sits a granite memorial not much bigger than an average-size tombstone. Leading up to it are twenty-five stepping stones. Framing the pathway are twenty-five matching crepe myrtle trees planted in a U-shaped formation. Maybe it's the sun. Maybe there is too much of it and too little shade, but the trees don't seem to be flourishing. They look thin and a little vulnerable, like a strong wind could snap them in half the next time it blows through. But, despite it all, they are still there.

Before the fire and the controversy over placing the Dobbins Heights fire-fighters on standby, and before the fights over the memorials, the lawsuits, and the building, Loretta Goodwin rented a house where squirrels raced back and forth across the attic floor. With the money from the lawsuits, she paid off her debts and settled into a modest 1950s-era bungalow on a quiet street with a church across the way and a school at the end of the block. She filled the place with leather couches and comfortable chairs and a matching dining room set almost too big for the space. Though no one would confuse her home with a mansion, it is big enough so that her children, grandchildren, and extended family have been able to live with her there on and off over the last two-plus decades.[117]

Twenty years after the fire, on a bright autumn day, the cloudless sky a perfect shade of Carolina blue, Loretta Goodwin sat in her living room with the shades drawn tight over the windows. She used to walk every where, she said. But now she doesn't walk anywhere, not that there are many places to go in Hamlet these days. It's too hard for her to breathe, and her legs hurt all of the time. She has trouble remembering little things. But even as she loses track of her keys and her purse, the fire stays with her. She still can't sleep. Night after night, she stays up and stares at the television, trying to avoid the nightmares that might come. Sometimes she gets mad at network programmers if there isn't anything on for her to watch.

Goodwin is still trapped by the fire, just like her town and the rest of the country are all still trapped by the same system of cheap that was the mean and divisive force behind the tragedy of September 3, 1991.

EPILOGUE

When you're a historian, people ask you all the time what you are working on. Over the last six years, I have told them, "I'm writing a book about a fire in 1991 in a chicken processing plant in Hamlet, North Carolina, where John Coltrane was born, and where twenty-five people died behind locked doors."

After hearing this, I usually get two follow-up comments.

"What year was that again?"

"1991," I answer.

"Wow, that wasn't that long ago."

Then they say, "That sounds a lot like that fire in New York . . . at that sweatshop where all those people died."

They are, of course, right. The year 1991 wasn't all that long ago, and the fire at Imperial does seem like an eerie reprise of the disaster that took place at the Triangle Shirtwaist Factory in New York's Greenwich Village eighty years earlier, when an eighth-, ninth-, and tenth-floor factory that produced women's blouses caught fire.

As the workers in that cluttered facility heard the screams of "Fire!" on a March afternoon in 1911, they rushed to the stairwells and exits, only to find them locked. The doors had been shut, the owners later said, to stop the women on the line from stealing fabric and taking unauthorized breaks. Dozens of terrified laborers jumped out the windows to avoid getting burned alive. Down below, shoppers on their daily rounds, firefighters, and newspaper reporters looked on with horror as bodies seemed to drop down from the sky. The death toll from the fire reached 146, making this the worst industrial "accident" in the history of New York City. One hundred and twenty-three of the dead were women, most of them young and single; almost all of them Jewish and Italian immigrants.

The shock of the Triangle fire brought about a rash of new laws and a sweeping overhaul of industrial regulations in New York. Before he visited the victims' families, State Assemblyman Al Smith was a typical Tammany Hall operative. Politics, to him, were about transactions, about handing out favors, collecting graft, and staying in power. After the tragic fire, he governed, writes David Von Drehle in his gripping book, *Triangle: The Fire That Changed America*, "as though the ghosts of the Triangle were looking over his shoulder."[1]

Smith's political heirs, Frances Perkins (who watched from the street on the day of the fire and was the first woman ever to serve in the cabinet), Robert Wagner (longtime New York senator and sponsor of the most important labor legislation of the twentieth century), and, of course, his successor in the governor's office and later president of the United States, Franklin D. Roosevelt, carried this spirit with them. The ghosts of Triangle followed them to Washington and made their way into the New Deal.

Whatever the shortcomings of the rash of legislation passed between 1933 and 1938, from its refusal to confront Jim Crow laws and practices to its caving to fiscal conservatives to its building of a safety net that from the start was riddled with gaping holes, the New Deal did change the nation.[2] It established the principle, largely accepted by the mainstream of both the Democratic and Republican Parties for the next four decades, that the government's job was to protect the most vulnerable, provide a modicum of economic security, and foster equality, however vaguely defined.

The fire in Hamlet produced its own wave of reform. In the wake of the deadly blast at Imperial, North Carolina lawmakers enacted measures to authorize the hiring of new OSHA investigators and support staff, protect whistle-blowing employees against reprisals, increase fines for workplace safety violations, and require accident-prone businesses to institute in-house safety programs.[3] Local and state officials, meanwhile, made sure fire departments investigated workplaces at least once every three years and drew up and kept on file pre-disaster firefighting plans. At a memorial ceremony to mark the twenty-fifth anniversary of the Imperial fire, the state's current insurance commissioner and chief fire marshal, Hamlet native Wayne Goodwin, declared, "By the lessons learned, workplaces are safer. So are our public buildings and our homes."[4]

But the fire at Imperial did not, like the blaze at Triangle, change the statewide or national conversation. Cheap still reigned, a year after the fire, ten years after the fire, and today.

What happened at Imperial Food Products—the calculated neglect, deliberate lack of oversight, and piercing indifference to "folks like them"— was an extreme version of what was going on across the country at the time. Large swaths of the nation were being dragged back to the Gilded Age, back to a world of deregulation, monopoly control over labor markets, and mass economic and physical insecurity. What was new was the ideology—and the faith, really—behind the return of America, especially its small towns and rural crossroads, to yesterday.

Beginning in the middle of the 1970s, politicians, business leaders, and everyday people across the United States embraced the notion of cheap. They shared a collective belief in the power and virtue of cheap goods, cheap foodstuffs, cheap government, and cheap labor as the surest and fairest way to solve the most vexing problems that plagued the nation, from inflation to the loss of manufacturing jobs to government inefficiency to the need for greater personal responsibility to the push for less welfare spending. The wholesale acceptance of the social gospel of cheap, of getting more by paying less and worrying about the consequences later, shaped the decision making of economists, policy makers, consumers, and the Roes themselves. Cheap led food writers and chefs to herald the coming of cheap chickens without looking too closely at how these animals got so incredibly inexpensive in the first place. Cheap convinced policy makers that regulations cost too much and weren't worth the trouble. And cheap made some people more valuable than others were and some places harder to see than others.

As horrifying and shocking as it was, the Hamlet fire was the nearly predictable outcome of the reign of the system of cheap, which extended far beyond Emmett and Brad Roe and their out-of-the-way factory. It became the central logic for decision making in the United States from the middle of the 1970s onward. Food scientists offered cheap food as a solution to poverty. The answer to a business slowdown was cheaper government. Flagging profits could be fixed with cheaper labor. Cheaper labor could be expected to get by on cheaper goods. And those cheaper goods would, it seems, blunt any popular outrage against the system of cheap. But all of this cheapness was bound to explode—and that's what happened in Hamlet.

Hamlet is as ordinary as its name suggests. And it is, as locals joke, two hours from just about anywhere. But, at the same time, it is connected to everywhere and everything. Understanding what happened along Main Street and Bridges Street, why Emmett Roe opened a factory there in the early 1980s, why government officials left him and his plant managers alone, why his company processed the foods they did, the way they did, and why Loretta Goodwin needed a job so badly that she went to work somewhere where she couldn't go to the bathroom without having to ask permission means identifying and naming the most fundamental and far-reaching shift in America in the last five decades: the embrace of the idea of cheap as a paramount social good and viable solution to social problems. This meant that while Hamlet might have looked like a place stuck in time with its slow pace of life and old-timey downtown drugstore serving cream sodas at the counter, it was in 1991 at the cutting edge of the assault on the ghosts of Triangle and the spirit of Fordism and the New Deal, on the ideas that higher wages and robust consumption were positive economic forces and that the government existed, at least in part, to provide security and protection for those at the bottom of society.

The fire at Imperial Food Products grew out of the disappearance of well-paying jobs on the railroad and the spread of minimum-wage work into the voids left behind. The Hamlet story is, then, the story of the emergence over the last forty years of an economically and physically vulnerable working poor as the largest segment of the American working class. It is the story of feverish state and municipal competition for employers and jobs and the resulting movement of industry to the South and to the nation's hinterlands. In fact, it bears repeating that heavily rural North Carolina became, quite remarkably, the most industrial state in the nation by 1990. With the state government's help, businesses created a new industrial geography to shore up flagging profits and to take advantage of isolated labor markets and isolated laborers, like Loretta Goodwin. Relocating to rural areas allowed companies to effectively silence workers and prevent them from speaking out against hazardous conditions and low pay. As a result, it was nearly impossible for workers to organize durable unions or even to see them as a viable counterweight to management. At the same time, the political economy of cheap that brought new businesses to the countryside diluted working people's faith in government and government solutions to their problems because the government always seemed to be on the side of someone else. This is the story, then, of the origins of the world of today, a world marked by gaping inequalities and stunning political inertia.

This is the story of a company, like so many other companies in recent America, methodically assembling a cheap labor force. It couldn't have done so without both of the major political parties in the United States backing deregulation and the lax enforcement of labor laws. But it also would not have been possible without the unintended consequences of the civil rights movement, the women's movement, and larger liberal gains. Before the breakdown of legal Jim Crow, black women and men couldn't, for the most part, work inside southern factories tending machines or standing along assembly lines. If an African American laborer got an industrial job, he (and sometimes she) worked on the outside of the plant unloading coal or inside sweeping cotton dust. The twisted logic of white supremacy somehow came up with the idea that black people couldn't tend to machines. In the wake of the stirring marches and landmark legislation of the 1960s, legal segregation and some of the more explicit forms of gender discrimination ended, eliminating many racial and sexual categories of employment and creating a measure of equality of opportunity. But the breakdown of employment barriers did not generate economic equality in less-skilled jobs so much as it created larger pools of workers competing against one another in a world of dwindling prospects. In a sense, bosses like Emmett Roe could now exploit black and white labor, male and female labor, equally, and that meant that they got the labor they wanted cheaper, with some built-in divisions.[5]

Whatever equality black woman and men in Richmond County, North Carolina, gained at the employment bureau or under the warmth of Friday night lights, the roots, and many of the branches, of Jim Crow remained in place. Long after the passage of the Civil Rights Act of 1964 and long after the separate water fountains in the town's train depot got pulled out of the wall, Hamlet remained segregated, a place where black people lived, prayed, and drank on their side of town and white people lived, prayed, and drank on the other side of the divide. Cheap didn't change that or the suspicions and distrust that existed between white and black people, distrust bred by a lifetime of disregard, neglect, and small and large aggressions, ranging from harsh words to demeaning rituals to police harassment and abuse. Cheap meant that when the all-white Hamlet city council couldn't find the money in its budget to tear down the Imperial plant, black families thought the inaction was about race and how little black lives mattered. Addressing these sorts of inequalities had no place in the system of cheap, so little changed.

Still, like underpaid workers of all races across the world in the age of cheap, Loretta Goodwin knew that in this new order, with its holdovers from the old one, she was expendable. Indeed, Brad Roe and his Imperial plant managers reminded her every day of her vulnerability. If she complained, the foremen told her he would fire her. If he did, how would she support her family? Not with public assistance. That had been cut to reduce taxes and make things better for business. So she said nothing about the slippery floors, leaky connections from the conveyor belt to the machine box, absence of fire drills, or daily presence of mechanics who jerry-rigged machines with leftover parts to make sure that chicken parts kept zipping down the assembly line.

The Hamlet story is also the story of eating in the age of cheap. It stemmed from the triumph of convenience food, the spread of the microwave oven, and the falling-off in culinary knowledge in the United States. It is about the growing inequalities at the dinner table and about how the other half eats. Even more, it is about the glaring paradox of plenty in recent America where the wrong sorts of calories don't cost much, though they are almost always unhealthy, both for the hungry consumers eating them and the frenzied workers who make them.

But mostly the Hamlet story is about the unaccounted-for costs of cheap. Cheap was not simply a business strategy, nor was it a personal price calculation or a "perceptual shift," as the journalist Ellen Ruppel Shell maintains in her book *Cheap: The High Cost of Discount Culture*.[6] The rise of cheap amounted to a new(ish) and, in the end, fiercer and narrower social imagining than the one fashioned by Al Smith, Frances Perkins, Robert Wagner, and FDR—one that borrowed from the pre-Triangle past and rose out of what the historian Daniel Rodgers has called the "great fracture," a dividing line in American life between earlier notions of history and society that stressed collective sacrifice and common fate and a newer one that emphasized individual choice and personal outcomes.[7] The shock of Watergate, the defeat in Vietnam, steadily declining wages, vanishing industries, and rising oil prices and widespread inflation together stirred a slew of new anxieties. When the New Deal– and Great Society–inspired policies of the past couldn't fix these things in a hurry, a new and largely unstated accord emerged that borrowed from the business progressivism of North Carolina governor Jim Hunt and Hamlet mayor Abbie Covington and brought together Democrats and Republicans, the rich and the middle classes, northerners and southerners.[8] Far better, the new majority asserted, to exchange more business for less government, because if the pie was no longer going to expand, at least the essential pieces should cost less. This broadly shared ideological accord helped to sweep away union protections and support for higher wages as a social good and to stymie the regulatory state that had been built from the Progressive Era through the Nixon years. As it did, it replaced the New Deal ideals of protecting the weak, social security, and broad-based economic equality maintained through higher paychecks and robust levels of consumption with an alternative political economy of cheap. This new set of ideas stressed reduced levels of government intervention (in some areas, though not all); lower pay, especially at the bottom of the economic ladder, to create more overall jobs; and everyday bargains, putting the individual consumer and her or his "right" to have something inexpensive ahead of community and the common good. In the world of cheap, social fairness came not through grassroots organizing, decent pay for steady work, or state action to oversee factory safety and the health of water and airways, but rather through choices of discounted food, inexpensive clothes, and easily replaced TVs, washing machines, and microwaves.

On the surface, the new order seemed to work. Taxes fell. Government spending on social programs dropped along with factory inspections and the enforcement of health and safety regulations. As the proponents of cheap from both the Republican and Democratic Parties predicted, sticker prices did, in fact, fall during the 1980s. The average family of four spent 18 percent less on food during the Clinton years than it did during the Reagan years.⁹ Chicken, the era's most industrialized food product, cost no more in 1983 than it had sixty years earlier in real dollars.¹⁰ Lower-priced fried tenders and other items allowed low-paid workers to stretch their paychecks and buy more at K-Mart and Kroger.

Yet the new cost structure only made things *look* cheap. Scratch beneath the surface in Hamlet, or at a Walmart superstore today, and you will find the extremely high personal, communal, and political costs of cheap.¹¹

For working people, the regime of cheap was not an abstraction. It added stress and costs to every part of Loretta Goodwin's life, from the furniture and VCR she bought on credit with high interest payments at a store along the highway to the wobbly house with squirrels running across the attic floor where she lived. Cheap decided what she did for a living, what she and her kids ate for breakfast, lunch, and dinner, and when—or if—she went to see a doctor or dentist. As the relationship between Goodwin and the father of her children crumbled in a fog of disappointment, the railroad industry, long the mainstay of Hamlet's local economy, pulled out of town for the most part. As the switching yards and maintenance facilities scaled back, shedding hundreds, even thousands, of well-paying union jobs, Emmett Roe smelled the town's despair from afar. He bought the shuttered ice cream plant on Bridges Street and turned it into a chicken further-processing operation. This was happening just as Goodwin found herself alone and in need of money. Like so many in the world of cheap, she traded time at home with her children for time at work, relying on family, friends, and television programs for child care as she labored in the burgeoning fast food industry to produce low-cost, high-fat convenience foods for people just like her with low-paying jobs and little time to cook. She was paid poorly for this cooking and processing, so she depended on cheap food to get by. In fact, even with the overall drop in food prices in the 1980s, a substantial chunk of her paycheck went right back to food companies, like the one she worked for, to buy her family's inexpensive meals of chicken nuggets and microwavable fries. Goodwin and her co-workers relied on the cheap foods they made to get by at home in terms of cost, calories, and time. These same cheap foods, though, led them down an unhealthy road of dependence on sugar, fat, and salt and through the door of an uninspected food-processing plant where the hum of the line and bark of the foreman left almost everyone stiff and sore with carpal tunnel syndrome and tendinitis. What Goodwin's family ate for dinner wasn't a matter of personal choice, as the architects of cheap insisted. It was about what she could afford in terms of price and time and what was available along the aisles of a Food Lion store in a strip mall in a small town in North Carolina.

Cheap relies on one other essential factor—a carefully constructed cover-up. In 1991, three golden-fried chicken fillets made at Imperial Food Products along with an order of fries cost $1.99 at Shoney's.[12] This price, however, hid the real costs of the social system that allowed a company like Shoney's to charge so little for heaping plates of calorie-dense foods. Covered up were the costs incurred in farm subsidies and the piles of debt taken on by the chicken growers, some of whom had been turned into "modern-day serfs."[13] The price didn't include the cost of food stamps for the underpaid, road building for transport, the cleanup of waterways polluted by animal factories, or the health care outlays needed in order to address the myriad issues linked to obesity and the litany of other ills associated with chronic overexposure to sugary, salty, and fatty foods. At the same time, the system of cheap never paid a dime for the wanton cruelty it imposed on animals or the injuries suffered by workers while killing, processing, and further processing industrially produced chickens.[14]

What was covered up the most, though, was the government's role in creating the system of cheap. In North Carolina and across much of the rest of the country, a submerged yet powerful "cheap state" built highways and maintained ports, incarcerated tens of thousands, gave tax breaks to corporations, kept worker's compensation costs as low as possible, paid for inspections of food products and elevators but not workplaces, and made sure labor unions fought uphill at all times to get a foothold or just gave up because it wasn't worth trying to organize the most precarious areas of the economy. But the government largely remained behind the scenes, tucked behind the rhetoric of free trade and free choice and powerful and seductive narratives of individualism, self-help, and racial reconciliation. That cover-up made discovering alternatives to cheap difficult, and made it harder still to articulate the problem. Who wasn't in favor of the democracy of lower prices for everyone?

But this isn't just a story about past cover-ups. The tragedy in Hamlet brought a flood of national attention to poultry plant working conditions and the woeful lack of government regulation in the food industry. Yet it turned out to be a startlingly brief moment of concern. The suffering in Hamlet generated legislative reforms in North Carolina, but nothing compared to the sustained attention of the Progressive Era leading into the New Deal or the sea change in the government's role in industry generated by the deaths at the Triangle Shirtwaist Factory.

Six months after the Hamlet fire, unemployment benefits were running out for Imperial employees. Dozens still collected worker's compensation checks and waited for settlement payments to arrive from their lawyers' offices. A few took advantage of grants for retraining and vocational education. But those looking for work couldn't find much.

After getting by for weeks on United Way vouchers, Thomas Oates, who had survived the fire without extensive physical injuries, got hired on the overnight shift at the Perdue Farms chicken plant in Rockingham for $5.45 an hour. If he lasted until the next spring, he would make an additional sixty cents an hour.[15]

By then, though, the line speeds in poultry plants had climbed again. By 1992, less than a year after the fire, injury rates in the broiler industry hit a nineteen-year high. Yet, as a watchdog group reported, workers across the state were afraid to speak out for fear that they would lose their jobs. In fact, small-town poultry processors were already replacing African American and white laborers with immigrant workers, many of them undocumented and easily silenced, from Mexico, Guatemala, and, later, Haiti.[16] Workers weren't the only ones endangered.[17] With chickens racing by faster than ever on the line, USDA inspectors couldn't keep up. According to a *60 Minutes* report in 1987, more than 35 percent of industrial chicken contained traces of salmonella, a bacteria caused by the contact of meat with animal or human feces. Twenty-five years later, that number, according to *Consumer Reports*, rose to around 90 percent. Poultry capitalism, in other words, remained an unaccounted-for public health threat.[18]

Not long after the North Carolina General Assembly passed its spate of workplace reforms in 1992, the forces of cheap mounted their counterattack. One year after the fire, Republican lieutenant governor Jim

Gardner chided state lawmakers for going "overboard" with safety regulations. "We've gone from having too few inspections," he contended,
"to having the second highest number of any state in the country." Even
though his numbers didn't add up—North Carolina ranked at that point
in the middle of the states for its ratio of inspectors to workplaces—the
perception stuck.[19]

In the fall of 1991, Hickory, North Carolina, businessman and U.S.
representative Cass Ballenger told a reporter, "It's embarrassing that it
takes a fire like this . . . before the news media makes a big enough deal
that people will say, 'Okay, we'll pay more tax money' (for worker safety).
It's the squeaking wheel that needs the grease and this wheel apparently
hasn't been squeaking loud enough." Four years later, Ballenger and allies
like Speaker of the House Newt Gingrich didn't want to hear anything
about new spending. Both of these Republican congressmen rejected calls
from Jesse Jackson and their union-friendly colleagues to spend more
money to beef up OSHA. Instead, Ballenger launched a crusade against
what he called the agency's "gestapo" tactics and backed legislation that
supported lower penalties for workplace safety violations, "warning tickets" to first-time offenders, voluntary compliance, and a license to retaliate
against whistleblowers, as some read in the bill's language.[20]

But, this wasn't just about the Cass Ballengers or Jim Gardners or Newt
Gingriches of the world doing the bidding of business interests, and it
wasn't about new Democrat Bill Clinton, a friend to the Perdues and the
Waltons, refusing to make workplace safety a campaign issue in 1992.[21] It
wasn't even about the short memory of North Carolina lawmakers who in
1995, less than four years after the Hamlet fire, pushed to cut the state's
OSHA budget.[22] Nor was it about local school boards and federal officials who didn't think twice about making chicken nuggets and tenders
a staple of school lunches. Anything on the plate, they seemed to say, was
better than nothing for those didn't have much money. All of these proc-
lamations and (in)actions were about the ongoing triumph of cheap.

The truth was, and is, that most Americans before and after the fire
were unwilling or unable to give up on the apparent benefits of cheap or
to imagine an alternative system of buying. Many believed in what one
Walmart advertisement promised: "Save money. Live better."[23] While

working people counted on the world's largest retailer to provide them with discounts, most have, at the same time, lost faith in government. It just doesn't seem to be working for them or for anyone around them. As the fire's memory fades, this anti-statist thinking mixes with the growing faith in the power of lower prices. Together these forces make it hard to see how school lunch choices, cutbacks in spending on worker safety, tributes to post-racialism (and denials of the past), and Election Day decisions (including the decision not to vote) fueled the fire in Hamlet and made it an uncommonly common event in the expanding global order of cheap.

These connections, though, were made clear by a fire in 2013 in a remote poultry slaughterhouse in China's Jilin Province that killed 120 people and injured 60 more behind locked doors. This event tragically underscores the troubling fact that the murderous negligence of the social, political, and economic systems of cheap that lit the Hamlet fire in 1991 still burn in the world of today. It became painfully clear again, also in 2013, when a Bangladeshi clothing factory crumbled, killing more than a thousand workers who before the disaster had stitched together the inexpensive goods that, through a tangled web of jobbers and middlemen, filled the racks of Walmart and Benetton stores from Mexico City to Morehead City, North Carolina.[24] The company that made these shirts and blouses had deliberately moved to where labor was abundant and where it faced little competition in hiring and firing. That way it could pay workers next to nothing and not worry about any interference from labor organizations or government officials. Like the Imperial plant, these out-of-the-way factories existed in closed worlds where elected, business, and press leaders created meticulously crafted silences, the kinds of silences that the system of cheap depends on to mute the voices of its victims, grind out steady profits, and pass along as much of the costs of production and distribution as possible to others, including to the government it says it doesn't need and to the underpaid workforce it exploits and says is expendable.

The most effective silencing, though, is the one that insists that these events, that these recurrent killing floors from North Carolina to China, are not part of a pattern or a system, but rather are disconnected accidents perpetuated by greedy individuals who exist outside of history. This is the sort of cheap analysis that disregards any alternatives and just continues to trumpet the virtues of low-cost lives and low-cost government over everything else. Retelling the story of the Hamlet fire with cheap at the core is one way to break the narrative cycle.[25]

That's why Loretta Goodwin is willing to push past her own personal pain, the piercing screams she still hears in her head and the thick black smoke she still feels in her lungs, to tell her story. She knows there is no happy ending just yet. But there *is* the hope that her story and the story of the Hamlet fire will be told over and over, like a prayer, so it won't be repeated and no one will ever again have to die to work.[26]

ACKNOWLEDGMENTS

This is a book about loss. Partway through the research and writing, it became more than a deep dive into the past as loss came to my family in several wide and sorrowful waves.

Just after my dad died suddenly, Sharon Norteman, a close high school friend of mine, wrote me a condolence note. "Joy," she said, "is always multiplied but grief needs to be divided." She promised to carry a small piece of my pain, forever. Many others have done the same for me and my family over the last few years.

At the same time, people knowingly and unknowingly helped by carrying pieces of this book for me, telling me their stories and sharing with me their insights.

As I drafted the sections of this manuscript and struggled to find the right voice to unlock the larger meanings of the fire, I gave presentations at the University of Tokyo, University of Tubingen, Erfurt University, University of Delaware, University of Georgia, Princeton University, Mississippi State University, Vanderbilt University, and my alma mater, the University of North Carolina at Chapel Hill. Hopefully all, or at least most, of the smart comments, well-informed suggestions, and telling critiques I received in these seminar rooms and lecture halls found their way into the final version of the book.

Lots of colleagues and friends walked with me while I did my research and sat down to write. Lila Berman was the first person to read the first full draft of this book. In her characteristically funny and brilliant way, she told me just where I had been and where I needed to go. Geri Thoma read the last version and the first proposal and steered me in the right direction, toward Carl Bromley, my editor, and the other terrific people at The New Press.

In between, Kevin Kruse, Alex Cummings, Beth Hale, and Roger Horowitz read drafts of chapters and whole sections and shared with me their voluminous knowledge of all things North Carolina, American politics, and chicken. My model of a department chair, Jay Lockenour, has been endlessly supportive. Gary Scales dropped his own work and amazing teaching to help me map the story. Jeff Cowie, Josh Cole, Jane Dailey, Glenda Gilmore, Tyler Greene, Beth Bailey, Tom Sugrue, Joe Crespino, Martha Hodes, Steve Estes, David Farber, Robert Devens, Jim Giesen, Anne Marshall, Dave Grazian, Sarah Igo, Moshe Sluhovsky, Jim Cobb, Kat Charron, Peter Siskind, Susan Herbst, Richard Immerman, Drew Isenberg, Charles Fishman, Christian Lentz, Walter Licht, Alex Macauley, Tom Grimes, Sarah Milov, and Nina Mackert listened to me at conferences and over coffee and gently, and sometimes not so gently, pointed me in so many of the right directions. Usually the same directions that Peter Coclanis, Bob Korstad, and Jacquelyn Hall have been pointing me toward for years, decades even. One of my favorite people to talk to, Stephanie McCurry, just listened, and so did Heather Thompson, and Michael Kwass and Laura Mason, and so did my newer friend Juergen Martschukat. And thanks to Matt Lassiter for his steady quiet on the longest walk ever. And finally, I'm sad I won't walk again with Michael Goldberg, but his voice and advice on commas and writing history is, hopefully, sprinkled across these pages.

Steve Kantrowitz, Bill Deverell, and Doug Flamming taught me everything I needed to know about the possibilities of a text message or a quick note. On a Thursday at 3:30 p.m. or a Sunday at 8:45 a.m. or during the Duke-Carolina game, they would write a few short words to check in and remind me of the power of our connections.

To me, every book has a soundtrack, and John Coltrane (that Hamlet man) and Jason Isbell provided the music for this project.

To my West Philly people, to the boys at Donna's and the families crowded around Local 44 afterwards, to the dreams of shore houses bought with lottery tickets, to the bouncing of basketballs in the alley and Little League dreams that came true, to Christmas Eve and Super Bowls in various living rooms, you carried way, way more for me and my family than any of you can know.

Faith, I trust, is what connects joy and grief, and my faith is in my friends and family. In my brothers, Steve, John, and Jeffrey, sisters, Libby, Rachel, and Jessica, and sister (in-law) Margo, who always, and I mean always, stand with me. To my real brother Brad, thanks. Maria Reardon is the kindest and warmest person I know and that just helps. And to my momma, the best momma. We are still trying to figure out what to do now. We really are, and I guess it doesn't matter if it ever makes sense. But we have each other and that makes perfect sense, right?

What also makes perfect sense is the "loves" of Eli, Benjamin, and Ann Marie. It was either Eli or Benjamin, I can't remember which one of them, who first started to say the word "loves" when he left the house in the morning or checked in on his phone. Now it is the word that the four of us say to each other all the time. It is our word, and somehow, it gets at the loud, fussy, cantankerous, and fierce love(s) that hang over our house and last much, much longer than twenty-four frames. I will, I promise, multiply these pieces of loves and carry them back to you forever.

NOTES

Abbreviations used in the endnotes:

ACU—American Conservative Union
GSU—Georgia State University
NCOSHP—North Carolina Occupational Safety and Health Project
SHC—Southern Historical Collection
SHSW—State Historical Society of Wisconsin
UFCW—United Food and Commercial Workers Union
UNC—University of North Carolina at Chapel Hill
UNCC—University of North Carolina at Charlotte

Introduction

1. This account of Goodwin's life and what she saw and heard and experienced on the day of the fire is based on multiple author interviews with Goodwin. Information taken from sources other than these interviews will be noted below. For additional information on Goodwin's job history, see Steve Riley, "A Betrayal of Trust," *Raleigh News and Observer*, December 11, 1991. For more information on African American women in the poultry industry, see Kathleen C. Schwartzman, *The Chicken Trail: Following Workers, Migrants, and Corporations Across the Americas* (Ithaca, NY: Cornell University Press, 2013), 28; and LaGuana Gray, *We Just Keep Running the Line: Black Southern Women and the Poultry Processing Industry* (Baton Rouge: Louisiana State University Press, 2014). (A note on author interviews used in this book: I conducted all of my interviews either in person or over the phone between August 2011 and February 2017.)

2. On Imperial's bathroom policy, see "Testimony by Mary Bryant," June 1992, NCOSHP, SHC, Chapel Hill, NC; and Ben Stocking, "Life and Death at Imperial," *Raleigh News and Observer*, December 8, 1991. For a more general account on the regime of bathrooms and bodily control, see Linda Tirado, *Hand to Mouth: Living in Bootstrap America* (New York: G. P. Putnam's Sons, 2014), 18.

3. Doug Stark, "The South's Poultry Plants Thrive," *Baltimore Sun*, September 8, 1991.

4. Author interview with Annette Zimmerman. She remembers Goodwin telling her this unfinished story about an arrest on the morning of the fire.

5. Author interview with Ada Blanchard.

6. Author interview with William Morris. On the problem of the parts used to fix the line, see "Lack of Spare Parts May Have Led to Fatal Fire," *Chicago Tribune*, September 25, 1991; and

U.S. Department of Labor Worksheet, Inspection 18479204, December 30, 1991, in author's possession.

7. Department of Labor Investigation, miscellaneous reports, including accounts about Gagnon's aptitude for fixing things, previous experience with this problem, and Brad Roe's interventions over the intercom in author's possession; and Greg Trevor and Paige Williams, "Worker: Repairers Left Fryer On," *Charlotte Observer*, September 10, 1991. Martin Quick, who worked in maintenance, also talked about Gagnon's aptitude for fixing things and about Brad Roe's cursing at him to get stuff done and done quickly. See author interview with Martin Quick. Obituary for John Gagnon, n.d., Folder, Imperial, Richmond County Historical Society, Rockingham, NC.

8. Committee on Education and Labor, House of Representatives, "The Tragedy at Imperial Food Products, December 1991," Serial No. 102-N, p. 3; and "Maintenance Worker: Burners Routinely Left On During Fryer Repairs," *Richmond County Daily Journal*, September 10, 1991.

9. Author interviews with Loretta Goodwin. Goodwin Testimony, "Hearing on HR 3160, Comprehensive Occupational Safety and Health Reform Act," September 12, 1991, Serial No. 102-47, pp. 39–41.

10. For more on Gagnon and the maintenance crew replacing the hose, see Bobby Quick's Testimony, "Hearing on HR 3160, Comprehensive Occupational Safety and Health Reform Act," September 12, 1991, Serial No. 102-47, pp. 100–101; and Trevor and Williams, "Worker: Repairers Left Fryer On."

11. For an explanations of what happened to start the fire, see Jack Yates, "Chicken Processing Plant Fires, Hamlet North Carolina (September 3, 1991), North Little Rock Arkansas (June 7, 1991)," (Washington, DC: Federal Emergency Management Agency), available at www .usfa.fema.gov/downloads/pdf/publications/tr-057.pdf; and "Imperial Foods Processing Plant Fire, Hamlet, MC, September 3, 1991," Box, Imperial Fire, Hamlet City Hall, Hamlet, NC.

12. For some additional information on the fire, see "Fatal Plant Fire Leaves Children Without Parents," *Chicago Tribune*, September 8, 1991.

13. On the impact of carbon monoxide, see U.S. National Library of Medicine, "Carbon Monoxide," available at www.nlm.nih.gov/medlineplus/ency/article/002804.htm. For accounts of the fire full of telling details, see Paige Williams, "Seven Years of Silence," *Charlotte Observer*, October 25, 1998; and Yates, "Chicken Processing Plant Fires."

14. This conversation was reported by Jim Schlosser, "'We Are Going to Die': Plant Inferno's Survivors Relive the Horror," *Greensboro News and Record*, September 8, 1991. Additional details come from an author interview with Calvin White. On the timing of things that day, see "Statement from Robin Leviner," a Hamlet firefighter, Box, Imperial Fire, Hamlet City Hall, Hamlet, NC; and Yates, "Chicken Processing Plant Fires."

15. Goodwin's account of the cries she heard came from "Survivor Tells Panel of Screams for Help in Plant Fire," *Los Angeles Times*, September 13, 1991.

16. Author interview with Calvin White, who recalled the detail about the Trojan tractor.

17. That last detail about coughing up soot comes from C.E. Yandle, "Lawmaker Assails States' OSHA Programs," *Raleigh News and Observer*, September 13, 1991.

18. Schlosser, "'We Are Going to Die.'"

19. "Hearing on HR 3160, Comprehensive Occupational Safety and Health Reform Act," September 12, 1991, Serial No. 102-47, pp. 39–41.

20. Department of Labor Investigation, Goodwin Interview, in author's possession. This interview is redacted, but I determined based on my conversations with Goodwin that it is, in fact, her testimony. For more of Goodwin's account, see Yandle, "Lawmaker Assails States' OSHA Programs." For some pushback on her account, see "Officials Question Report of Living in Body Bags," *Richmond County Daily Journal*, September 13, 1991. Reporters later revealed that the body bags could only be opened from the outside, which seemed to challenge Goodwin's account, but she remained firm in her retelling. Hamlet mayor Abbie Covington tried to tamp down this rumor. See for example, Covington to Congressman William Ford, September 26, 1991, Box, Imperial Fire, Hamlet City Hall, Hamlet, NC.

21. On the legend of the fire and Barrington, see author interview with Lorrie Boyle and the following newspaper accounts: Karl Stark, "Sudden Horror of Fatal Fire Overwhelms Tiny N.C. Town," *Philadelphia Inquirer*, September 8, 1991; and Peter Kilborn, "In Aftermath of Deadly Fire, A Poor Town Struggles Back," *New York Times*, November 25, 1991.

22. Williams, "Seven Years of Silence."

23. For some background on Dawkins, see Jeff Holland, "Lance Route Salesman Philip Dawkins One of Fire Victims," *Richmond County Daily Journal*, n.d., in author's possession; and Jeff Holland, "None of Them Should Have Died," *Richmond County Daily Journal*, August 30, 1992.

24. There are a number of conflicting accounts of how Philip Jr. learned of his father's death. See, for instance, Holland, "Lance Route Salesman." The account here relies on several firefighters on the scene that day. See author interviews with Gus Bellamy, Frankie Moree, and Calvin White; and a letter from Henry L. Kitchin to Gary Johnson, January 27, 1993, Box, Imperial Fire, Hamlet City Hall, Hamlet, NC.

25. On Webb and his tastes, see Karl Stark, "Sudden Horror of Fatal Fire." See also Brad Isbell Photo, "Tragedy at Hamlet," Folder—Imperial Food Products Plant Other Employees, Photo Archives, *Raleigh News and Observer*, Raleigh, NC.

26. On the Moateses' story, see Jon Jefferson, "Dying for Work," *ABA Journal*, January 1993; Estes Thompson, "Blaze in Chicken Plant Smolders for Survivors," *The State*, September 14, 1992; Robin P. Teater, "Hamlet Fire Victims Can't Remember," *Richmond County Daily Journal*, October 27, 1991; and "Mildred Lassiter Moates: Summary of Injuries and Damages Resulting From September 3, 1991 Industrial Plant Fire," from records of Woody Gunter, in author's possession.

27. Author interview with Martin Quick. Kemlite Video, from Charles Bection Collection, Durham, North Carolina.

28. Author interviews with Berry Barbour.

29. On attempts to revive Gagnon, see "Imperial Food Processing Fire," Hamlet Fire Department, September 3, 1991, Box, Imperial Fire, Hamlet City Hall, Hamlet, NC.

30. Author interview at the diner with Neil Cadieu, Tom MacCallum, and Bert Unger.

31. Claudia Rankin, *Citizen: An American Lyric* (Minneapolis, MN: Graywolf Press, 2014), 114. Other accounts of the story of the Hamlet fire include a section of a chapter from

David Harvey, "Class Relations, Social Justice, and the Political Geography of Difference," in *Justice, Nature, and the Geography of Difference*, edited by David Harvey (Oxford: Blackwell, 1996), 334–41, 349–50; Lawrence Naumoff's novel, *A Southern Tragedy in Crimson and Yellow* (Winston-Salem, NC: Zuckerman Cannon Publishers, 2005); essay from Judy Aulette and Raymond Michalowski, "Fire in Hamlet: A Case Study of State-Corporate Crime," in *White Collar Crime: Class and Contemporary Views*, edited by Gilbert Geis, Robert F. Meier, and Lawrence M. Salinger (New York: Free Press, 1995), 166–90; Erik Loomis, "This Day in Labor History: September 3, 1991," *Lawyers, Guns, and Money Blog*, September 3, 2016, available at, www.lawyersgunsmoneyblog.com/2016/09/this-day-in-labor-history-september-3-1991; and the song from Mojo Nixon and Jello Biafra, "Hamlet Chicken Plant Disaster," available at www .youtube.com/watch?v=xyU-PvbOjlo.

1: Hamlet

1. E. Gordon Mooneyhan, "Hamlet, North Carolina," *Trains* (June 1992), 64; and Panel, "Hamlet's Boom Began," from Hamlet Depot Museum (visited on March 10, 2013). The two sources agree on the date of the town's founding and on the fact that there were two railroad lines that ran through it. They don't, however, agree on the names of these railroads. I drew on the Hamlet article in *Trains* here for the names.

2. On the development of the town, see author interview with Jane Mercer. For more on the history of Hamlet, see Richmond County Historical Society, *Mixed Blessings: Richmond County History, 1900–2000* (Rockingham, NC: Richmond County Historical Society, 2010), 36; City of Hamlet website, www.hamletnc.us/cityhistory.html; and Dan Bennett, "Magazine Features Historic Hamlet Station," *Hamlet News*, February 4, 1982.

3. Riley Watson interviewed by Abbie Covington, August 19, 2009, Hamlet Depot Museum Oral History Project, Hamlet, NC.

4. Mooneyhan, "Hamlet, North Carolina," 64–65.

5. On the power of the breadwinner ideal, see Robert Self, *All in the Family: The Realignment of Democracy Since the 1960s* (New York: Hill and Wang, 2012).

6. Clark Cox, *Deadly Greed: The McEachern Murders in Hamlet, North Carolina* (Boone, NC: High Country Publishers, Ltd, 2003), 32.

7. Burnell McGirt interviewed by Glenn Sumpter, July 21, 2009, Hamlet Depot Museum Oral History Project, Hamlet, NC.

8. Nate Campbell interviewed by Abbie Covington, n.d., Hamlet Depot Museum Oral History Project, Hamlet, NC.

9. Author interview with Ron Niland.

10. United States Census, Richmond County Master Area Reference, 1980, available at digital.ncdcr.gov/cdm/compoundobject/collection/p15012coll4/id/2312/rec/1.

11. On the minstrel shows, see interview with Nate Campbell by Abbie Covington, August 14, 2009, Hamlet Depot Museum Oral History Project, Hamlet, NC. On race and ongoing tensions with the police, see Hamlet native Jody Meacham's novel set in the town in the 1970s, *Through the Heart of the South* (San Jose, CA: Doodlebug Publishing, 2010).

12. Author interviews with Harold Miller and Mike Quick. For more on the city's racial geography, see Cox, *Deadly Greed*, 33. For more on segregation in Hamlet, see interview with J.W. Mask, February 15, 1991, Southern Oral History Project, available at docsouth.unc.edu/sohp/M-0013/M-0013.html.

13. On African American laborers on the railroad in Hamlet, see interview with Walter Bell by David Adeimy, August 20, 2009, Hamlet Depot Museum Oral History Project, Hamlet, NC.

14. See McDonald's obituary and more details about his life, available at www.findagrave.com/cgi-bin/fg.cgi?page=gr&GRid=64493504.

15. Author interview with Joseph Arnold.

16. Author interview with Josh Newton.

17. Author interview with Mike Quick.

18. Interview with Walter Bell by David A. Adeimy, August 20, 2009, Hamlet Depot Museum Oral History Project, Hamlet, NC; Tom Lawton, "The Life and Times of a RR Town," *Fayetteville Observer*, February 28, 1982.

19. Interview with Neil Cadieu by Abbie Covington, n.d., Hamlet Depot Museum Oral History Project, Hamlet, NC.

20. *Mixed Blessings*, 30. On the bowling alley, interview with Wingate Williamson by Glenn Sumpter, July 22, 2009, Hamlet Depot Museum Oral History Project, Hamlet, NC.

21. On Hamlet hospital, see *Mixed Blessings*, 137; interview with Burnell McGirt by Glenn Sumpter, July 21, 2009, Hamlet Depot Museum Oral History Project; and author interview with Ron Niland.

22. On the railroad mergers and other changes in the industry, see MDC, Inc. (Chapel Hill, NC), "Three Faces of Rural North Carolina: A Summary Report to the North Carolina Commission on Jobs and Economic Growth," (December 1986), 1, North Carolina Collection, UNC, Chapel Hill, NC. Interview with Burnell McGirt by Glenn Sumpter, July 21, 2009; interview with Ed Snyder by Glenn Sumpter, August 5, 2009; and interview with Nate Campbell by Abbie Covington, August 14, 2009, Hamlet Depot Museum Oral History Project, Hamlet, NC.

23. *Mixed Blessings*, 173–74.

24. MDC, Inc., "Three Faces," 12. See also Peter A. Coclanis and Louis M. Kyriakoudes, "Selling Which South?: Economic Change in Rural and Small-Town North Carolina in an Era of Globalization, 1940–2007," *Southern Cultures* 4 (Winter 2007): 96; and Jane Ruffin, "A World Apart: Economic growth of North Carolina's rural areas," *Business North Carolina* (April 1992): 92. See also George Packer, especially the sections set in North Carolina, *The Unwinding: An Inner History of the New America* (New York: Farrar, Straus, and Giroux, 2013).

25. Interview with Riley Watson by Abbie Covington, August 19, 2009, Hamlet Depot Museum Oral History Project, Hamlet, NC. Author interview with Josh Newton.

26. Account of the riot drawn from the following sources: "Arrest Raises Controversy," *Richmond County Daily Journal*, June 6, 1975; "Hamlet Curfew Imposed After Racial Violence," *Greensboro Daily News*, June 8, 1975; "Hamlet Unrest Continues," *Richmond County Daily Journal*, June 9, 1975; and *Mixed Blessings*, 175–76.

27. Tim Tyson, *Blood Done Sign My Name: A True Story* (New York: Crown, 2004).

28. Author interview with Harold Miller. For details on the look and feel of the town, see Karl Stark, "Sudden Horror of Fatal Fire Overwhelms Tiny N.C. Town," *Philadelphia Inquirer*, September 8, 1991.

29. Jane Ruffin, "Dreams of Better Days," *News and Observer*, December 9, 1991; and B. Drummond Ayres Jr., "Factory Fire Leaves Pall Over All-American City," *New York Times*, September 5, 1991.

30. Ruffin, "Dreams of Better Days," and Ayers, "Factory Leaves Pall."

31. Peter Kilborn, "In Aftermath of Deadly Fire, A Poor Town Struggles Back," *New York Times*, November 25, 1991; and Ruffin, "Dreams of Better Days." Author interview with Ron Niland; and interviews with Riley Watson by Abbie Covington, August 19, 2009, and Bert Unger by Glenn Sumpter, August 7, 2009, Hamlet Depot Museum Oral History Project, Hamlet, NC.

32. Ruffin, "Dreams of Better Days."

33. Ruffin, "Dreams of Better Days"; *Mixed Blessings*, 123–34; MDC Inc., "Three Faces," Appendix C, 13; and Riley Watson interviewed by Abbie Covington, August 19, 2009, and Neil Cadieu interview by Covington, Hamlet Depot Museum Oral History Project, Hamlet, NC.

34. Author interview with Ada Blanchard.

35. Bruce J. Schulman, *The Seventies: The Great Shift in American Culture, Society, and Politics* (Cambridge, MA.: Da Capo Press, 2001), 5.

36. "Voiceless Workers?" *Charlotte Observer*, October 29, 1991. See also Jacquelyn Dowd Hall, et al., *Like a Family: The Making of the Southern Cotton Mill World* (Chapel Hill: University of North Carolina Press, 2000); and Bryant Simon, "Rethinking Why There Are So Few Unions in the South," *Georgia Historical Quarterly* 81 (Summer 1997): 465–84.

37. Interviews with Burnell McGirt by Glenn Sumpter, July 21, 2009, Walter Bell by David Adeimy, August 20, 2009, Jimmy Stricklin by David Adeimy, July 20, 2009, Hamlet Depot Museum Oral History Project, Hamlet, NC. Author interview with Josh Newton. For a survey of union locals in Hamlet and information about the town's Central Labor Union, see Carey Haigler to William F. Schnitzler, July 12, 1962, Box 10, Folder, Hamlet, North Carolina, AFL-CIO Records, Department of Organization, RG-28-006, Special Collections, University of Maryland, College Park, MD.

38. Thomas Holt, *The Problem of Race in the 21st Century* (Cambridge, MA.: Harvard University Press, 2002), 104.

39. Greg Trevor, "Work-Safety Advocates Buck Anti-Union Sentiment," *Charlotte Observer*, October 27, 1991; and Courtney Smith (Program Coordinator of the NC Workplace Reform Mission, a program of the NC Council of Churches) to Susan Collins, August 30, 1993, Box 33, Folder, Fundraising, NCOSHP, SCH, UNC. See also, "North Carolina Highly Attractive for Manufacturers, National Study Shows," *Chapel Hill News*, February 14, 1982; and *A Study of Manufacturing Business Climates of the Forty-Eight Contiguous States of America, 1980* (Chicago: Alexander Grant and Company, 1981).

40. Richard Lacayo, "Price of Neglect," *Time*, September 28, 1992.

41. On Goodman's background, see Rob Christensen, *The Paradox of Tar Heel Politics: The Personalities, Elections, and Events That Shaped Modern North Carolina* (Chapel Hill: University of North Carolina Press, 2008), 188–89; Cox, *Deadly Greed*, 9–12; Rick Nichols, "Richmond Political Tension Matches the Heat," *Raleigh News and Observer*, April 25, 1976. And the probably very best published piece on Goodman is David Perlmutt, "Richmond County's Goodman: The Last of the Old Style Sheriffs," *Charlotte Observer*, May 26, 1991.

42. Godfather quote from Hamlet Meeting, November 18, 1991, Box 35, Folder, Hamlet Organizing Contacts, NCOSHP, SHC, UNC, Chapel Hill, NC; and Annie Brayboy of Rockingham to Hunt, December 1, 1977, Box 81, Folder, Richmond, James B. Hunt Papers, North Carolina State Archives, Raleigh. On holiday turkeys and governing, see author interviews with Frankie Moree and Gus Bellamy; and Christensen, *The Paradox of Tar Heel Politics*, 188–89.

43. For more on Goodman, see author interviews with Joseph Arnold, Harold Miller, Ron Niland, Frankie Moree, and Annette Zimmerman.

44. On the rumors about Goodman's illicit activities, see *Mixed Blessings*, 139; interview with Wingate Williamson by Glenn Sumpter, July 22, 2009, Hamlet Depot Museum Oral History Project, Hamlet, NC.

45. Author interviews with Martin Quick and Mike Quick.

46. "Ground Broken for New Clark Plant," *Richmond County Daily Journal*, September 23, 1974; Clark Cox, "Clark to Phase Out Rockingham Plant," *Richmond County Daily Journal*, March 4, 1985.

47. "Union Loses Vote," *Richmond County Daily Journal*, July 16, 1979. See also Jay Hensley, "State, Plant Officials Say Unions Not Needed," *Asheville Citizen*, June 23, 1978.

48. Author interviews with Martin Quick and Mike Quick.

49. Ruffin, "Dreams of Better Days."

50. Author interview with Bob Hall.

51. Author interview with Abbie Covington.

2: Silence

1. Quotes and information on Emmett Roe's background in this paragraph come from author interview with Bill Sawyer; and C.E. Yandle and Jim Barnett, "The Road to Ruin," *Raleigh News and Observer*, December 10, 1991.

2. Biographic details in the above account come from Paige Williams, "Seven Years of Silence," *Charlotte Observer*, October 25, 1998; and "Hamlet Fire Latest in a Long List of Imperial Setbacks," *Richmond County Daily Journal*, September 16, 1991.

3. Author interview with John Joseph Shanley.

4. Yandle and Barnett, "The Road to Ruin."

5. "Hamlet Fire Latest in a Long List of Imperial Setbacks."

6. Yandle and Barnett, "The Road to Ruin."

7. "Why You Need the Amalgamated," in a brochure in a packet called "Your Union Welcomes You," circa 1975, Box 5, Folder, Our Union Welcomes You, circa 1975, UFCW Papers, SHSW, Madison, WI.

8. Yandle and Barnett, "The Road to Ruin."

9. Erik Loomis, *Out of Sight: The Long and Disturbing Story of Corporations Outsourcing Catastrophe* (New York: The New Press, 2015), 58.

10. "Hamlet Fire Latest in a Long List of Imperial Setbacks," and author interview with Sawyer.

11. On the Roe family and its businesses, Paul Hendrickson, "Reverberations of a Town's Tragedy," *Washington Post*, October 22, 1991; "Hamlet Fire Latest in a Long List of Imperial Setbacks," *Richmond County Daily Journal*, September 16, 1991; "Imperial Officials Released on Bond," *Richmond County Daily Journal*, March 13, 1992. See also author interview with Bill Sawyer.

12. Neil Cadieu to author, email, August 11, 2011.

13. Author interview with Abbie Covington. See also Richmond County Historical Society, *Mixed Blessings: Richmond County History, 1900–2000* (Rockingham, NC: Richmond County Historical Society, 2010), 78–79; Jane Ruffin, "Dreams of Better Days," *Raleigh News and Observer*, December 9, 1991; and interview with Burnell McGirt by Glenn Sumpter, July 21, 2009, Hamlet Depot Museum Oral History Project, Hamlet, NC.

14. Jane Ruffin, "Dreams of Better Days." See also author interviews with Abbie Covington, Jane Mercer, and Wayne Goodwin.

15. Ruffin, "Dreams of Better Days."

16. Yandle and Barnett, "The Road to Ruin."

17. Tony Horwitz, "Nine to Nowhere," *Wall Street Journal*, December 1, 1994; Doug Stark, "The South's Poultry Plants Thrive," *Baltimore Sun*, September, 8, 1991. On the emergence and timing of the southern chicken industry, see Kathleen C. Schwartzman, *The Chicken Trail: Following Workers, Migrants, and Corporation Across the Americas* (Ithaca: Cornell University Press, 2013); and Steve Striffler, *Chicken: The Dangerous Transformation of America's Favorite Food* (New Haven, CT: Yale University Press, 2007), 93–96.

18. On the crucial relationship between labor costs and "capital moves," see Jefferson Cowie, *Capital Moves: RCA's 70-Year Quest for Cheap Labor* (New York: The New Press, 2001).

19. Paul Gaston, *The New South Creed: A Study of Southern Myth Making* (Baton Rouge: Louisiana State University Press, 1976).

20. James C. Cobb, *The Selling of the South: The Southern Crusade for Industrial Development, 1936–1990* (Urbana and Chicago: University of Illinois Press, 1993), 229–30.

21. For more on the idea of the South as a forerunner to globalization, really to neoliberalism, see Mary E. Frederickson, *Looking South: Race, Gender, and the Transformation of Labor from Reconstruction to Globalization* (Gainesville: University of Florida Press, 2011). On the globalization of the South, see Leon Fink, *The Maya of Morganton: Work and Community in the Nuevo New South* (Chapel Hill: University of North Carolina Press, 2003).

22. On Hunt and his role in North Carolina politics, see Tom Eamon, *The Making of a Southern Democracy: North Carolina Politics from Kerr Scott to Pat McCrory* (Chapel Hill: University of North Carolina Press, 2014), 168; Rob Christensen, *The Paradox of Tar Heel Politics: The Personalities, Elections, and Events That Shaped Modern North Carolina* (Chapel Hill:

University of North Carolina Press, 2008), 140–50; Paul Luebke, *Tar Heel Politics: Myths and Realities* (Chapel Hill: University of North Carolina Press, 1990), 74–76. See also Gary Pearce, *Jim Hunt: A Biography* (Winston-Salem, NC: James F. Blair Publishers, 2010). On the ideas and importance of business progressives to southern history, see George B. Tindall, *The Emergence of the New South, 1913–1945* (Baton Rouge: Louisiana State University Press, 1967); Cobb, *The Selling of the South*, 3–4; and Christensen, *The Paradox of Tar Heel Politics*, 10. See also Judy Aulette and Raymond Michalowski, "Fire in Hamlet: A Case Study of State-Corporate Crime," (early draft of article), p. 11, Box 35, Folder, Judy Aulette Paper, NCOSHP, SHC, UNC, Chapel Hill, NC.

23. LaGuana Gray, *We Just Keep Running the Line: Black Southern Women and the Poultry Processing Industry* (Baton Rouge: Louisiana State University Press, 2014), 14–15; and author interview with Larry Lee.

24. Luebke, *Tar Heel Politics*, 29.

25. Cobb, *The Selling of the South*, 5–34.

26. Tom Wicker, "A Governor's Dilemma," *New York Times*, December 8, 1991.

27. "The Candidates: Governor, James B. Hunt, Jr," *We the People of North Carolina* (April 1980): 34. See also, Hunt to E.G. Matheson, plant manager, Rheem Manufacturing Comp (Apex), August 23, 1977, Box 38, Folder, Labor, Department of, K–Z, James B. Hunt Papers, North Carolina State Archives, Raleigh, NC.

28. "Interview with Larry D. Cohick: The State's New Economic Development Chief," *We the People of North Carolina* (November 1978): 42.

29. Arnold Brackett, Asheboro, to Hunt, October 3, 1977, Box 37, Folder, Labor, Department of, A–J,; George A. G. Browder, Rockingham, to Hunt, May 29, 1978, Box 174, Folder, Port Strike, James B. Hunt Papers, North Carolina State Archives, Raleigh, NC.

30. "Address to North Carolina Citizens Association, Raleigh, March 24, 1977," Memory F. Mitchell, ed., *Address and Public Papers of James Baxter Hunt Jr. Vol I, 1977–1981* (Raleigh: Division of Archives and History, 1982), 83.

31. On right-to-work laws, see Hunt to E.G. Matheson, plant manager, Rheem Manufacturing Comp (Apex), August 23, 1977, Box 38, Folder, Labor, Department of, K–Z, James B. Hunt Papers, NC State Archives, Raleigh, NC; and Proposal For NC Occupational Safety and Health Act of 1992–93, February 27, 1992, Box 33, Folder, Legislative Proposals, NCOSHP, SHC, UNC, Chapel Hill, NC.

32. For this data and an impressive examination of the state's economy, see Edward Martin, "The Great Divide: Haves and Have-Nots in North Carolina," *Business North Carolina* (February 2001), 18–19.

33. Luebke, *Tar Heel Politics*, 71–73.

34. John Herbers, *The New Heartland: America's Flight Beyond the Suburbs and How It Is Changing Our Future* (New York: Times Books, 1986), 28–29. See also Tyler Greene's terrific dissertation, "Accessible Isolation: Highway Building and the Geography of Industrialization in North Carolina, 1934–1984" (Temple University, 2017).

35. Luebke, *Tar Heel Politics*, 85–87; and Courtney Smith to Susan Collins, August 30, 1993, Box 33, Folder, Fundraising, NCOSHP, SHC, UNC, Chapel Hill, NC.

36. News Release from the Governor's Office, "Hunt Announces German Plant to Locate in Richmond County," April 5, 1978, Box 148, Folder, B, Industrial Development, Division of Industrial Commission, James B. Hunt Papers, North Carolina State Archives, Raleigh, NC; and Memory F. Mitchell, ed., *Addresses and Public Papers of James Baxter Hunt Jr. Vol I, 1977–1981* (Raleigh: Division of Archives and History, 1982), 820. See also Janet Guyon, "Hamlet to Get German Plant," *Raleigh News and Observer*, April 6, 1978.

37. Lester Suss (President of BeA Fasteners) to Hunt, November, 13, 1978, Box 174, Folder, B, Industrial Development, Division of Industrial Commission, James B. Hunt Papers, North Carolina State Archives, Raleigh, NC. For more on the company and its past, see the website, www.beafastenersusa.com/company/.

38. "Governor's Remarks," Box 279, Folder, Remarks, Ribbon Cutting—BeA Fasteners Company, September 22, 1978, James B. Hunt Papers, North Carolina State Archives, Raleigh, NC.

39. John Hechinger and John Drescher, "Does N.C. Send the Wrong Message," *Charlotte Observer*, October 7, 1991.

40. "Greetings from Progressive Hamlet at the Crossroads of the Carolinas," pamphlet from the Hamlet Depot Museum, Hamlet, NC.

41. Cobb, *The Selling of the South*, 108.

42. Jane Ruffin, "A World Apart: Economic Growth of North Carolina's Rural Areas," *Business North Carolina* (April 1992): 92.

43. "Unemployment Here Declines," *Richmond County Daily Journal*, November 1, 1983; Jennifer French Parker, "Poultry Industry's Boom in N.C. Has A Price Tag," *Charlotte Observer*, September 9, 1991.

44. Martha Quillin, "Grief Runs Deep," *Raleigh News and Observer,* September 2, 2001.

45. Bruce J. Schulman, *The Seventies: The Great Shift in American Culture, Society, and Politics* (Cambridge, MA: Da Capo Press, 2001), 161–62.

46. Richard Lonsdale, "Unlike the Northeast: NC an 'Industrial State, But Not Industrialized,'" *Raleigh News and Observer*, January, 28, 1968.

47. Author interview with Abbie Covington.

48. Author interview with Mark Schultz.

49. Ruffin, "A World Apart."

50. Yandle and Barnett, "The Road to Ruin."

51. Author interview with Niland.

52. "Imperial Food Products Had a Dozen Violations," *Richmond County Daily Journal*, November 15, 1991.

53. On the lack of permits, see U.S. Department of Labor Worksheet, Inspection Number 18479204, December 30, 1991, in author's possession. On building violations, see "Imperial Food Products Had a Dozen Violations," and author interview with Tom MacCallum.

54. James Greiff, "Imperial Foods Fined in 80s Over Fire Doors," *Charlotte Observer*, September 17, 1991.

55. Hamlet Fire Department, Run Report(s), November 1, 1980, May 27, 1983, Box, Imperial Fire, Hamlet City Hall, Hamlet, NC. See also Steve Riley, "A Betrayal of Trust," *Raleigh News and Observer*, December 11, 1991.

56. The first Thompson quote comes from Paige Williams and John Drescher, "County Officials Had Authority But Didn't Inspect Hamlet Plant," *Charlotte Observer*, September 10, 1991. The second Thompson quote is from Paul Taylor, "Ashes and Accusations," *Washington Post*, September 5, 1991. See also, "County Inspectors Missed Chance to Upgrade Imperial's Safety Procedures," *Richmond County Daily Journal*, September 22, 1991. In the fire department's official report on the 1983 fire at the Imperial plant, the building was valued at $150,000. Hamlet Fire Department, Run Report, May 27, 1983, Box, Imperial Fire, Hamlet City Hall, Hamlet, NC. See also, John Drescher, "In Hamlet Fire, Government Safety Nets Gave Way," *Charlotte Observer*, September 22, 1991.

57. On the wells, see author interview with Ron Niland and Department of Labor Investigation, in author's possession. James D. Monroe, a water treatment plant consultant, told Mayor Abbie Covington in a letter that he found what he called three "unauthorized wells" in the plant after the fire. See Monroe to Covington, October 25, 1991, Box, Imperial Fire, Folder, Imperial Fire File, Hamlet City Hall, Hamlet, NC.

58. Author interview with Ron Niland.

59. Greiff, "Imperial Foods Fined in 80s"; Steve Riley, "Imperial Pa. plant was cited—Serious violations found twice in '80s," *Raleigh News and Observer*, September 14, 1991.

60. Yandle and Barnett, "The Road to Ruin."

61. The information in this paragraph was drawn from Pennsylvania OSHA Report obtained through Freedom of Information Act (FOIA) request, in author's possession. See also Greiff, "Imperial Foods Fined in 80s." For a general description of how an OSHA investigation works, see "After the Fire: A Review of the North Carolina Occupational Safety and Health Program," October 15, 1991, Box 7, Folder—Hamlet, NC, Imperial Foods, UFCW Local 204, GSU, Atlanta, GA.

62. Steve Riley, "A Betrayal of Trust," *Raleigh News and Observer*, December 11, 1991.

63. "Imperial Never Licensed to Operate in N.C.," *Richmond County Daily Journal*, October 3, 1991. See also author interview with John Brooks.

64. "Hamlet Fire Latest in a Long List of Imperial Setbacks," *Richmond County Daily Journal*, September 16, 1991.

65. "Imperial Food Products Had a Dozen Violations," *Richmond County Daily Journal*, November 15, 1991.

66. Hamlet Fire Department, Run Reports, November 1, 1980, May 27, 1983, Box, Imperial Fire, Hamlet City Hall, Hamlet, NC.

67. Author interview with confidential source.

68. On the back-and-forth over this issue, see Ron Niland to Brad Roe, June 22, June 27, July 24, September 19, October 1, October 15, November 29, 1990, May 1, 1991, Box, Imperial Fire, Hamlet City Hall; and Hamlet City Council Regular Meeting, January 5, March 12, 1991, Hamlet City Hall, Hamlet, NC. See also John Hechinger, "Chicken Processing Under Attack," *Charlotte Observer*, September 4, 1991.

69. Author interview with Ron Niland; and Hechinger, "Chicken Processing."

70. Author interview with Ron Niland.

71. Quote from Brooks can be found in Randy Diamond, "Plant Never Had Safety Inspection," *Raleigh News and Observer*, September 4, 1991. On the USDA men's daily routine, see

Department of Labor Investigation, Interview with USDA Inspector, pp. 5, 7, 16, in author's possession.

72. These quotes are from the USDA's inspection reports. Each time the inspector noted a problem, it was listed in a report that was called, "Process Deficiency Record." I obtained copies of these reports from Steve Riley, a reporter for the *Raleigh News and Observer*, and they are in my possession. For confirmation of this policy, see Riley's excellent reporting, "US Agency Knew About Locked Door," *Raleigh News and Observer*, November 12, 1991; and Department of Labor Investigation, interview #4, pp. 20, 22, in author's possession. The final quote is from U.S. Department of Labor, "Imperial Food Products, Inc.: Accident Investigation Report," p. 12, Inspection Number 18479204, December 30, 1991, in author's possession. In another document from this inspection, a complaint filed by lawyer Woody Gunter on behalf of Mildred and Olin Moates charges that "Grady Hussey and Kenneth Booker . . . approved the locking and blocking of doors at the IFP plant . . . for 'fly control.'" (Complaint in author's possession.)

73. Author interview with Nellie Brown.

74. "Dateline NBC," n.d., in Charles Becton Files, Private Collection, Durham, NC; Steve Riley, "US Agency Knew About Locked Door," *Raleigh News and Observer*, November 13, 1991; John Hood, "Over-reaction to Hamlet Tragedy Will Only Create Additional Victims," *Atlanta Journal Constitution*, September 3, 1992.

75. Author interview with Nellie Brown.

76. Author interview with William Morris. See also a description of the locking of the door from an unnamed Imperial maintenance man in Department of Labor Investigation, in author's possession.

77. For information on theft at the plant and comments about it, see John Drescher and Ken Garfield, "Worker: Doors Kept Locked," *Charlotte Observer*, September 5, 1991. Roe quoted by Paige Williams, "Seven Years of Silence," *Charlotte Observer*, October 25, 1998. Department of Labor Investigation, Interview with Plant Manager, pp. 16, 22, in author's possession. Author interviews with confidential source, William Morris, and Abbie Covington.

78. See also notes and reports of an interview with William Morris in U.S. Department of Labor, "Imperial Food Products, Inc.: Accident Investigation Report," p. 12, Investigation Number 18479204, December 30, 1991, in author's possession. This is where he talks about OSHA. For other comments from Morris, see author interview with William Morris.

79. Author interview with Annette Zimmerman.

80. Henry L. Kitchin to Gary M. Johnson, January 13, 1993, Box, Imperial Fire, Hamlet City Hall, Hamlet, NC. On Fuller's reputation as a good old boy, see interview with Ron Niland.

81. On Fuller's denial of this rumor, see author interview with Gary Johnson.

82. Greg Trevor and Paige Williams, "Ex-Worker: Locked Door Was OKD, Hamlet Fire-fighter Given Key, He Says," *Charlotte Observer*, October 10, 1991; and in *NBC Dateline* episode on the fire, episode in author's possession. See a corroborating account about Fuller having a key, Department of Labor Investigation, interview #4, p. 22, in author's possession.

83. Glenn Sumpter, "Fire Chief Denies Department Okayed Locking Plant Door," *Richmond County Daily Journal*, October 10, 1991; "Allegations in Letter Are Denied," *Richmond*

County Daily Journal, September 23, 1991. Author interviews with Ada Blanchard and Gary Johnson.

84. C.E. Yandle, "OSHA adviser ties stealing to Hamlet deaths," *Raleigh News and Observer*, November 21, 1991. See also, "Sad Chapter in Tragedy," *Richmond County Daily Journal*, November 26, 1991. And see, in addition, "No Death Penalty for Workers Just Trying to Make a Living: Demand to Have Bradford Barringer Removed from the NC OSHA Council," Box 35, Folder—Barringer Petitions, NCOSHP, SHC, UNC, Chapel Hill, NC.

85. Annette Zimmerman remembered seeing Fuller in the plant a couple of times before the fire. Author interview with Zimmerman. See also author interview with Calvin White. White believes that Fuller had surely been to the plant before the fire.

86. Author interview with Frankie Moree.

87. Fuller quotes from "Phantom Fire Inspections," *Raleigh News and Observer*, September 6, 1991; and Steve Riley, "Betrayal of Trust," *Raleigh News and Observer*, December 11, 1991. Last quote from *Our Jobs, Our Lives: A Work in Progress*, documentary (Black Workers for Justice, 1991), available at American University. See also Randy Diamond, "Panel Will Consider Fire Inspection Rules," *Raleigh News and Observer*, September 9, 1991; John Drescher, "In Hamlet Fire, Government Safety Nets Gave Way," *Charlotte Observer*, September 22, 1991; David Perlmutt, "Owner May Reopen Plant Hit by Fire," *Charlotte Observer*, September 18, 1991.

88. Jonathan Kozol, *Amazing Grace: The Lives of Children and the Conscience of a Nation* (New York: Harper Perennial, 1995), 53.

89. Author interview with Frankie Moree.

90. Land quoted by Ruffin, "Dreams of Better Days." On Roe's reliance on "employment services," see the documentary *Out of the Ashes* (O2 Productions, 1994), available at the North Carolina Department of Labor, Raleigh, NC.

91. "Poultry Plant Fire Victims Mourned in North Carolina," National Public Radio, September 6, 1991.

92. Author interviews with Goodwin, Zimmerman, and Lorrie Boyle; Paul Taylor, "Ashes and Accusations," *Washington Post*, September 5, 1991; and *Out of the Ashes* (O2 Productions, 1994).

93. *Out of the Ashes* (O2 Productions, 1994).

94. Author interview with Ada Blanchard.

95. John Drescher and Ken Garfield, "Workers: Doors Kept Locked—Plant Owner Could Face Criminal Charges," *Charlotte Observer*, September 5, 1991.

96. Author interviews with Abbie Covington and William Sawyer.

97. Emmett Roe to Employee, n.d., Box, Imperial Fire, Hamlet City Hall, Hamlet, NC.

98. Rose DeWolf, "Philaposh Targeting Owner of Plant Hit by Deadly Fire," *Philadelphia Daily News*, November 20, 1991. John C. Brazington, "Victim's Kin Asks for Penalty for Death," *Philadelphia Tribune*, November, 22, 1991.

3: Chicken

1. Shoney's menu circa 1990, purchased on eBay, in author's possession.

2. Some put this date at 1987, but others put it at 1992. On the latter date, see Pew Environmental Group, "Big Chicken: Pollution and Industrial Poultry Production in America," (2011), available at www.pewtrusts.org/~/media/legacy/uploadedfiles/peg/publications/report/pegbig chickenjuly2011pdf.pdf; and "History of Poultry Production," available at www.uspoultry.org /educationprograms/PandEP_Curriculum/Documents/PDFs/Lesson2/HistoryofPoultryPro ductionver3Pres.pdf. On chicken's triumph in 1987, see David Amey, "PCC—Bone of Contention," *Broiler Industry*, (August 1989), 54; and Peter Applebome, "Worker Injuries Rise in Poultry Industry as Business Booms," *New York Times*, November 6, 1989. See also Donald Stull, Michael J. Broadway, and David Griffith, eds., *Any Way You Cut It: Meat Processing and Small-Town America* (Lawrence: University of Kansas Press, 1995).

3. Marlon Manuel, "Chicken Coup: Beef? Pork? Nope, it's power to the poultry as we scarf tons of the meat that definitely has legs," *Atlanta Journal Constitution*, January 25, 2004.

4. Daniel Gross, "The Poultry Boom: It's never a good time to be a chicken, but now is really awful," *Slate*, January 26, 2005, available at www.slate.com/articles/business/moneybox /2005/01/the_poultry_boom.html.

5. On the price in 1923, see Timothy Smith, "Changing Tastes: By End of This Year Poultry Will Surpass Beef in the US Diet," *Wall Street Journal*, September 17, 1987. On the historic shift in prices and choices of meat, see Clement E. Ward, "Twenty-Five Year Meat Consumption and Price Trends," Oklahoma State Report, AGEC-603.

6. On the innovations in poultry production, see among other sources, William Boyd and Michael Watts, "Agro-Industrial Just-In-Time: The Chicken Industry and Postwar American Capitalism," *Globalising Food: Agrarian Questions and Global Restructuring*, edited by David Goodman and Michael J. Watts (London: Routledge, 1997), 192–93; and Annie Potts, *Chicken* (London: Reaktion Books, 2012), 139–40.

7. Lu Ann Jones, *Momma Learned Us to Work: Farm Women in the New South* (Chapel Hill: University of North Carolina Press, 2002); LaGuana Gray, *We Just Keep Running the Line: Black Southern Women and the Poultry Processing Industry* (Baton Rouge: Louisiana State University Press, 2014), 22–23; Wenonah Hauter, *Foodopoly: The Battle Over the Future of Food and Farming in America* (New York: The New Press, 2012), 199.

8. On wartime eating and rationing, see Amy Bentley, *Eating for Victory: Food Rationing and the Politics of Domesticity* (Urbana: University of Illinois Press, 1998); and Steve Striffler, *Chicken: The Dangerous Transformation of America's Favorite Food* (New Haven, CT: Yale University Press, 2007), 43–46.

9. The history of Cagle's is drawn from Paige Bowers, "Cagle's," *New Georgia Encyclopedia* (original entry 2008), available at www.georgiaencyclopedia.org/articles/business-economy /cagles; and "History of Cagle's," available at www.fundinguniverse.com/company-histories /cagle-s-inc-history/. For extremely useful overviews of the history of the chicken industry in the United States, see John Steele Gordon, "The Chicken Story," *American Heritage* (September 1996), 52–67; Roger Horowitz, *Putting Meat on the American Table: Taste, Technology, Transformation* (Baltimore: Johns Hopkins University Press, 2006), 103–28; Andrew C. Godley

and Bridget Williams, "The Chicken, the Factory Farm, and the Supermarket," in *Food Chains: From Farmyard to Shopping Cart*, edited by Warren Belasco and Roger Horowitz (Philadelphia: University of Pennsylvania Press, 2008), 47–61; and Striffler, *Chicken: The Dangerous Transformation*.

10. On the independent streak of the southern yeomanry, see Steve Hahn, *The Roots of Southern Populism: Yeomen Farmers and the Transformation of the Georgia Upcountry, 1850–1890* (New York: Oxford University Press, 2006); and Bethany Moreton, *To Serve God and Wal-Mart: The Making of Christian Free Enterprise* (Cambridge, MA: Harvard University Press, 2010).

11. Monica Richmond Gisolfi, "From Cotton Farmers to Poultry Growers: The Rise of Industrial Agriculture in Upcountry Georgia, 1914–1960," (PhD dissertation, Columbia University, 2007), 105, 110, 121–22, 125; Striffler, *Chicken: The Dangerous Transformation*, 40–48; and Potts, *Chicken*, 150.

12. Christopher Leonard, *The Meat Racket: The Secret Takeover of America's Food Business* (New York: Simon & Schuster, 2014), 237.

13. On the rise of the poultry industry in the South, see "Southeast Economic Justice Network," September 7–9, 1990, December 2, 1988, Box 35, Folder, Southeast REJN September 1990, NCOSHP, SHC, UNC, Chapel Hill, NC. See also Applebome, "Worker Injuries Rise in Poultry Industry"; Tony Horwitz, "Nine to Nowhere," *Wall Street Journal*, December 1, 1994; and Susan Traylor, "Poultry Worker Tells Panel She Was Disabled on Job," *USA Today*, September 12, 1991. See also a more detailed story from Human Rights Watch, "Blood, Sweat, and Fear: Workers' Rights in US Meat and Poultry Plants" (New York: Human Rights Watch, 2004), 40.

14. For more information on the shifting geography and scale of chicken production, see Pew Environmental Group, "Big Chicken."

15. David Kirby, *Animal Factory: The Looming Threat of Industrial Pig, Dairy, and Poultry Farms to Humans and the Environment* (New York: St. Martin's Press, 2010).

16. Solomon Iyobosa Omo-Osagie II, *Commercial Poultry Production on Maryland's Lower Eastern Shore: The Role of African Americans, 1930s to 1990s* (Lanham, MD: University Press of America, 2012), 79.

17. Gisolfi, "From Cotton Farmers to Poultry Growers," 128 (Jewell quote), 155 (second quote). On indentured servitude and modern-day serfs, see Leonard, *The Meat Racket*, 3. See also the insightful John Oliver show, "Chickens," available at www.youtube.com/watch?v=X9wHzt6gBgI.

18. Boyd and Watts, "Agro-Industrial Just-In-Time," 198; Hauter, *Foodopoly*, 199; Mark Schatzker, *The Dorito Effect: The Surprising New Truth About Food and Flavor* (New York: Simon & Schuster, 2015), 23.

19. William Boyd, "Making Meat: Science, Technology, and American Poultry Production," *Technology and Culture* (October 2001), 637; Horowitz, *Putting Meat on the American Table*, 132; and Striffler, *Chicken: The Dangerous Transformation*, 43.

20. Leonard, *Meat Racket*, 5–6; Hauter, *Foodopoly*, 199; and Potts, *Chicken*, 150.

21. N.R. Kleinfield, "America Goes Chicken Crazy," *New York Times*, December 9, 1984.

22. Kleinfield, "America Goes Chicken Crazy"; Nicholas Kristof, "Arsenic in Our Chicken," *New York Times*, April 4, 2012; Potts, *Chicken*, 153–58; and Deena Shanker, "Chicken Is Killing the Planet," *Salon*, September 16, 2013, available at www.salon.com/2013/09/16/chicken _is_killing_the_planet. On de-beaking, see Maneka Gandhi, "Here's Why Beak Trimming of Chicks Is a Senseless Act of Cruelty," FirstPost, August 22, 2016, available at http://www.first post.com/living/heres-why-beak-trimming-of-chicks-in-poultry-farms-is-a-senseless-act-of-cru elty-2969954.html; and "Debeaking," available at www.upc-online.org/merchandise/debeak _factsheet.html.

23. See a reprint of the brochure, "What's Wrong with McDonald's," as well as additional background information, at www.mcspotlight.org/case/factsheet.html.

24. Most of the documents for the McLibel Case are available at www.mcspotlight.org/case /trial/verdict/verdict_jud2c.html. See also George Ritzer, *The McDonaldization of Society* (Thousand Oaks, CA: Pine Forge Press, 2000), 124–25; Eric Schlosser, *Fast Food Nation: The Dark Side of the All-American Meal* (Boston: Houghton Mifflin, 2001), 234–37; and *McLibel*, (Spanner Films, 2005).

25. For more on this, see Gabriel Thompson, *Working in the Shadows: A Year of Doing Jobs (Most) Americans Won't Do* (New York: Nation Books, 2010), 142–43. See also Timothy Pachi-rat, *Every Twelve Seconds: Industrial Slaughter and the Politics of Sight* (New Haven, CT: Yale University Press, 2013).

26. See also Thompson, *Working in the Shadows*, 137.

27. Kathleen C. Schwartzman, *The Chicken Trail: Following Workers, Migrants, and Corporations Across the Americas* (Ithaca, NY: Cornell University Press, 2013), xiii; and Sarah Miller, "What We Don't Know About Chicken and Fish," *Grist*, available at grist.org/food/what -we-dont-want-to-know-about-chicken-and-fish.

28. Richard Behar and Michael Kramer, "Something Smells Foul," *Time*, October 17, 1994; Newsletter: "Hamlet Response Coalition for Workplace Reform," September 1994, Box 31, Folder, Hamlet Response Coalition, 1995, Federal OSHA Reform, North Carolina Occupational Safety and Health Project, SCH, UNC, Chapel Hill, NC. On the fecal soup, see "Five Little Known Facts About Chicken Meat That Affect Your Health," *Healthy Habits Hub*, August 12, 2016, available at healthyhabitshub.com/5-little-known-facts-about-chicken-meat-that -can-affect-your-health; and Linda Carney, "Chicken 'Fecal Soup' Contamination," August 20, 2013, available at www.drcarney.com/blog/entry/chicken-fecal-soup-contamination. For more on line speeds, see Judy Mann, "Hard Times at Perdue's Plant," *Washington Post*, March 10, 1989.

29. In addition to the data cited by Peter Applebome, "Worker Injuries Rise in Poultry Industry as Business Booms," *New York Times*, November 6, 1989; see Frank Swoboda, "U.S. Act to Reduce Repetitive Motion Injuries," *Washington Post*, August 31, 1990; Susan Traylor, "Poultry Worker Tells Panel She Was Disabled on Job," *USA Today*, September 12, 1991; C.E. Yandle, "OSHA Adviser Ties Stealing to Hamlet Deaths," *Raleigh News and Observer*, November 21, 1991; "North Carolina Poultry Worker Fact Sheet," Box 65, Folder: 1910, Southerners for Economic Justice Records, SHC, UNC, Chapel Hill, NC.

30. Applebome, "Worker Injuries Rise."

31. Manuel, "Chicken Coup." On price trends in meat, Ward, "Twenty-Five Year Meat Consumption and Price Trends." The phrase "chickenized" to imply a relentless downward pressure on meat prices comes from Leonard, *The Meat Racket*.

32. See this scene from *The Wire* at https://www.youtube.com/watch?v=1e10ZPVafUA.

33. Douglas Martin, "Robert Baker, Who Reshaped Chicken Dinner, Dies at 84," *New York Times*, March 16, 2006.

34. The information on Baker and his background is drawn from Kleinfield, "America Goes Chicken Crazy"; Martin, "Robert Baker"; "Robert C. Baker: Creator of Chicken Nuggets and Cornell Barbeque Sauce, Dies at 84," *Cornell Chronicle*, March 16, 2006; Maryn McKenna, "The Father of the Chicken Nugget," *Slate*, December 28, 2012, available at www.slate.com/articles/life/food/2012/12/robert_c_baker_the_man_who_invented_chicken_nuggets.html; and Colin Schultz, "Love Chicken Nuggets? Thank Cornell Poultry Professor Robert C. Baker," *Smithsonian Magazine* (December 31, 2012).

35. Author interview with Regenstein and "Free Bird: Remembering Robert Baker," *Cornell Alumni Magazine* (May/June 2006). For a good description of chicken preparation in rural communities in the early part of the last century, see Lu Ann Jones, "Work Was My Pleasure: An Oral History of Nellie Stancil Langley," in *Work, Family, and Faith: Rural Southern Women in the Twentieth Century*, edited by Melissa Walker and Rebecca Sharpless (Columbia: University of Missouri Press, 2006), 31–33.

36. See Baker's co-authored article with C.A. Bruce, "Further Processing of Poultry," in *Processing of Poultry*, edited by G.C. Mead (Boston: Springer, 1995).

37. On budgets and how they vary by class and on the figures showing that the poor spend as much as 30 percent of their income on food even after food prices fall, see Michael Carolan, *The Real Cost of Cheap Food* (London: Routledge, 2011), 75; Kathryn Edin and Laura Lein, *Making Ends Meet: How Single Mothers Survive Welfare and Low-Wage Work* (New York: Russell Sage Foundation, 1997), 88–119; Derek Thompson, "Cheap Eats: How America Spends Money on Food," *The Atlantic*, March 8, 2013, available at www.theatlantic.com/business/archive/2013/03/cheap-eats-how-america-spends-money-on-food/273811; Economic Research Service, USDA, "Household Food Spending by Selected Demographics in the 1990s," available at www.ers.usda.gov/webdocs/publications/aib773/31731_aib773e_002.pdf; and USDA, "Food Prices and Spending: Food Spending as a Share of Income, 2014," available at www.ers.usda.gov/webdocs/charts/40096_foodprices_fig10png/food-prices_fig10.png?v=42472.

38. Gerald J. Fitzgerald and Gabriella M. Petrick, "In Good Taste: Rethinking American History with Our Palates," *Journal of American History* 95 (September 2008), 392–404; and Laura Shapiro, *Something from the Oven: Reinventing Dinner in 1950s America* (New York: Penguin Books, 2005). For more on convenience and cooking, see Harvey Levenstein, *Revolution at the Table: The Transformation of the American Diet* (Berkeley: University of California Press, 2003); Warren J. Belasco, *Appetite for Change: How the Counterculture Took on the Food Industry* (Ithaca: Cornell University Press, 2006, originally published 1989), 124–25; and Hank Cardell, *Stuffed: An Insider's Look at Who's (Really) Making America Fat and How the Food*

Industry Can Fix It (New York: Ecco, 2009), 4. On the impact of this trend on chicken production and producers, see author interview with Scott Russell.

39. On household labor, see Kathryn Edin and Laura Lein, *Making Ends Meet: How Single Mothers Survive Welfare and Low-Wage Work* (New York: Russell Sage Foundation, 1997). See also Melanie Warner, *Pandora's Lunchbox: How Processed Food Took Over the American Meal* (New York: Scribner, 2013), 206; and David K. Shipler, *The Working Poor: Invisible in America* (New York: Vintage Books, 2005), 201, 216.

40. Warner, *Pandora's Lunchbox*, 205–6. See the chicken industry's response, David Amey, "Competitive Challenge for Frozen Foods," *Broiler Industry* (March 1990): 70–71.

41. "Future in Fast Foods," *Broiler Industry* (November 1989): 70–71. On the microwave and the transformation of cooking, see Margaret Visser, "The Meaning of Meals: A Meditation on the Microwave," *Psychology Today* (December 1989). See also Harvey Levenstein, *Paradox of Plenty: A Social History of Eating in Modern America* (New York: Oxford University Press, 1993), 249; and Michael Pollan, *Cooked: A Natural History of Transformation* (New York: Penguin Press, 2013), 188.

42. Greg Crister, *Fat Land: How Americans Became the Fattest People in the World* (Boston: Houghton-Mifflin, 2003), 32; and Tracie McMillan, *The American Way of Eating: Undercover at Walmart, Applebee's, Farm Fields and the Dinner Table* (New York: Scribner 2012), 197.

43. Pollan, *Cooked*, 186–87.

44. For an example of one of these waves of price competition, see Chip Pearsall, "Overstocked Poultry Processors Losing Millions as Prices Drop," *Raleigh News and Observer*, April 13, 1980. See also Marj Charlier, "Chicken Growers Face Leaner Earnings as Salmonella Publicity Takes Its Toll," *Wall Street Journal*, July 20, 1987; and Boyd and Watts, "Agro-Industrial Just-In-Time," 199.

45. Shapiro, *Something from the Oven*, 26.

46. Charlier, "Chicken Growers Face Leaner Earnings"; and Horowitz, *Putting Meat on the American Table*, 117–18. For more on the question of taste, see Schatzker, *The Dorito Effect*.

47. Charlier, "Chicken Growers Face Leaner Earnings"; Kleinfield, "America Goes Chicken Crazy"; and Striffler, *Chicken: The Dangerous Transformation*, 22–23.

48. Horowitz, *Putting Meat on the American Table*, 76.

49. McKenna, "The Father of the Chicken Nugget," and Kleinfield, "America Goes Chicken Crazy."

50. Author interview with Regenstein.

51. Michael Moss, *Salt, Sugar, Fat: How the Food Giants Hooked Us* (New York: Random House, 2013).

52. McKenna, "The Father of the Chicken Nugget."

53. Kevin G. Salwen, "McDonald's Revenue Flow with Franchisees May Help It Profit from Prolonged Drought," *Wall Street Journal*, June 21, 1988.

54. John F. Love, *McDonald's: Behind the Arches* (New York: Bantam Books, 1995), 340–43; and "Rene Arned," available at mcdonalds.wikia.com/wiki/Rene_Arend.

55. John Bryan Hopkins, "A History of Chicken Nuggets," *Foodimentary*, March 15, 2102, available at foodimentary.com/2012/03/15/history-chicken-nuggets. On the Tyson/

McDonald's deal, see Leonard, *The Meat Racket*, 95; Schlosser, *Fast Food Nation*, 140–42; and Striffler, *Chicken: The Dangerous Transformation*, 26–28.

56. Doug Stark, "The South's Poultry Plants Thrive," *Baltimore Sun*, September 8, 1991; and Marlon Manuel, "Chicken Coup."

57. Carole Sugarman and Tom Sietsema, "Nugget Mania: The Low-Down on the Country's Hottest Snack," *Washington Post*, November 5, 1986; Schatzker, *The Dorito Effect*, 38–39. On hot dogs as exemplars of industrial meat, see Horowitz, *Putting Meat on the American Table*, 75–77.

58. Moss, *Salt, Sugar, Fat*, 105 (quote), 305 (on salt 302–18); and James Hamblin, "Look Inside a Chicken Nugget," *The Atlantic*, October 21, 2013, available at www.theatlantic.com /health/archive/2013/10/look-inside-a-chicken-nugget/280720.

59. Quote from Sugarman and Sietsema, "Nugget Mania," and author interview with Scott Russell.

60. Author interview with unnamed source.

61. On competition in poultry capitalism, Kleinfield, "America Goes Chicken Crazy"; and Leonard, *The Meat Racket*.

62. Author interview with Scott Russell. On early profits for poultry companies derived from nuggets, see Scott Kilman, "R.J. Reynolds Net Doubled in 4th Quarter," *Wall Street Journal*, February 15, 1985.

63. David Zuckerman, "Chicken Tenders Advertising Blitz Unleashed by Burger King," *Nation's Restaurant News*, April 7, 1986. On the notion of chicken and healthiness as opposed to red meat, see Striffler, *Chicken: The Dangerous Transformation*, 27, 30–31.

64. Peter O. Keegan, "Chicken Chains Leap Out of the Frying Pan," *Nation's Restaurant News*, August 5, 1991.

65. On the content of Imperial food, see Ben Stocking, "She Hid in Prayer to Flee Fumes," *Raleigh News and Observer*, September 15, 1991. On food trends in 1991, see "Hormel Expands Chicken by George," *Broiler Industry* (July 1989): 18.

66. On the increased pace of work at Imperial in the months leading up to the fire and on cutbacks by the company, see author interviews with Martin Quick and Georgia Quick.

67. Reference to maggots from Steve Riley, "Labor Agency Called Negligent—Panel Releases Report on Hamlet Tragedy," *Raleigh News and Observer*, December 4, 1991, while Ben Stocking reported on Oates's encounter with Brad Roe in his article, "Life and Death at Imperial," *Raleigh News and Observer*, December 8, 1991. For additional accounts of the processing of green and rancid chicken, see author interview with Martin Quick and various interviews from Department of Labor Investigation, in author's possession.

68. C.E. Yandle and Jim Barnett, "The Road to Ruin," *Raleigh News and Observer*, December 10, 1991. On the Mrs. Kinser operation, see author interview with Bill Sawyer. Still, this section on the state of the Roes' businesses relies heavily on the deep and thorough research of Yandle and Barnett and a subsequent author interview with Yandle.

69. Yandle and Barnett, "The Road to Ruin."

70. Ben Stocking, "Life and Death at Imperial." On school lunches and budget cuts, see Susan Levine, *School Lunch Politics: The Surprising History of America's Favorite Welfare Program* (Princeton, NJ: Princeton University Press, 2010).

71. Steve Riley and Randy Diamond, "U.S. Probing Safety at Imperial Plant in Georgia," *Raleigh News and Observer*, September 5, 1991; Steve Riley, "Imperial Pa. Plant Was Cited—Serious Violations Found Twice in '80s," *Raleigh News and Observer*, September 14, 1991; and "Poultry Firm Earlier Fined for Violations," *The State*, September 15, 1991.

72. The history of Haverpride presented here is, again, largely drawn from the excellent reporting of Yandle and Barnett, "The Road to Ruin."

73. On Lyle's actions, see Yandle and Barnett, "The Road to Ruin," and interview with confidential company source.

74. On the demise of Haverpride and its impact on workers, see Yandle and Barnett, "The Road to Ruin"; and Judy Aulette and Raymond Michalowski, "Fire in Hamlet: A Case Study of State-Corporate Crime" (early draft of article), p. 21, Box 35, Folder, Judy Aulette Paper, NCOSHP, SHC, UNC, Chapel Hill, NC.

75. "Hamlet Fire Latest in a Long List of Imperial Setbacks," *Richmond County Daily Journal*, September 16, 1991; and Hamlet Meeting, n.d., Box 35, Folder, Hamlet Organizing Contacts, NCOSHP, SHC, UNC, Chapel Hill, NC.

76. John Hechinger, "Chicken Processing Under Attack," *Charlotte Observer*, September 4, 1991. Author interview with Niland.

77. See again Yandle and Barnett, "The Road to Ruin." See also "Hamlet Plant Owners Weigh Bankruptcy," *Rock Hill Herald*, September 29, 1991.

78. Author interview with Martin Quick.

79. For a larger framing of these issues, see Jacob S, Hacker, *The Great Risk Shift: The New Economic Insecurity and the Decline of the American Dream* (New York: Oxford University Press, 2008).

4: Labor

1. The spine of this chapter is based on an author interview with Georgia Quick; supporting documents were supplied by her lawyer, Woody Gunter, in the author's possession; and genealogical research into Quick's background was conducted by Diane Richard, also in author's possession. For some similar stories of women working in the food industry and with a framing around the idea of cheap, see Dale Finley Slongwhite, *Fed Up: The High Costs of Cheap Food* (Gainesville: University of Florida Press, 2014).

2. On cotton production in North Carolina, see North Carolina Business History, "Cotton," available at www.historync.org/cotton.htm. See also Peter A. Coclanis and Louis M. Kyriakoudes, "Selling Which South? Economic Change in Rural and Small-Town North Carolina in an Era of Globalization, 1940–2007," *Southern Cultures* 4 (Winter 2007): 86–102.

3. On the decline of steady work for men in the countryside, see Cynthia M. Duncan, *Worlds Apart: Poverty and Politics in Rural America* (New Haven, CT: Yale University Press, 1999), 123.

4. It seems like this was a somewhat widely used tool against working people, at least that was what some in the AFL-CIO believed. "Policy Resolutions, November 1981," p. 73, AFL-CIO Records, AFL-CIO Bound Pamphlets, RG-34-002, Box 23, Folder 30, Special Collections, University of Maryland, Silver Spring, MD.

5. Department of Labor Investigation, Interview Number 4, p. 7, in author's possession.

6. Department of Labor Investigation, Interview Number 4, pp. 11, 22, in author's possession; and "Some Facts on the Imperial Food Products Murders in Hamlet, NC," Box 35, Folder, Hamlet Organizing Contacts, NCOSHP, SHC, UNC, Chapel Hill, NC.

7. Author interview with Lorrie Boyle.

8. On the gloves, see Ben Stocking, "Life and Death at Imperial," *Raleigh News and Observer*, December 8, 1991. See also, on the chicken policy, Jim Schlosser, "We Are Going to Die," *Greensboro News and Record*, September 8, 1991.

9. Department of Labor Investigation, various interviews, in author's possession.

10. Department of Labor Investigation, Interview Number 6, pp. 15–17, in author's possession.

11. In addition to the author interview with Georgia Quick, see "Testimony by Mary Bryant," June 1992, NCOSHP, SHC, UNC, Chapel Hill, NC.

12. B. Drummond Ayres Jr., "Factory Fire Leaves Pall Over All-American City," *New York Times*, September 5, 1991.

13. Paul Taylor, "Escape from Fire Is a Rare Piece of Luck for Poultry Worker," *Washington Post*, September 6, 1991.

14. On the rules about slips and falls, see Hamlet Meeting, n.d., Box 35, Folder, Hamlet Organizing Contacts, NCOSHP, SHC, UNC, Chapel Hill, NC. See also author interviews with Mark Schultz and Lorrie Boyle.

15. Department of Labor Investigation, Interview Number 5, p. 23, in author's possession.

16. Details about Gail Campbell come from Kemlite Video, Charles Becton Personal Files, Durham, NC, copy in author's possession.

17. For similar descriptions of shopfloor friendships and relationships among poultry workers, see LaGuana Gray, *We Just Keep Running the Line: Black Southern Women and the Poultry Processing Industry* (Baton Rouge: Louisiana State University Press , 2014), 84.

18. Gregg LaBar, "Hamlet, N.C.: Home to a National Tragedy," *Occupational Hazards* (September 1992): 29.

19. "Testimony by Mary Bryant," June 1992, NCOSHP, SHC, UNC, Chapel Hill, NC. See a similar view expressed by an Imperial worker in Bob Edwards, "Poultry Plant Fire Victims Mourned in North Carolina," NPR, *Morning Edition*, September 6, 1991.

20. Author interview with William Morris.

21. Author interview with Joseph Arnold.

22. Bobby Quick, no relation to Georgia, quoted by Judy Aulette and Raymond Michalowski, "Fire in Hamlet: A Case Study of State-Corporate Crime," p. 23, Box 35, Folder, Judy Aulette Paper, NCOSHP, SCH, UNC, Chapel Hill, NC.

23. Lee May, "Plant Fire Unlikely to Spur Major Reforms," *Los Angeles Times*, September 11, 1991.

24. On the movement back to the South, see James Cobb, *The South and America Since World War II* (New York: Oxford University Press, 2011), 190–91; and Dan Bilesky, "New Life, Blacks in City Head South," *New York Times*, June 21, 2011.

25. Information about Bellamy comes from Ben Stocking, "Life and Death at Imperial," *Raleigh News and Observer*, December 8, 1991. See also Dave Moniz, "New Life Cut Short in Hamlet Fire," *Columbia State*, September 6, 1991.

26. Taylor, "Escape from Fire," and Doug Stark, "The South's Poultry Plants Thrive," *Baltimore Sun*, September 8, 1991.

27. Osha Gray Davidson, "The Rise of the Rural Ghetto," *The Nation*, June 15, 1986, 820.

28. Cobb, *The South and America*, 190.

29. Anderson quoted by Ray Suarez, *The Old Neighborhood: What We Lost in the Great Suburban Migration, 1966–1999* (New York: Free Press, 1999), 67.

30. Davidson, "The Rise of the Rural Ghetto"; and Osha Gray Davidson, *Broken Heartland: The Rise of America's Rural Ghetto* (Iowa City: University of Iowa Press, 1996). See also Coclanis and Kyriakoudes, "Selling Which South?," 86–102. See also the portrait of a small town in crisis in Nick Reding, *Methland: The Death and Life of an American Small Town* (New York: Bloomsbury, 2009). See similar accounts of the struggles in small towns during this period in Nate Blakeslee, *Tulia: Race, Cocaine, and Corruption in a Small Texas Town* (New York: Public Affairs, 2005); and Richard Rubin, *Confederacy of Silence: A True Tale of the New Old South* (New York: Atria Books, 2002), 31.

31. For a profile of the economy of Richmond County, see MDC, Inc. (Chapel Hill, NC), "Three Faces of Rural North Carolina: A Summary Report to the North Carolina Commission on Jobs and Economic Growth" (December 1986): i. On unemployment, see Taylor, "Escape from Fire."

32. William Julius Wilson, *When Work Disappears: The World of the New Urban Poor* (New York: Vintage, 1997).

33. "Hamlet's Streak of Misfortune Began on Friday," *Richmond County Daily Journal*, April 12, 1991; "Seems Like Crime Is on the Rise," *Richmond County Daily Journal*, September 3, 1991; Karl Stark, "Sudden Horror of Fatal Fire Overwhelms Tiny N.C. Town," *Philadelphia Inquirer*, September 8, 1991.

34. Author interview with Cordelia Steele.

35. Jane Ruffin, "Dreams of Better Days," *Raleigh News and Observer*, December 9, 1991; and MDC, Inc., "Three Faces," Appendix C, p. 12.

36. Author interview with Reverend Harold Miller; and Coclanis and Kyriakoudes, "Selling Which South?" 96.

37. Author interview with Josh Newton.

38. MDC Inc., "Three Faces," Appendix C, p. 12. Coclanis and Kyriakoudes, "Selling Which South?," 96; and Jane Ruffin, "A World Apart: Economic growth of North Carolina's rural areas," *Business North Carolina* (April 1992). See also George Packer, *The Unwinding: An Inner History of the New America* (New York: Farrar, Straus and Giroux, 2013).

39. Gordon Edes, "From Hamlet to Megalopolis: Dodgers' Franklin Stubbs Seems to Have Arrived to Stay," *Los Angeles Times*, June 18, 1996; and author interview with Martin Quick.

40. Author interview with Martin Quick.

41. Author interview with Martin Quick; and Taylor, "Escape from Fire."

42. Author interview with Larry Lee. See also William Julius Wilson, *The Truly Disadvantaged: The Inner City, the Underclass, and Public Policy* (Chicago: University of Chicago Press, 1980).

43. David Sirota, *Back to Our Future: How the 1980s Explain The World We Live in Now— Our Culture, Our Politics, Our Everything* (New York: Ballantine Books, 2011), 175, 197.

44. Michelle Alexander, *The New Jim Crow: Mass Incarceration in the Age of Colorblindness* (New York: The New Press: 2010), 50–51. See also Heather A. Thompson, "Why Mass Incarceration Matters: Rethinking Crisis, Decline, and Transformation in Postwar American History," *Journal of American History* 97 (December 2010): 702–34.

45. On Detroit, see Thomas Sugrue's classic book, *Origins of the Urban Crisis: Race and Inequity in Postwar Detroit* (Princeton, NJ: Princeton University Press, 2005).

46. Douglas S. Massey and Nancy A. Denton, *American Apartheid: Segregation and the Making of the Underclass* (Cambridge, MA: Harvard University Press, 1993), 166. See also on the point of men and family, Elijah Anderson, *Streetwise: Race, Class, and Change in an Urban Community* (Chicago: University of Chicago Press, 1992), 112–37; Elijah Anderson, *Code of the Street: Decency, Violence, and the Moral Life of the Inner City* (New York: W.W. Norton, 2000); and, of course, Wilson, *The Truly Disadvantaged*. Cynthia M. Duncan makes a similar link between urban and rural ghettos in her book, *Worlds Apart*, 126–27.

47. Author interview with Annette Zimmerman. On welfare spending, see Cobb, *The South and America*, 202. On Imperial, see "Some Facts on the Imperial Food Products Murders in Hamlet, NC," Box 35, Folder, Hamlet Organizing Contacts, NCOSHP, SHC, UNC, Chapel Hill, NC.

48. Gray, *We Just Keep Running the Line*, 70.

49. Jesmyn Ward, *Men We Reaped: A Memoir* (New York: Bloomsbury 2013), 83–84, 131. For more on Richmond County and the rise of single-parent households, see "Richmond Shows Gain in Families Headed by Women," *The News*, June 16, 1975, Charles McClean Papers, Box 2, Folder 6, UNCC, Charlotte, NC. See also U.S. Bureau of the Census, Census of Population and Housing, 1990: Social and Economic Characteristics North Carolina, Table 2: Summary of Labor Force and Commuting Characteristics, available at www.census.gov/prod/cen1990/cp2 /cp-2-35-1.pdf. See also Dean Bakopoulos's novel that explores the disappearance of working-class men, in this case white men, as their jobs disappear, *Please Don't Come Back From the Moon* (Orlando, FL: Harvest Books, 2005).

50. On the larger phenomenon, see Robert Putnam, *Our Kids: The American Dream in Crisis* (New York: Simon & Schuster, 2015), 68–69; and Robert O. Self, *All in the Family: A Realignment of America* (New York: Hill and Wang, 2013), 110–11.

51. Ward, *Men We Reaped*, 131.

52. Andrew J. Cherlin estimates that 75 percent of undereducated women sought employment in 1990. That was up from 38 percent thirty years earlier. This again explains something of the jump in the labor market participation. See Cherlin, *Labor's Love Lost: The Rise and Fall of the Working-Class Family in America* (New York: Russell Sage Foundation, 2014), 148.

53. In his book on the 1970s, Thomas Borstelmann makes an interesting argument about the egalitarian impulse coming out of the 1960s and its somewhat counterintuitive impact

on inequality; see *The 1970s: A New Global History from Civil Rights to Economic Inequality* (Princeton, NJ: Princeton University Press, 2012), 6.

54. Katherine Newman, *No Shame in My Game: The Working Poor in the Inner City* (New York: Vintage, 2000), xiv. See also Gray, *We Just Keep Running the Line*, 64–65.

55. Vanesa Ribas uses this term in her book on hog-processing workers in a small town in North Carolina, *On the Line: Slaughterhouse Lives and the Making of the New South* (Berkeley: University of California Press, 2015), 62.

56. Lillie Belle Davis, *A New Beginning: It's a Blessing to Be Alive* (lulu.com books, 2004), 11–14.

57. Author interview with Zimmerman. See a similar response in Gray, *We Just Keep Running the Line*, 53.

58. Budget estimates drawn based on what the survivors of the fire reported their needs were after the fire, Reverend James Bailey, Disaster Relief Fund Treasurer, January 28, 1992, Box 33, Folder, Correspondence, NCOSHP, SHC, UNC, Chapel Hill, NC; Peter Kilborn, "In Aftermath of Deadly Fire, A Poor Town Struggles Back," *New York Times*, November 25, 1991; and Lawrence Naumoff, *A Southern Tragedy in Crimson and Yellow* (Winston-Salem, NC: Zuckerman Cannon Publishers, 2005), 46, 52. See also Kathryn Edin and Laura Lein, *Making Ends Meet: How Single Mothers Survive Welfare and Low-Wage Work* (New York: Russell Sage Foundation, 1997), 88–119; and Anne Draper, "Crisis in the Family Budget," (1980) AFL-CIO Records, AFL-CIO Bound Pamphlets, RG-34-002, Box 23, Folder 58, Special Collections, University of Maryland, College Park, MD.

59. "Testimony of Conester Williams," June 23, 1992, NCOSHP, SHC. See also "Some Facts on the Imperial Food Products Murders in Hamlet, NC," Box 35, Folder, Hamlet Organizing Contacts, NCOSHP, SHC, UNC, Chapel Hill, NC.

60. Author interview with Ada Blanchard.

61. Edin and Lein, *Making Ends Meet*, 56–57.

62. Author interview with Zimmerman.

63. Ada Blanchard noticed the same problems with the equipment and the overworked maintenance crew. Author interview with Ada Blanchard.

64. Quick's pregnancy is revealed in a court document, "Georgia Anne Quick: Summary of Injuries and Damages Resulting from September 3, 1991 Industrial Plant Fire," Woodrow Gunter Files, in author's possession, and from an unnamed source in an author interview.

5: Bodies

1. These reports can be found in Imperial Foods File, Office of Medical Examiner, North Carolina Department of Environment, Health, and Natural Resources, Raleigh, NC.

2. Harvey Levenstein, *Paradox of Plenty: A Social History of Eating in Modern America* (New York: Oxford University Press, 1993), 101–15.

3. This draws on a point made by Eric Schlosser, *Fast Food Nation: The Dark Side of the All-American Meal* (Boston: Houghton Mifflin, 2001), 113. See also Mark Schatzker, *The Dorito Effect: The Surprising New Truth About Food and Flavor* (New York: Simon & Schuster, 2015), 18, 73, 81–82, 110–11; Michael Moss, *Salt, Sugar, Fat: How the Food Giants Hooked Us* (New

York: Random House, 2013), xvi; and Greg Critser, *Fat Land: How Americans Became the Fattest People in the World* (Boston: Houghton Mifflin, 2003). For engaged and critical readings of these numbers, see J. Eric Oliver, *Fat Politics: The Real Story Behind America's Obesity Epidemic* (New York: Oxford University Press, 2006); and Julie Guthman, *Weighing In: Obesity, Food Justice, and the Limits of Capitalism* (Berkeley: University of California, 2011).

4. The medical term for this is slipped capital femoral epiphysis.

5. John Hoffman and Judith A. Salerno, *The Weight of the Nation: To Win We Have to Lose* (New York: St. Martin's Griffin, 2012), 22–23.

6. Hoffman and Salerno, *The Weight of the Nation*, 22–23; Michael Carolan, *The Real Cost of Cheap Food* (London: Routledge, 2011), 75; and Kelly D. Brownell, *Food Fight: The Inside Story of the Food Industry, America's Obesity Crisis, and What We Can Do About It* (New York: McGraw Hill, 2004), 3.

7. Prepared by the Staff of the Select Committee on Nutrition and Human Needs, United States Senate, "Dietary Goals for the United States" (Washington: February 1977), 1, 9.

8. Alton Ochsner, *Smoking: Your Choice Between Life and Death* (New York: Simon & Schuster, 1970), 110.

9. Hoffman and Salerno, *The Weight of the Nation*, 81.

10. Moss, *Salt, Sugar, Fat*, 328.

11. Levenstein, *Paradox of Plenty*, 10, 242, 262.

12. "Kids Weigh in on Growing Waistlines," *Atlanta Journal Constitution*, May 20, 2007.

13. Hoffman and Salerno, *The Weight of the Nation*, 11.

14. Levenstein, *Paradox of Plenty*, 204.

15. For a detailed treatment of this bill and its fate, see Jefferson Cowie, *Stayin' Alive: The 1970s and the Last Days of the Working Class* (New York: The New Press, 2012), 262–80. See also Marisa Chappell's smart reading of this measure in *The War on Welfare: Family, Poverty, and Politics in Modern America* (Philadelphia: University of Pennsylvania Press, 2010), 126–27.

16. Sarah Wu, *Fed Up with Lunch: The School Lunch Project* (San Francisco: Chronicle Books, 2011), 81. Laura Moser, "Physical Education in American Schools Is Getting Lapped," *Slate*, April 12, 2016, available at www.slate.com/blogs/schooled/2016/04/12/most_states _are_shortchanging_kids_on_physical_education_study_finds.html. See also Division of Public Health, North Carolina Department of Health and Human Services, "The Burden of Obesity in North Carolina," (Raleigh, 2009), available at www.eatsmartmovemorenc.com /ObesityInNC/Texts/OBESITY_BURDEN_2009_WEB.pdf.

17. Critser, *Fat Land*, 48.

18. Susan Levine, *School Lunch Politics: The Surprising History of America's Favorite Welfare Program* (Princeton, NJ. Princeton University Press, 2000), 150–70.

19. Aaron E. Carroll, "How Restricting Food Stamp Choices Can Fight Obesity," *New York Times*, September 22, 2016; Government Accounting Office, "Food Stamp Program: Options for Delivering Financial Incentives to Participants for Purchasing Targeted Foods" (July 2008), available at www.gao.gov/new.items/d08415.pdf; and Olga Khazan, "Should Food Stamps Buy Soda," *The Atlantic*, November 11, 2013.

20. Michael Pollan, *Omnivore's Dilemma: A Natural History of Four Meals* (New York: Penguin Press, 2006); and Amelia Urry, "Our Crazy Farm Subsidies, Explained," *Grist*, April 20, 2015, available at grist.org/food/our-crazy-farm-subsidies-explained.

21. Carolan, *The Real Cost of Cheap Food*, 103.

22. Quoted by Schatzker, *The Dorito Effect*, 145.

23. James Hamblin, "Look Inside a Chicken Nugget," *The Atlantic*, October 21, 2013, available at www.theatlantic.com/health/archive/2013/10/look-inside-a-chicken-nugget/280720.

24. Carole Sugarman and Tom Sietsema, "Nugget Mania: The Low-Down on Country's Hottest Snack," *Washington Post*, November 5, 1986.

25. The American Heart Association, "The Effects of Excess Sodium," available at www.heart.org/HEARTORG/HealthyLiving/HealthyEating/HealthyDietGoals/The-Effects-of-Excess-Sodium-Infographic_UCM_454384_SubHomePage.jsp; and Michael F. Jacobson, "Salt: The Forgotten Killer" (2005), available at cspinet.org/new/pdf/salt_report_with_cover.pdf.

26. Schatzker, *The Dorito Effect*, 73. Second quote from Hoffman and Salerno, *The Weight of the Nation*, 71–73.

27. Striffler, *Chicken; The Dangerous Transformation of America's Favorite Food* (New Haven, CT: Yale University Press, 2007).

28. "North Carolina Health News," available at www.northcarolinahealthnews.org/interactive-physical-activity-health-in-north-carolina-county-data.

29. "The State of Obesity in North Carolina," available at stateofobesity.org/states/nc.

30. Diane Duston, "Kids Prefer to Eat Pizza," *Richmond County Daily Journal*, September 12, 1991.

31. Ann Vileisis, *Kitchen Literacy: How We Lost Knowledge of Where Food Comes From and Why We Need to Get It Back* (Washington, DC: Island Press, 2008), 7, 8–9.

32. Michael Pollan, *Cooked: A Natural History of Transformation* (New York: Penguin Press, 2013), 191. See also Levenstein, *Paradox of Plenty*, 105.

33. "The State of Obesity in North Carolina," and "The Burden of Obesity in North Carolina."

34. Author interview with Blanchard.

35. J.D. Vance, *Hillbilly Elegy: A Memoir of a Family and Culture in Crisis* (New York: HarperCollins, 2016), 138.

36. Tracie McMillan, *The American Way of Eating: Undercover at Walmart, Applebee's, Farm Fields and the Dinner Table* (New York: Scribner, 2012), 1. On the working poor and the difficulty they typically have finding time to cook, see also David K. Shipler, *The Working Poor: Invisible in America* (New York: Vintage Books, 2005), 36–37; and Linda Tirado, *Hand to Mouth: Living in Bootstrap America* (New York: G. P. Putnam's Sons, 2014), xv.

37. Pollan, *Cooked,* 193. Laura Shapiro, *Something From the Oven: Reinventing Dinner in 1950s America* (New York: Penguin Books, 2005), 253; and Helen Zoe Veit, "Time to Revive Home Ec," *New York Times*, September 5, 2011.

38. Author interview with Zimmerman.

39. Thomas Borstelmann, *The 1970s: A New Global History from Civil Rights to Economic Inequality* (Princeton, NJ: Princeton University Press, 2012), 60–61.

40. Peter Coclanis and Louis M. Kyriakoudes, "Selling Which South? Economic Change in Rural and Small-Town North Carolina in an Era of Globalization, 1940–2007," *Southern Cultures* 4 (Winter 2007): 94.

41. Wilbur Hobby, President of NC AFL-CIO, to Holshouser, December 30, 1975, Box 332, Folder, "Labor, Department of, A–J," Governor James E. Holshouser Papers, North Carolina State Archives, Raleigh, NC.

42. Ted Genoways, *The Chain: Farm, Factory, and the Fate of Our Food* (New York: Harper Collins, 2014), 42. On the larger shift in meatpacking, see Donald D. Stull and Michael J. Broadway, *Slaughterhouse Blues: The Meat and Poultry Industry in North America* (Belmont, CA: Wadsworth Publishing, 2012).

43. On the importance of this way of thinking, see Lizabeth Cohen, *A Consumer's Republic: The Politics of Mass Consumption in Postwar America* (New York: Knopf, 2003), 54–56.

44. Cowie quoted by E.J. Dionne, "Fighting Nostalgia and Amnesia in America's Search for Greatness," *Washington Post*, July 6, 2016. See also Cowie, *The Great Exception: The New Deal and the Limits of American Politics* (Princeton, NJ: Princeton University Press, 2016), 153–54.

45. Christopher Leonard, *The Meat Racket: The Secret Takeover of America's Food Business* (New York: Simon & Schuster, 2014), and Guthman, *Weighing In*, 134.

46. Nestle quoted in *A Place at the Table* (Motto Pictures, 2012); See also Marion Nestle, *Food Politics: How the Food Industry Influences Nutrition and Health* (Berkeley: University of California Press, 2007).

47. Author interview with Annette Zimmerman. See also the interviews in *A Place at the Table* (Motto Pictures, 2012).

48. Eric Finkelstein and Laurie Zuckerman, *The Fattening of America: How the Economy Makes Us Fat, If It Matters, and What to Do About It* (Hoboken, NJ: Wiley, 2008), 128.

49. Quote from *A Place at the Table*. See also Brownell, *Food Fight*, 201–2.

50. In general, CHOP has a terrific website describing the problems associated with obesity. Interestingly enough, beginning in 2005, their data suggests that there is no longer a linear relationship between poverty and obesity. "Being wealthy," add John Hoffman and Judith Salerno, "is not nearly as protective against obesity as it used to be." Hoffman and Salerno, *The Weight of the Nation*, 11.

51. The discrimination that goes along with the appearance of alleged "fat-ness" and body shaming is one of the central insights of the emerging scholarly field of "fat studies." See for instance, Esther D. Rothblum, "Fat Studies," in *The Oxford Handbook of the Social Science of Obesity*, edited by John Cawley (New York: Oxford University Press, 2011), 176–77.

52. In 2011, this McDonald's outlet was eventually closed. See Don Sapatkin, "Children's Hospital Is Closing Its McDonald's Restaurant," *Philadelphia Daily News*, September 16, 2011.

53. Charlotte Biltekoff, *Eating Right in America: The Cultural Politics of Food and Health* (Durham, NC: Duke University Press, 2013), 120, 124; Brownell, *Food Fight*, 45, 46; and Carolan, *The Real Cost of Cheap Food*, 75.

54. Author interview with Bob Hall.

6: Deregulation

1. Randy Diamond, "Plant Never Had Safety Inspection," *Raleigh News and Observer*, September 4, 1991.

2. On this inaction, see John Conway, "Feds Took No Action Despite N.C. Safety Violations," *Greensboro News and Record*, September 4, 1991.

3. NBC News, September 4, 1991, Vanderbilt Television News Archive, Vanderbilt University, Nashville, TN. See also for more on this report on North Carolina's OSHA enforcement, Committee on Education and Labor, House of Representatives, "The Tragedy at Imperial Food Products, December 1991, Serial No. 102-N, pp. 6–7.

4. "A Handy Reference Guide to The Williams-Steiger Occupational Safety and Health Act of 1970," in a brochure in a packet called, "Your Union Welcomes You," circa 1975, UFCW Papers, Box 5, Folder, Our Union Welcomes You, circa 1975, SHSW, University of Wisconsin, Madison, WI. By far the best book, and really the only quality monograph on OSHA, is Charles Noble, *Liberalism at Work: The Rise and Fall of OSHA* (Philadelphia: Temple University Press, 1986).

5. I.W. Abell to President Lloyd, May 7, 1971, Frame 650, Reel 280, Frame 653, Folder, "UFCW Action Photos," UFCW Papers, SHSW, University of Wisconsin, Madison, WI. And I.W. Abel, President, Industrial Union Department, AFL-CIO, to Brother Gorman, August 31, 1972, Reel 280, Frames 469–70, Folder, "UFCW Action Photos," UFCW Papers, SHSW, University of Wisconsin, Madison, WI.

6. H.W. Brands, *Reagan: The Life* (New York: Doubleday, 2015), 178. See also Erik Loomis, *Out of Sight: The Long and Disturbing Story of Corporations Outsourcing Catastrophe* (New York: The New Press, 2015), 66–67.

7. "Martin Plan: Start Hot Line," *Charlotte Observer*, September 12, 1991. Mike Casey, "Safety Penalties Less in Carolinas: Serious Violations Costlier to Firms in 39 Other States," *Charlotte Observer*, October 26, 1991.

8. Harry Bernstein, "Fatal Fire May Stir OSHA Action," *Los Angeles Times*, September 7, 1991; Martin Gensler, Letter to the Editor, *Washington Post*, October 17, 1991; and *NBC Nightly News*, September 4, 1991.

9. Casey, "Safety Penalties Less in Carolinas." See also Russ Bargmann, "OSHA: The Urgency of Revival" (1977), AFL-CIO Records, AFL-CIO Bound Pamphlets, RG-34-002, Box 20, Folder 27, Special Collections, University of Maryland, College Park, MD.

10. Michael Steward Foley, *Front Porch Politics: The Forgotten Heyday of American Activism in the 1970s* (New York: Hill and Wang, 2014), 23. On the timing and substance of this shift in attitudes, see also Daniel T. Rodgers, *Age of Fracture* (Cambridge, MA: Belknap Press of Harvard University Press, 2011), 122.

11. "The National Economy," AFL-CIO Records, AFL-CIO Bound Pamphlets, RG-34-002, Box 23, Folder 54, Special Collections, University of Maryland, College Park, MD.

12. Foley, *Front Porch Politics*, 23.

13. Rick Perlstein, *The Invisible Bridge: The Fall of Nixon and the Rise of Reagan* (New York: Simon & Schuster, 2014), 478. On the broader currents of economic thinking going on in the United States and Europe during the last century, see Angus Burgin, *The Great Persuasion:*

Inventing Free Markets Since the Great Depression (Cambridge, MA: Harvard University Press, 2012). On independent truck drivers, in particular, and their break with the New Deal, see Shane Hamilton, *Trucking Country: The Road to America's Wal-Mart Economy* (Princeton, NJ: Princeton University Press, 2014).

14. Charlotte Montgomery, "Pressure to Scrap Key U.S. Health Laws Forecast," *The Globe and Mail*, May 26, 1981.

15. Edwin McDowell, "OSHA, EPA: The Heyday Is Over," *New York Times*, January 4, 1981; Laura Kalman, *Right Star Rising: A New Politics, 1974–1980* (New York: Norton, 2010), 240; and the final quote from W. Edwards Deming to Congressman George Hansen, July 11, 1978, ACU Papers, Brigham Young University, Provo, UT.

16. Kim Phillips-Fein, *Invisible Hands: The Businessmen's Crusade Against the New Deal* (New York: Norton, 2009), 210. See also for a similar point, Kalman, *Right Star Rising*, 41.

17. On this key point, see Meg Jacobs, *Pocketbook Politics: Economic Citizenship in Twentieth-Century America* (Princeton, NJ: Princeton University Press, 2005).

18. Joseph A. McCartin, *Collision Course: Ronald Reagan, the Air Traffic Controllers, and the Strike That Changed America* (New York: Oxford University Press, 2011); and Jefferson Cowie, *Stayin' Alive: The 1970s and the Last Days of the Working Class* (New York: The New Press, 2010). Reagan quote from Cody Carlson, "This week in history: Ronald Reagan fires 11,345 air traffic controllers," *Deseret News*, August 5, 2012, available at www.deseretnews.com /article/865560028/This-week-in-history-Ronald-Reagan-fires-11345-air-traffic-controllers .html?pg=all.

19. For information on rates of union membership, see data available at digitalcommons.ilr .cornell.edu/cgi/viewcontent.cgi?article=1176&context=key_workplace.

20. Jim Larkee (Arden) to Holshouser, Holshouser to Larkee, July 21, 1976, Box 433, Folder, "Safety and Health Review Board, Labor Department of," Governor James E. Holshouser Papers, North Carolina State Archives, Raleigh, NC.

21. HJB to Harley F. Shuford, President of Shuford Mills in Hickory, May 19, 1980, Beard Papers, Box 4, Folder 28, UNCC, Charlotte, NC; Draft letter on yellow legal paper, Addressed to "Dear Fellow . . . ," n.d., Box 34, Folder 31, UNCC, and Affidavit, State of NC, County of Mecklenburg, Box 34, Folder 23, Beard Papers, UNCC, Charlotte, NC; and George Hansen to Dear (blank), February 14, 1979; Beard to Bill Keyes, September 25, 1979, ACU Papers, BYU, Provo, UT.

22. Phillips-Fein, *Invisible Hands*, 208–9.

23. Phillips-Fein, *Invisible Hands*, 208–9. See more on the values of the ACU, available at conservative.org/who-we-are.

24. Damon Stetson, "Carter Backed by State Labor Federation," *New York Times*, August 26, 1980; Memorandum to the President, From Charles L. Schulze (Chair, Council of Economic Advisors), Stu Eizenstat, (Assistant to the Pres for Domestic Affairs and Policy), and Bert Lance (Office of Management and Budget), May 27, 1977, Council of Economic Advisors, Charles L. Schulze's Subject Files, Box 59, Folder, OSHA Reform, Carter Presidential Library, Atlanta, GA. On Ford, see "Tennessee and Kentucky: A Profile," Ford campaign memo, 1976, available at www.fordlibrarymuseum.gov/library/document/0204/1512257.pdf.

25. Jimmy Carter, "Statement of OSHA," circa 1976, Box 5, Carter Presidential Library, Atlanta, GA.

26. Philip J. Simon, "Reagan in the Workplace: Unraveling the Health and Safety Net" (Washington, DC: Center for Study of Responsive Law, 1983), 6; "Eula Bingham," Wikipedia. com, available at en.wikipedia.org/wiki/Eula_Bingham; Nolan Hancock, "Employer Retaliation Can Chill Workers' Support for OSHA," AFL-CIO Records, AFL-CIO Bound Pamphlets, RG-34-002, Box 23, Folder 17, OSHA: A 10 Year Success Story, Special Collections, University of Maryland, College Park, MD.

27. Michael Verespej, "OSHA: Under New Management," *Industry Week*, November 2, 1981.

28. Hancock, "Employer Retaliation."

29. Press Release: Council on Wage and Price Stability, "Council Criticizes OSHA Approach," September 22, 1976, Council of Economic Advisors, Charles L. Schultze's Subject Files, Box 59, Folder, OSHA, Carter Presidential Library, Atlanta, GA.

30. Memorandum to the President, May 27, 1977.

31. On Carter's drift toward deregulation, see Bruce J. Schulman, *The Seventies: The Great Shift in American Culture, Society, and Politics* (Cambridge, MA: Da Capo Press, 2001), 125. See also Daniel Steadman Jones, *Masters of the Universe: Hayek, Friedman, and the Birth of Neoliberal Politics* (Princeton, NJ: Princeton University Press, 2012), 217.

32. "The President's Anti-Inflation Program," Box 5, Folder, Special Advisor—Inflation Kahn, "Anti-Inflation—Brochure, 6/79–8/79," Carter Presidential Library, Atlanta, GA.

33. Dominic Sandbrook, *Mad as Hell: The Crisis of the 1970s and the Rise of the Populist Right* (New York: Knopf, 2011), 333.

34. Perlstein, *The Invisible Bridge*, 560.

35. Seth S. King, "Labor Dept. Proposes Voluntary Worker Safety Plans," *New York Times*, January 19, 1982; and Charlotte Montgomery, "Pressure to Scrap Key U.S. Health Laws Forecast," *The Globe and Mail*, May 26, 1981.

36. Douglas Kneeland, "A Summary of Reagan's Positions on the Major Issues of This Year," *New York Times*, July 16, 1980.

37. Robert Collins, *Transforming America: Politics and Culture During the Reagan Years* (New York: Columbia University Press, 2009), 81.

38. Jules Tygiel, *Ronald Reagan and the Triumph of American Conservatism* (New York: Pearson Longman, 2005), 124.

39. On the record of Donovan's firm, Schiavone Construction, including its OSHA fines and infractions, see Warren Brown and Philp J. Hilts, "Labor's Nominee's Firm Has Mixed OSHA Record," *Washington Post*, December 23, 1980. See also Philip J. Hilts, "OSHA Has Fears Successor Will Kill Rules," *Washington Post*, November 23, 1980; and Susan Garland, "OSHA's New Tack: Letting Firms Design OWN Ways to Deal with Safety," *Christian Science Monitor*, August 20, 1981.

40. See quotes (and some background) from Michael A. Verespej, "OSHA Shuffles Deck on Health Standards," *Industry Week*, April 20, 1981; and David Pauly, "Reagan's War on Regulation," *Newsweek*, April 20, 1981. On fines faced by Auchter's company, see Joann S.

Lublin, "Choice to Head OSHA Is Thorne Auchter, A Proponent of Less Federal Regulation," *Wall Street Journal*, February 12, 1981. See also "A Construction Executive Is Picked to Head OSHA," *Chemical Week*, February 18, 1981; and Michael Verespej, "OSHA: Under New Management," *Industry Week*, November 2, 1981.

41. On Auchter's response to the pamphlet, see "Towards a 'Neutral' Role for OSHA," *New York Times*, March 29, 1981. Quote from the factory inspector is from Simon, "Reagan in the Workplace," 2. See also Fred Barbash, "OSHA Will Seek to Relax Rules on Cotton Dust," *Washington Post*, March 27, 1981; and Fred Barbash, "OSHA to Review Work-Exposure Rules," *Washington Post*, March 28, 1981.

42. Peter Behr, "Reagan Team Takes Stock of Prospects for Reshaping Regulations," *Washington Post*, February 6, 1981.

43. Douglas D. Feaver, "In a Turnabout, States Find Things Easier Under OSHA," *Washington Post*, October 21, 1981; Peter Earley, "OSHA Shift Means Cutbacks in Its Inspections," *Washington Post*, February 3, 1982; John Conway, "Fed Took No Action Despite N.C. Safety Violations," *Greensboro News and Record*, September 20, 1991; Simon, "Reagan in the Workplace," 9, 11, 33, 46; and Noble, *Liberalism at Work*.

44. Richard Lacayo, "Price of Neglect," *Time*, September 28, 1992. On increased injuries during the 1980s, see Cass Peterson, "Injuries Unreported, Unions Say," *Washington Post*, March 20, 1987; and Frank Swoboda, "'Unbearable Pain' on the Job," *Washington Post*, October 25, 1988.

45. "Policy Resolutions, November 1981," p. 73, AFL-CIO Records, AFL-CIO Bound Pamphlets, RG-34-002, Box 23, Folder 30, Special Collections, University of Maryland, College Park, MD.

46. Sandra Evans Teeley, "OSHA Under Siege," *Washington Post*, April 12, 1981.

47. Martin Tolchin, "Nader Says OSHA Is Shackled," *New York Times*, September 5, 1983; and Simon, "Reagan in the Workplace," 10.

48. On the politics of North Carolina in the 1980s, see John Hood, *Catalyst: Jim Martin and the Rise of North Carolina Republicans* (Winston-Salem, NC: John F. Blair Publishers, 2015).

49. Jerry Adams, "The Bad Boy of State Politics," *We the People* (October 1979): 32.

50. For more on Brooks, see C.E. Yandle, "Fire Creates Furor About Inspections—Brooks Cites Growing Lack of Staff," *Raleigh News and Observer*, September 7, 1991; Van Denton, "Hamlet Fire Puts Brooks Squarely in the Limelight," *Raleigh News and Observer*, September 17, 1991; and Greg Trevor and John Drescher, "N.C. Champion of Worker Safety Takes a Lashing, Gives It Back," *Charlotte Observer*, September 16, 1991.

51. For one of his requests see, John C. Brooks, N.C. Department of Labor, Requests for Appropriation Changes for the Fiscal Year 1978–1979, January 13, 1978, Box 174, Folder, B, Industrial Development, Division of Industrial Commission, James D. Hunt Papers, North Carolina State Archives, Raleigh, NC. See also, New Release, John R. Brooks, "State on OSHA Fund Reversions," September 13, 1991, Box 7, Folder—Hamlet, NC, Imperial Foods, UFCW Local 204, GSU, Atlanta, GA.

52. Van Denton, "Wreath, Blame Placed at State's Doors—Luring Businesses to State Fosters Lack of Safety Concern, Some Say," *Raleigh News and Observer*, September 7, 1991. On the

total number of workers in the state in 1980 and 1990, see Joseph Menn, "N.C. Labor Official Puts Blame on Legislature," *Charlotte Observer*, September 6, 1991. For more on the number of safety and health inspectors, see "After the Fire: A Review of the North Carolina Occupational Safety and Health Program," October 15, 1991, Box 7, Folder—Hamlet, NC, Imperial Foods, UFCW Local 204, GSU, Atlanta, GA.

53. "North Carolina OSHA in Violation," December 2, 1988, Box 35, Folder, NCOSH Advisory Council, NCOSHP, SHC, UNC, Chapel Hill, NC.

54. Jennifer F. Parker, Joseph Menn, and Kevin O'Brien, "Inspection Need Overwhelms Tiny NC Staff," *Charlotte Observer*, n.d, in author's possession; Yandle, "Fire Creates Furor."

55. Paul Taylor, "Ashes and Accusations," *Washington Post*, September 5, 1991; John Conway, "Labor Department Under Fire for Inspector Ratio," *Greensboro News and Record*, September 8, 1991; and Leonard Larsen, "Government's 'Dead Hand' Can Save Lives," *St. Louis Post-Dispatch*, September 13, 1991.

56. John Drescher, "State Hadn't Checked Plant for Violations," *Charlotte Observer*, September 4, 1991.

57. Paul Taylor, "City Officials Urge Criminal Probe of Safety Lapses at Fatal Fire Scene," *Washington Post*, September 7, 1991; "The Horrors of Hamlet," *Washington Post,* September 7, 1991; Joseph Menn and Kevin O'Brien, "N.C. Labor Official Puts Blame On Legislature," *Charlotte Observer*, September 6, 1991; and C.E. Yandle, "Brooks Cites Budget Constraints," *Raleigh News and Observer*, September 19, 1991.

58. On Brooks, see Adams, "The Bad Boy of State Politics"; Yandle, "Fire Creates Furor;" and Van Denton, "Hamlet Fire Puts Brooks Squarely in the Limelight," *Raleigh News and Observer*, September 17, 1991. Author interviews with John Drescher and Ruth Sheehan.

59. John Drescher, "In Hamlet Fire, Government Safety Gave Way," *Charlotte Observer*, September 22, 1991. On the USDA, see author interview with William Morris.

60. Department of Labor Investigation, miscellaneous interviews, in author's possession.

61. On the relationship between management and the USDA, see author interview with Georgia Quick.

62. Department of Labor Investigation, USDA investigator, p. 15, in author's possession.

63. Albert Shanker, "The Hamlet, N.C., Fire: A Postmortem," *The New Republic*, February 17, 1992, 27.

64. First quote can be found in Les Leopold, "Recent Explosion Reveals Fatal Double Standard for Workers," Alternet.com, February 20, 2008, available at www.alternet.org/story/77353 /recent_explosion_reveals_fatal_double_standard_for_workers; and the second in Simon, "Reagan in the Workplace," 9.

65. A number of workers recalled the changes taking place on the shop floor; see for examples author interviews with Ada Blanchard, Martin Quick, and Georgia Quick.

66. Susan Garland, "OSHA's New Tack."

67. William Serrin, "After Years of Decline, Sweat Shops Are Back," *New York Times*, October 12, 1983. See also Loomis, *Out of Sight*, 66–67.

68. Author interview with Mark Schultz. Nationally, see Loomis, *Out of Sight*, 66–70.

69. "State Inspectors Visited Ice Cream Plant Three Times," *Richmond County Daily Journal*, November 24, 1991; Van Denton, "Low Funds Blamed for OSHA's Woes," *Raleigh News and Observer*, December 3, 1991.

70. Correspondence between Avery and Hair, re. OSHA Complaint No. 70816616, attached to letter from Chanel Brown to Bryant Simon, October 15, 2015, in author's possession.

71. Hamlet City Council Regular Meeting Minutes, June 18 1991, Hamlet City Hall, Hamlet, NC.

72. "Testimony by Conester Williams," June 23, 1992, NCOSHP, SHC, UNC, Chapel Hill, NC.

73. Department of Labor Investigation, Interview # 4, p. 16, in author's possession. "Preliminary Report: A Closer Look at NC OSHA, Summary, Blowing Rock, North Carolina, November 14, 1987," Box 31, Folder—11/87, NCOSHP Preliminary Report, North Carolina Occupational Safety and Health Project, SCH, UNC, Chapel Hill, NC.

74. On the relationship between the Roes and USDA men, author interviews with William Morris and Ada Blanchard. On the USDA men's routines, see also Department of Labor Investigation, with USDA Inspector, in author's possession.

75. LaGuana Gray noticed a similar mind-set among the workers she studied; see her book, *We Just Keep Running the Line: Black Southern Women and the Poultry Processing Industry* (Baton Rouge: Louisiana State University Press, 2014), 157.

76. Lacayo, "Price of Neglect."

77. Simon, "Reagan in the Workplace," 47.

78. On the similarities between Martin and Hunt, see Paul Luebke, *Tar Heel Politics: Myths and Realities* (Chapel Hill: University of North Carolina Press, 1990); and Tom Eamon, *The Making of a Southern Democracy: North Carolina Politics from Kerr Scott to Pat McCrory* (Chapel Hill: University of North Carolina Press, 2014), 217, 285. Author interview with John Drescher. For more on Martin, see Hood, *Catalyst*.

79. Press Release, James G. Martin, September 11, 1991; and "Log of Events Transcribed by Lynn B. Gilliam, September 18–19, 1991," Box, Imperial Fire, Hamlet City Hall, Hamlet, NC; "Governor Outlines Plans to Improve Workplace Safety," James Martin Papers, Office of General Counsel, Box 61, Folder—Department of Labor, OSHA, Hamlet Fire, 1991; and on "federal intrusion," Martin to Elizabeth Dole, Secretary of Labor, March 6, 1990, North Carolina State Archives, Raleigh, NC. On the recruitment of Imperial, Governor Martin Papers, Governor's Press Office, Press Conference Transcript, 1985–1991, Box 7, Folder—Press Conference Transcript, September 9, 1991; Kevin O'Brien, "Martin Questions Need for More Inspectors," *Charlotte Observer*, n.d.; Chief of Staff, Special Files, Box 43, Folder Labor/Audit, Martin Papers, North Carolina Department of Labor, Raleigh, NC. Author interview with Mike Okun.

80. John Hechinger, "Fire's Legacy: Sweeping Change," *Charlotte Observer*, September 8, 1991.

81. "Chicken Processors Fines," *Washington Post*, January 29, 1992.

82. Mark Barrett, "Hamlet Plant Fire Shines Spotlight on Labor Race," *Asheville Citizen Times*, April 26, 1992. See also an assessment of the legal changes produced by the fire, Emily

Kuo, "Occupational Safety and Health in North Carolina: Before and After the Fire" (Honors Thesis, University of North Carolina at Chapel Hill, 1994).

7: Endings

1. Fran Arrington, "Dobbins Heights, Hamlet Worlds Apart," *Raleigh News and Observer*, December 9, 1991.

2. This information comes from Arrington, "Dobbins Heights."

3. For more information on the community's history and Pastor Jim Dobbins, see Keith Parsons, "Town's History Began Long Before It Was Incorporated in 1984," *Richmond County Daily Journal*, n.d., Vertical File, Dobbins Heights, Richmond County Historical Society, Rockingham, NC; and "The Town That's Moving Forward," available at www.dobbinsheights .com/town-history.

4. Channie McManus, "A Brief History of the Dobbins Heights Community," n.d.; and Parsons, "Town's History Began."

5. Author interview with Calvin White.

6. Arrington, "Dobbins Heights," and Jack Yates, "Chicken Processing Plant Fires, Hamlet North Carolina (September 3, 1991), North Little Rock Arkansas (June 7, 1991)," (Washington, DC: Federal Emergency Management Agency), available at www.usfa.fema.gov/downloads /pdf/publications/tr-057.pdf.

7. Author interviews with Frankie Moree, Gus Bellamy, and Calvin White. For more on how the fire was fought that morning, see Yates, "Chicken Processing Plant Fires"; "Testimony from Robin Leviner," and typed sheet, "Imperial Plant Fire, Hamlet, North Carolina, September 3, 1991: Sequence of Events," Box, Imperial Fire, Folder, Fatalities Imperial, Hamlet City Hall, Hamlet, NC.

8. Tom MacCallum, "Hamlet Fire Chief Disputes Charges of Discrimination," *Richmond County Daily Journal*, September 5, 1991.

9. Documentary, *Our Jobs, Our Lives: A Work in Progress* (Black Workers for Justice, 1991), available at American University Library, Washington, DC.

10. "Carolina Poultry Plant Inferno," *Workers Vanguard*, September 13, 1991.

11. Arrington, "Dobbins Heights."

12. "Carolina Poultry Plant Inferno," and Arrington, "Dobbins Heights."

13. MacCallum, "Hamlet Fire Chief Disputes Charge."

14. Hamlet Meeting, n.d., Box 35, Folder, Hamlet Organizing Contacts, NCOSHP, SCH, UNC, Chapel Hill, NC. Mayor Abbie Covington backed Fuller's decision to keep the Dobbins Heights Fire Department on standby, see "Log of Events Transcribed by Lynn B. Gilliam," September 18–19, 1991," Box, Imperial Foods, Hamlet City Hall, Hamlet, NC.

15. *Our Jobs, Our Lives.*

16. Author interviews with Ruth DeRosa and Annette Zimmerman. See also author interview with Stephen Frye. Representatives of the North Carolina Occupational Safety and Health Project heard similar charges of racism against the fire department at a meeting in Hamlet after the fire. See Hamlet Meeting, n.d., Box 35, Folder, Hamlet Organizing Contacts, NCOSHP,

SHC, UNC, Chapel Hill, NC. It came up again when Jesse Jackson visited town. "Jackson: Keep Striving for Safe Workplace," *Charlotte Observer*, November 26, 1991.

17. Hamlet City Council Regular Meeting, September 10, 1991, Hamlet City Hall, Hamlet, NC.

18. Author interviews with Martha Barr and Berry Barbour. On City Lights, see Letter to the Editor from David Andrews, "Anger over the Fire," *Richmond County Daily Journal*, October 13, 1991.

19. Dannye Romine, "Passing Days," *Charlotte Observer*, September 6, 1991.

20. Author interview with Berry Barbour. Miscellaneous Papers from Ministerial Alliance sent to author by Reverend James Bailey, in author's possession.

21. See an accounting of the ministerial group's spending in Rev. James Bailey, Disaster Relief Fund Treasurer, January 28, 1992, Box 33, Folder, Correspondence, NCOSHP, SHC, UNC, Chapel Hill, NC. See also Karl Stark, "Sudden Horror of Fatal Fire Overwhelms Tiny N.C. Town," *Philadelphia Inquirer*, September 8, 1991; Peter Kilborn, "In the Aftermath of Deadly Fire, A Poor Town Struggles," *New York Times*, November 25, 1991; "Log of Events Transcribed by Lynn B. Gilliam, September 18–19, 1991," Box, Imperial Fire, Hamlet City Hall, Hamlet, NC; and "Coors Relief Fund to Aid Imperial Victims," *Richmond County Daily Journal*, October 1, 1991. See also pictures of donations being delivered in *Richmond County Daily Journal*, September 26, 30, October 21, 1991. On the Christmas party, see Hamlet City Council Regular Meeting Minutes, December 10, 1991, Hamlet City Hall, Hamlet, NC. Author interviews with Covington and Barbour.

22. Author interview with Covington.

23. On what happened between Brad Roe and Liberty Mutual and the flow of information, see author interview with Martha Barr. On some snags encountered getting Imperial officials to hand over the needed materials, see "Log of Events Transcribed by Lynn B. Gilliam, September 18–19, 1991," Box, Imperial Fire, Hamlet City Hall, Hamlet, NC. According to this record, Brad Roe provided access to application files with addresses, zip codes, phone numbers, SSNs, DOB, and contact persons, but when asked for additional information, he reportedly said, according to the log cited above, "Sorry, but all our personnel records have been taken to GA by the Workman's Comp carrier, insurance carrier." This, by the way, constituted a violation of OSHA policy. Records of workplace injuries were supposed to be stored on-site.

24. For an explanation of worker's compensation benefits, see Glenn Sumpter, "Officials Issue Conflicting Statements," *Richmond County Daily Journal*, September 5, 1991. See also author interview with Martha Barr.

25. The above paragraphs are drawn from author interviews with Martha Barr. Martha Barr, "A Love Song to Hamlet," lyrics and tape in author's possession thanks to Barr.

26. Author interview with DeRosa. See also "Post-Fire Stress Studied in Hamlet," *Charlotte Observer*, December 19, 1991.

27. "Log of Events Transcribed by Lynn B. Gilliam, September 18–19, 1991," Box, Imperial Fire, Hamlet City Hall, Hamlet, NC.

28. "Blaze in Chicken Factory Plant Smolders for Survivors," *Chicago Tribune*, September 14, 1992.

29. Ruth R. DeRosa, "Post-Traumatic Stress Disorder and the Subjective Experience of Disaster: The Hamlet Fire," (PhD dissertation in psychology, Duke University, 1994), 38.

30. DeRosa, "Post-Traumatic Stress Disorder," 38–39; and author interview with Annette Zimmerman.

31. Wil Haygood, "Still Burning: After a Deadly Fire, a Town's Losses Were Just Beginning," *Washington Post*, November 10, 2002. Author interview with DeRosa; and email, Ruth DeRosa to author, June 3, 2015.

32. Author interview with Lisa Amaya-Jackson. Testimony about Terrell Quick from Kemlite Video, Charles Becton Files, in author's possession. See also Ben Stocking, "Shock and Suffering Are Etched Forever on Hamlet's Soul," *Raleigh News and Observer*, September 8, 1991; and Joe Drape, "Pain Smolders Long After Fatal NC Plant Fire," *Atlanta Journal Constitution*, January 19, 1992.

33. Haygood, "Still Burning."

34. Ben Stocking, "Some Scars Are Slow to Heal," *Raleigh News and Observer*, December 11, 1991.

35. John S. March, Lisa Amaya-Jackson, Robert Terry, and Philip Costanzo, "Posttraumatic Symptomatology in Children and Adolescents After an Industrial Fire," *Journal of the American Academy of Child and Adolescent Psychiatry* 36 (August 1997), 1080–88. See also, for an overview of PTSD diagnosis and research, Matthew J. Friedman, *Post-Traumatic Stress Disorder* (Salt Lake City, UT: Compact Clinicals, 2003).

36. Author interviews with Reverend Harold Miller, Cordelia Steele, and Annette Zimmerman.

37. Martha Quillin and Julie Powers Rives, "A Year Later, Hamlet Blaze Binds, Divides," *Raleigh News and Observer*, September 4, 1992.

38. WRAL Broadcast, n.d., Martha Barr Personal Papers, in author's possession.

39. Quillin and Rives, "A Year Later."

40. James Greiff, "Jesse Jackson to Visit Survivors Today," *Charlotte Observer*, September 10, 1991.

41. Author interview with Abbie Covington; and "Log of Events Transcribed by Lynn B. Gilliam, September 18–19, 1991," Box, Imperial Fire, Hamlet City Hall, Hamlet, NC. On perceptions of Jackson at the time, see "The Parachute Politician" reprinted in *Charlotte Observer*, n.d., UFCW, Box 7, Hamlet Folder, GSU, Atlanta, GA. See also Marshall Frady, *Jesse: The Life and Pilgrimage of Jesse Jackson* (New York: Random House, 1996).

42. Author interview with Abbie Covington. On Jackson linking Hamlet to the civil rights struggle, see "Jackson Revisits Hamlet," *Raleigh News and Observer*, November 26, 1991.

43. Letter from Martha Barr to author, n.d., in author's possession, and author interviews with Ruth DeRosa and Stephen Frye.

44. Hamlet City Council Regular Meeting Minutes, August 28, 1992, Hamlet City Hall, Hamlet, NC; Ricki Morell, "Ceremonies Divide Survivors," *Raleigh News and Observer*, September 4, 1992; and Haygood, "Still Burning."

45. Author interview with Harold Miller.

46. Ricki Morell, "Ceremonies Divide Survivors," *Raleigh News and Observer*, September 4, 1992; Haygood, "Still Burning," and author interviews with Blanchard and Zimmerman.

47. On Zimmerman's recent reflections on the past, see Melonie McLaurin, "Memories of a Fatal Tragedy," *Richmond County Daily Journal*, September 1, 2016.

48. Quillin and Rives, "A Year Later."

49. Quote from Michael Etts, "Trauma and the Desire for Revenge," available at www.adaptivetherapy.com/Trauma%20and%20the%20desire%20for%20revenge.pdf. On these incidents and others like them, see author interviews with Franke Moree, Ada Blanchard, and Annette Zimmerman, and on more fire-related vandalism, see Paige Williams, "Seven Years of Silence," *Charlotte Observer*, October 25, 1998.

50. Author interview with Lisa Amaya-Jackson. For more on this dynamic, see Thane Rosenbaum, *Payback: The Case for Revenge* (Chicago: University of Chicago Press, 2013).

51. Author interview with Loretta Goodwin.

52. Author interview with Lisa Amaya-Jackson.

53. Ibid.

54. "Chicken Plant Operators Indicted," *New York Times*, March 10, 1992. On Black Workers for Justice and the group's involvement in Hamlet after the fire, see author interviews with Ashaki Binta and Loretta Goodwin.

55. "Chicken Plant Operators Indicted."

56. For this quote, see Matt Tomsic, "Cheshire Defends Rights of Those in Big Trouble," *Wilmington Star-News*, February 1, 2011. Author interview with Joe Cheshire.

57. On Lowder, see Stephanie Banchero, "Case Closed: Retiring DA Adjourns to Private Life," *Charlotte Observer*, January 3, 1995.

58. For the ACLU, see Motion for Appropriate Relief filed in *State of North Carolina v. Guy Tobias LeGrande*, available at www.aclu.org/files/assets/LeGrande_RJA_motion-r.pdf. On similar charges, see John H. Tucker, "Did a Prosecutor and Police Send an Innocent Teenager to Prison for Murder," *The Independent*, January 5, 2015. On good old boy tag, see Banchero, "Case Closed."

59. Author interview with Joe Cheshire. Heather Thompson heard Cheshire tell the same story at a public forum in North Carolina in 2014. Author interview with Thompson.

60. E-mail Joseph Cheshire to author, February 13, 2017.

61. "Meat-Plant Owner Pleads Guilty in a Blaze That Killed 25 People," *New York Times*, September 15, 1992.

62. "Some Survivors Unhappy with Plea Bargain," *Chicago Tribune*, September 15, 1992.

63. "Owner Gets 20 Years in Fatal Poultry Plant Fire," *Chicago Tribune*, September 15, 1992.

64. Jeff Holland, "None of Them Should Have Died," *Richmond County Daily Journal*, August 30, 1992.

65. Pouncey quoted by Estes Thompson, "Plant Owner Sentenced to Prison," *The State*, September 15, 1992; Quick quoted in "Plant Owner Pleads Guilty in Fatal Fire," *Chicago Tribune*, September 14, 1992; and Ratliff quoted in "Convicted Hamlet Plant Owner in Buncombe Jail," *Hendersonville Times News*, September 26, 1992.

66. "Poultry Plant Owner Gets 20 Years in Deadly Blaze," *Jet* (October 1992): 29.

67. Author interviews with Miller, Georgia Quick, and Berry Barbour.

68. Author interview with Ada Blanchard; and "16 Million Payoff Approved in Fatal Chicken Plant Fire," *Washington Post*, December 17, 1992.

69. "First Lawsuit is Filed," *Richmond County Daily Journal*, September 11, 1991. Robert Miller Photograph, Folder—Imperial Food Products Plant, Victims' Families and Victims Funerals, Photo Archives, *Raleigh News and Observer* Archives, Raleigh, NC. See also James Greiff, "Imperial Foods Fined in 80s Over Fire Doors," *Charlotte Observer*, September 17, 1991.

70. "State Bar Charges D.C. Attorneys," *Richmond County Daily Journal*, October 2, 1991. Author interview with Woody Gunter.

71. Jane Ruffin, "Hamlet Fire Suit Says Profits Topped Safety," *Raleigh News and Observer*, October 18, 1991. See also, Rachel Buchanan, "Lawyers Quest Draws Charges," *Raleigh News and Observer*, October 3, 1991; and Henry J. Reske, "Lawyer Charged with Soliciting: Accused Calls North Carolina Bar Officials 'Sanctimonious Yah-Hoos,'" *ABA Journal* 77 (December 1991): 26.

72. Jeff Holland, "Fourth Lawsuit Is Filed Against Imperial Foods," *Richmond County Daily Journal*, October 7, 1991; Jeff Holland, "Fifth Lawsuit Filed Here," *Richmond County Daily Journal*, October 11 1991; "Tentative Plant Fire Settlement," *Washington Post*, November 7, 1992.

73. Ed Shur, "Cold Hard Winter Settles In," *Baltimore Sun*, December 26, 1991.

74. For the report, which runs several hundred pages, see North Carolina Department of Labor, Citation and Notification of Penalty, Inspection No. 018479204, December 30, 1991. See also Scott Bronstein, "Poultry Company Is Fined $32,326 Per Life Lost in the Fire," *Atlanta Journal Constitution*, December 31, 1991; and Dennis Patterson, "N.C. Plant Fined $808,150 After Fatal Fire," *Washington Post*, December 31, 1991.

75. "Poultry Plant Owner Objects to Fine Imposed in Fatal Fire," *Washington Post*, January 24, 1992.

76. "State's Work-Safety Changes Could Help OSHA Reform," *Richmond County Daily Journal*, July 20, 1992.

77. "Families of Victims Have No Sympathy for Those Indicted," *Richmond County Daily Journal*, March 10, 1992.

78. United States Bankruptcy Court for the Middle District of North Carolina, Re. Imperial Food Products, Inc., Debtors, Filed July 21, 1992, Case No., B-92-12380C-7G; and "Imperial Foods Will Not Reopen," *Richmond County Daily Journal*, October 9, 1992.

79. "Roe Tells Judge He's Broke," *Richmond County Daily Journal*, August 7, 1992.

80. For Roe's filing, see Charles M. Ivy, Trustee for *Imperial v. PNC Bank*, Schedule B—Personal Property Case No., B-92-12380C-7G. On the subsequent search for Roe's funds, see "G-man turns into fee man," *Business North Carolina*, December 11, 1992, 57.

81. On the reluctance at first to settle, see "Victims of Poultry-Plant Fire to Get $16.1 Million," *New York Times*, November 8, 1992. "Fire Victims to Get $16.1 Million," *Richmond County Daily Journal*, November 8, 1991. The actual breakdown of settlement payments comes

from the following document, "Exhibit A: Settlement Offers," Box, Imperial Fire, Hamlet City Hall, Hamlet, NC.

82. "Lawsuit Seeks Damages from Plant's Suppliers," *The State*, July 25, 1993. "Hamlet Fire Victims Sue 41 Companies," *Fayetteville News*, July 25, 1993. Kemlite Video from the Personal Files of Charles Becton, in author's possession.

83. Author interviews with Woody Gunther and Loretta Goodwin; and email from Annette Zimmerman to author, September 15, 2015.

84. Author interview with Gary Johnson. See also William Anderson to Abbie Covington, September 14, 1993, Box, Imperial Fire, Hamlet City Hall, Hamlet, NC

85. "Hamlet Decision Is Painful, but Sound," *Greensboro News and Record*, February 10, 1998. "*Stone III v. North Carolina Department of Labor*," No. 81P97, Decided February 6, 1988. This decision is available at Open Jurist, available at openjurist.org/948/f2d/1295/stone-v-united-states-department-of-labor.

86. In his detailed and moving article, "Still Burning," Haygood reported that Wall received $200,000, but according the settlement offer sheet found in the records at Hamlet City Hall, Wall got $109, 423.14.

87. Author interview with Amaya-Jackson; Haygood, "Still Burning"; and Williams, "Seven Years of Silence."

88. Author interview with Georgia Quick.

89. Author interviews on the settlements with Blanchard and Loretta Goodwin; and Haygood, "Still Burning." See quotes from Lillie Bell Davis in *A New Beginning: It's a Blessing to Be Alive* (Lulu.com, 2004), 50. See also author interview with Stephen Frye.

90. Author interview with Stephen Frye.

91. Griffin quoted by David Perlmutt, "Owner May Reopen Plant Hit by Fire," *Charlotte Observer*, September 18, 1991.

92. Author interviews with Loretta Goodwin and Annette Zimmerman. For more on Griffin, see "Imperial Foods Will Not Reopen."

93. Police reports contained in an email from Tim Reid to Bryant Simon, July 27, 2015, in author's possession; *State v. Albert Griffin*, File Number 98CR5003566, Rockingham Superior Court, Rockingham, NC; and Haygood, "Still Burning."

94. Author interview with Frankie Moree.

95. Details of Wendy Dawkins's murder come from author interview with Frankie Moree and Wil Haygood, "Still Burning." See also *State of North Carolina v. Philip Ray Dawkins, Jr.*, No. COA02-1637, January 20, 2004, available at caselaw.findlaw.com/nc-court-of-appeals/1339589.html.

96. For Quick and Frye's stories, see author interviews with them as well as Amy Rogers, "Rising from the Ashes" in *No Hiding Place: Uncovering the Legacy of Charlotte-Area Writers. Anthology*, edited by Frye Gaillard, Amy Rogers, and Robert Inman (Asheboro, NC: Down Home Press, 1999), 218–24; quote, 221–22.

97. Davis, *A New Beginning*, 47–48; and Rogers, "Rising from the Ashes," 221. The actual amount of the settlement was $87,358.50.

98. On triggers, see Sutter Health, "On Coping with Memories, Triggers, and Reminders," available at www.pamf.org/teen/life/trauma/memories/; Freidman, *Post-Traumatic Stress Disorder*. On the building, see Rogers, "Rising from the Ashes," 223; and author interview with Stephen Frye.

99. Author interviews with Ruth DeRosa and with Joseph Arnold, Stephen Frye, and Annette Zimmerman.

100. David Perlmutt, "Owner May Reopen Plant Hit by Fire," *Charlotte Observer*, September 18, 1991; Shur, "Cold Hard Winter Settles In"; "Fire," no paper, July 26, 1992, Folder—Imperial, 1992, Richmond County Historical Society, Rockingham, NC. Author interview with Covington. For more on Bobby Quick, see Jeff Holland, "Imperial Foods Worker Saved Lives," *Richmond County Daily Journal*, September 10, 1991; and "Hearing on HR 3160, Comprehensive Occupational Safety and Health Reform Act," September 12, 1991, Serial No. 102-47, 100–01.

101. Author interviews with DeRosa and Zimmerman. Also see Gregg LaBar, "Hamlet, N.C.: Home to a National Tragedy," *Occupational Hazards* (September 1992): 29.

102. "Blaze in Chicken Factory Plant Smolders for Survivors," *Chicago Tribune*, September 14, 1992.

103. Author interview with Miller.

104. "Judge Orders Plant Sealed," *Richmond County Daily Journal*, September 15, 1991. On Brad Roe's post-fire life, see Williams, "Seven Years of Silence" and "Imperial Officials Released on Bond," *Richmond County Daily Journal*, March 13, 1992. The following article talks about Roe's subsequent career as a bartender in the Atlanta suburbs without mentioning his earlier career in Hamlet: H.M. Cauley, "Around Town: Old Pub Is Back as Central City," *Atlanta Journal Constitution*, April 9, 1998.

105. Allen Mask to Governor Hunt, November 17, 1998, Imperial File, Richmond County Historical Society, Rockingham, NC.

106. For background on Legrand, see author interview with Legrand; and Matt Harrelson, "Pastor Marks 50 Years of Ministry," *Richmond County Daily Journal*, June 20, 2014.

107. Author interviews with Robin Hayes and Tommy Legrand.

108. Hamlet City Council Regular Meeting Minutes, July 14, 1998, Hamlet City Hall, Hamlet, NC.

109. Mask to Jesse Jackson, March 9, 1999, Imperial File, Richmond County Historical Society, Rockingham, NC.

110. Memorandum, Representative Wayne Goodwin to Tom McCullan (*sic*), July 6, 2000, Imperial File, Richmond County Historical Society, Rockingham, NC; "Hamlet Dropped Ball on Imperial Funding," *Richmond County Daily Journal*, September 29, 2000. See also author interview with Wayne Goodwin.

111. "Imperial Food Products," *Business North Carolina* 20 (2000): 19. Background from author interview with Robin Hayes.

112. Tom MacCallum, "Monday Is Deadline for Imperial Cleanup to Begin," *Richmond County Daily Journal*, October 1, 2000; Editorial, "Hamlet Dropped Ball on Imperial Funding," *Richmond County Daily Journal*, September 29, 2000. See also how Futrell lays out the issues about the property in his letter, Stephan Futrell to Marchell David, Interim City Manager,

January 22, 2002, Box, Imperial Fire, Folder, Imperial Food File, Hamlet City Hall, Hamlet, NC.

113. Author interview with Goodwin; Hamlet City Council Regular Meeting Minutes, March 10, 1992, Hamlet City Hall; author interview with Legrand.

114. Author interviews with Miller, Legrand, and Zimmerman. Letter to the Editor from Mask, *Richmond County Daily Journal*, September 24, 2000.

115. Kimberly Harrington, "Imperial Building Declared Public Nuisance," *Richmond County Daily Journal*, August 1, 2001. Legrand quote from "Disaster Site Being Demolished," *Raleigh News and Observer*, September 18, 2001.

116. Author interviews with Legrand and Hayes. See also Howie Paul Harnett, "Healing, Step by Step: 12 Years After Disaster Breaks Ground on Memorial," *Charlotte Observer*, April 25, 2003.

117. Author interview with Goodwin. On her rental house, see author interview with Steven Frye.

118. Author interview with Goodwin.

Epilogue

1. David Von Drehle, *Triangle: The Fire That Changed America* (New York: Grove Press, 2004), 262–63. For another important study of this event, see Richard Greenwald, *The Triangle Fire, the Protocols of Peace, and Industrial Democracy in Progressive Era New York* (Philadelphia: Temple University Press, 2005). On the significance of the Triangle fire over time, see "Twenty-Five Moments That Changed History," *Time*, January 4, 2015, available at time.com/3889533/25-moments-changed-america. At the time of the Hamlet fire, a number of commentators also made comparisons between Triangle and Imperial. See, for a few examples, "Deadly Complacency," *Denver Post*, September 5, 1991; Osha Gray Davidson, "It's Still 1911 in America's Rural Sweat Shops," *Baltimore Sun*, September 7, 1991; and Albert Shanker, "The Hamlet, N.C., Fire: A Postmortem," *The New Republic*, February 17, 1992, 27.

2. On the limits of the New Deal, see two assessments spanning two different eras and perspectives: William Leuchtenburg, *Franklin D. Roosevelt and the New Deal, 1932–1940* (New York: Harper Perennial, 2009); and Jefferson Cowie, *The Great Exception: The New Deal and the Limits of American Politics* (Princeton, NJ: Princeton University Press, 2016).

3. "Blaze in Chicken Factory Plant Smolders for Survivors," *Chicago Tribune*, September 14, 1992. See also James Martin to Henson P. Barnes and Daniel Blue, September 25, 1991, Office of General Counsel, Box 61, Folder—Department of Labor, OSHA, James Martin Papers, Hamlet Fire, 1991, North Carolina State Archives, Raleigh, NC.

4. Notes taken at this event by the author. See also Melonie McLaurin, "Emerging from the Darkness," *Richmond County Daily Journal*, September 2, 2016. In February 1992, a Hamlet city council member urged his colleagues to begin a fire inspection program and allocate money to send someone from the fire department to fire inspection school, someone other than Chief Fuller. See Hamlet City Council Regular Meeting Minutes, February 11, 1992, Hamlet City Hall. On the fire inspection reforms locally, see "City of Hamlet Fire Prevention, Protection, and Inspection Ordinance," April 13, 1992, Box, Imperial Fire, Hamlet City Hall, Hamlet,

NC; and statewide, see Ben Stocking, "Fire Inspections Ordered for All N.C. Businesses," *Raleigh News and Observer,* December 11, 1991.

5. Thomas Borstelmann, *The 1970s: A New Global History from Civil Rights to Economic Inequality* (Princeton, NJ: Princeton University Press, 2012), 3. See also Nancy MacLean, *Equality Is Not Enough: The Opening of the American Workplace* (Cambridge, MA: Harvard University Press, 2008). On the breakdown of segregation in two key southern industries, see, Timothy J. Minchin, *Hiring the Black Worker: The Racial Integration of the Southern Textile Industry, 1960–1980* (Chapel Hill: University of North Carolina Press, 1999); and Minchin, *The Color of Work: Civil Rights in the Southern Paper Industry, 1945–1980* (Chapel Hill: University of North Carolina Press, 2001).

6. Ellen Ruppel Shell, *Cheap: The High Cost of Discount Culture* (New York: Penguin Press, 2009). For other key notions of cheap, each different from the one presented here, see David Bosshart, *Cheap: The REAL Cost of the Global Trend for Bargains, Discounts and Consumer Choice* (London and Philadelphia: Kegan Page, 2005). Lauren Weber, *In Cheap We Trust: The Story of a Misunderstood American Virtue* (New York: Little, Brown, and Company, 2009); Michael Carolan, *The Real Cost of Cheap Food* (London: Routledge, 2011); and Jason Moore, "Cheap Food and Bad Money: Food, Frontiers, and Financialization in the Rise and Demine of Neoliberalism," *Review* (2012), available at www.jasonwmoore.com/uploads/Moore_Cheap _Food_and_Bad_Money.pdf.

7. Daniel T. Rodgers, *Age of Fracture* (Cambridge, MA: Belknap Press of Harvard University Press, 2011).

8. For an example of this kind of thinking about the broader shift in American politics beyond the Democratic-Republican, liberal-conservative divide, see Matthew Lassiter, "Political History Beyond the Red-Blue Divide," *Journal of American History* 98 (December 2011): 760–64.

9. Shell, *Cheap*, 3.

10. Timothy Smith, "Changing Tastes: By End of This Year Poultry Will Surpass Beef in the US Diet," *Wall Street Journal*, September 17, 1987.

11. On the political economy of Walmart, see Nelson Lichtenstein, *The Retail Revolution: How Wal-Mart Created a Brave New World of Business* (New York: Metropolitan Books, 2010).

12. Mark Schatzker, *The Dorito Effect: The Surprising New Truth About Food and Flavor* (New York: Simon & Schuster, 2015), 25.

13. Wenonah Hauter, *Foodopoly: The Battle over the Future of Food and Farming in America* (New York: The New Press, 2012), 191–95.

14. In his book, Roger Horowitz talks about some of these "perils of convenience," *Putting Meat on the American Table: Taste, Technology, Transformation* (Baltimore: Johns Hopkins University Press, 2006), 145–52.

15. Joe Drape, "Pain Smolders Long After Fatal NC Plant Fire," *Atlanta Journal Constitution*, January 19, 1992. See also Memo Regarding Former Imperial Food Products Workers, n.d. Box 32 , Folder, Hamlet Response Coalition: Minutes from Meetings, NCOSHP, SHC, UNC, Chapel Hill, NC; "Blaze in Chicken Factory Plant Smolders for Survivors," *Chicago Tribune*, September 14, 1992; and Ben Stocking, "Displaced Workers Struggling," *Raleigh News and Observer*, December 10, 1991.

16. On changes in the southern labor force, see Leon Fink, *The Maya of Morganton: Work and Community in the Nuevo New South* (Chapel Hill: University of North Carolina Press, 2003); and Kathleen C. Schwartzman, *The Chicken Trail: Following Workers, Migrants, and Corporations Across the Americas* (Ithaca, NY: Cornell University Press, 2013).

17. Lucinda Wykle to Sabrina McDonald, September 27, 1994, Box 33, Folder, Correspondence, NCOSHP, SCH, UNC; and "Statement to the General Baptist Convention," Box 33, Folder, Education/Road Show, NCOSHP, SHC, UNC, Chapel Hill, NC.

18. On salmonella, see Marj Charlier, "Chicken Growers Face Leaner Earnings As Salmonella Publicity Takes Its Toll," *Wall Street Journal*, July 20, 1987; "Southeast Economic Justice Network," September 7–9, 1990, December 2, 1988, Box 35, Folder, Southeast REJN September 1990, NCOSHP, SHC, UNC, Chapel Hill, NC. See also LaGuana Gray, *We Just Keep Running the Line: Black Southern Women and the Poultry Processing Industry* (Baton Rouge: Louisiana State University Press, 2014), 9. On the effects of salmonella, see www.webmd.com/food-recipes /food-poisoning/tc/salmonellosis-topic-overview. "The High Cost of Cheap Chicken," ConsumerReports.org, January 2014, available at www.consumerreports.org/cro/magazine/2014 /02/the-high-cost-of-cheap-chicken/index.htm.

19. "Gardner Blames Hunt for Bringing Imperial Plant to Hamlet," *Raleigh News and Observer*, September 4, 1992. See also, John Hood, "Overreaction to Hamlet Tragedy Will Only Create Additional Victims," *Atlanta Journal Constitution*, September 3, 1992.

20. "Ballenger calls for major OSHA reform," *Occupational Hazards* 57 (1995): 19. Reverend Jesse L. Jackson Testimony before The Senate Committee on Labor and Human Relations, June 10, 1992, Box 35, Folder, Jesse Jackson Testimony, NCOSHP, SHC, UNC, Chapel Hill, NC; and Sarah Anderson, "OSHA Under Siege," *The Progressive*, December 1995.

21. Carl Bloice, "Big Demonstration Planned for Democratic Convention," *Amsterdam News*, June 27, 1992.

22. "Hamlet Response Coalition for Workplace Reform," Jan 20, 1995, Box 31, Folder, Hamlet Response Coalition, 1995, Federal OSHA Reform, NCOSHP, SHC, UNC, Chapel Hill, NC.

23. As heard by author on television, September 23, 2016.

24. Chris Buckley, "Over 100 Die at Fire at Chinese Poultry Plant," *New York Times*, June 3, 2013; and "Bangladesh Factory Collapse Toll Passes 1,000," bbc.com, May 10, 2013, available at www.bbc.com/news/world-asia-22476774. On the Benetton connections, see Rebecca Smithers, "Benetton Admits Links with Firm in Collapsed Bangladesh Building," *The Guardian*, April 29, 2013; and on Walmart, see "Wal-Mart: Bangladesh Factory in Deadly Fire Made Clothes Without Our Knowledge," CBS News, November 26, 2012.

25. See a related argument in Jacob S. Hacker and Paul Pierson, *American Amnesia: How the War on Government Led Us to Forget What Made America Prosper* (New York: Simon & Schuster, 2016).

26. For other reminders of the importance of retelling the Hamlet story, see author interview with Georgia Quick and former North Carolina labor commissioner Harry E. Payne's powerful editorial on the twentieth anniversary of the fire, "Have We Forgotten the Hamlet Fire?," *Raleigh News and Observer*, September 2, 2011.

INDEX

ABOUT THE AUTHOR

Bryant Simon is a professor of history at Temple University. He is the author of *Boardwalk of Dreams: Atlantic City and the Fate of Urban America* and *Everything but the Coffee: Learning About America from Starbucks*. His work and commentary have been featured in the *New Yorker*, the *Washington Post*, the *New Republic*, and numerous other outlets. He lives in Philadelphia.

Celebrating 25 Years of Independent Publishing

Thank you for reading this book published by The New Press. The New Press is a nonprofit, public interest publisher celebrating its twenty-fifth anniversary in 2017. New Press books and authors play a crucial role in sparking conversations about the key political and social issues of our day.

We hope you enjoyed this book and that you will stay in touch with The New Press. Here are a few ways to stay up to date with our books, events, and the issues we cover:

- Sign up at www.thenewpress.com/subscribe to receive updates on New Press authors and issues and to be notified about local events.
- Like us on Facebook: www.facebook.com/newpressbooks
- Follow us on Twitter: www.twitter.com/thenewpress

Please consider buying New Press books for yourself; for friends and family; and to donate to schools, libraries, community centers, prison libraries, and other organizations involved with the issues our authors write about.

The New Press is a 501(c)(3) nonprofit organization. You can also support our work with a tax-deductible gift by visiting www.thenew press.com/donate.